WEST GERMAN REPARATIONS TO ISRAEL

West German Reparations to Israel

by Nicholas Balabkins

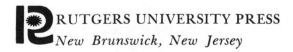 RUTGERS UNIVERSITY PRESS
New Brunswick, New Jersey

Copyright © 1971 by Rutgers University, the State University of New Jersey

Library of Congress Catalog Card Number: 70-152724
ISBN: 0-8135-0691-3

Manufactured in the United States of America by Quinn & Boden Company, Inc.,
Rahway, New Jersey

Contents

WEST GERMAN REPARATIONS TO ISRAEL

1

Germany's Road into Industrial Genocide

The signing of the Luxemburg Treaty in 1952 marked the beginning of an official German-Israeli-Jewish triologue. The Federal Republic of Germany pledged to make good, within the limits of its capacity, the material damage suffered by the Jews under the government of the Third Reich.

Since the Federal Republic of Germany was built upon the moral ruins of the Third Reich, Chancellor Konrad Adenauer wanted to demonstrate to the international community that his government was of a different moral fiber. He made it clear by word and deed that the Bonn government and all decent Germans were ashamed of the Nazi past and wanted to offer large-scale remedial action for the material damage suffered by Jews at the hands of the Nazis. And that attitude toward restitution and compensation prevailed at the top levels of government in West Germany.

To understand what the Bonn government was paying for, it may be useful to examine the social order of the Third Reich and survey the forces that conceived, financed, and carried out the destruction of European Jewry.

The Nazi Social Order

In general, a given social order can be explained in terms of the ideological, political, institutional, and economic arrangements that govern the operations of that particular society. Here, therefore, the social order is conceived as consisting of *four-dimensional social space,* namely, ideological, political, institutional, and economic. In all totalitarian societies, ideologies act as the fountainhead of ideals and as guides for policies. Ideologies also serve as substitute religions and justify discrimination against and punishment of all those who do not accept the sacredness of the "official faith." [1]

The ideological dimension of the Nazi social order was set in terms of the "iron laws of nature," which manifested themselves basically in the concept of struggle, or eternal war, and the purity of blood.[2] The Nazi racist theory was developed on the basis of blood, bad or good. Heredity, blood, and biology were the three major factors of the Nazi racial doctrine,[3] which held that the Aryan race was superior to all others, and that the Jews represented the most inferior race and therefore had to be exterminated.

This Nazi race creed has been analyzed as an outgrowth of Christian theology, German Volkish ideology, and the pseudo-scholarly anti-Jewish literature of nineteenth-century Europe. Since the majority of all Christians, the argument went, always had been and continued to be anti-Jewish,[4] denigration and hatred of the Jews was probably as old as Christianity itself.[5] Discriminatory Church laws, designed to undermine the Jews socially, politically, and economically, went back to the Roman Empire.[6] Jews were, among other things, forbidden to intermarry or to have sexual intercourse with Christians; they were not allowed to hold public office, to employ Christian servants, or to be plaintiffs or witnesses against Christians. The Christian Church also decreed the marking of Jewish clothes with a badge in 1215, and the erection of compulsory ghettos.[7]

In addition to the existing anti-Jewish legislation of the Christian Church, all European nations, including Germany, had developed their own brands of national Judaeophobia. In Germany, it manifested itself in the form of Volkish ideology,[8] and was based on the medieval notion that the Jew was an alien in the land of the Germanic peoples.[9] In the popular image, a Jew was dishonest and ruthless, consumed by a lust for power. Jews were not to be trusted because they practiced "a subversion from within." But the most important part of the Volkish view of the Jewish stereotype was the assertion that the lust of the Jewish parasite for Aryan women was as strong as his lust for money.[10] By intermarriage the Jew contaminated the German race, it was said. But Church *teaching* about the Jews was far more important than anti-Jewish legislation, because the latter directly affected relatively few Christians in premedieval and medieval society. Anti-Jewish teaching, by means of "pictorial" representation in Church sculpture and stained-glass windows, and in regular Sunday sermons, reached millions and was particularly potent in its effects in the European nations. It also affected rulers as individuals and as Christians. Regardless of the fact that attitudes toward Jews differ among the several European nations, all the stereotypes can be traced back ultimately to the Church's view, which pervaded all of Christendom, that the Jewish people were outside the pale of civilized society. Because the Jews rejected Christ (that is, God) and murdered Him, God had crossed them off. And if God no longer cared for them, then men should equally abhor them. In many pictorial representations adorning churches and museums, Jews became representatives of Satan. From this came the idea of contamination. The Church's attitude toward Jews has been simple: convert, leave, or die. For whatever the race theorists and nationalists could contrive in the nineteenth century, they had a firm foundation in the Church's legislation and in its daily teaching and preaching.

To the disabilities resulting from the anti-Jewish attitude of the Church could be added numerous other unfavorable stereotypes, the result of the efforts of a few European intellectuals to dress popular notions about the Jews in pseudo-scientific trappings. The Frenchman Count Joseph Arthur de Gobineau was probably the first modern race theorist. His work, *The Inequality of Human Races,* published in 1853, is a comprehensive exposition of white racial supremacy, and in his writings the concept of race becomes the focus for all human history. Gobineau's theory boils down to three basic ideas: differences in racial characteristics, miscegenation, and race contamination as producing the inevitable decline of civilization. He divides mankind into white, yellow, and black races. The white race supposedly possesses all such noble qualities as energy, leadership, and superiority; the yellow races have fertility and stability; the blacks are endowed with sensuality and artistic impulse. The salient feature of this theory is the assertion that civilization occurs only when two races mix. But unfortunately, argues Gobineau, civilization leads to more and more mixing of "inferior blood" with that of the ruling race. The process of blood mixture bastardizes the ruling class and decadence is inevitable.[11]

Gobineau's writings were largely ignored by the French, but his influence was strong among German teachers, "who were in a position to disseminate the racist ideas in the schools." [12]

Another writer whose work on racial questions had immense influence on the masses was Houston Stewart Chamberlain, a naturalized German of English parentage and birth. He combined the theories of Gobineau with Friedrich Nietzsche's concept of the superman, and this aggregation, with his additions, resulted in his *The Foundations of the Nineteenth Century,* published in 1899. In this volume, according to one scholar, "the highly inventive pseudo-science of Teutonic racial superiority and its correlate, Jewish baseness, were pushed to their limits." [13] Chamberlain's volume became the bible of the anti-Jewish academicians and of the Jew-baiting, Volkish ideologists.

The next major work in the pseudo-scientific literature of Aryan racism, which added still a new dimension to it, was a two-volume work by another Frenchman, Edouard Drumont. His *La France Juive* (Jewish France), published in 1886, charged that the Jews had been responsible for French woes since the Middle Ages. From this work the Jew emerges as the eternal conspirator-felon, the pariah of nations. The diabolical Jew, a man of superior cunning, is claimed to be the real enemy of all peoples. Nations beware, says Drumont, and unite in your fight against Jews! [14]

The most important work of anti-Jewish literature, which fully revealed the collective psychopathology of European Christianity, was Sergei Nilus's *The Protocols of the Elders of Zion,* published in 1903.[15] It was manufactured between 1894 and 1899 at the behest of Rachkovsky, head of the Russian secret police in Paris. This work spread the myth of a global Jewish conspiracy designed for the spiritual and physical subversion of the Christian world. The legend was well received by those Christians who for centuries also believed in the tale of Jewish ritual murder of Christian children.[16] Although the *Protocols* was exposed as a crude forgery, the work became a best-seller between the two World Wars. After the Russian Revolution, and especially after the lost civil war, White Russian refugees, primarily officers and nobility, presented the Revolution of 1917 as the concrete manifestation of a world-wide Jewish plot.[17] Kaiser Wilhelm II and his supporters were also impressed with the *Protocols.* In Germany it sold extremely well, going through thirty-three editions up to 1933. It provided the frustrated German middle classes, officer corps, and bureaucrats with handy explanations for the loss of the war, the hyperinflation that followed, and the disastrous reparations settlement, all in terms of the world-wide Jewish plot. In short, this work became a cornerstone of Nazi propaganda.

The pseudo-scientific race theories, the popular stereotypes of the Jew-baiters, and the essentially negative attitude toward all Jews because they were implicated in the death of Jesus were manifestations of a prevailing Judaeophobia in Germany.

The work that "ennobled" anti-Jewish feelings and elevated violence against the Jews to a German civic duty was Alfred Rosenberg's *The Myth of the Twentieth Century,* first published in 1930.[18] This Nazi spokesman "exalted the Volk, or folk, a people of unmixed racial origins who were mystically bound together in a primitive community of blood and soil which recognized no artificial boundaries. . . ." [19] The author eventually called for the complete elimination of the Jews from all walks of life.[20] In 1933, when the Nazis came to power, Rosenberg's anti-Semitic *Weltanschauung* was transformed into a vehicle for political action. Total anti-Semitism had finally arrived and the gas chambers were in sight.[21]

Of the four dimensions of the Nazi social order, the political dimension was characterized by totalitarianism. As soon as Hitler took over in 1933, the existing multiparty system of the Weimar Republic was eliminated. The Nazi Party became the only legitimate political party.[22] Parliamentary processes were scrapped, and one-man authority was substituted for majority rule. With the Nazi Party firmly in the saddle, the "One Realm, One Nation, One Führer" slogan subordinated everybody and everything to the commands of the state. The individual was effectively deprived of his former constitutional rights and given only Nazi-coined obligations instead.[23] Free speech and freedom of assembly were either suspended or eliminated from political life as was the right to disagree with the officials of the Nazi Party. In the new one-party system, Hitler's responsibility to the voting public was replaced by his or his party's responsibility to the Nazi ideology, the "iron laws of nature." [24] The establishment of the totalitarian political structure was accompanied by the inevitable process of the fragmentation of German society. An omnipresent secret police ruthlessly eliminated all opposition. Since the courts were quickly transformed into institutions for meting out punishment instead of justice, people ceased

to speak out or even to talk to each other. Being tight-lipped became a way of life. People soon learned that resistance and protests
were brutally dealt with by the new Nazi lords. Of course, a few
thousand resisted openly because they could not live otherwise.
Some of them committed suicide, though more often the opponents
of the new regime ended up in concentration camps. But the majority of all Germans in the 1930s wanted simply to live, to have a
job again, and to see public order restored and preserved.[25]

The third dimension of social space, under the Nazi order, may
be said to be the institutional. This refers to the particular legal
and administrative framework within which the totalitarian state
operated, into which were built such factors as government interference with and regulation of economic activity, changes in the
extent of private and corporate ownership of industry, and the
establishment of the so-called "economic crimes against the state"
subject to capital punishment. All of these are institutional arrangements, "ways of doing things," not purely economic, but without which the unique economic processes that take place in a particular social order at a given period cannot be properly understood.
German economists have used "economic sociology" as an umbrella
term to cover all social institutions relevant to economic behavior
(including property rights, inheritance, contract, economic misbehavior), as well as those motivating economic actions. All of the
above do not constitute economic history; they merely explain why
people behave as they do.[26]

Nazi economic arrangements were conservative. For the most part,
they upheld the existing economic institutions of the Weimar
period. For instance, both private and corporate ownership of the
means of production were recognized, and wholesale expropriation
never took place.[27] Such economic conservatism avoided duplication
of the Soviet experience. However, the preservation of private property rights was subject to many qualifications. The Nazi concept of
private property had nothing to do with customary subjective
property rights. The property laws of the Third Reich safeguarded
the rights only of those persons who had acceptable status, defined
in terms of race and blood.[28] All politically unreliable Germans and
all Jews were deprived of their property within a few short years.

The fourth dimension of the Nazi social order concerns the
manner in which it solved the basic problems of economic rational-

ity, such as the task of coordination and the quest for efficiency. Coordination in a market economy deals with the achievement of a balance between the amounts demanded and supplied, the elimination of shortages, and the prevention of surpluses. Goods in short supply enjoy rising prices, which encourage the production of the scarce commodity, and vice versa. In addition to coordination of demand and supply, everything must be produced in the most efficient way; for instance, a given output must be produced with the smallest possible input of resources. The capitalist "profit whip" is an effective scale on which to weigh available market alternatives; if a firm does not pay attention to production costs and fails to earn profits, it is not producing "efficiently" and is, in fact, too costly for the society. It must give way to another firm, which will use scarce resources more economically.

In addition to preserving private and corporate property, the Nazis did not subject the economy to the quantitative output planning of the Soviet type. This does not imply that the "free enterprise system" of the Weimar Republic was retained intact. True, German businessmen continued to operate their firms, but subject to supervision by a number of government agencies.[29] During the Nazis' first five years in power, their economic policy was primarily concerned with eliminating mass unemployment,[30] controlling foreign trade and foreign exchange, maintaining monetary stability, creating favorable profit opportunities for big business, and stimulating capitalist-type institutions.[31] To achieve these objectives, Dr. Hjalmar Schacht, the economic czar of the Third Reich, used direct and indirect controls. To make the most important industrial sectors of the economy profitable, German corporations were permitted to limit dividend payments, and the undistributed corporate profits were not taxed if invested in war-related industries.[32] At the same time, the Nazi destruction of free labor unions on May 2, 1933, enhanced the managerial prerogative.[33] The manager, in fact, was elevated to a power-control position, with the unrestricted right to enforce personal and technical subordination in the plant. The introduction of an unfettered managerial prerogative restored a medieval-like patriarchal order in German industry.[34] To eliminate excessive competition and to maintain stable prices, many small businesses were forced into cartels.

In addition to this stimulation of capitalist institutions, all businesses were required by law to become members of appropriate organizations, related both horizontally and vertically. The various economic groups and subgroups were instruments of functional control, while the respective economic chambers represented institutions of territorial control.[35] Reorganized in this fashion, German industry and agriculture were made subject to the new controlled leadership principle. One reason behind the compulsory membership in the various agencies was the Nazi quest for economic self-sufficiency. It was hoped that a totalitarian state, with an economy organized along hierarchical lines of authority, would be in a position to improve the raw material situation rapidly by developing materials which were close substitutes, by eliminating the use of scarce materials in civilian production, and by rigorous stockpiling measures.[36] In addition, the various economic groups also carried on their former trade association activities. Thus reorganized, the free enterprise system was transformed into a politically implemented capitalism in which the economic helplessness of labor, the predicament of stockholders, and the political impotence of the middle class were effectively exploited by German big business. In league with the General Staff, big business (except for close government regulation of foreign exchange, the capital market, and industrial relations) was relatively free from Nazi influence and regulation.[37] As long as profits continued to swell, German big business wore blinders and ignored the rising Nazi brutalities.[38] Despite much talk and confusion, the Nazi rearmament program up to 1936 was quite moderate. Until 1936 such military expenditure claimed roughly 11 per cent of the gross national product; [39] it rose to 15 per cent in 1938.

To recapitulate the four dimensions of the social order of the Third Reich: at the ideological level, it was racism, cast in terms of blood, biology, and heredity—to be a full citizen of the Third Reich one had to prove full Aryan ancestry. On the political side, it was totalitarianism, with the Nazi party holding a monopoly of political power. Institutionally, the Nazis preserved private and corporate property ownership under a controlled managerial system for all "acceptable" and "reliable" citizens. Economically, the Nazis stimulated and encouraged capitalist big business with a view toward building up the industrial war potential.

The Destruction of Jewish Life and Property

From the Darwinians the Nazi racist theoreticians drew the conclusion that human fate and the political life of a nation are partially rooted in its biological stock. Given this hypothesis, the racist-scientists of the Third Reich inferred that certain European ethnic groups were inferior to the Germanic nations and that they either had no right to exist at all or must be reduced to a service caste. The Nazi ideologists, in fact, viewed their "New Europe" as a garden from which all weeds had to be eliminated.[40] The weeds consisted of all "asocial" ethnic groups or individuals who were classified as "useless" or "inferior" and could therefore not possibly acquire an "acceptable" status in the new biological hierarchy of the Nazi state. For this reason, the Nazis had no compunction about using euthanasia or sterilization, about transplanting populations, and in some cases about "Germanizing" (by fiat) portions of non-Germanic groups; "useless" elements were doomed. The Jews were regarded as vermin, subhumans, a bacillus to be exterminated from the body politic of European nations. The Nazis' treatment of the Jews was unique and differed from their treatment of the Poles and Russians, for instance, in the following respects: [41] the Third Reich aimed at total extermination of all Jews, but only portions of inferior Aryan nationalities were to die; the "Final Solution" for the Jews was to take place during the war, while the fate of Slavs and other inferiors was to be postponed until after the Nazi victory; the Nazi campaign against the Jews had priority over the campaigns against all other racial or national groups; the elimination of the Jews justified the use of any and all available means.

The destruction of European Jewry started immediately with Hitler's rise to power in 1933.[42] Before the beginning of World War II in 1939, this process took the form of disfranchisement, stigmatization, forced emigration, and outright plunder of Jewish property. Since for more than a decade the ideologists of the Nazi party had blamed the Jews for "stabbing the fighting effort in the back" during World War I, for the misery of the middle classes during the hyperinflation of the early 1920s, for the onerous reparations burden, and for the Communist threat, it was only to be expected that when they came to power the Nazis had to make good some of their early promises to retaliate for these "wrongs." [43]

Persecution of the Jews started on April 1, 1933, when Julius Streicher organized the first boycott of Jewish shops, businesses, and professional people. A week later, the Nazis promulgated the Law for the Restoration of the Civil Service, which contained an Aryan paragraph. This law made mandatory the pensioning-off of all civil servants of non-Aryan descent. The Aryan paragraph was soon extended to include all lawyers, public-health physicians, artists, writers, university and even high-school students. It was followed by the Law Concerning the Revocation of Naturalization and the Annulment of German Nationality, on July 14, 1933. Then in 1935 came the Reich Citizenship Law and the Law for the Protection of German Blood and Honor, the so-called Nuremberg race laws,[44] which made sexual intercourse between Aryans and non-Aryans a criminal offense.[45] All of these laws were discriminatory in nature, but they were still a far cry from the physical depredations which started in the fall of 1938 and the mass destruction initiated in 1941.[46] In 1938, all Jewish doctors lost their licenses and those Jewish lawyers still practicing, chiefly patent attorneys, were disbarred. Most trades were closed to Jews. Passports held by Jews were ordered stamped with a "J." Also in 1938, the Nazis passed a regulation that every German Jew must add either Israel or Sara to his or her name.[47] By the summer of 1939, German Jews were no longer allowed to take part in German cultural events or to appear at given hours in certain public places. They were also forbidden to drive a car. Without the necessary certificate of "Aryan proof" the German Jew, within a few years, was relegated to a position of social inferiority, cut off from the normal channels of political, intellectual, and economic life. Consigned to outcast status, many Jews left Germany, but many others had insufficient funds to pay their passage. Above all, no country really wanted to receive them.[48]

To someone who has never been really hungry for a long period of time and who does not know what torture is, the idea of starvation does not convey very much; it is just a word, a situation to avoid. In the same vein, the preceding paragraph mentions legislation which for many readers will seem to deal with discrimination, disfranchisement, stigmatization, and spoliation in the abstract, in the mass. Though the literature on the Third Reich is enormous, there is a way to get a sense of the enfolding tragedy in terms of individual life, and that is for the reader to consult some of the numerous memorial volumes on the fate of the Jews in various German cities.[49]

The Nazi Genocide

To elaborate further the roots of anti-Semitism, for centuries European Jewry had been subject to many forms of canonical discrimination, social alienation, and sporadic but savage pogroms. The expulsion of Jews from Spain was legalized in 1483, for instance, and the forced emigration of 300,000 Jews from Spain in 1492, with only nine days to get out, taking virtually nothing along, was an attempt to eliminate the Jews from all areas of Spanish life.[50] Although *autos da fe* were not unusual, this government-inspired eviction was not accompanied by organized and state-financed mass killing of Jews. In addition to its religious background, Spanish anti-Semitism probably received impetus from the envy on the part of the Spanish nobility and the emerging middle class, who wanted the place and position earned by the Jews. Thus, the Inquisition became a vehicle, a means to an end, for the elimination of Jewish influence in response to popular sentiment.

By contrast, in Czarist Russia, the government-inspired pogroms primarily served to intimidate the Jew, as an alien, unreliable element residing in the Slavic community, and thus to mobilize Russian nationalism. Yet in spite of the discrimination, alienation, and infliction of periodic damage to Jewish life and property, it is clear that the Russians never dreamt of any Nazi-style "Final Solution" for their Jews.

The wholesale extermination of people on racial grounds alone was a German invention of this century. It was unprecedented in scope and magnitude.

The Nazi ideology represented, in reality, a bundle of resentments stemming from antiliberalism, antiparliamentarianism, antisocialism, anti-Marxism, anticlericalism, and a large dose of chauvinism. Added to this was the decades-long Volkish indoctrination into anti-Semitic feeling and the existence of canonical legislation concerning the Jews. All of this encouraged intense hatred of the "parasitic Jew." The notion that a Jew, by definition, must be a "Jewish parasite" was very pervasive.[51]

The destruction of European Jewry by the Third Reich, in the final analysis, can be traced to two basic elements: the existence of rampant anti-Semitism and the establishment of a totalitarian political structure in 1933.[52] Without a one-party political regime, it would have been impossible to carry out the mass slaughter, financed by tax money, of innocent people for reasons of race and religion. By the same token, and this is of utmost importance, without the presence of a latent but virulent anti-Semitism, the Nazi dictatorship could hardly have proceeded against the Jews.[53]

The history of the "Final Solution" has already been partially recorded.[54] Out of the detailed chronicles emerges the frightful human and material toll of the Nazi blood bath. The systematized murder perpetrated by the Third Reich exterminated twelve million men, women, and children, of whom seven million were non-Jews, and five million were Jews.[55]

The Germans as a whole, not just the Nazis, profited immensely from the criminal activity of their Nazi government. Between 1933 and 1945, looted Jewish property, in terms of prewar prices, came to $12 billion, according to one authority,[56] and to $32 billion (1933 prices), according to another.[57] These sums do not include the value of the stolen personal property of deportees, the various ransom payments, special Jewish taxes, the purely monetary values involved in the killing of millions of breadwinners, and accumulated interest. The monetary value of the material losses suffered by European Jewry, in terms of prewar prices, estimated by the Jewish Agency in 1945, was $8 billion,[58] while in 1966 Chancellor Konrad Adenauer used a $6 billion figure.[59] But it is impossible to calculate such material losses precisely.

Having branded all Jews subhumans with no right to live, the Nazis then turned their industrial machinery and managerial know-how to the task of exterminating them. This gigantic operation, designed to destroy a national, ethnic, racial, or religious group, for whatever reason, was recognized, when the time for punishment arrived after the war, as a new phenomenon needing its own name, "genocide." Genocide is, of course, a form of war, a form of intra-state war, but genocide differs from war in that the intent is the physical destruction, not just the defeat, of an entire group, however defined. "The victim was born into it; once placed in an undesirable category, he could not escape." [60] But genocide is, of course, not a new phenomenon. From the dawn of history men have been at war with each other. The victors have slaughtered whole populations of losers and destroyed or carried off the possessions of the vanquished captives. These have been the time-honored rights of the winner in an *interstate* conflict.

In the twentieth century, however, purposeful mass murder has taken the form of intrastate war, aimed at physical destruction of the adversary, while in interstate war the objective now is the defeat, not the extermination, of the adversary. Massacre is something else again. Although it signifies indiscriminate killing of human beings in barbarous warfare or in cases of persecution, it does not imply systematic and purposeful extermination. The two major cases of genocide in this century are the Nazi extermination of the Jews and the Stalinist elimination of Soviet "socially unacceptable" elements. The government of the Third Reich used sophisticated and technologically advanced methods for the mass killings, using the techniques of modern organization. The factories of human death with their gas chambers and incinerators were located at a safe distance from urban centers. In them, men in charge "produced" and "managed" death in just about the same way that others manufactured articles for daily use.

In Stalin's Soviet Union of the 1930s, 1940s, and early 1950s, individuals and entire ethnic groups, found unacceptable to the regime, for whatever reason, or simply singled out, were either shot or sent to Siberia for "reeducation," as it was euphemistically called in the U.S.S.R. The Stalinist-type reeducation was by no means identical with Hitler's Final Solution. The remnants of the Russian nobility, officer corps, merchants, and kulaks, and, after May 1934, most of the non-Russian Communists, were not gassed by Zyklon B, but were sent for reeducation to the Siberian tundra. Thousands of the particularly dangerous were sentenced by "flying troikas" and executed the next morning. However, if one could survive the rigors of Siberian work camps indefinitely, one might die on a camp's bunk and not in the gas chamber. The destruction of Stalin's opponents was neither total nor rapid, but it exacted an enormous toll in human life; estimates run from fifteen to twenty million people.[61] As another example of mass murder, Stalin's reeducation program must also be considered as a form of intrastate war. Thus, genocide, a form of intrastate war, in which the bureaucracy and the armed forces have purposefully and systematically destroyed millions of human beings, is probably the salient feature of the twentieth century. The definition of the legal term "genocide" is well known, but its implications and impact are not yet fully understood and have not been studied systematically. To understand why the Bonn government made collective payments to Israel and paid individual compensation to former victims of Nazi persecution, it is necessary, I believe, to turn attention to the study of what I call *socio-teratology*, the study of genocide in a totalitarian, industrialized state.

"Teratology" stems from the Greek word for monster, *teras*. In biology, teratology is the science or study of monstrosities or abnormal formations in plant or animal life, and was probably first named by the French surgeon Ambroise Paré in the sixteenth century.[62] It has been used in other connections, such as in literary studies of monstrosities—Frankenstein or Jekyll and Hyde, for example. The combined word, socio-teratology, then, I suggest for use in dealing with the manifestations of such social monstrosities as the Nazi "Final Solution" or Stalinist-type "purges," as referring to the production of death in industrial, totalitarian societies. In this connection, the small Center for Research in Collective Psychopathology at the University of Sussex, United Kingdom, is encouraging.[63]

Since the Soviet as well as the Nazi totalitarian regime has practiced industrialized genocide, Stalin's holocaust deserves as much attention as Hitler's holocaust. Both were crimes of incredible immensity, atrocities without parallel. Yet, Stalin's holocaust continues to be veiled by big-lie explanations, justifications, and rationalizations as to why it was necessary to remove so many million "asocial" elements.

In conventional terms, "warfare" refers to interstate war, and is defined as "a violent contact of distinct but similar entities." [64] The violent contact represents a legal condition that is characterized by the use of force. More simply, war represents "violence organized on a national basis." [65]

Violent conflicts between organisms of the same species probably began with the emergence of organic nature. Animal warfare has been interpreted in the past as a consequence of psychic elements of at least one of the fighting animals, urging it "(a) to obtain food, (b) to satisfy sex, (c) to secure a home territory, (d) to be active, (e) to preserve its own body and life, (f) to preserve the society of which it is a member, (g) to dominate over others, (h) to free itself from control." [66] One or several of these urges may be the cause of a particular conflict.

A recent work on animal warfare, by the zoologist-physician Konrad Lorenz,[67] suggests that animals fight primarily to defend their territory. As an instance, he demonstrates that fish are far more aggressive toward their own species than toward any other, especially in their own territory. All vertebrates, including man, fight their own species on their own territory. Birds mark territory acoustically, mammals by depositing urine and feces, and the readiness to fight is greatest in the most familiar place. Hence, according to Lorenz, the instinct of aggression is common to man and animals, and manifests itself in so-called intra-specific aggression where members of one species fight each other. The behavior of all vertebrates shows that aggression has deep roots in nature.[68]

It is next to impossible to say whether political, economic, religious, or other considerations represent the *casus belli* in a particular war, but history to some extent does repeat itself. From 3000 B.C. to the present century, interstate war was considered "a stable social institution, and for mankind as a whole a tolerable one." [69]

Before the advent of the Nuclear Age, during one thousand years of their history, the French were at war close to 80 per cent of the time; and of approximately nine centuries of English history, 72 per cent were war years.[70] The average percentage of time at war for the eleven principal European powers—France, Austria, Great Britain, Russia, Prussia, Spain, Netherlands, Sweden, Denmark, Turkey, and Poland—from 1100 to 1900, may be shown in a table: [71]

Century	*Average time at war (percentage)*
12th	45.0
13th	42.0
14th	53.5
15th	64.0
16th	63.5
17th	60.0
18th	36.0
19th	29.5

Thus for eight centuries of European experience, the element of continuity can be observed alongside the element of contingency. Of twenty-six previous civilizations identified by Toynbee, war has been the downfall of all. Since the dropping of the A-bomb at Hiroshima, however, war has ceased to be a viable means of settling interstate disputes, and all-out war may have become a thing of the past,[72] leaving only "limited wars," like the ones in Korea and Vietnam. Nuclear weapons seem to offer mankind a simple choice: permanent peace or universal suicide.[73] The technological changes produced by the scientific revolution have increased the destructive power so much that today, for instance, the Soviet Union and the United States "have the power to do unacceptable damage to each other, and each from points well within its own boundaries." [74] Thus, in the second half of the twentieth century, a nuclear interstate war has become an inappropriate social institution. A thermonuclear war will surely turn the globe into a vast ruin, reduce mankind to barbarism, and result in genetic degeneracy.[75] Such a catastrophe must be avoided. But can mankind also prevent a repetition of Hitler's and Stalin's industrial genocide?

2

Reparations in Perspective:
The Victor-Vanquished Relationship
in Interstate Wars

Historically, the vanquished have always been at the victor's mercy. From the dawn of history, the winner has carried off the possessions of the vanquished, gutted buildings, burned harvests, destroyed cities, razed walls, slaughtered captives or led them into slavery. Such behavior was a time-honored right of the victor, who took what he wanted both during the fighting and after the end of the war. It was not until the late eighteenth century that Rousseau proclaimed "a state wages war only against the other state and not against its population and that, accordingly, hostilities may only be directed against fighting forces and organs of the state, and cannot affect the life and property of private persons." [1] All European countries soon subscribed to Rousseau's principle that a state "was not allowed to confiscate or to destroy, without reason, private enemy property either on the proper territory of the belligerent state or on the battlefield." [2] In 1907, at the Second Hague Conference, all major European land powers agreed upon the inviolability of private property during a state of belligerency.[3] Thus, Rousseau's doctrine of private property was made a binding part of international law.

The practice of levying tribute upon the defeated is as old as organized political life. From the Stone Age on, martial, pastoral, seminomadic, and maritime peoples have exacted tribute from those more settled and less bellicose.[4]

Rome, for instance, levied upon the conquered Italic peoples the so-called *stipendium,* originally to cover the military expenses incurred in the conquest. With the growth of the Roman Empire, however, the *stipendium* was collected regularly in all the new provinces; it thus became a tribute. Originally, the Latin term *tributum* referred to a head tax on Roman citizens—a tax levied at times of special need, as in war—but with the reign of Augustus it was levied regularly upon all non-Roman subjects.[5] With the emergence of national states in the fifteenth and sixteenth centuries, the feudal and medieval practice of pillaging the vanquished was partly abandoned and tributes in kind were replaced by monetary indemnities. These national states, governed by absolute rulers, were expanding their colonial empires overseas and trying to consolidate the domestic economy in an attempt to become self-sufficient.[6]

This quest for economic self-sufficiency resulted in the policy known as mercantilism. The mercantilist ideal implied that a strong national state must be able to produce the basic necessities of life as well as manufactured goods; in addition, it must have the ability to maintain and equip a large army, navy, and merchant marine. Foreign trade was looked upon as a way of importing goods and raw materials that could not be produced at home. Precious metals were indispensable for monetary purposes and for settling adverse trade balances.[7] The accumulation of gold and silver, per se, was a way to, not the goal of, the mercantilist economy. More gold in a country meant higher prices, which stimulated domestic activity; but, above all, a large "war chest" in the national treasury assured essential supplies in the event of war. During the mercantilist era, war was regarded as virtually the normal state of international affairs. In the fifteenth, sixteenth, and seventeenth centuries, periods of peace lasted less than forty years in each century. In so bellicose a world, each nation wanted to be independent economically and as strong as possible militarily.

With the professionalization of European armies in the seventeenth century, the more gold an absolute ruler had, the more soldiers he could array to fight. The strength of the national state, in the final analysis, rested upon its mercenary army and navy. Gold was the very sinew of war.

Mercantilist wars were usually settled by the transfer of territory, mostly overseas, and by monetary indemnities. Since national treasuries had paid for the war, the victors reclaimed some or most of the costs of war by imposing a military indemnity on the vanquished state.[8] The feudal practice of pillage, looting, and taking booty was abandoned in theory, and private property rights were given increasing protection and recognition.

The legal concept of indemnity is usually associated with compensation for damages suffered in a context of justice being exercised. But military indemnity had to do with payments arbitrarily levied by the victor and exacted from the vanquished. Such exactions, based solely on military defeat, had nothing to do with justice. In these terms, indemnity became the victor's way of recovering the costs of a successful military operation. The Peace of Westphalia of 1648, which ended the Thirty Years' War, introduced monetary indemnities.[9] Cromwell exacted one million guilders from the Dutch in the Treaty of Westminster of 1654. The major confrontation of the leading powers in the eighteenth century ended with the Peace of Paris, signed in 1763. Called the first world-wide conflict, the war saw France, England, and Spain, and their allies, engaged in settling colonial accounts. According to the terms of the treaty, France lost Canada and gave up her claims to all territory east of the Mississippi, together with the right of navigation on the Mississippi River. Louisiana, the Philippines, and Cuba were returned to Spain; England received Florida from Spain.[10] Once the French threat was removed from the North American continent, Great Britain became its undisputed master. She now imposed tax levies upon the colonials as their just share of expenses for the defense of the American colonies. The government in London felt that the mother country was entitled to recoup some of the war costs of protecting the colonies, costs that had been borne chiefly by the taxpayers in the British Isles up to 1763. Thus, Roman-type tributes remained part and parcel of the eighteenth-century mercantilist creed. At the risk of oversimplification, it may be said that these impositions led through bitter controversies to the outbreak of the American Revolutionary War in 1775.

The first two decades of the nineteenth century were stormy. Napoleon was the scourge of Europe and his armies roamed all over the Continent. Tottering kingdoms and dukedoms paid what the Corsican demanded as submission money. Such exactions were particularly high from wealthy commercial cities. From defeated adversaries the French Emperor collected indemnities, mostly in gold.

After the defeat of Napoleon, no major wars of long duration took place on the Continent until the outbreak of World War I. The Crimean War (1854–1856) and the Franco-Prussian War (1871) were brief interruptions in an otherwise peaceful era. It was a century of relative peace, based essentially on a doctrine of balance of power. Balance of power was not a balance at all, but rather a Continental balance, with Great Britain serving as the balancer. In diplomatic confrontations she always threw her support behind the weaker party. It was a delicate, constantly shifting arrangement of alliances, but it somehow worked. Once a balance was established, however, there was war, as in 1914 when Germany felt that its strength in conjunction with the Austro-Hungarian Empire was roughly equal in military potential to that of the Entente. In 1939, under Hitler, Germany was again tempted to overrun the weak Eastern European countries, thus destroying the prevailing Eurasian power balance and launching World War II.

Economics of Cash Reparations

The most striking example of cash reparations in the nineteenth century resulted from the Franco-Prussian War, which ended in the defeat of the French. The Treaty of Frankfurt, signed on May 10, 1871, imposed upon her an indemnity of 5 billion francs, cession of territory, and German occupation of certain parts of France until the obligation was paid.[11] It was to be paid within five years in gold, silver, and bills of exchange.

Although the sequestration of Alsace and Lorraine was most humiliating to France, and Bismarck's demand for an indemnity of 5 billion francs appeared astronomical at the time, in other respects the Germans treated their defeated adversary with respect. The peace treaty, for instance, was not a document of capitulation, but a convention between two powers, "which indicated only a negotiated settlement between two equals."[12] It left the French colonial empire intact and placed no limitations upon the size of the French armed forces. For the two belligerents, private and corporate property had remained inviolable throughout the conflict and the peace treaty was most careful not to alter this situation.[13] In fact, the large indemnity aside, France remained one of the Great Powers.

The ability of a defeated country, the debtor, to discharge an obligation in an external currency or gold depends upon two distinct factors: first, its ability to raise the necessary sums in domestic currency, through taxes, levies, or domestic loans; and second, its ability to convert the monies raised in domestic currencies to specified foreign currency or gold.[14]

The debtor can effect real conversion, or transfer, of domestic funds into the creditor's (victor's) currency only if the paying country can generate export surplus and the creditor country permits a corresponding import surplus.

The lightning speed with which the French discharged the 5 billion franc war indemnity made them unique in the history of indemnity payments. The case became the classic textbook example of successful unilateral transfers. Humiliated by the defeat and aroused by the peace terms, the French government mobilized the country's efforts. It raised the necessary sums in two large loans and by the end of 1873 the entire indemnity was paid in full.[15] During the two-year period, to meet its obligation, Paris turned over to Berlin gold, stocks, bonds, and German banknotes and bills of exchange.[16]

The successful transfer of cash reparations can be accomplished only if the receiving country expands its effective demand for all types of goods and services, roughly according to the amount of reparations owed.

The mechanism according to which large foreign payments of a noncommercial kind could be discharged was developed by the classical economists. Under the gold standard, the payment of a war indemnity usually started with an initial gold shipment to the creditor country. The reduction of the amount of gold meant a reduction in the debtor's monetary circulation, accompanied by a fall of price level. For the receiving country, the influx of gold meant an increase of bank reserves and demand deposits, and a rise in the general price level. For the debtor country, the falling price level, in turn, was likely to increase exports and reduce imports.[17] According to this classical theory, the creditor country benefited in two ways from an indemnity: by receiving from the debtor country a specific sum, and by receiving "all other imports from the debtor country at a lower price."[18] For the debtor country, on the other hand, the indemnity payment entailed a loss of foreign exchange on the goods shipped and a further loss on all exports on account of the lower prices generated by the outflow of specie.

In France, a gold standard country, loss of the precious metal inevitably brought a deflation. Conversely, the influx of gold into Germany led to a rise of its general price level. Deflationary tendencies created a French export surplus and generated a German import surplus, "thus transferring capital in the real sense from the debtor to the creditor." [19] For instance, from 1872 to 1875, France had substantial export surpluses, running, on an average, to 510 million francs a year. In four years, theoretically, the French should have been able to generate a trade balance equal to less than half the entire indemnity, while the other half could be realized by gold and currency exports, imports of capital, and the liquidation of investments abroad.[20] Actually, however, sale of government securities abroad and of foreign securities held in France, plus the sacrifice of income from foreign investment, yielded 60 per cent of the entire indemnity sum, while net commodity exports accounted for only 10 per cent.[21] Thus, the French discharged their indemnity obligation not so much by export surpluses but by liquidation of claims on wealth (foreign investments) and by going into debt. The immediate effect of cash reparations on the creditor was to enlarge the amount of currency, and to raise prices, profits, and the level of employment. Under the gold standard, economic expansion of the gold-receiving country continued until, ultimately, the unfavorable trade balance brought about a loss of specie, a decrease in profits, and a decline in employment.[22] In the early 1870s, the indemnity payments were responsible for artificial stimulation of the economic life of Germany, while defeated France was going through a deflationary period. The massive influx of French payments led to a substantial rise in the German price level and was undoubtedly the main factor for the subsequent near-boom conditions, which in turn were terminated by the so-called "Founder's Crash" of 1873.[23] The aggregate business losses of this German economic disaster exceeded the entire indemnity received from the French.

The Treaty of Versailles

The Armistice of November 1918 imposed upon the German government an indemnity *for all damages inflicted upon the civilian population in the victorious countries.* The Versailles Peace Treaty of 1919 which formally ended hostilities was a *Diktatfrieden,* based on onerous terms, if not impossible conditions.[24]

Versailles required that Germany surrender her entire navy and most of the merchant marine, accept stringent limitations on the production of certain strategic goods, have her army reduced to 100,000 men, and pay "a war indemnity unheard of in the history of any country." [25] In addition, she was to cede territory with some million inhabitants, 40 per cent of her blast furnaces, 30 per cent of her steel mills, and 28 per cent of her rolling mills. The proposed reparations bill was so huge that, according to Lloyd George, "no civilized nation has ever been forced to shoulder anything comparable." [26] As a military power, Germany was to be reduced to the level of Greece and, as a naval power, to the level of Argentina.

At the end of 1917, the Soviet government had announced that it would make peace without "contributions and annexations." Since the former meant indemnities, which in the past usually meant victor's vengeance and exploitation of the vanquished, the peacemakers at Versailles dropped this term and coined a new one: reparations. Regardless of this semantic adjustment, it still meant payments by the vanquished. The Allied demands were based essentially on the concept of compensation for injury done. During the Armistice period, they demanded that Germany make "reparation for the damage done in Allied territory." [27] What exactly constituted damage was left undefined. The German delegates accepted the obligation for direct injury to civilians and property; the Armistice rested on it. However, this obligation was greatly inflated at the Versailles Peace Conference. From the published record of the private conversations of Wilson, Lloyd George, Clemenceau, and Orlando, it is now known that the four principal peacemakers agreed that reparations for damages to property and persons suffered by the civilian populations included pensions as well.[28] Since Germany was made morally responsible for all the consequences of the war, Lloyd George felt that if the Germans refused to accept this formula, "we shall resume our unlimited right to compensation for all damages suffered." [29] Keynes reminded the victors that the inclusion of capitalized pensions in the reparations bills was a breach of faith and warned that such exorbitant demands would probably make it impossible to collect anything.[30] However, the public-opinion makers, politicians, and generals in France and England wanted to exact maximum reparations. For instance, Lloyd George fought the 1918 general election on the campaign slogan that he would "Make the Germans Pay"; he would "search their pockets to the uttermost farthing." [31] The French were primarily concerned with weakening Germany as much as they could. They were afraid of the Reich and pointed out to the world that in 1870 and again in 1914 the Germans had penetrated into the heart of France. What Paris was demanding now was that Germany be kept in military, economic, and financial chains.

It took the victorious Allies almost two years to decide how much Germany owed. On May 1, 1921, the Reparations Commission announced that this obligation had been set at 132 billion gold marks (equivalent to $31.5 billion).[32] This charge on Germany represented Allied claims to compensation for physical destruction of property and pensions to soldiers.[33] The final reparations bill was presented to the German authorities on May 5, 1921, and it was accepted a few days later.[34] Supporters of the so-called "fulfillment policy" insisted on making all possible efforts to meet the payments and to show the world Germany's good faith. They hoped that such a policy of faithful execution of the treaty obligations would eventually result in a more favorable public opinion abroad toward Germany and would slowly lead to the lowering of the GM 132 billion indemnity.

The Peace Treaty contained a large array of devices for the exaction of payments, among them the threat of occupation of the Ruhr, economic reprisals, and a general "first charge" on the assets and revenues of the Reich.[35]

There is no question that the reparation demands were excessive, but what lamed the will of the Germans to discharge this obligation was Paragraph 231 of the Versailles Treaty. Whatever the intention behind it, this paragraph was generally interpreted to mean that Germany was morally responsible for the war, and therefore had to pay for the damages.

In contrast to Bismarck's peace terms of 1871, in which equals settled accounts, the Versailles terms treated German delegates "as representatives of a criminal people, which was merely to be sentenced." [36] Germany was made solely responsible for the war and became subject to moral defamation. The noted economist John

Maynard Keynes, in his *The Economic Consequences of the Peace* (1919), produced probably a lasting testimonial to how not to make peace. He predicted that the imposed indemnity was not in the best economic interests of the victors because the Germans would have to flood these countries with their goods to earn the required foreign exchange. Professor F. W. Taussig of Harvard University felt that the 132 billion indemnity represented "sums quite beyond anything heretofore known in international transactions on government account." [37] He also recalled that the indemnity imposed on the French in 1871 was no precedent for the situation facing the Germans after World War I, because the 1871 indemnity had been discharged by France in a very short stretch of time mainly "by utilizing the foreign securities then held by her people, constituting potential assets distributed widely over the world." [38] Since Germany held no such assets, the only way to discharge its indemnity would be to generate a great and constant favorable trade balance.

President Wilson strongly admonished the aging Clemenceau during the sessions of the Council of Four that ". . . Germany could not make very large payments without a greater place in world markets than she had before the war." [39] "Can this be in our interest?" he asked. "Would it not be better to seek to earn this money ourselves in the world markets, rather than to encourage Germany to wrest them from us?" [40] But common sense, so soon after the heady victory, did not have great appeal to the French. As victors they wanted to be reimbursed for some of their war costs. They also felt that the German funds would be handy for paying the heavy war-connected debt owed to the United States. The victors expected to "collect" the indemnity in the form of gold and foreign exchange. The French pointedly insisted that now it was the German turn to tighten the belt and "make good" in the same fashion as the French had settled the 5 billion franc indemnity in 1871. French statesmen could not envision how collecting the indemnity would be possible, but for the time being they did not care. They wanted the "Boche" to pay.

Again Keynes admonished the world that the Versailles Treaty "outraged Justice, Mercy, and Wisdom." [41] He demanded a reduction of the Allied demands to GM 36 billion, a sum he considered to be just enough for the Germans to accept. Keynes also pleaded for the cancellation of all occupation costs and all interest claims.[42]

However, his pleas, for the most part, fell on deaf ears. Hjalmar Schacht, the influential German banker and later Minister of Economics under Hitler, called the Versailles Treaty a "model of ingenious measures for the economic destruction of Germany." [43]

The Implementation of the Versailles "Cash" Indemnity

The actual implementation—that is, the various attempts to discharge the GM 132 billion obligation—falls into four distinct periods. The first and most difficult phase extended from the surrender in 1918 to the end of the inflation crisis in 1923. The second stage ran from August 16, 1924, to August 31, 1929, during the Dawes Plan. The third period extended from September 1, 1929, to the Hoover Moratorium of July 1931; these were the years of the Young Plan. The Hoover Moratorium called a halt for one year to all reparation payments by Germany and all payments on debts owed to the United States by France, England, and others.[44] In late summer of 1932, all German reparations ended. The world economy was in the throes of a depression.[45]

How could Germany have generated the necessary foreign exchange to pay off the GM 132 billion obligation? What were the possible ways of getting dollars, francs, and pounds sterling? First, the Germans, unquestionably, might have obtained foreign exchange by exporting their gold holdings. But the vaults of the Reichsbank held very little gold, and no substantial sums could be mobilized in this way. Second, the liquidation of German foreign investments might have been a source of substantial amounts of foreign exchange had not the Allies seized them during the war. Third, exports of German bonds and currency abroad might have been possible. Unfortunately, the German credit rating was very low in the early 1920s and nobody really wanted German bonds. The only asset they could sell for foreign exchange was in the form of German paper marks. Fourth, German diplomats presumably could have attempted to convince some rich nation that unless they got foreign aid they would turn Germany over to some supposed threatening power to use to launch a conquest of the world. A number of nations, of course, used this type of argument successfully after World War II, thereby receiving many billions in aid from Washington for the purpose of preventing a presumed communist take-over. But, alas! America was not in the "foreign-aid business" at that earlier date. The only way Germany could generate foreign exchange was by large-scale exportation of goods. But this was precisely what the victors did not want. So it was that Germany's "capacity to pay reparations" became a stumbling block.[46]

The capacity of an industrial nation to pay an indemnity in the form of cash reparations depends upon two interrelated factors: its ability to raise funds domestically, whether by taxation or other levies, and its having the opportunity to convert these domestic funds into foreign currency.[47] For reparations funds, however collected, "can be transferred to other countries only by means of an export surplus."[48] The gigantic GM 132 billion indemnity could ultimately be discharged in goods only. The limit of yearly remittances was governed by the "excess of merchandise exports over merchandise imports,"[49] while the extent of the indemnity that could be extracted depended upon the availability of exportable merchandise.

As early as 1921, when Western European countries and the United States were in the throes of a short but very pronounced recession, Allied demands for German ships, coal, machinery, reconstruction materials, and chemicals had disturbing effects on the economies of the victors. For instance, while German shipyards were busy day and night building ships for delivery to England, British yards were idle. Furthermore, the German-delivered ships increased the excess capacity of the already under-utilized British merchant fleet.[50] In addition, German coal deliveries to France deprived the British coal-mining industry of its market, again with adverse consequences for the British economy. Similarly, the French government was forced to recognize that its labor unions and industrial firms had no interest in receiving large amounts of German machinery, consumer goods, or coal because such shipments deprived Frenchmen of their jobs and depressed the profit margin of their business establishments.[51] France and other victor nations wanted cash (gold, dollars, francs, or pounds sterling), and not German-made goods. To stem the influx of German goods and to protect their own labor and industry, France and Italy began erecting higher tariff walls.

Of course, in the early 1920s Germany might have earned the necessary foreign exchange for reparations by engaging in so-called triangular trade and transferring the accrued proceeds to France, Britain, and Italy.[52] Such a trade pattern would have involved German exports to the "rest of the world." However, "the rest of the world" could have meant only the United States. Had this happened, the Germans would have flooded the U.S. market and, incidentally, destroyed the American chemical industry which had come into being only during World War I. They would also have earned several hundred million dollars, but at the expense of great injury to American firms and serious aggravation of the American unemployment situation. The crux of the matter was that, although the German industrial capacity to pay reparations was large enough, there remained the consideration (to cite John Foster Dulles) that "capacity to give is immaterial unless there is a corresponding willingness and capacity to receive." [53] The victors showed no such capacity. Only slowly did it dawn upon the Allies that they must ask the question: "How much German-made goods are we willing to accept?"

Before that question was asked, however, the German government had to search for gold and foreign exchange, because the first installment of a billion gold marks was due at the end of May 1921, in other words within 25 days after the Allies made known the figure of the entire German indemnity. The Reichsbank vaults were empty of gold and foreign exchange. But, since the leaders of the Weimar Republic were firm in their resolve to honor their pledge to pay reparations, the Reichsbank was instructed to buy foreign exchange and borrow abroad. Credits were arranged with some Dutch banks, on rather onerous terms, and the first billion gold marks was finally deposited to the Allied account.[54] Indicative of the difficulties that were to follow, this sum was made up of three-month treasury bills endorsed by the Dresdener, Deutsche, Discontgesellschaft, Darmstädter, and National banks.[55] The loan from the Dutch banks amounted to almost 300 million marks.

But all this was just the beginning. The London Reparations Agreement specified a yearly payment of two billion marks, plus 26 per cent of Germany's yearly exports.[56] With difficulty the German government made one more cash payment—only partial—in the amount of GM 500 million in November 1921. The inability to raise the necessary foreign exchange as installments fell due led, on December 14, 1921, to a request for a moratorium. From 1922 on,

Germany was allowed to pay reparations in kind by making deliveries of coal, chemicals, and other products.

An important question that has often perplexed the student of the period is: Was the reparations amount of GM 132 billion directly responsible for the hyperinflation and collapse of the German currency in 1923? The answer to this question is probably no. Indirectly, however, the enormous Allied-imposed obligation undoubtedly created negative psychological influences which ultimately undermined internal confidence in the future of Germany. These influences helped to give rise to a "flight from the mark," as people tried to convert funds to a ready supply of foreign exchange. Of course, the danger of revolutionary leftist or rightist movements plus the desire to avoid heavy taxation were additional factors which aggravated the "flight from the mark." The actual cash payments amounted to about GM 1.5 billion by 1921. It is not likely that these payments, by themselves, could have brought about the ruin of the German mark. However, it can be noted that November 1921, following the partial payment of the second installment, marked the point when the continuous rise in the dollar rate spread panic among the Germans and led to the quickening, widespread attack on the mark.[57] Earlier, it must be recalled, strong inflationary pressures had become evident with the termination of hostilities in 1918. In particular, the prices of imported goods rose much more rapidly than domestic prices, and the mark depreciated in terms of the dollar. Germany became a "cheap country" as Americans and foreigners eagerly bought up large amounts of paper marks in the hope of making windfall gains when the inflationary pressures should subside. In fact, some writers felt that there was at the time an "insatiable foreign demand for paper currency." [58] According to this account, the Germans sold close to 8 billion in paper marks for hard currency. Exports of the paper marks became a foreign exchange earner and helped to pay for imports. However, foreign exchange obtained in this way did not necessarily accrue to the government, since most of it was acquired by individuals and corporations. For this reason, the government itself sold paper marks abroad to obtain foreign exchange.[59] In spite of these developments, the dollar rate of the mark throughout 1920 remained relatively stable and reached over 60 marks for the dollar on June 1, 1921. The real attack on the mark had begun in September 1921 partly because of the reparations bill and partly on account of the division of Upper Silesia between Germany and Poland, which was heralded in the German press as a threat of economic ruin. Thus, even before 1921, exports of paper marks were reflected in falling quotations for the mark. As the dollar became more expensive, import prices rose sharply. This, in turn, was reflected in higher export prices and a rise in the domestic price level.

In addition to these developments, purely domestic considerations also generated forces that undermined the value of the currency. The government of the Weimar Republic had to support millions of people living close to subsistence level because of physical inability to make a living. Orphans, war widows, mutilated civilians, crippled war veterans, all had to be supported from the public purse. The government also paid for public-works programs to enable people to eke out an existence. In view of the weak financial structure of the newly established Weimar Republic, budget deficits became the rule, and these were met by continued issues of paper money. Keynes calculated, for instance, that by taxing 43 per cent of the prevailing per capita income it might have been possible to obtain enough marks for reparations and probably to avoid budget deficits as well. But, he predicted, any government "which makes serious attempts to cover its liabilities will fall from power." [60] Keynes reasoned that since such a rate of taxation for political reasons was virtually impossible, public deficits and note-printing were bound to follow hand in hand.

From 1922 on, Germany paid reparations in kind. These deliveries became mandatory by decision of the Reparations Commission, which fixed such terms as prices, quantities, and delivery dates. Reparations in kind did not require any foreign exchange because the German producers were paid in paper marks out of the budget. This form of reparations bypassed the so-called transfer problem of converting paper marks into foreign exchange. However, the fixing of delivery prices was a source of friction between the Reparations Commission and the German government. Since these deliveries were started in considerable quantities prior to the establishment of any adequate system of accounts and supervision, bitter disputes were inevitable. For example, the Allies by 1922 had supposedly credited the German government with only slightly more than 20 per cent of all the deliveries it had made.[61] The question of setting prices for deliveries in kind led to protracted negotiations. Should these prices be fixed in gold, German paper marks, or the currency of the receiving country? It was finally decided to fix prices in the currency of a third country and to have the payor and payee assume the risk of fluctuations in the exchange rate. The exchange rate prevailing on the day when the Reparations Commission accepted the German delivery would be used for accounting purposes.[62]

Deliveries in kind, however, were a mixed blessing for both parties. It is true that such payments did not call for foreign exchange, and the Reichsbank was under no pressure to sell paper marks abroad. If the German budget had been balanced and the payments for these deliveries been made out of tax receipts, they would not have been a contributory factor of an open inflation. But instead of budget surpluses, the governments of the Weimar Republic in the early 1920s were operating with chronic budget deficits. Insufficient tax receipts were made up by letting the banknote printing presses run. To pay German suppliers of reparations commodities, the government needed more revenue. Thus, the larger the mandatory deliveries, the greater the deficits, and the more notes were issued. In this fashion, reparations in kind contributed to the already rapid depreciation of the mark.

In 1922, the German government paid hardly any cash reparations—primarily deliveries in kind—but the depreciation of the paper mark accelerated; and in the fall hyperinflation set in.[63] A new wave of pessimism about Germany's future seized the nation and a renewed attack on the paper mark got under way. Nearly every German was buying and hoarding foreign bills of exchange and currency as a protection against the evaporation of the domestic mark.[64] Industrialists were the biggest hoarders of gold and foreign currency.[65]

Given the reparation-induced depreciation of the mark, German industrial and commercial interests learned how to turn the continued decline of the paper mark into a profitable proposition. Businessmen obtained credits from the Reichsbank by discounting commercial paper. The loan's proceeds were invested in foreign exchange, inventories, or plant and equipment, and the debt was repaid at maturity with handsome profits in paper marks. The Reichsbank's policy of easy credit was duplicated by all commercial banks and became general practice.[66] Heavy industry was particularly adroit at exploiting inflationary credits for building bigger firms and industrial empires. Concentration in German industry proceeded at a rapid pace during these years.[67]

From January 1919 to January 1921, the average dollar price declined from 8.9 to 64.9 paper marks.[68] After the payment of one billion gold marks of reparations in the summer of 1921, the paper mark probably lost its function as a "store of value." The business community and the populace in general came to believe that price increases were to continue indefinitely. By July 1922, more than 400 paper marks were being paid for one dollar; in September the price jumped to 1,500 marks and in November had tripled to 4,550 marks.[69] In the late fall of 1922, the paper mark ceased to be a "unit of account" in terms of the usual function of money in an economy. From then on, contracts were made either in dollars or in other commodities. The paper mark, however, was still used as "a medium of exchange." As long as feverish business activity continued, the paper mark was accepted, but it was quickly disposed of or converted. While numerous industrial empires were being built in the vortex of inflation, the Paris government believed that the government of the Weimar Republic was deliberately evading its reparations obligations. In 1922, Germany had paid only GM 450 million out of the assessed GM 720 million; France and Belgium also felt that the German government was deliberately slackening in the delivery of reparations in kind. They therefore decided to occupy the Ruhr Valley, the industrial heart of Germany.[70] French and Belgian troops marched into the Ruhr in January 1923,[71] to exact by force what was their "proper due." The occupation of the Ruhr struck the last blow at the paper mark; it broke the camel's back, so to speak.

Germany's response to this action was the suspension of all deliveries in kind to France and Belgium. The government also prohibited the taking of orders from the occupation authorities by any German official. It also financed the "passive resistance" of the population, including business firms. This subsidy swelled the public deficit enormously and ultimately led to the complete collapse of the paper mark. Before the occupation of the Ruhr, during November 1922, "only" 9,000 paper marks were needed to buy one dollar. With the occupation of the Ruhr, however, the price jumped to almost 18,000 to the dollar; in July 1923 it rose to 353,000; a month later to 4.6 million; in October it reached 23 billion. By November 1923, at the height of hyperinflation, the price of the dollar had soared to the astronomical figure of 4.2 trillion marks.[72]

Three hundred paper mills supplied paper to one hundred and fifty printeries with 2,000 presses and, working around the clock, they printed currency, but even this herculean effort could not satisfy the insatiable demand for notes. The demand rose so fast that the issuing authorities were physically unable to keep up with it. Overprinting old notes with higher denominations was one way to help matters; another method saw cities, provinces, and even business corporations issuing their own note currency. All this made it patently obvious that the German hyperinflation was marked by an acute shortage of currency relative to the demand for it.[73]

German authors, as a rule, have placed the blame on the reparations burden as a primary cause of the hyperinflation, while Allied experts have felt that the chronic budget deficits, by swelling the money supply, eventually brought about the eclipse of the mark. Again the question arises: What was the real cause of the inflation? Was it the work of the government of the Weimar Republic, of the big industrialists, of the underground General Staff?[74] By pleading poverty and social chaos, the German government could assert that it was unable to pay reparations, even while the industrialists were building greater empires than ever. Was the cause of inflation the exchange depreciation or the chronic public deficits? Probably all these forces were at work and, at some stage, one or another predominated. In 1921, exchange depreciation was the major force behind inflation; after the occupation of the Ruhr, the public deficits became the more important factor. Then, too, the prevailing pessimistic mood of the German people was an important part of the total picture. However, the answer to the question of what sustained the inflationary process is a key, a missing link, in the explanation of the phenomenon.

Joan Robinson, the noted British economist, believed that continuous "rise in money wages" provides the explanation of the hyperinflation, and she insisted that "whatever starts a violent rise in money wages starts inflation."[75] According to the argument, the rapid depreciation of the mark in 1921 raised import prices, which, in turn, pushed domestic prices up as well. The higher cost of living led to the demand for higher wages. Unemployment was low, profits were rising, and wage demands were met. Rising wages increased money incomes and costs of production. Every round of wage increases "precipitated a further fall in the exchange rate, and each fall in the exchange rate called forth a further rise in wages." [76] As long as the expectation of rising prices continued, it stimulated investment in plant and equipment. However, the stimulating element of inflation on economic activity began to lose its force. Everybody wanted to buy and nobody wanted to sell. Goods were much more valuable than paper marks. Shopkeepers did not know whether they would be able to replenish goods they sold, regardless of the price at which they were sold. Firms were not anxious to sell to domestic buyers, so they hoarded most of their output. Manufacturers were allowed to acquire foreign exchange to import raw materials. They kept their plants going, but output went into inventories. Merchants treated buyers almost like enemies, because they deprived them of goods that could not be replaced. "Buying, like kissing, went by favor." [77] In the summer of 1923, the monetary economy had virtually broken down. Barter was practiced in many areas of economic life and division of labor became well-nigh impossible. In August of that year, unemployment rose sharply and by September it had assumed alarming proportions. The fires of inflation had burnt themselves out. Only the introduction of the Rentenmark in mid-October 1923 brought any semblance of order to the monetary chaos.

The redistributive impact of the monetary crisis on various social groups was irreparable. The process of hyperinflation penalized wage earners, salaried people, rentiers, and dealers in nominal claims (banks); it favored businessmen, the profit-takers. [78] The savings of the German middle class disappeared in the monetary vortex and with them went the source of independent incomes. The proletarianization of the middle class contributed very substantially to the destruction of the Weimar Republic. [79] The middle classes lost not only their financial status but their social position as well. The politically conservative element of the Weimar Republic was *the* victim of the monetary upheaval. [80] Many a recruit to the Nazi Party came from the ranks of these German *déclassé* elements—bitter, frustrated, alienated. On the other hand, the industrialists, landowners, merchants, and speculators of all sorts profited from the inflation.

The big industrialists discovered in no time at all how to use the sustained depreciation of the paper mark for their own purposes. They borrowed paper marks and sold them for the sake of depressing the mark's value; they hoarded whatever foreign exchange they could obtain. The political weakness of the Weimar Republic made it virtually impossible to catch the speculators and industrialists in a "short" position. In addition to speculation, the industrialists rapidly expanded productive capacity, especially of heavy industry. At the end of the hyperinflation, the industrial capacity of German heavy industry was larger than it had been in 1914. Thus, in a period of open inflation, the fixed income groups paid an "inflationary tax" to the profit-takers who built gigantic industrial empires.

From the Armistice in 1918 to the introduction of the Rentenmark in October 1923, Germany had paid reparations in cash and in kind out of her own resources. After the stabilization of the mark, it dawned on many Western statesmen and the public at large that the economic provisions of the Versailles Treaty were both malignant and downright silly. The victorious Allies had condemned Germany to pay what Winston Churchill called "reparations on a fabulous scale." [81] The victors wanted to squeeze Germany till the pips squeaked.[82] After the end of the hyperinflation period, the Reparations Commission recommended the Dawes Plan, a new system of collecting the required reparations sums in Germany out of specific revenues and then transferring these sums to the creditor countries.[83] The German budget contributions were obtained by the so-called "controlled revenues" in the form of revenues from customs, beer, tobacco, and sugar taxes, and the alcohol monopoly. These sums were to be paid in German currency into the account of the General Agent, held by the Reichsbank. Thereafter the "Transfer Committee" of the General Agent would transfer the funds into foreign currencies as long as such transfers did not undermine the stability of the mark.

The Dawes Plan was to go into effect on September 1, 1924. Reparation payments were to begin again in 1924–1925 at the rate of GM one billion a year and were to rise to GM 2.5 billion a year by 1928–1929. Again, the principal difficulty for the Germans was the task of transferring the necessary payments into foreign currencies, because such transfer called for "an extension of the German export trade." [84] For this reason, deliveries in kind continued to play a major role, even during the Dawes Plan years.[85] The necessary foreign exchange was obtained from the proceeds of American loans.[86] In other words, it was not the Germans, but their American creditors, who were actually paying reparations. The problem of how these debts would eventually be paid remained unsolved for the time being. Numerous experts analyzed the thorny transfer problem, but, as long as Germany made all reparations payments punctually, the lender, creditor, and borrower were all reconciled.[87]

At the beginning of 1930, the Dawes Plan was replaced by the Young Plan, which was set up for the Germans to pay annuities for almost sixty years, until 1988. On January 1, 1930, all foreign control over the German economy was removed and the country was finally free from what she considered the dictates of the victors.[88]

Under these new arrangements, the so-called "present value" of all German payments was computed at GM 37 billion, only one-third of the unrealistic sum of GM 132 billion set by the Reparations Commission in 1921. The General Agent for Reparations was replaced by the Bank for International Settlements in Basel, Switzerland, which was to supervise the execution of the German reparation payments. After two years of operation, the Young Plan had to be suspended on account of the deepening world-wide depression. Germany was subject to severe withdrawal of funds from abroad and had to beg for standstill agreements. To stem the spreading financial panic, President Hoover called a moratorium, suspending all international debt payments for one year from June 30, 1931. However, Congress refused to legislate a debt reduction. After the year had passed, the depression was even more acute. Finally, the Lausanne Agreement of July 9, 1932, scuttled the Young Plan and virtually wiped out all reparations claims, except for a token sum.[89]

From 1925 to 1932, German reparation payments (deliveries in kind, payments for the armies of occupation, and payments in foreign currency), according to Professor Fritz Machlup of Princeton University,[90] amounted to 11.3 billion marks; according to the Reparations Commission, the sum was almost 21 billion marks. The official German estimates of total amounts paid as reparations was 68 billion.[91] During this period, Germany's public and private indebtedness abroad increased by some 20 billion marks.[92] Such development meant that after the stabilization of the mark, foreigners, especially Americans, bought German bonds and other promises to pay, and the Berlin government used the proceeds of the loans to

meet the annual reparations bill. The French and British governments, in turn, sent these receipts to Washington, to pay back their
war debts. As long as the American credits were flowing to Germany,
this atmosphere of euphoria anesthetized politicians and money
lenders. However, as soon as credits were recalled from Germany,
this "merry-go-round" of New York-Berlin-Paris-London-Washing-
ton stopped, and the whole scheme collapsed.

Reparations After World War II

The German reparations impasse was one of the major unsolved
economic and political problems of the 1920s. Victors and vanquished alike learned from long and painful experience that Germany's ability to raise the necessary funds domestically through
taxes was not enough; these sums had to be converted into foreign
currencies, and that could be done only by deliberate stimulation
of exports and reduction of imports.[93] Germany's attempt to earn
foreign exchange resulted in a scramble for world markets. Neutral
countries, which had nothing to do with the war, reparations, or
war debts, were hurt as much as the victors themselves, but notably
affected were France, Belgium, Italy, and Great Britain. These
countries had at that time basically laissez-faire economies and their
capacity to absorb German goods depended upon what the internal
employment picture was.[94] Since considerable unemployment prevailed, these countries were diligently erecting protective tariff walls
to shelter home markets.

From what had happened after World War I, Allied statesmen
knew that large reparations obligations were, to a large extent, responsible for the rebuilding and modernization of Germany's heavy
industry.[95] But after World War II they were determined to destroy
the Reich's war potential, that is, its heavy industry.

At the Yalta Conference in early 1945, the Big Three Allies decided that reparations would be taken in three forms: (a) German
industrial equipment, machine tools, ships, rolling stock, and investments abroad; (b) annual deliveries of goods from current production, and (c) use of German labor.[96] The total reparations claim
against the Reich was set at $20 billion, with 50 per cent of this sum
destined for the Soviet Union. The Potsdam Agreement of August 2,
1945, further provided that the allotted shares of reparations could

be taken from the respective zones of occupation and from German-owned assets abroad. The Soviet Union was also promised 15 per cent of all removable plant and equipment located in the Western zones of occupation (this against food shipments), and another 10 per cent without any *quid pro quo*.[97]

Since the delivery obligations were stated in terms of specific sums of, for example, tons of coal per year, the Allies wanted to price the commodities as cheaply as possible, whereas the Germans wanted to price them as high as possible so as to obtain maximum credit on the reparations books.

The concept of reparations in kind was not an innovation of World War II. It was the inability of the Weimar government to raise enough foreign exchange for cash reparations in 1922 that had led to the introduction of such payments.

All armistices terminating belligerency during and after World War II made payments in kind the "exclusive method of reparations."[98] Aside from Germany, the various peace treaties signed in 1947 provided for many different forms of payments in kind for reparation purposes.

The Soviet-Finnish armistice of September 1944 had imposed an obligation of $300 million to be paid within six years in seventy-two equal installments, entirely in kind.[99] The commodities to be delivered were divided into 199 categories and, for late deliveries of any of the specified items, the Finns had to pay a fine of 5 per cent a month.[100] The salient feature of this reparations agreement was that the Finnish obligations toward the Soviet Union were specified in commodities for which Finland had hardly any productive equipment or skills. In 1938, for example, 80 per cent of Finland's exports were timber and forest products, but they constituted only 30 per cent of the goods to be delivered to the Soviet Union. Machinery, ships, heavy equipment, and cables, items which accounted for only 2 per cent of Finnish exports in 1938, constituted more than 70 per cent of all mandatory deliveries.[101]

Next to the problem of the composition of the reparations deliveries, the question of pricing was of crucial importance. The Finns were asked to pay $300 million in terms of 1938, not 1944, prices, which raised the total sum to be paid by 20 per cent.[102] And, finally, the Soviet technical requirements, in terms of quality and specifications, were considerably higher than those prevailing in the West. The reparations weighed heavily on the Finns during the first five postwar years. For example, in 1945, reparations as a percentage of Net National Product was 7.6 per cent and constituted 20.9 per cent of state expenditure; in 1948, the corresponding values were 3.2 and 10.7 per cent. In 1952, the last year of Finnish payments, reparations constituted 1.1 per cent of N.N.P. and 4.1 per cent of state expenditure.[103] Since Finland's reparations were mostly in machinery, equipment, and ships, these industries experienced very substantial expansion. In fact, at the end of the payments to the Soviet Union, these capacities were just about double those of the prewar years,[104] and the Finns had to look hard for new markets.

The Soviet Union also took reparations from Hungary, Romania, Bulgaria, and Italy. The peace treaty with Hungary required it to deliver 300 million gold dollars' worth of diversified goods over a six-year period. Goods worth $200 million were to be delivered to the Soviet Union, $50 million to Czechoslovakia, and $50 million to Yugoslavia.[105] Romania had to pay 300 million gold dollars' worth of reparations goods, half in oil and oil products, the rest in industrial equipment and agricultural produce. Bulgaria's obligations were 75 million gold dollars' worth, of which one-third went to Yugoslavia, and two-thirds to Greece. Later, the Soviet Union extended the delivery period by two years, changed the composition of the mandatory payments, raised the price of goods to be turned over, and, in mid-1948, halved the balance. From Italy the Soviet Union collected $100 million, also in goods. The Soviet Union exacted heavy reparations from East Germany in the form of war booty, official dismantling of plants and equipment, and deliveries from current production. From 1945 to 1960, the value of such exactions amounted to RM-DM 63 billion at current prices.[106]

The rationale of the Soviet reparations policy thus was replacement by the aggressor state of damages suffered by the invaded state. In contrast to the Versailles Treaty, where the Allies formally demanded compensation for damages to the civilian population while, in effect, pressing for an indemnity, the Soviet Union demanded merely partial replacement of damages to her economy. For instance, Italy paid only $100 million, which represented one-twentieth of all damages directly inflicted upon the Soviet Union by the Italian armed forces during World War II. According to the Soviet Union, such modest demands rose from consideration for the vanquished nation's ability to pay. This compensation was fixed not in cash but in kind, partly in industrial plants, equipment, and deliveries from current production, and, to some extent, from the liquidation of the vanquished nation's foreign investments.[107] Reparations in kind also eliminated the need for foreign loans and the scramble for markets abroad, as demonstrated by the German experience after World War I. In total, the Soviet Union collected close to $900 million from her former adversaries.[108] The total estimate of Soviet losses came to $128 billion. But the $900 million figure must be looked at with the recognition of Soviet insistence on 1938 prices. Also, the demands for quality in the goods to be delivered frequently tripled the price of many mandatory deliveries.

The Soviet reparations demands were nominally modest, but actually Hungary, Romania, Bulgaria, Poland, and later Czechoslovakia were transformed into Soviet-type societies. Moscow installed governments in which Communists held all strategic posts. With one-party dictatorships firmly in control, the Soviets proceeded to develop centrally administered economies with heavy emphasis on capital-goods industries.

Soviet-type industrialization went hand-in-hand with reparations demands. First, priority in industrialization was for reparations. Second were the so-called joint companies, which mostly grew out of former German holdings in these countries. Third was the transfer of former German-held assets back to these countries. The joint stock companies became vehicles for obtaining large amounts of high-quality products at low prices. The re-acquiring of former German holdings from the joint companies was costly, and the Soviets demanded high-quality commodities of all sorts at low prices.[109] The interesting aspect of Soviet exactions was that they stressed reparations from current production at low prices. Since Hungary, Bulgaria, and Romania were firmly in the Soviet orbit, it was also claimed that reparations from current production facilitated the industrialization of these countries. In other words, the vanquished made good their material responsibility to the victor and at the same time developed and diversified their economies. Since these countries had changed from essentially market-type economies to quantitative-output planning, the end of reparations did not leave them with excess capacity. The Soviet-style, forced-draft industrialization kept all the facilities available in use.

In Germany, during the first two years of occupation, the three victorious powers and France wanted to destroy the German war potential in all its forms. At that time, military security was still the primary objective of the occupation and the four Allies were supposedly building a better future for the Continent, making it safe from future German aggression. In 1944 and 1945, the American policy-makers believed that as long as Germany possessed heavy industry peace in the world was impossible. Henry Morgenthau, Jr., the wartime Secretary of the Treasury, and President Roosevelt were the most outspoken proponents of this view, and complete destruction of German heavy industry after the end of hostilities was decided upon at the second Quebec Conference in September 1944.[110] Even though this drastic policy was never implemented, the Americans and British dismantled many plants completely or in part and sent them abroad.[111] The so-called "war plants" were simply blown up. They also strangulated German industrial production by imposing low production ceilings as a means of controlling retained industrial capacity, as we shall see in the next chapter. At this point, it is merely important to keep in mind that reparations in kind (in the form of machinery, equipment, entire plants, mandatory delivery of patents and trade secrets, prohibitions against certain kinds of industrial production, and the imposition of production ceilings) were a corollary of industrial disarmament.

3

From Ruin to Reconstruction: 1945–1952

In 1952, West Germany's economic recovery was well under way, but by no means complete. Substantial injections of American aid had helped speed revival, but Germany's obligations, external and internal, were staggering. For instance, as one of the conditions for the creation of the Federal Republic, the Western Allies had demanded that the new German government acknowledge its responsibility for the prewar debts of the former Reich, both public and private. In addition, Chancellor Adenauer was seeking a settlement with Israel and world Jewry of Jewish "global claims." He was also ready to promulgate comprehensive legislation on indemnification. Occupation costs had to be paid. Ten million refugees had to be absorbed into the rump state that was now West Germany. Structural readjustment of the entire economy still lay ahead, although no one really foresaw how foreign trade would develop. With the overvalued exchange rate, experts were pessimistic about the future of the balance of payments.[1]

The emphasis of the new government's economic policy was upon the stability of its currency and equilibrium in its balance of payments. In fact, throughout 1950 and 1951 an intense balance-of-payments struggle took precedence over everything else, prodded by the scheduled decline of American aid by the end of 1952. Nevertheless, by January 1952, the balance-of-payments crisis was almost over and, in the spring of that year, a government team headed by Dr. Hermann J. Abs, Chairman of the Board of the Deutsche Bank, was in London negotiating the foreign debt settlement, while still another West German delegation was discussing a settlement of Jewish global claims in Wassenaar in the Netherlands. As the following chapters will show, the Wassenaar talks were long and difficult.

The West German plea of limited ability to pay poisoned the atmosphere at first and resulted in a hostile press. Abs insisted that the London debt talks and the Wassenaar negotiations were inseparable. His position was a difficult one; for, while he was proposing a reduction of West Germany's total indebtedness (not so much the principal as accrued interest), Adenauer was preparing to create an unprecedented new debt. Abs felt that it was unfair to ask former creditors to cut back their claims and, at the same time, permit West Germany to incur substantial new financial commitments. He was particularly concerned about the nation's ability to pay any new obligations, whether they were the renegotiated earlier debts of the Reich or something else. He was sensitive to the fact that in 1952 West Germany still suffered from a dollar shortage.

While the London Debt Conference dealt primarily with economic matters, the Wassenaar preoccupations were chiefly political. But the outcome of both conferences was of crucial importance to the Adenauer government. The London settlement was supposed to restore Bonn's financial credit standing; the Wassenaar settlement was designed to give West Germany a better moral image. Both entailed a considerable outlay of funds. For this reason Abs insisted that the two conferences were interrelated, as indeed did Adenauer himself.[2] Abs feared that if the London talks failed, Bonn's credit standing would not be restored and the government would not have the means to pay other obligations. The Israeli government and the Jewish Claims Conference resisted this argument, insisting that the Wassenaar negotiations had nothing in common with the talks in London. The Israelis reminded the Germans that they had entered the Netherlands talks on purely moral grounds and not to haggle. Moral claims were, they contended, above and beyond the bargaining techniques appropriate to Dr. Abs' conference in London. Abs, on the other hand, was inclined not to give the Israelis any preferential treatment. Thus a clash was inevitable, and it reverberated throughout the world, making headlines and agitating minds on both sides. How legitimate was Abs' claim?

From Unconditional Surrender to Cold War

By the spring of 1945, Hitler's dream of a Thousand-Year Reich had evaporated in smoke and ruin. The decimated remnants of the German armed forces were no match for the combined American,

British, and Soviet might. On May 7, 1945, the German High Command surrendered unconditionally at General Dwight D. Eisenhower's headquarters in Reims. The following day, a similar document was signed with the Soviet High Command in Berlin.[3]

Shortly thereafter, the Allied Control Council in Berlin assumed authority in the defeated Reich. The country was to be divided into four zones of occupation, each subject to the supreme rule of the American, British, Soviet, or French commander. The four commanders would jointly and unanimously exercise legislative, judicial, and executive authority within Germany.

The dream in 1945 was that the mighty East-West partnership that had destroyed Hitler's armies would remain united in building a lasting peace. Hopes, yearnings, for peace ran high. Some skeptics had certain misgivings, but the more optimistic planners pointed out that on the day of Germany's surrender the Soviets in San Francisco were helping to bring into being the Charter of the United Nations. As the generals faced the task of making sure that the Germans would never again disturb the equilibrium of the world, the Allies felt that holding down the defeated enemy economically and militarily was the surest way to guarantee the newly won peace. Similarly, they saw unity of purpose in following this policy as the surest way to preserve the wartime alliance and maintain it as a workable peacetime coalition.

Peace, as it exists in the 1970s, is founded on the fear of thermonuclear bombs and missiles and not, as mankind had hoped in 1945, on mutual trust, cooperation, and confidence. What went wrong? Who or what was responsible for this unexpected cooling off of the warm relationship among the wartime Allies? When did it all start?

To judge from the intentions and actions of the American and British governments as revealed in the records, these two allies wanted to carry the wartime partnerships over into peacetime. Statesmen in the West were ready to coexist with the Soviet Union in the consolidation of victory and the establishment of peace.[4]

The over-all orientation of American policy toward the defeated Reich was based upon President Franklin D. Roosevelt's "Grand Design" for the postwar world, which assumed that the Soviet Union and the United States could become partners in peace because the struggle against Nazi Germany had made them partners in war.[5] Throughout the war, Roosevelt did everything possible to win the confidence of the Russian premier, Joseph Stalin. To demonstrate American good will and his sincere desire to cooperate with the Soviets, the President insisted that the occupation of Germany become a proving ground of Moscow-Washington cooperation. He felt that without a strong Soviet-American partnership lasting peace would be impossible. The Grand Design offered a prospect of worldwide peace, and for that everybody yearned.

Nobody knows for sure exactly when the Cold War started, but the first and strongest manifestations were noted in Germany while the ruins of the Third Reich were still smoldering. A number of salient reasons can be cited for its outbreak, the first undoubtedly the ideological differences. Marxist-Leninist ideology regarded the capitalist West as an enemy.[6] During the war, Soviet theoreticians played down the ideological incompatibility of the Allies, but after victory Moscow's antagonism came to the fore at once. It quickly became evident that the Soviet quest for security involved expansion toward the center of Europe.[7] Where the line between legitimate security needs ends and an openly expansionist policy begins is, of course, difficult to say under any circumstances. But the spread of the Soviet sphere of influence from 1939 on was substantial and alarming to the Western powers. For, after consolidating its post-World War II territorial gains, the U.S.S.R. dominated Europe east of the Trieste-Stettin line. The Western powers looked upon this rapid expansion of Soviet influence as a permanent threat to their safety. Thus, the fundamental conflict between concepts of what really constitutes national security was probably the second basic factor of the Cold War. The third factor was America's monopoly of the atomic bomb, an advantage that magnified Moscow's suspicions about U.S. imperialist intentions throughout the world.

By 1945, the power relationships were considerably altered from those of 1939. Germany was a power vacuum at the end of the war. Britain and France emerged as titular victors, but were in fact second-rate powers. The Soviet Union marched from the brink of defeat at the hands of the Nazi armies to the status of superpower.[8] The United States, in 1945, stood momentarily as the undisputed dominant world power. But after 1945, mankind witnessed a drift toward what has been called a "bipolar world," with Washington facing Moscow on all major issues. For whatever reasons, including those suggested above, the Cold War started. The United States

cannot be held solely responsible for it, despite the contentions of
certain American "New Left" writers and of others determined to
lay the blame squarely on Washington. These men have argued that
the United States has been so obsessed with the Communist threat
that American foreign policy has become rigid and devoid of prag-
matism. As a result of its fear of Communism, they reason, America
interferes anywhere and everywhere to protect the so-called *Pax
Americana.*[9] This position, however, must be challenged on the
ground that the arguments do not stand the test of scholarly scrutiny.

Can the Cold War be explained solely in ideological terms? According to one noted analyst, the breakdown of the wartime collaboration among the United States, the Soviet Union, and Great
Britain was actually a clash of the "universalist" and the "sphere-
of-influence" views of world order.[10] The universalists claimed that
the national security of a country could be best guaranteed by an
international agency. The United States was among the first to cham-
pion a concept of high idealistic principles whereby the United
Nations would solve all the problems. The sphere-of-influence view,
on the other hand, which maintained that national security would
best be assured by a balance of power, was insisted on by the Soviet
Union as the best guarantee of future peace.

These were the irreconcilable differences. The United States adhered to legal and moral principles as preconditions for settling the
problems of postwar Europe; the Soviet Union was equally adamant
in demanding spheres of influence. This led to mounting friction
between the two great powers and mutual suspicion of each other's
motives. By the time the Potsdam Conference was held in August
1945, the seeds of the Cold War were already sown.[11]

With the gradual crumbling of the Third Reich's military might
and the concomitant fading of its threat, collaboration diminished
bit by bit at first, then by leaps and bounds. The feeling of mutual
suspicion was already quite perceptible even before Germany was
defeated. Mutual distrust was intensified when the American government failed to grant the Soviet Union a $6 billion credit for
postwar reconstruction. On the heels of this, the abrupt termination
of American lend-lease shipments in May 1945 was viewed by the
Soviets as an outright act of blackmail. According to Professor
Schlesinger, the wartime "Grand Coalition" had been created "by
one thing, and one thing alone: the threat of Nazi victory." [12]

To launch a new era of collaboration, Winston Churchill (and for a few days Clement Attlee), Stalin, and Harry Truman met in Potsdam from July 17 to August 2, 1945. But this conference produced only vague and troublesome agreements. As the heads of state posed for pictures on the eve of their departure, they smiled, but all the participants knew that the agreements were inconclusive, that the most pressing problems had been swept under the rug.

The Potsdam Protocol outlined some of the immediate short-term Allied objectives in occupied Germany. To deprive the defeated Reich of all war-making potential, the agreement called for a drastic reduction of German heavy industry. Germany was to have only light, "peaceful industries," as they were designated at the time, and a highly developed agriculture. The new generation of Germans were to be farmers and dairymen, not steel-makers, chemists, and physicists. During the period of occupation Germany was to be treated as an economic unit, with central administrative agencies for industry, agriculture, finance, transport, communications, and a joint export-import agency. Another important charge of the Potsdam communiqué was preparation of "a level of industry" plan to determine which plants were to be left in Germany and to earmark capital equipment and plants for reparations. The Allied Control Council was given six months to prepare this plan.[13]

The magnitude of reparations, however, remained unsolved. At the Yalta Conference in early February 1945, the Soviets proposed $20 billion worth of goods in prewar prices in the form of removal of plants, annual deliveries from current production, and the use of German labor, half for the Soviet Union and half for the Allies.[14] This proposal supposedly was never accepted by the Western powers.[15] The Potsdam provisions on reparations dealt only with the removal of industrial plants and equipment,[16] and it soon became obvious that the Soviets interpreted the reparations provisions of the Yalta and Potsdam agreements differently from the Western powers. The British and Americans argued that the Potsdam agreement had replaced all previous ones, including that of Yalta, and deliveries from current production were illegal. The Soviet Union, on the other hand, claimed that the Potsdam agreement represented a supplement to the Yalta reparations proposals.[17] A prolonged confrontation was inevitable. Strangely enough, the Potsdam document said nothing about Germany's future economic and social system.

It referred to the creation of a democratic Germany, but it did not
indicate whether this would be predicated upon a one-party or two-
party system. This omission led to different interpretations of the
Potsdam agreement and very quickly became the apple of discord
among the wartime Allies.

Consequences of the Defeat

After the unconditional surrender, most German territory was
held by Allied armies, except for a small area in northern Germany
under the jurisdiction of a successor government, headed by Admiral
Karl Dönitz. The admiral believed that the unconditional surrender
implied neither the elimination of the German state nor of his government. General Eisenhower, believing that the existence of the
Dönitz government was likely to make trouble between the Americans and the Russians, ordered the arrest of all its cabinet members
on May 23, 1945.[18] Its last vestiges of sovereignty eliminated, Germany became an occupied country where the four Allied commanders reigned supreme in their respective zones of occupation.[19]

The Allies were supposed to govern the country "as a whole," but
the idea of Germany "as a whole" was a fiction almost from the first
moment of occupation. The former German Reich was, in fact, cut
up into six parts (not to be confused with the occupation zones):
(1) the territories east of the Oder and Neisse rivers were placed
under temporary Polish administration; (2) northern East Prussia,
including the city of Königsberg, was incorporated into the Soviet
Union; (3) the Americans occupied the southern sections of Germany, consisting of Bavaria, Hesse, and parts of Württemberg and
Baden, (4) the British took over Lower Saxony, north Rhine-West-
phalia, and Schleswig-Holstein, (5) the Russians took Saxony,
Mecklenberg, and Thuringia,[20] (6) the French were assigned a zone
of occupation adjacent to Alsace.

Germany's population loss, excluding her Jews, as a result of
World War II and its immediate aftermath was more than six million people: 3.7 million killed in battle, one half million dead as the
result of Allied bombing raids, and another 2.2 million who perished in the course of expulsion from Poland, Czechoslovakia, Hungary, and Romania.[21]

The Allies felt it necessary to impose upon the defeated Reich a "harsh" peace. The Germans were not to be allowed ocean-going ships or airplanes. The German merchant fleet, which at the outbreak of the war registered a 4.5 million gross tonnage, the fifth largest in the world at that time, had been severely depleted during the war.[22] The ships that survived the war were taken over by the Allies without compensation. Germany was also deprived of its foreign assets, and much of its industrial and social capital was used up, destroyed, or hauled away. Estimates are that Germany lost from one-half to about two-thirds [23] of its national wealth. Parenthetically, the national wealth of a country is considered to comprehend all natural resources, land and the improvements upon it, factories, office buildings, dwellings, railways, highways, canals, sewers, communications network, and so on. It also includes ships, planes, automobiles, railway cars and locomotives, machinery, farm implements, livestock, raw materials, goods in process of manufacture, consumer durable goods, clothing, furniture, net foreign assets, gold, and silver. A complete inventory would list a country's wealth as drawn up at a given date.

The outcome of World War II was the worst defeat in Germany's history,[24] as witnessed not only by the death of more than six million people and the loss of one-half of its national wealth, but by the loss of its political unity as well. The Third Reich, or rather its smoldering ruins, emerged from the war a "shrunken, devastated and divided mockery of her former self, devoid of domestic government, occupied by foreign troops, and her population in the large part uprooted and demoralized." [25]

In the Soviet-occupied zone, a totalitarian political structure and central planning were introduced in the fall of 1945,[26] while in the American, British, and French zones, basic human rights were written into newly established constitutions. For the U.S. government, the objective of the occupation consisted principally of seeking the destruction of the remaining German war potential at the same time as undertaking the reeducation of the people. Generals Eisenhower and Lucius D. Clay felt that, with firmness and determination, the Germans could eventually be converted into a democratic nation.[27] In the early stages of occupation, American officials in Germany were disposed to favor a tough policy in their zone, particularly in economic matters.[28] To make sure that the Germans could never again wage war, the Americans advocated considerable deindustrialization and, judging by their early actions, what the Americans really wanted was to impose almost indiscriminate revenge on the German people as a whole.[29]

The British occupation policy, considerably less harsh than the American, showed a strong preference for moderation. The British spent much time and effort in opposing the extreme policy measures of some overzealous Americans on the Allied Control Council and in the Military Government of the zone. Since, by 1946, the Allied Control Council had virtually broken down and "Germany as a whole" had proved to be a fiction, the British took another tack. They became primarily concerned with the economic re-integration of Germany into the Western European economy and the reduction of the dollar costs of food imports into the British zone. Their aim was to make the heavily industrialized zone self-supporting and to return the responsibility for managing the economy into German hands.[30]

France's approach to the German problem was matter-of-fact, although its position was that of a courtesy member of the Allied Control Council. A guest victor, France was neither economically nor militarily a Big Power. To weaken the traditional enemy as effectively as possible, the French insisted on a sweeping decentralization of economic and political life in Germany "as a whole" and in their zone of occupation. With the former adversary—whose armies in June 1940 had imposed a crushing defeat upon the French army—now on its knees, France tried to reestablish itself as a dominant power on the Continent.[31]

Within a year after the unconditional surrender of the Nazi generals, the Allied Control Council became an arena where the British-American teams "slugged it out" with their Soviet counterparts. Germany "as a whole" under the Allied Control Council resembled one of Krylov's immortal fables, in which a swan, a lobster, and a pike decided to pull a hay wagon. Instead of pulling in unison, the swan pulled up, the pike pulled toward the water, the lobster crawled backward, and the wagon did not move an inch. So it was in Germany. The country remained cut into six parts, but "only two regions of virtual partition, divided by the Iron Frontier" [32] existed. The façade of Allied unity in Germany "as a whole" crumbled for good in March 1948 when the Russians instituted a blockade of Berlin. In June, American planes started the Berlin Airlift, and the Cold War was on in earnest.

The Emergence of the Federal Republic of Germany

To cope with the economic chaos in the British and American zones, the two zones were fused into a "Bizone" on January 1, 1947.[33] According to Robert Murphy, "Bizonia really laid the foundation for western Europe's most powerful state, West Germany. . . ."[34] The reluctant French joined the Bizone in April 1949, turning it into Trizonia.[35] On September 21 of that year, the American, British, and French military governments were replaced by three High Commissioners, and the first West German government, under the chancellorship of Konrad Adenauer, took over the reins of the newly created Federal Republic of Germany. It covered an area of 245,000 square kilometers, exclusive of West Berlin, with a population of 46.7 million. On this occasion, Adenauer told the Allied High Commissioners, who still held supervisory control, that his government would do all it could to concentrate upon solving the pressing social problems. Without new homes and proper jobs for the millions of bombed-out people and refugees, he said, a stable society within the country would be impossible.[36]

What were the social problems the Chancellor spoke of and how serious were they? The American and British air raids on Germany, designed to undermine the Third Reich's "motivational potential," had been successful. The blanket bombings had destroyed most of the German cities.[37] In 1945 they looked like "eerie moonscapes of destruction." [38] It has been estimated that in the large cities in the territory of the Federal Republic of Germany, almost 50 per cent of all apartments were destroyed.[39] In Cologne, for example, 70 per cent of all apartments went up in smoke; in Dortmund, 65.8 per cent; in Hamburg, 53.5 per cent, and in Hanover, 50.5 per cent.[40] In West Berlin and West Germany, 5.4 million people had been completely bombed out and were without homes or possessions.[41] The survivors lived either in cellars or air-raid shelters, or doubled and tripled up in the houses that remained standing, while many others moved to the countryside.

In 1939, the territory comprised in the Federal Republic of Germany had had an estimated population of 39.3 million. By the fall of 1946, it was 43.9 million, and on January 1, 1948, it had risen to 45.2 million. In 1950, it was 47.7 million, and three years later it was up to 49.0 million.[42] This phenomenal increase in population was due to an unprecedented movement of people into West Ger-

many. More than 10 million impoverished, bitter, and frustrated
Germans living in hundreds of camps throughout rump Germany
were without jobs or hope in the prevailing milieu of political pa-
ralysis, administrative chaos, and economic stagnation. They represented a dangerous package of political dynamite. If not dealt with
quickly and effectively, these refugee camps might have developed
into something like the issue of the second Arab-Israeli refugee
problem.[43] Some of the people involved represented expellees from
former Reich territory east of the Oder-Neisse line, forced to leave
their established homes as the result of the Allied wartime agreements at Yalta and Potsdam.[44] But earlier, the relentless flood of
refugees had started in the fall of 1944 when millions of Germans
and non-Germans fled before the Red Army.[45] The expulsion of
millions of Germans was done with "a mercilessness surpassed only
by the previous brutalities perpetrated upon many of these countries by the Nazis. . . ." [46] Czechoslovakia drove out 2.2 million
Germans,[47] and Poland 0.54 million. From Silesia, under Polish
administration, 2.7 million were expelled; from East Prussia, 1.4
million; from Pomerania, 1.2 million. The horrors of forced trans-
plantation of this kind had been vividly told to the world in the
powerful novel by Franz Werfel, *The Forty Days of Musa Dagh*
(1933), which described the sufferings of the Armenians. The Germans experienced these horrors first-hand ten years after Werfel
published his novel.[48]

By March 31, 1953, at the time the Shilumim Agreement was
ratified by the Israeli and West German governments, the 8.3 million
expellees and 1.9 million refugees living in the Federal Republic
of Germany represented almost 20 per cent of the total population.[49]
In rural Schleswig-Holstein, they constituted more than one-third
of the population. In southern Bavaria and Lower Saxony, the
"new" population, living mostly in barracks-type towns, represented
slightly less than 30 per cent of the population.

In addition to refugees and expellees, 3.6 million people fled to
the Federal Republic from the "hated system" prevailing in Communist Germany.[50] This flood of Germans from East Germany,
seeking better jobs and housing in the West, reached 400,000 people
in 1953, and, by the time the Berlin Wall was built in 1961, the
figure had reached approximately one-third of a million a year.[51]
Further, during the first three postwar years, as a result of lack of

building materials, coal, and transportation, and the inertia resulting from undernourishment, the program of repair of damaged buildings was quite inadequate. A survey showed that, on the average, 3.18 persons shared one bedroom in the Federal Republic of Germany in 1949.[52] The problem of housing this distended population was overwhelming. Roughly 20 per cent of all urban buildings in the Federal Republic of Germany had been destroyed during the war.[53] Thus, overcrowding was inevitable, a condition which led to a rapid spread of tuberculosis and other diseases, social friction, and discontent. Former President Herbert Hoover, in his winter 1947 survey of the Bizonia situation, reported: ". . . the housing situation in the two zones is the worst that modern civilization has ever seen." [54]

Food: The Major Bottleneck

Immediately after the unconditional surrender, the Western Allies informed the German public that their available agricultural resources should enable them to produce and feed themselves, at a per capita rate of 2,000 calories a day, without Allied assistance.[55] Only in extreme emergencies were the Americans ready to consider sending food to the Germans. Such was the situation during the pre-occupation policy of a "hardhearted attitude about the German people." [56] There is a Russian saying, "One never eats food as hot as when it is cooked"; and so the initial policy was scrapped as soon as the British and American military government officials had time to take careful stock of the existing food reserves. Two factors were mainly responsible for the reversal.

First, the loss of Germany's former breadbasket, located east of the Oder-Neisse line and placed under Polish administration in 1945, aggravated the food deficit in the American and British zones. This territory had produced 25 per cent of the country's prewar agricultural output. Second, the millions of German refugees and expellees settled in the two Western zones after the war, had greatly increased food requirements. The British and American zones of occupation were soon desperately short of food.

The early postwar program of food assistance to the Western zones of Germany can be divided into two phases. The first extended from mid-1945 to mid-1946, when the British and American military gov-

ernments were engaged primarily in so-called disaster relief. This
early aid helped to tide the country over the lean months until the
first peacetime harvest was reaped. In the fall of 1945 wheat imports
provided under a joint Anglo-American arrangement gave impetus
to the strenuous efforts that made it possible to keep the German
food ration at the 1,550-calorie level.[57] From June 1, 1945, to June
30, 1946, the British military government imported 1,245,900 tons
of foodstuffs into the British zone. Only this aid prevented a famine
in the Ruhr.[58] During the same period, 461,000 tons of food were
brought from Army stocks into the American-occupied zone, making
the total for the year 1,706,900 tons. This massive assistance to a
former enemy was without parallel in recorded history. Undoubtedly, millions of Germans owe their lives to these early imports of
food by the Western powers.

The second phase of the Allied food assistance program began in
1946, when the U.S. Congress voted special funds to prevent "disease
and unrest" in occupied Germany. The "Government and Relief in
Occupied Areas" appropriations stipulated that the funds might be
used to finance only the imports of food, petroleum, and fertilizers.[59]
During the first three years of occupation, the American and British
governments together spent close to $1.5 billion for the shipment of
relief food to Germany.[60] American Congressional investigators estimated that in the early years food production within the British and
American zones was 975 calories per person daily, less than two-thirds
of the "normal" ration of 1,550 calories that prevailed from mid-1945
to mid-1948. The missing third had to be imported.[61] Although there
can be no doubt that the British and American relief shipments prevented mass starvation in the Western zones of Germany, the prevailing subsistence rations left the Germans desperately hungry.

Food shortages, industrial disarmament and repressed inflation, as
the major bottlenecks in the postwar recovery of Germany, form the
subject of my book on *Germany Under Direct Controls*.[62] The subject matter is so relevant to an understanding of the problem at hand,
and so many new sources have emerged since 1962 (the cut-off date
of *Germany Under Direct Controls*), that it has been deemed of
major importance to carry the analysis forward past 1948, even at the
risk of repetition.

It has been estimated that the human "basal energy requirement"
(as differentiated from "minimum daily requirement") ranges from

1,400 to 1,800 calories every 24 hours, just to stay alive.[63] If work must be done, more calories are needed. For example, merely to sit requires 15 calories an hour over basal metabolic needs; to walk, 200 additional calories an hour are needed; to climb stairs calls for 1,000 calories more. If they are not available to the body, three things happen: people get hungry, they do less work, and they use up the reserve substances of the body. From 1945 to 1948, the prevailing legal rationing levels were so low that they did not provide enough energy for basal metabolism. One competent observer on the scene remarked that the German people had become "thin and under-weight and incapable of doing a good day's work." [64]

Not only was the caloric intake low, but the food itself was inadequate and nutritionally of poor quality. Cereals and potatoes made up as much as 80 per cent of the total ration, and proteins and fats were particularly deficient. Men of responsibility and authority admitted that the rations actually distributed "represented a fairly rapid starvation level." [65] To anyone who has never known critical hunger over a prolonged period of time, the theoretical figure of 1,550 calories means little. What became apparent, however, was that living on such a ration for a prolonged period sapped the physical strength of the German population.[66] Under such conditions, it was small wonder that the principal concern of most Germans was how to get additional food. Sociologists and historians who have studied the effects of prolonged hunger on man have reported that "until hunger is relieved, it tends to dominate our behavior by means of food-seeking and food-consuming activities." [67] Thus, efforts to stay alive in spite of everything became a way of life in occupied Germany. It has been estimated that during these years the Germans in the British and American zones consumed daily roughly 500 calories of nonrationed foods. This food was obtained either by bartering possessions for it in the countryside, by raising food in small garden plots, or by black-market purchases.[68] Food became an obsession.[69]

For the individual, of course, these activities seemed absolutely necessary to stay alive, but from an economic point of view they were sheer waste. Instead of rebuilding their destroyed cities, homes, and factories, the Germans spent most of their time trying to get enough calories to stay alive. Inadequate nutrition made sustained work very difficult and all attempts to stimulate even permissible industrial activities failed. This experience suggests that economists and poli-

ticians are free to choose between "guns and butter." With given
resources, manpower, and technology, and assuming full employment, more guns or capital goods can be produced only at the expense of butter or consumer goods. This is one of the basic postulates
of economics. But when an entire highly industrialized country
suffers from semistarvation, orderly economic exchanges and division of labor become impossible. Continued search for additional
food leads to a primitivization of all economic activity. People do
more work, but the output in both industry and agriculture stag-
nates. At the end of 1946, competent observers summed up the situation in one sentence: "Reconstruction is a problem of calories." [70]

The Effects of Industrial Disarmament on the Economy

The debacle produced by the Versailles Treaty's reparations provisions in the 1920s left an indelible impression upon statesmen and
economists. Today, it is agreed by all that the treaty was unworkable.
J. M. Keynes predicted the Versailles fiasco in his *The Economic
Consequences of the Peace,* almost a decade before the statesmen
recognized their folly. The breakdown was not caused because the
Germans were ordered to make "cash reparations." In fact, 40 per
cent of the German government's payments were made in *kind.*[71]
The Allied governments soon discovered that the only way the Germans could "pay" was by maintaining a favorable trade balance, by
borrowing abroad, by liquidating investment abroad, or by making
payments in domestic currency. That commercial policy intensified
competition throughout the world; it aggravated the unemployment
situation in reparations-receiving countries; and it disrupted the
British, French, and American export markets. After World War II,
Western statesmen were determined to pursue a more sensible policy.
They strove not only to avoid a situation that would cause the vanquished Germans to begin to compete furiously again on the world
markets, but above all to insure that the taking of reparations would
restructure German industry in such a way that it could never wage
another war. In other words, reparations policies were "centered
'round security." [72]

To take away from Germany forever the sinews of war required
the destruction of the industrial power of "the eternal warmonger
among nations," as Germany was called at that time. Effective elimi-

nation of its industrial war potential was deemed indispensable. In the name of security a gigantic dislocation, in the nature of an industrial pogrom, was advocated.[73] Germanophobia was so much in vogue throughout the world that almost nothing was considered too punitive for Germany.

The most far-reaching proposal for the elimination of the war potential of German industry was developed by Henry Morgenthau, Jr., the wartime Secretary of the Treasury of the United States. In the view of one observer, it was the "crudest reparation scheme malevolent planning could devise." [74] Morgenthau felt that so long as Germany had heavy industries there would never be peace in the world. To eliminate Germany as a potential aggressor, the Morgenthau proposal called for the complete destruction of the country's metallurgical, chemical, and electrical industries within six months after the end of World War II.[75] All factories were either to be blown up or dismantled and sent to the victorious countries as reparations; all coal mines were to be flooded and the entire Ruhr Valley turned into a "ghost territory." The Ruhr was, in effect, to be "put out of business," wiped out as an industrial area, regardless of what happened to millions of Germans.[76] Subsequently this proposal was officially accepted in a somewhat modified form by Roosevelt and Churchill at the Second Quebec Conference in September 1944. Shortly thereafter, however, both Churchill and Roosevelt repudiated the plan. Nevertheless, its basic principles dominated official thinking in Washington for almost six years after the defeat of Hitler's Thousand-Year Reich. Government officials in both America and Great Britain continued to treat Germany in "moralizing categories" and the public-opinion makers remained fixed in the stereotypes established in the "hate the Germans" milieu of the two world wars.[77]

When the United States Army took over its zone of occupation, the widespread feeling among Americans at home and in the military government was that Germany "should be reconstructed on an agricultural basis, with industry drastically curtailed." [78] The economic policy for the American occupation zone was clearly spelled out in a directive of the Joint Chiefs of Staff (JCS 1067) in April 1945.[79] This directive, which for two years remained nominal law for American military government officials, was aimed at keeping Germany down and making sure that it could never wage another war. This normative orientation of the American occupation policy rested on the assumption that the "incurably bellicose" Germans could not be trusted and that Germany must be made "so impotent that she cannot forge the tools of war." [80] Further, destruction of German industry was initially regarded as a potential blessing to the rest of the European economy. Thus, in the early stages of occupation, the Americans gave moral reasons among other rationalizations for the plea to engage in large-scale industrial dis-development of Germany.[81] The specific objectives of the American occupation were given as industrial disarmament, demilitarization, denazification, and administrative decentralization.[82]

To implement the industrial program, which had priority over reparations, Paragraph 32 of the directive of the Joint Chiefs of Staff permitted only minimum industrial production of iron and steel, nonferrous metals, machine tools, radio and electrical equipment, automotive vehicles, heavy machinery, and their related parts. Furthermore, to debilitate German potential in physics, chemistry, and engineering, the framers of JCS 1067 spelled out in detail techniques of "technological disarmament." Paragraph 31 prohibited virtually all research activities and required abandonment of all laboratories, research facilities, and similar technical establishments, except those considered necessary for protection of public health. In addition, Paragraph 8 prescribed arrest categories for security reasons on the basis of position held, and "not the particular culpability of the individual occupying the position." [83] Many German businessmen and government officials were taken into custody for this reason. According to Robert Murphy, at the time when the U.S. forces moved into their zone of occupation JCS 1067 had supposedly "prescribed thirty-three automatic arrest categories, mostly on account of membership, high or low, in a Nazi organization. . . ." [84] Those who remained free were subjected to the removal-from-office program that virtually denuded the German economy and government of skilled and trained manpower.[85] Even though JCS 1067 permitted the arrest of important businessmen for security reasons, it said nothing about their punishment.[86]

The directive was such a strange document that General Clay's advisors William H. Draper and Lewis W. Douglas "were shocked by the detailed prohibitions . . . ," and Douglas supposedly exclaimed that JCS 1067 "was assembled by economic idiots." [87]

No matter how brutal the initial American occupation policy was, the Germans took it comparatively well because they were fully aware how fortunate they were in having Americans for their conquerors instead of Russians. The initial, stringent form of JCS 1067 determined the over-all policy in the American zone *only* in the fall of 1945; from then on, a drift in policy led eventually to formal repudiation of the directive in July 1947. However, as long as JCS 1067 was not formally revoked and the lower administrative echelons in Germany and the various policy-making agencies in Washington (such as the State Department and the Foreign Economic Administration) were staffed by adherents of Mr. Morgenthau's implacable policy, its provisions were enforced.[88] For this reason, U.S. Military Government officials were quite reluctant to take responsibility for allowing German plants to resume production or even to repair damages to prepare the way. The British were considerably more circumspect in their zone; they wanted no part of the American-inspired program of making Germany an industrially impotent nation.[89]

Beyond the various zones of occupation, the fiction of Germany "as a whole" still existed in the minds of public-opinion makers in London and New York, willfully blinded intellectuals, and bureaucrats. In 1945 and 1946, American officials in Berlin "were leaning over backward to get along with the Russians." [90] Germany was still considered the proving ground for postwar Soviet-American cooperation.[91] Americans were frequently disposed to favor "the hardest possible economic policy vis-a-vis Germany." [92] They were bent on bringing about substantial de-industrialization of the German economy without regard for the consequences. And they pushed this policy, as one observer put it, "with more enthusiasm than knowledge." [93] "Hard-nosed" attitudes toward Russians were immensely unpopular at that time.[94]

Security from future German aggression required that its war potential be thoroughly destroyed. The Potsdam Protocol charged the Allied Control Council of Berlin to prepare a plan for a "permissible" future level of German industry and to determine which plants could be removed as reparations. This plan was to be ready within six months.[95]

The Allied Control Council experts released their document, a landmark of the intended industrial emasculation of Germany, in

March 1946; it was called the "Control Council Plan for Reparations and the Level of Postwar German Economy." [96] The political aspect of security dominated the economic principles of this document, which called for the complete elimination of the aircraft and ship-building industries and a drastic reduction in the metallurgical, chemical, and engineering industries. The four Allies also agreed on a reduction in the German standard of living.[97] It has been estimated that the German prewar standard of living was "about thirty per cent above the European average (the United Kingdom and the USSR excluded)," [98] and it was anticipated that the German national income would probably amount to half of the prewar figure if the plan was implemented.

In over-all terms, the Allied reparations plan aimed at reducing Germany's aggregate industrial production to roughly 55 per cent of its 1938 output. If this plan were to be put into effect the German living standard would be lower than that of 1932.[99] But nobody really knew whether this standard of living would be a ceiling or a floor.[100] The reparations plan specified that some 1,600 industrial plants were surplus to Germany's future needs and "were consequently to be available as reparations." [101] An American official, an economist by profession, who was very much involved in bringing this plan about, stated that the "task of deliberately reducing production and holding down the standard of living . . . went contrary to all habits of thought in the Western world." [102] Or, in the view of Dr. Calvin B. Hoover, Director of the German Standard of Living Board in Berlin, the proposed plan "would have meant the permanent reduction of German productive powers even for peaceful purposes far below their prewar level." [103]

But this "Luddite-type" machine-smashing project was never im-plemented because the four incompatible Allies could not agree on setting up the necessary administrative agencies for treating Germany "as a whole." The objectives of the British and American industrial disarmament policy changed substantially in mid-1947, when General Clay, the U.S. Military Governor, was instructed from Washington to proceed with the economic reconstruction of Bizonia in order to achieve a self-sustaining economy. The new directive, JCS 1779, conceded that under the terms of the First Level of Industry Plan, Germany could neither become economically viable nor con-tribute her part to the economic recovery of Western Europe.[104]

However, this document still called for reparations in the form of capital equipment to eliminate Germany's war potential; the "Morgenthau effect" was still influential.

On August 19, 1947, the American and British military governments released a new document, "The Revised Plan for Level of Industry in the Anglo-American Zones." [105] This new plan officially admitted the bankruptcy of the former policy by stressing that the two united zones of Germany could not regain economic health under prevailing reparation procedures. The Revised Plan provided for the retention of sufficient industrial capacity to approximate roughly the 1936 level of industrial output and aimed at providing for a self-sustaining economy in the Bizonal Area and enabling this area to make an economic contribution to the rehabilitation of Western Europe. Consequently, the Revised Plan was significantly less restrictive than the initial Carthaginian measures. However, machines, plants, and equipment that should be declared in excess of the permitted industrial level were to be removed in the form of reparations. Accordingly, in the fall of 1947, the British and American military governments published a list of plants or portions of industrial facilities available for reparations. For the Bizonal Area, 682 plants were scheduled for dismantling.[106] From the heavily industrialized British Zone, 496 plants were on the removal list, the majority either steel-producing or steel-processing. Factories earmarked for removal were classified as either "war plants" or "surplus plants."

On the part of the Western Allies, the logic of arguing for reparations in the form of plants and equipment, even as late as 1947, continued to suffer from the restrictive and shortsighted mentality of those of the Morgenthau persuasion. They still claimed that European security would be enhanced if certain "war" plants were to be removed from Germany. Reassembly of such plants abroad, the argument went, would accelerate the economic rehabilitation of the recipient countries and such removal would improve the West German cost structure.[107] Whatever the merits of these rationalizations or justifications, they sounded empty and artificial to German ears.[108] After all, the U.S. Congress insisted that reparations removals from the French, British, and American zones could take place *only* if such removals would best serve the purpose of the European Recovery Program. However, the so-called surplus-plant loophole in the Marshall Plan framework enabled British and French and, to a very

limited extent, American policy-makers in West Germany to continue the destruction of those plants. They proceeded to select and
remove or destroy the best and most modern facilities, which could
threaten certain French and British industrial interests. The Germans felt that these removals were designed to eliminate competition,
not existing "war potential." [109] As one astute economist has observed, "Had the entire prewar potential of the western zones remained intact, it could not be worked without huge foreign imports"
(of raw material).[110]

Under the existing conditions of grossly inadequate steel capacity,
the intended dismantlings of plants producing plate, hot strip, seam-
less tubes, forgings, and electrical and stainless steel represented a
substantial blow to Germany's engineering industries. It was feared
that "surplus" plant dismantlings might wreak havoc on the European Recovery Program. For this reason, pressure mounted to stop
reparations completely. In the spring of 1949, the Humphrey Committee requested that 159 plants slated for reparations removal
should be left in Germany.[111] Even after these concessions, the most
efficient and significant German steel-producing units remained on
the list for eventual removal or destruction. But the so-called Petersburg Agreement between the Federal Republic of Germany and the
Western High Commissioners on November 22, 1949, led to a virtual
suspension of reparations. The death knell for reparations was
sounded in the spring of 1951. However, the Petersburg Agreement
stipulated that dismantled works should not be rebuilt without permission, nor could certain "sensitive" plants be expanded without
the consent of the Allied Military Security Board.[112]

The Western powers received little in the way of reparations from
the defeated western zones of the Third Reich. According to one
Allied source, at the final reckoning in 1951 the aggregate value of
all plant removals, in terms of 1938 values, came to 708.5 million
marks, or one-half their current worth.[113] Such meager reparations
benefits were in marked contrast with the $2 billion actually paid by
Germany during the first two years after World War I.[114] Because
the plants dismantled were reckoned in terms of "residual values,"
obtained after deductions for depreciation over a number of years,
the Allied figures did not reflect adequately their true value. German
valuations of the plants removed were considerably higher, ranging
from 2 to 5.4 billion marks, allowing for price increases.[115] In terms

of existing industrial capacity, the Inter-Allied Reparation Agency reported that actual removals came to 1.3 per cent, while German estimates ranged from 3 to 4 per cent.[116] According to Professor Rolf Krengel of the Deutsches Institut für Wirtschaftsforschung, West Berlin, Allied dismantling in the western parts of Germany eliminated 5.7 per cent of the 1936 capacity.[117] His findings show that dismantling of entire plants in the producer and investment-goods industries constituted from 4 to 5 per cent of the existing 1945 capacity, while corresponding values for the dismantling of equipment in the above-mentioned industries came to 10 and 15 per cent, respectively.[118] At the time of the currency reform of mid-1948, the fixed assets of West German industry "had a current value of 56,000 million DM [Deutsche Mark] (at 1950 prices) which was still about the same as the average for 1939." [119] The war damage was far greater "in its immediate effects on output than when measured by permanent effect on the equipment itself." [120] It was easy to put industrial plants out of action, but very difficult to destroy them completely.

The short-term effects of dismantling might be measured in macro-economic and micro-economic terms. The former focus on the relationship between the removal of capital equipment and its impact on the level of employment and the Gross National Product. The micro-economic approach stresses the impact of the dismantling on a particular industry and its market structure. The important point, however, is that economic losses from dismantling were greater than the simple summation of all plants and equipment removed.[121] Furthermore, the effects of destroying certain "bottleneck" industrial capacities and of forbidding their rebuilding were felt by many branches of industry.

Twenty years after the end of the Allied industrial-disarmament program, it became evident that the wartime blanket bombings of German cities, the destruction of factories and farms in the course of the fighting in 1945, and the subsequent dismantling, demolition, and neglect of industrial facilities represented an accelerated capital destruction. Normally, all capital diminishes slowly and in stages through wear and tear, as John Stuart Mill observed; but war and other calamities greatly accelerate the pace.[122] During the first three postwar years, Germany's infrastructure, or social capital, in the form of roads, canals, communication systems, educational facilities, government offices and bureaucracy, availability of skilled manpower, entrepreneurial talent, and "calculating spirit" on the part of the general public remained virtually intact, although latent. These factors could not be easily removed for reparations purposes. The massive bombings of German cities, however, swept away the remnants of the medieval towns and cities, with their winding streets, atrocious plumbing, and poor access roads. Today, of course, West Germany is a country of beautiful and modern cities, built after the wartime holocaust. Although difficult to measure, the spill-over effects of renovation on over-all productivity, in terms of better housing for the workers and easier access roads for industry, must be substantial. The aim of industrial disarmament was specifically directed at industrial capital and Germany retrogressed, as desired by the Western powers. For instance, the level of gross fixed assets in industry declined from DM 58.6 million in 1945 to DM 55.9 in 1948.[123]

Here again, dismantling represented accelerated capital destruction. It actually meant the replacement of old by newer equipment that eventually raised German output per machine or man and that gave German industry a competitive edge in the international markets.

What would have been the effect on West Germany's ability to make restitution and pay indemnification and collective compensation to Israel, had the four wartime Allies not fallen out with each other? Had the Cold War not divided Europe and the world into two hostile camps, it is probable that the victorious Allies might have proceeded to emasculate Germany economically. In such a case, a so-called "Potsdam Germany" would have emerged by 1949. It would have been a country "without war potential," lingering at a prescribed RM 3 billion level of exports and imports.[124] Economic stagnation most likely would have led to political polarization, and the country would have been a trouble spot in the heart of Europe, poisoning the political atmosphere as much as did the Versailles Treaty after World War I. But more important, a semipastoralized Potsdam-type Germany would not have been able to generate any balance-of-payments surplus to pay the Jewish material claims. The German balance-of-payments miracle certainly would not have plagued the world, as it did in the 1950s and 1960s. A Potsdam Germany would have been the triumph of those who stoked the fires of hatred and suspicion of Germany, but it would have done no service for those who suffered most from the biological warfare of the Nazi government: the Jews. The Soviet Union would have been most happy to see the Ruhr Valley in shambles, but the Jews would have gone empty-handed.

The incompatibility of the Allies necessitated the dropping of Morgenthauism by the American government. The emergence of an economically viable West Germany, the rump of what remained of the Third Reich, and in particular its spectacular balance-of-payments strength, has made possible the payment to Israel of more than $2.5 billion in indemnification payments and collective compensation. This never would have been possible had the four wartime Allies managed to create a postwar Germany along the lines suggested at Potsdam. The Jews, in that event, would have lost more than anyone else.

Repressed Inflation and the System of Physical Controls, 1945–1948

Military occupation during and after World War II built up a new kind of economic system: a retrogressing economy.[125] In most of the occupied countries where Hitler was building a new empire based on the German race, Nazi political hierarchy, and a self-sufficient economy, Nazi Germany invented and perfected this system. The conquered nations were assigned a role serving the German masters.[126] Given this orientation, the Nazis practiced compulsory exportation of raw materials to Germany; they removed capital equipment and conscripted certain types of skills. In all occupied countries, price, rent, and wage controls, coupled with rationing, floor-space controls, and labor conscription, became the order of the day. The food rations were low, bringing about widespread malnutrition. Lack of raw materials resulted in considerable under-utilization of the available productive capacity. The standard of living declined sharply. Despite differences in over-all policy objectives, the Allies used almost identical forms of direct or physical controls. The Nazis used such controls for purposes of economic exploitation; the Allies used them for the industrial disarmament of Germany.

The Allied closure of the economic annals of the Third Reich in June 1945 was halfhearted. Though they eliminated the Dönitz government, they preserved virtually the entire body of Nazi economic legislation on fixing prices, wages, and rents; on rationing consumer goods and foodstuffs; on conscription of labor and the licensing of raw materials, capital goods, and intermediate goods; on compulsory delivery quotas in both industry and agriculture; on housing controls; and on foreign-exchange controls and the tight supervision of exports and imports.

In recent history, direct controls have been used primarily either for economic mobilization during major wars or for purposes of "forced draft" industrialization (in the Soviet orbit). The Nazis used various combinations of direct controls for economic exploitation of the occupied countries in Europe. Had the four Allies been unanimous on a policy of maximum reparations in kind, from current German production, they also could have employed direct controls. But organized restoration and renovation of German industry for purposes of reparations was abhorrent to Germany's Western neighbors; they all dreaded the thought. Military security being the paramount consideration of all the Allied nations in 1945, such a course was unacceptable.

To make sure that Germany would not have the means to wage an aggressive war, the Allies decided on industrial disarmament; to implement it, they used the entire gamut of direct controls. The Allies could have used a similar system of physical controls to exact the maximum of reparations, mostly from current production. Of course, such a policy would have meant rebuilding German industry. Direct controls would have assured that the population was adequately fed, the machinery and equipment kept in good working order, and incentives preserved. The rest of annual G.N.P. would have been surplus, which could have been used for reparations. Such a system would also avoid monetary chaos. If, furthermore, the victors could maintain a continuous high level of employment, the system of direct controls would enable them to collect substantial reparations.[127] Instead, their policy aimed at limiting output in most sectors of the economy and setting production ceilings in many industries. Specifically, it curtailed drastically the output of the engineering industries. At first, the industrial rollback was intended to affect most sectors of the economy, across the board, by roughly 50 per cent of a given base year. For instance, in the machine-tool industry, Germany was scheduled to retain only 11 per cent of its 1936 capacity, according to the 1946 plan. These projected disproportionate cuts had far-reaching consequences. "Expanded reproduction," as it is known in the Soviet-type societies, implies that, first, the yearly rate of investment in heavy industry exceeds the rate of investment in light industry, and, second, the yearly investment rates in the machine-tool and other privileged industries exceed the investment rate of heavy industry as a whole. Since industrial disarmament was the opposite of economic growth, the announced disproportionate cuts in certain strategic industries produced unexpected spill-over effects throughout Europe. As a result, in 1946 and in 1947 the German industrial economy operated well below permissible levels. For the year 1946, the monthly average of industrial production of the combined British and American zones was one-third that of 1936; in 1947, the average was 38 per cent.[128]

Another reason for the retention of the entire gamut of direct controls of the Nazi period was that without them it would have been impossible to control the existing inflationary potential.[129] That meant, of course, that physical controls were intended to prevent capital accumulation in the form of industrial plant and equipment out of the forced savings created in an open inflation. Stability of prices and wages, together with rationing, assured rough justice in the distribution of food. And since industrial disarmament implied a considerable cutback in production in many lines of industrial activity, the three-year-long stagnation of the bizonal economy under the postwar regimen of maximum prices lends considerable support to the view that, actually, physical controls were used to bring about the weakening of the German economy.[130] Since the actual reparations removals were small, the reason for low-key production was lack of effective utilization of existing capacity. Ex-Chancellor Ludwig Erhard once explained that the low-key production prevailing up to mid-1948 would have enabled every German to buy "one plate every five years; a pair of shoes every twelve years; a suit every fifty years." [131] Near-starvation made a mockery of efforts to increase production to the permissible levels because people were primarily concerned with getting more food. Since nobody really knew which plants would eventually be removed or destroyed, entrepreneurial initiative was virtually crippled; the Germans simply marked time.

To keep the inflationary potential in check, the Western powers retained price and wage controls and rationing of all essential goods.

The unconditional surrender of the Nazi armies destroyed all hope for full convertibility of wartime savings into goods. The protracted negotiations on currency reform destroyed the Reichsmark as a store of value, although it remained a "unit of account." It was rumored that up to 90 per cent of the existing money supply would be destroyed by monetary conversion. Fear that existing monetary claims would be drastically scaled down resulted in a flight, by individuals and by business, from the Reichsmark into material values.[132] When 1946 arrived, the hoarding of goods had become an accepted feature of the economic landscape in the bizonal area. The U.S. Military Governor reported month after month that companies were keeping unusually large inventories of raw materials and finished products because of the uncertain currency situation.[133] Various German chambers of industry and trade also reported that the widely expected currency reform was the principal reason for hoarding. To preserve the working capital of the firm, everybody kept as much in the form of goods as possible, and a reluctance to sell was widespread.[134]

Given the unsettled currency situation, the German business community pleaded forcefully and eloquently that hoarding of consumer goods was indispensable to the success of any future currency reform. Many high German administrators, including Ludwig Erhard, openly encouraged the storing of consumer goods. In fact, hoarding increased the appearance of success of currency reform, since it had the effect of heightening inflationary pressure in the period preceding currency reform, during which goods were held off the market, and of causing goods to be released when the new money arrived.

It is difficult to quantify the extent of hoarding out of current production during 1947 and the first half of 1948, but it is safe to say that 50 per cent of current output either went into inventories or was used for bartering purposes, the other 50 per cent being produced for the legal market.[135] Workers entitled to "incentive" goods, such as coal miners and railway employees, consumed almost the entire legally available output of consumer goods, leaving nothing for the average German.[136] With material values preferred to monetary values, the cigarette emerged as new currency, without its being legal tender. Cigarettes frequently bought goods the Reichsmark could not and were preferred to it. In fact, the cigarette became such "good" money that it drove out, to some extent, the "bad."

The Reichsmark remained a unit of account and a medium of

exchange, although it bought virtually nothing more than the highly inadequate food ration. Distrust of its future value led, especially during the last half of the year prior to the currency reform, to flagrant hoarding of goods.[137] Under the prevailing administrative near-chaos, the interests of the business community ran counter to the wishes of the consuming public, and in the absence of a strong hand it was impossible to cope with the hoarding spree. The Allied-imposed price freeze at the Nazi level did its share to turn the German economy into chaos. The zonal split, shortages of fuel and power, low productivity caused by malnutrition, lower output per machine caused by obsolescence and lack of repairs, the damage to industrial plants, and over-all stagnation of West German industry—all combined to produce sharply raised production costs. And with legal prices often much lower than the costs of production, losses were inevitable.

For the time being, however, the Allies were unwilling to revise prices upward; hence the only way for a firm to avoid financial ruin was to circumvent the outdated price-freeze by manufacturing "new," formerly unknown goods. During the three years from the surrender to currency reform, more than 5,000 price increases were granted, mostly for the production of "new" goods.[138] Ash trays, fancy lamps, dolls, chandeliers, and other low-utility items poured forth while the production of cups, pails, pots, knives, forks, plates, needles, shoelaces, and other daily necessities stagnated.[139] The price-freeze made the incentive to produce directly inverse to the social utility of the product. The more useless a proposed "new" product, the greater the probability that it had not been available before the war and thus the easier to get the authorities to agree to a profitable price. As a result, the Western zones of occupation before currency reform had what one Swiss economist called a "hair-oil, ash-tray, herb-tea, economy." [140] The German economy was at the end of its rope, so to speak. In the view of *The London Economist,* the first three postwar years were "utter economic hell." [141]

Mid-1948: The New Phase of Economic Reconstruction and Political Integration with the West

By 1946, the industrial production of Western Europe was down to two-thirds of the 1938 level. With the Ruhr almost not functioning, the prewar pattern of European economic integration and intra-

European division of labor was in fact destroyed and a high degree of economic fragmentation, similar to conditions prevailing in the depressed early 1930s, reappeared.[142] For more than half a century, Germany had been intimately involved in the health of the European economy. The prosperity of the Low Countries, Italy, Denmark, France, and Sweden had been inextricably tied to the prosperity of Germany, which was a supplier of a great variety of industrial goods, coke, and coal, as well as a purchaser. If Germany could not produce and sell capital goods to the Italians, the Dutch, the Danes, the Norwegians, and the French, then these nations, in turn, could not sell their goods to Germany. This meant that the intra-European division of labor, the basis of prewar European economic well-being, would come nearly to a halt, which is precisely what happened.

The Morgenthau-oriented occupation policy inflicted hardships not only on the defeated Reich, but on the other Western European nations as well. Keeping Germany in economic chains meant keeping Europe in rags, as former President Herbert Hoover said of American policy in Germany in early 1947.[143] The Western European balance-of-payments position deteriorated constantly. In the absence of supplies of German capital goods, Western European nations were forced to import from America, but their ability to export was seriously out of balance. Furthermore, prewar earnings from overseas investments were gone, and Western Europe was critically short of United States dollars.

In 1947 the economic difficulties were compounded by political instability, especially in Italy and France.[144] With Moscow openly threatening America's position, Washington feared that communism might spread in Western Europe and take possession of the Ruhr Valley, the industrial hub of Western Europe. To forestall that possibility quickly and effectively, Congress passed a large-scale assistance program, called the European Recovery Program or Marshall Plan, which was to run from April 1948 to December 1951. Thus, the Americans eventually set up what that old Germany hand, John Maynard Keynes, had demanded during World War II: ". . . a Reconstruction Fund to be supported by the United States, on terms of unprecedented generosity, as soon as Hitler was overthrown, to prevent the spread of communism in Germany." [145]

The basic objectives of the ERP were to increase the production of the participating Western European countries and to solve their balance-of-payments problems. The quickest way to raise industrial production was to eliminate the basic causes of postwar dislocation and economic distress by putting the Ruhr Valley back into production. In the early months of 1948, the American government decided to integrate the Western parts of Germany economically and politically with the West. The first steps taken to implement the new American-led policy of integration were the currency and economic reforms of June 20, 1948.[146] It was these reforms which ended the "three nightmare years." [147] The Germans themselves had nothing to do with this drastic policy change on the part of the victors. In fact, it might be said that German geography did it for them. For the motivation of the Western Allies was inspired by the desire to make sure that the new Germany did not go communist or become a neutral country.

The salient feature of the monetary reform was a drastic contraction of the currency supply. In fact, RM 122.4 billion were presented for conversion in June 1948.[148] Initially, 10 per cent of the Reichsmark holdings were to be converted into the new Deutsche Mark, but later on certain cancellations were made, so that the net effect resulted in a new conversion rate of 100:6.5. This scaling-down applied to savings accounts as well as to demand deposits and led to much bitterness among fixed-income receivers. With one stroke of the pen, so to speak, the former "waiting purchasing power" was eliminated.[149] But the introduction of a new currency was the first prerequisite for the revival of the economy.

The much more important question of whether to create a production-oriented or a demand-oriented economy was settled in favor of the former by Ludwig Erhard, at that time Director of the Bizonal Department for Economic Affairs.[150] He reckoned that by eliminating the price ceilings on many goods he would liberate the economy from stifling bureaucratic controls, and supply would increase and make the economy viable again. On the day of the currency reform, 400 items were removed from price controls; and a month later, 90 per cent of the price ceilings in existence since 1936 were abolished.[151] The economy was given a chance to test its competitive vigor in an atmosphere that heavily favored the producer and the seller.

The impact of currency reform was profound. It elevated the spirit of the hungry and defeated people overnight. On Monday, June 21,

1948, Germans went on a spending spree.[152] Over the weekend, hoarded goods were displayed in shop windows and sold for the new marks, without any coupons or purchase permits. The new mark, at least for manufactured and decontrolled goods, was endowed with legal purchasing power *only*. Before decontrol, when the purchase of a shirt, for example, required both currency and a permit, the mark had legal and illegal purchasing power. Now, it was a thrilling sensation for shoppers to be able to buy goods they had wanted for years.

For the time being, however, all essential foodstuffs and raw materials remained price-fixed; also, rent controls and the strictest floorspace controls remained on the books because of the unbelievable overcrowding. All wage controls were retained as well.[153]

The economic and currency reforms created strong incentives for businessmen at the expense of the economically weak and unproductive classes who lived on fixed incomes. To eliminate the vast stores of manufactured goods left over from the period before currency reform, the business community was given a very small quota of new marks on the day of the currency reform. To obtain working capital, businesses had to unload hoarded goods. Credit was kept strictly rationed by a newly created Central Bank. Some tax relief was also accorded the business community. In short, all the active, ambitious, and daring elements of Germany were encouraged to make as much money as possible.

Industrial production rose rapidly, accompanied by a rapid increase in prices and a substantial growth in registered unemployment. But Western-occupied Germany had no indigenous raw materials, except coal, and was a grossly food-deficient area. For the time being, it had virtually nothing to export and, for this reason, American and British authorities had to assume responsibility for keeping the economy on an even keel.

Introduction of the new currency was the first step in the over-all integration of the new German state with the West, but vengeful military bureaucrats still could not grasp the essential policy change in Washington and London. The bureaucracies still thought and acted in stereotypical wartime fashion—that is, in terms of controlling "die unheimlichen Deutschen" (the unspeakable Germans). For their part, American authorities were eager to keep Germany as a buffer against the Soviets.[154] They wanted to make sure that the new Germany would not make a deal with the Soviet Union to exchange reunification for neutralization and thus, *de facto,* destroy the incipient North Atlantic Treaty Organization.

Alongside preparations for economic reconstruction went political reorganization. The first and probably the most important step was the Allied-sponsored fusion of the American and British zones of occupation. This merger had taken place on January 1, 1947. At that time the Allies hoped that pooling the resources of the two zones would produce considerable economic benefits. London and Washington argued that this merger should be considered as a first step toward the economic unity of the entire country. And after the failure of the Moscow Conference on Germany in March 1947, the American and British military governments began negotiations on strengthening the bizonal administration. In May of the same year, an Economic Council and an Executive Committee and five executive directors were created.[155]

The Economic Council consisted of fifty-two members, elected by the legislatures of the Länder in proportion to their division by parties and in the ratio of one member for each 750,000 of population.[156] The Council was to enact the necessary ordinances to cover all permitted fields of economic reconstruction. These ordinances were binding upon the Länder for implementation, because the new bizonal agencies still had no executive organs of their own. Every piece of legislation of the Economic Council had to be approved by the Allied Bipartite Board. The Germans were still living under a conqueror's regime up to the fall of 1949.

After currency reform, reorganization of the government proceeded quickly. On May 8, 1949, the Parliamentary Council ratified the draft of what soon became the German constitution, the Basic Law of the Federal Republic. In August, Dr. Adenauer won the first Federal election and became the first Chancellor. The first Minister of Economics was Ludwig Erhard, and the first Minister of Finance was Fritz Schäffer, to mention only two high appointments. The British and American military governments were replaced by a civil administration. In place of the military governors, the Allied High Commissioners became the chief officers of the occupation regime. On the American side, the High Commissioner was John J. McCloy, well-known New York banker and lawyer.[157] Sir Brian Robertson represented the United Kingdom, and André François-Poncet was the French High Commissioner.

In November 1949, Chancellor Adenauer and the Allied High

Commissioners signed the Petersburg Agreement, which granted the Federal Republic of Germany the right to establish consular offices abroad, reduced the number of plants to be dismantled, and removed restrictions on building ships of over 7,200 tons.[158] The Allies stressed that the new Germany was to be brought into the community of nations as an equal partner. Nevertheless, the Federal Republic of Germany was still not in a position to determine its own foreign policy. In this field it was completely dependent upon the Americans. That was the price Chancellor Adenauer paid for the political integration of the new Germany with the West as an equal member, the most important goal of his entire diplomatic activity.[159] Indeed West Germany was not to become a fully sovereign state until May 5, 1955.

The Balance-of-Payments Struggle and the
End of Reconstruction, 1949–1952

The Federal Republic was created and kept going by Marshall Plan funds. Nobody really knew whether the new Germany would be able to pay its way after the end of the Marshall Plan in 1952.[160] Many Germans were very skeptical. The future course of balance of payments was the most difficult item for them to reckon with. Yet the new policies of widespread industrial decontrol, tax relief, and currency reform were to bring immediate results.

In June 1948, the industrial production index stood at 54 per cent of the 1936 level; by December it had risen to 79, an increase of 46 per cent! The total production index for 1948 was 63 per cent of the 1936 level; in 1949, it rose to 89.8; in 1950, it stood at 113.7; by 1951 it had reached 136: [161] truly a remarkable and rapid growth in industrial production. However, to keep the revived industry going, the Federal Republic needed foreign exchange for the import of raw materials and foodstuffs. From the fall of 1945, British and American funds had kept the Germans alive to the extent that millions of them owe their very lives to the unprecedented generosity of their erstwhile enemies and conquerors. On the other hand, during the first three years of occupation, when the policy of industrial disarmament was in force, the Western occupation zones exported coal and other available raw materials, especially timber and scrap. The available figures for 1946, 1947, and the first half of 1948 show that the combined Anglo-American zone was transformed from a raw-material importing area into a raw-material exporting area.

This complete reversal of the prewar pattern of trade was indicative of the postwar economic dislocation in the Western parts of Germany. In 1936, for instance, 80 per cent of the Third Reich's exports consisted of manufactured goods and only 9 per cent took the form of raw materials, primarily coal. In 1946, on the other hand, raw materials exports constituted 90, and in 1947, 79 per cent of the total.[162]

The Western occupation authorities not only denuded the bizonal economy of raw materials, but they also underpriced German exports. For instance, from May 1945 to September 1947, German coal was exported at $10.50 a ton, while the world price fluctuated between $25 and $30 a ton.[163] In September 1947, the Allies raised the coal export price to $15 a ton, still from $5 to $7 less than the price of Polish and American coal. Estimating that some 25 million tons of coal were exported in this period, the net loss of hard-currency proceeds was roughly $150 million. During 1946 and 1947, the import surplus was $483 and $525 million, respectively.[164] Massive injections of Marshall Plan funds in 1948 and 1949 raised the import surplus to $946 million and $1.1 billion for those years.[165] For the entire period, the import surplus amounted to the stupendous sum of $3.1 billion; in 1949 alone, after recovery was well under way, the import surplus was still more than $1 billion a year.

The revival of German industrial exports was difficult. From 1947 on, the entire export business was in the hands of the Allied Joint Export and Import Agency. One commentator observed that the "fabulous complications of licensing did their share to discourage export business." [166] Low prices paid by JEIA to the exporters was another export-inhibiting factor.[167] However, after December 1, 1948, German firms were freed from many bureaucratic hindrances, and the 1949 export proceeds amounted to over $1 billion.[168] But the Federal Republic of Germany was still far from self-sufficiency.

During the first year of the Marshall Plan—that is, up to mid-1949—West Germany had received in aid a massive injection of $600 million worth of food, raw materials, and industrial machinery, which refilled the empty industrial pipelines and created some food stocks.[169] Despite this unprecedented generosity, however, the future of West Germany's industry was by no means certain.

Although the United States government wanted to see the Federal Republic firmly established within its political orbit, various bureaucracies were slow to adjust themselves to the requirements of the new policy. France, because of its innate fear of "les boches," was particularly apprehensive about the establishment of the German Republic. To assuage French fears, the Americans agreed to the formation of the International Authority for the Ruhr.[170] An agreement to this end, signed on April 28, 1949, had as its basic objectives to keep a lid on German industry and to control coal exports from the Ruhr.[171] By the terms of the agreement for the Ruhr International Authority, the Germans were not only given unequal voice in voting arrangements but, worse, they were in no sense even treated as equals. It was only after the signing on April 18, 1951, of the treaty establishing the Schuman Plan that all restrictions on steel production were lifted and the Germans became economic equals in a quasi-sovereign state.

By mid-1950, Marshall Plan deliveries had amounted to more than $1 billion.[172] But the Germans were hamstrung by the fact that while it is easy to expand domestic output, it is difficult to export.[173] The need for rapid expansion of exports was particularly pressing because, in 1949, West Germany had 21 per cent more people than lived in comparable territory in 1936, but the volume of exports was still only 40 per cent of the prewar level;[174] particularly ominous was the fact that 20 per cent of all exports continued to be raw materials, primarily coal.[175]

In 1950, the Korean War led to a world-wide scramble for raw materials. When prices soared, the Germans had to pay higher costs for raw materials and semifabricates. Higher import prices in relation to given amounts of exports are generally referred to as deteriorating terms of trade. In December 1950, the price index for the import of raw materials was 400 per cent compared with 1936, while the price index for the export of finished goods was only 251 per cent.[176] These divergent trends augured ill for the development of foreign trade. For the time being, however, West Germany was still receiving dollar aid from Marshall Plan funds. In 1951, the growth of German exports slowed down and it was feared that West Germany's export power had "reached a point which, for the time being, cannot be surpassed."[177] Exports apparently could not be expanded because of bottlenecks in the production of coal, iron, steel, and energy.[178] The German authorities feared that, in 1952, after the end of Marshall Plan aid, the dollar gap would become very conspicuous because throughout 1951 more dollars were needed than were earned.[179] In the first quarter of 1952, the import surplus from the dollar area was still $180 million.[180]

The Germans knew that by 1952 West Germany had to become economically independent, but how the necessary rapid expansion of exports would be accomplished with the prevailing rate of exchange of 30 cents for the Deutsche Mark, nobody was able to foretell. In the view of many experts, the DM was considerably overvalued and this Allied-set exchange rate was "the greatest single handicap for German exports," [181] at least for the time being. It may be recalled that in 1949 the Allies devalued the West German mark by 20.6 per cent as compared with 30.5 per cent for the British pound sterling.[182] By so doing, German goods were made relatively more expensive abroad than the British goods, while domestically imports into Germany rose less in price than did imports into the United Kingdom. In addition to gloomy forecasts about the future ability of the Federal Republic to earn enough foreign exchange to pay for the indispensable imports, the domestic situation was tense on account of high unemployment.

Immediately after the currency reform of mid-1948, many formerly employed in name only were compelled to make an honest living. In spite of rapidly rising industrial production, unemployment rose from about half a million in June 1948 to 1.28 million in June 1949.[183] In proportion to the total number of wage and salary earners, unemployment fluctuated as follows during the next five years: [184]

Year	Percentage Unemployed
1949	8.5
1950	10.3
1951	9.0
1952	8.4
1953	7.5

Unemployment was particularly heavy among the refugees and expellees. In March 1949, for instance, this category accounted for 37 per cent of total unemployment.[185] At the end of 1952, the proportion of expellees among the unemployed in West Germany was still 29.5 per cent.[186]

Despite considerable exhortation by American economic advisers to do something about the high level of unemployment, Minister of Economics Erhard opposed all advice on "artificial" stimulation of the economy by way of a public works program.[187] He believed that a stable currency was much more important than full employment. Rapid increase of production, to him, was of greater significance than the academic preoccupation with "fair shares." For this reason, his monetary and fiscal policy favored all productive groups, while the unproductive groups were kept alive by the comprehensive social security system. Increasing production and safeguarding the stability of the Deutsche Mark were the two basic goals of the German economic policy.

By June 1952, West Germany had received $1.5 billion in Marshall Plan Aid,[188] but the Gross National Product, per capita, was still 6 per cent below the level of 1938.[189] Nevertheless, from May 1945 to September 30, 1950, the various German states and the Bundesrepublik paid out a total of RM-DM 24,819 billion in occupation costs; and from October 1, 1950, to the end of the budget year 1952–1953, an additional DM 19,274 billion were so spent.[190] To be able to meet these expenditures demonstrated that, by the end of 1952, West Germany was economically a going concern. The country was also on the way to near-sovereignty politically. However, political and economic recovery were incomplete without moral recovery. In most parts of the Western world, West Germany was still considered a pariah among nations. Public-opinion makers continued to write editorials and make movies in terms of the wartime stereotypes. The legacy of the Third Reich weighed heavily upon Bonn's shoulders. The German escutcheon was still covered with disgrace and infamy, and the revolting vision of the *furor teutonicus* remained deeply ingrained in millions of minds.

Only a bold, fresh, sincere, and massive effort could soften the prevailing antagonism against the Germans in many other countries, especially America and England.[191] Bonn's ratification of the Luxemburg agreements of September 1952 was the first step toward a better public image of the Federal Republic abroad. The meticulous and sincere implementation of the "conscience reparations" that was to follow would bring added respect to the Bonn government.

4

The Moral Question:
To Claim or Not to Claim?

The issue of restitution and compensation for European Jewry was raised formally in the United States in the spring of 1940, when the American Jewish Committee appointed a Committee on Peace Studies under Professor Morris R. Cohen.[1] His charge was to conduct research on the promotion of "a more intelligent understanding of the Jewish situation and aid in the defense of the rights of Jews in the free forum of the world's conscience, as well as to formulate the necessary plans for its execution." [2] In March 1941, the Institute of Jewish Affairs of the World Jewish Congress was established as a research agency in Jewish war and postwar problems, with Dr. Jacob Robinson in charge.[3] In the same year, Dr. Nahum Goldmann broached this problem at an assembly of the World Jewish Congress in Baltimore.[4] At that time Nazi Germany stood at the peak of her power and military success. Most Germans believed that Hitler's armies were invincible. German tanks had annihilated Poland, crushed the French, and swallowed up all of the Balkan states. Most of the western part of the Soviet Union was under German occupation, and Moscow and Leningrad were expected to fall any day. Despite this gloomy outlook, Dr. Goldmann raised questions based on the eventual destruction of the Third Reich, liberation of Nazi-occupied countries, and payment to former owners of compensation for or restoration of Nazi-sequestrated property.

The first official declaration on the postwar restitution problem was made by eighteen Allied governments meeting in London on

January 5, 1943.[5] At that time the Allies warned the Germans that they would have to return all property seized, for whatever reason, no matter how such sequestrations had been legalized.

As the war went on, a number of Jewish scholars, chiefly refugees from Germany residing in the United States, Palestine, and England, worked intensively on the postwar claims against Germany. This work acquired a sense of urgency when the Allies turned the fortunes of war against the Axis Powers.

In the fall of 1943, Dr. George Landauer, an influential German Zionist living in Palestine, wrote a memorandum in which he stressed that, after the victory, Jews as a nation should be allowed to press claims against Germany.[6] He was aware that it would be extremely difficult for the victorious powers to recognize a collective demand, but since the Jews and Germans had special accounts to settle the claim had to be made. In fact, he elevated this objective to be the principal goal of the political activity of the Jewish Agency.[7]

In support of Dr. Landauer's work, Dr. Siegfried Moses, future comptroller of the State of Israel, published a small pamphlet on the subject early in 1944.[8] In it he raised questions of restitution and compensation and made concrete proposals for their implementation. Dr. Moses emphasized that in 1944 the Jews were a nation without a state and thus not subject to international law.[9] Yet, he argued, the Jews had a collective claim against Germany based on a moral justification rather than a legal one. He further insisted that the Jewish community of Palestine should be the creditor of that collective claim.[10] Gillis and Knopf also argued that all the property of the so-called "absent persons" should not be allowed to revert to the successor government of Germany, but instead should go to help build up Palestine, in the form of a collective Jewish claim.[11]

To insure that Jewish refugees from Germany would have adequate representation in pressing their claims after the war, Dr. Moses was instrumental in setting up in December 1944 the Council for the Protection of Rights and Interests of Jews from Germany.[12] The influence of his work on the terms of the Shilumim Agreement and on West German legislation providing individual compensation was of inestimable importance. Dr. Felix E. Shinnar, first head of the Israel mission in Cologne, said of Dr. Moses' pamphlet that eight years before the Luxemburg Treaty it had already settled virtually all basic aspects of the German reparation (*Wiedergutmachung*). According to Shinnar, Dr. Moses' analysis demonstrated the reality as well as the vision of what was possible, and this paved the way for the success of the Shilumim operation.[13]

The problem of restitution, that is, the return of identifiable property, was not very difficult because there had been several major cases of restitution in modern history that could serve as models for Jewish postwar restitution claims. For instance, the Peace of West-phalia of 1648 contained clauses for restitution of confiscated prop-erty; and after Napoleon's downfall, the restoration of the Bourbon dynasty returned 1 billion francs worth of expropriated property.[14] But cases of restitution had also occurred in antiquity.[15]

The problem of how to obtain idemnification for irrecoverable Jewish property was much more difficult. But regardless of the pre-vailing legal difficulties, most Western Jews felt that their claims against the successor government of the Third Reich would be based on legal as well as moral grounds. For example, the Swiss Jewish Community, in a memorandum in October 1944, stressed that the Germans would have to make restitution and pay individual as well as collective compensation.[16] The formal inheritance laws were to be disregarded; all Jewish property with "absentee or missing owners" was to be claimed and the proceeds used for "collective Jewish reconstruction work." [17] At the War Emergency Conference of the World Jewish Congress, in November 1944, Dr. Goldmann demanded that all Jewish property be restored and that a Jewish commonwealth be established.[18] During the same conference, Dr. Moses made the point that idemnification was the first and foremost political problem of Jewish organizations.[19] Indemnification was to be demanded in the form of individual claims, claims of Jewish communities, and the collective claim of the Jewish people as a whole. The proceeds of the latter category were to be used for the rebuilding of Palestine as the Jewish national homeland. Dr. Noah Barou, the dynamic and distinguished vice-president of the World Jewish Congress, British Section, also reiterated that Jewish or-ganizations demanded, among other things, claims for general dam-ages from the successor government of the Third Reich for the same purpose.[20] The demand for postwar compensation for general damages, caused by the genocidal warfare of Nazi Germany against all Jews, was a *res nova,* based on moral grounds. According to Dr.

Goldmann, it was a truly revolutionary concept.[21] The conference also decided to request UNRRA (United Nations Relief and Rehabilitation Administration) assistance for European Jews of ex-enemy nationality.[22]

That same year, Dr. Nehemiah Robinson, head of the Institute of Jewish Affairs of the World Jewish Congress, a refugee from Lithuania, published an important study on all aspects of Jewish postwar claims against the future German government.[23] He insisted that the Germans would have to pay individual compensation, restore all sequestered property, and make collective compensation for material damages to the Jews as a nation as well. He and his brother Jacob were "among those who conceived the very idea of demanding from Germany payments for idemnification and restitution." [24] Dr. Robinson's estimate of material damages sustained by the Jews at the hands of the Nazis came to $12 billion.[25]

Once the war was over, and with the groundwork laid on the matter of restitution and compensation, Dr. Chaim Weizmann, the future first president of Israel, sent a letter to the victorious powers on September 20, 1945. In the name of the Jewish Agency, he demanded restitution, idemnification, and compensation from Germany for the crimes against the Jews.[26] His estimated value of the material losses was $8 billion.[27] Dr. Weizmann requested that all buildings, art treasures, and valuables of every kind be restored to their former owners or their heirs. All property for which no heirs could be traced was to be turned over to the Jewish Agency for Palestine, as the official representative of the Jews. Furthermore, since the majority of the survivors of the concentration camps were likely to go to Palestine, he presented a global Jewish claim against Germany, demanding funds to be used for the purpose of compensating the cost of resettling Jewish refugees in Palestine.

Jewish wartime hopes were rudely shaken by the Paris Reparations Conference at the end of 1945. It virtually disregarded all Jewish demands for individual and collective compensation, except for a $5 million token fund for the benefit of nonrepatriable victims of Nazi concentration camps. In addition, Jewish agencies were offered a maximum of $25 million of German assets in neutral countries, plus the assets of the victims of the Nazis who had died without heirs.[28] Despite bitterness and disappointment on this score, the Jewish leadership in the Diaspora did not despair. After the

Holocaust, the Jews had learned to shift for themselves, and the driblets doled out at the Paris Reparations Conference in 1945 merely mobilized their energies to continue the fight for restitution and idemnification, both individual and collective.

From 1945 to 1949, there was no Germany or German government, merely four zones of occupation. In their zones, the Americans, British, and French had initiated some legislation for restitution and compensation, but under the prevailing conditions of repressed inflation these measures remained grossly inadequate. It was only in the fall of 1949 that the Federal Republic of Germany came into being.

The dreams of a lasting peace based on American-Soviet partnership turned out to be illusory and the Cold War enveloped and divided the world. New alliances emerged, and the remnants of the Third Reich were cut up into two states: the Federal Republic of Germany and the German Democratic Republic. The former became an integral part of the West, allied with the United States, while the latter was a puppet state of the Soviet Union. As West German economic recovery got under way, the Americans decided to put the Germans into uniform once more, this time on the side of the United States. West Germany was not yet sovereign, but she was well on her way to becoming so again.

Equally important, in another part of the world, on May 14, 1948, in Palestine as a mandate trusteeship of the League of Nations, the last high commissioner departed, and the Jewish State of Israel was proclaimed at Tel Aviv by joint action of the Jewish National Council and the General Zionist Council. David Ben-Gurion was appointed prime minister and Chaim Weizmann was elected president, at first provisionally and, in 1949, officially.[29]

Events moved quickly. Chancellor Adenauer was hardly eight weeks in office when he publicly ushered in his policy of restoring German relations with the Jews.[30] On November 11, 1949, he offered Israel DM 10 million worth of German-made goods. Adenauer was aware that his offer constituted only a symbolic gesture of material amends, but that by it he was taking a first step in placing responsibility for the Holocaust on the German people. It became one of his foremost objectives, both as man and as chancellor of the Federal Republic of Germany, to make material amends. Others, like Kurt Schumacher, the head of the Social Democratic Party, Theodor

Heuss, the first president of West Germany, and Carlo Schmidt, the much-respected parliamentarian, to mention only a few, were very much aware of the moral obligation of all Germans toward the Jews. The consciences of a few responsible men and women were clearly not dormant, but the majority of Germans remained passive, silent, and too preoccupied with making a living.[31] For the time being in 1949, however, there was no response from Israel to Adenauer's offer.[32]

Despite their bitter disappointment with the Paris Reparations Conference, many Jewish organizations, but especially the World Jewish Congress, discussed in numerous meetings the moral nature of Jewish demands against the future German government.[33] The Jews wanted redress, and Adenauer's speech of November 1949 left an impression upon the Jews and Israelis. The real question was how to begin exploratory meetings. It is difficult, of course, to reconstruct who made the first move and then the countermove that eventually led to the Shilumim agreement. The available documentation suggests, however, that the first major step was taken in December 1949 at the meeting of the World Jewish Congress in New York City, when a five-point declaration was issued demanding from the West German parliament: (a) acceptance of moral and political responsibility for Nazi deeds toward Jews; (b) material indemnification; (c) legislation against anti-Semitism; (d) reeducation of German youth; and (e) a check upon nationalistic tendencies in the West German government.[34] The German press was cool to these demands.

The year 1950 was marked by quiet, exploratory talks among Jewish, Israeli, and West German officials; officially, however, diplomatic activity was limited to the exchange of notes. Thus, on January 18, 1950, the Israeli government sent an *aide-mémoire* to the four occupying powers, restating Dr. Weizmann's claims of 1945.[35] The first informal contacts between the Israelis and West Germans, which took place in the spring of 1950, led to no concrete results.[36] But talks continued throughout the year.

The person who in 1950 initiated and for a long time alone and tirelessly conducted talks with Bonn's officials on Germany's moral obligations to make collective indemnification to the Jewish people was Dr. Noah Barou.[37] A colleague of Dr. Barou, Mr. A. L. Easterman, the head of the Political Department of the World Jewish

Congress, observed later that Dr. Barou continued his exploratory talks "impervious to the fierce and widespread Jewish opposition to accepting 'blood money' from Germany, and to the many doubts in Israel and in the Jewish world, as well as in Allied Government circles, of the legal and practical feasibility of obtaining Jewish reparations from a defeated, destroyed and impoverished Germany." [38] He made more than forty trips on this mission. [39] In early 1950, Dr. Barou established contact with Dr. H. Blankenhorn, at that time director of the Political Department of the Foreign Ministry in Bonn, who confirmed that the declaration of the World Jewish Congress of December 1949 could serve as a basis for negotiations. [40] Further contacts took place in Istanbul and other places, without any tangible results. [41]

Despite these seemingly futile efforts, two important documents on the subject of the Jewish collective claims against Germany made their appearance in 1950. The first was by Dr. Hendrik van Dam, an influential Jewish lawyer residing in West Germany, whose study, *The Problem of Reparations and Indemnification for Israel,* was published on July 1, 1950. In this memorandum Dr. van Dam reminded the Jews and Israelis that "the corresponding factor of the German people's *moral obligation* is the *moral claim* of the Jewish people." [42] It was, incidentally, Dr. van Dam, who as early as mid-1948, stated that "Israel can ill afford to give up material claims against Germany because of understandable Jewish revulsion in dealing with the Germans." [43] He urged the Jews then and in 1950 not to burden their claim upon Germany with futile rationalizations and to accept what was long overdue.

The other major document on collective Jewish claims was submitted by Mr. A. L. Easterman of the World Jewish Congress to Lord Henderson, Undersecretary of State for Foreign Affairs at the British Foreign Office, on July 25. [44] The author reiterated that Nazi genocide "created a responsibility on the part of the German people, which the German Government must discharge on a collective basis, as a measure of indemnification to the Jewish people. The German Federal Republic should, therefore, assume an obligation in an instrument of agreement with the Allied Powers, to indemnify the Jewish people by material compensation in goods, services or otherwise, commensurate with its share of responsibility for the German State as a whole." [45] On January 11, 1951, Lord Henderson,

accompanied by Mr. Harold Wilson, discussed at length the problem
of collective indemnity, and he inquired as to what would be regarded as acceptable to the Jewish people.[46] Mr. Easterman, speaking for himself only, estimated "an acceptable offer by the German
Government to be £500,000,000." [47] It was a prophetic guess, for it
was this sum that was later rationalized at the Wassenaar negotiations.[48] On January 16, 1951, Israel repeated its claims to the four
occupying powers,[49] followed on March 12 by another note, in
which it advanced claims in the amount of $1.5 billion and requested
Allied support for its position.[50] This note, which reviewed the
story of the Holocaust, made clear that no amount of material compensation would ever expiate the Nazi crimes against the Jews.

Nevertheless, the Israeli leaders were convinced that material
compensation could and should be obtained. The Allies whole-
heartedly approved their claim in theory, but apart from sympathy
Israel got no effective support. The American government replied
that it could not officially "impose on the Government of the German Federal Republic an obligation to pay reparations to Israel." [51]
In other words, for various specified and unspecified reasons, the
United States, Great Britain, and France abstained from any direct
action to further Israel's claim against Germany.

The government of the Soviet Union did not even reply to the
Israeli note, a position it has maintained up to the present day.
The German Democratic Republic has also continued to reject all
responsibility for injuries to Jews in the Nazi years. The East German government has consistently acted as though the men and
women living under its banner today had really never lived in the
Third Reich, and as if sufficient amends for the past could be
made by loud denunciations of former Nazis living or holding
public office in West Germany. Of course, part of the explanation
for such an attitude is that, in theory, no fascist elements exist in
the German Democratic Republic, and consequently its government
has no responsibility for the Nazi past. Communist doctrine recog-
nizes only class problems. For this reason, neither the Soviet nor
any other East European government has ever paid a penny for
the expropriated property of its former "bourgeois" classes. Nor
have they ever paid or made plans to pay for the loss of life and
limb of the millions of "class" enemies.

Under these circumstances, the leaders of Israel were in a quandary. They realized that they would have to take the initiative themselves, and the question "of direct contact with Germany, with all its emotional implications, became a political necessity." [52] Although finding themselves at the mercy of Big-Power politics, they refused to give up. Men like Ben-Gurion, Goldmann, Barou, Giora Josephthal, and Moshe Sharett, to mention just a few, unquestionably had strong reservations about what loomed ahead, but they were statesmen and patriots. They were determined to pursue the matter in spite of the prevailing doubt among the majority of their own people—doubt as to the moral and ethical justification of entering into any agreements with West Germany that might absolve the Germans collectively of their "crime against humanity." For, seven years after the Nazi depredations against the Jews, the Germans and Germany still represented the incarnation of evil to most Jews. With few exceptions, Israelis believed that it would be sacrilegious to negotiate with the Germans on the collective claim.[53] Joseph Sprinzak, the president of the Israeli Parliament, declared that "the honor of the Jewish people precluded any acceptance of restitution from Germany even if it were voluntarily and spontaneously offered." [54]

Ben-Gurion and his cabinet, supported by a number of Israeli officials and Zionists of stature and vision, were determined to go ahead. For instance, Israel's first comptroller, Dr. Siegfried Moses, wanted to save as much as possible of remaining European Jewish wealth in order to meet absorption costs.[55] On July 1, 1951, Israel's Foreign Ministry set up a section called "Geltendmachung der Ansprüche des jüdischen Volkes gegen Deutschland" (in English it would be The Claims Office of the Jewish People Against Germany). Dr. Felix E. Shinnar was appointed to head it.[56]

Officially, nothing happened after the Israeli note of March 12, 1951, was turned down by the Western Powers. The government of Israel was becoming increasingly convinced that it would have to deal with the Germans directly. "Money by cable," to use the metaphor of the American prosecutor at the Nuremberg trials, Robert M. W. Kempner, was out of the question; [57] and so, for the time being, were direct talks between Israel and the West Germans.

The private talks had been going on for more than fifteen months and were still deadlocked in early summer of 1951.[58] But Dr. Barou, with dogged persistence, carried on. His principal link with Dr.

Adenauer was Dr. Herbert Blankenhorn, a clever official who never contradicted his Chancellor.[59] Once again, it was Dr. Barou who convinced Blankenhorn that speeches admitting the responsibility of the German people for the crimes of the Nazi regime would never be enough.[60] Dr. Barou also demanded that the West German government assume a binding obligation to make collective reparation and accept the moral, political, and material responsibility for the deeds of the Third Reich.[61] He told Blankenhorn that Israel would negotiate with the Bonn government only after Adenauer had solemnly acknowledged before the West German parliament his nation's responsibility for the acts of the Nazi regime against the Jews. Another precondition was a public declaration of West Germany's intent to make amends for the material losses suffered by European Jewry, and still another was that representatives of Israel and world Jewry be officially invited to discuss the matter. These terms were accepted by Adenauer. The West Germans prepared the first draft of such a declaration in July 1951, but it took almost three months of negotiating in Israel, London, New York, and Bonn, to agree on a text which satisfied "justified Jewish demands." [62] It was again Dr. Barou who convinced Adenauer that he and other political leaders realize "that Israel must be the main beneficiary of collective compensation." [63] The draft of Adenauer's forthcoming speech was rewritten many times and "it included 31 points of special interest." [64]

West Germany's Social Democrats took an active part in these behind-the-scenes activities. The first official contact between Israelis and Germans came in May 1951 at the Hotel Bristol in Paris, when Adenauer met with the Israeli Ambassador to France, Maurice Fischer, and Dr. David Horowitz, Governor of the Bank of Israel.[65] This meeting was kept top secret. It turned out to have been quite dramatic when the facts became known. Adenauer received the two Israeli officials and listened with monumental patience to their passionate account of Nazi crimes. At the close of their testimony, he promised them to reexamine the entire question of material compensation.[66]

Finally, it was Chancellor Adenauer's Bundestag address of September 27, 1951, that made direct German-Israeli talks possible.[67] He emphasized that the Bonn government was not only aware of the crimes perpetrated against the Jews but would do everything possible to make amends. The majority of Germans, Adenauer said, were not accomplices to these crimes and, with some few exceptions,[68] abhorred what the Nazis had perpetrated; but since unspeakable crimes had been committed in the name of all Germans, his government felt obliged to do penance in the form of moral and material amends to Israel and the Jews at large.

The amounts that West Germany could pay were limited. She had not yet fully recovered from the war and its aftermath. Millions of refugees, expellees, war-crippled veterans, and bombed-out people were kept alive on the dole. But the Chancellor assured the world and his fellow Germans that regardless of budgetary and balance-of-payments difficulties, he would do everything "zur seelischen Bereinigung unendlichen Leides." He also committed himself to relentless prosecution of all those who might still be spreading anti-Semitic hate. The speech was approved by all members of the Bundestag except those of the extreme left and right. As an added tangible demonstration of the good will and sincerity of the German lawmakers, the members of the Bundestag rose from their seats in sympathy for the Jewish victims. The event represented an official invitation to the Israeli government for direct negotiations.

Dr. Adenauer's speech evoked instant and overwhelmingly favorable response from all over the world. The *Washington Post* called it "the best thing that came from Germany since before 1933." The *New York Times* termed Adenauer's offer "A Sign of Decency," and the Manchester *Guardian* took it for a "Sign of German Change of Heart." In the London *Economist*'s view it was an "Act of Courage," and for the *Montreal Daily Star* it was simply a "Necessity." [69]

In Germany all major newspapers voiced equally strong approval. The *Süddeutsche Zeitung* hoped that Adenauer's offer would usher in an era of a possible peace with Israel. The *Hamburger Echo* looked at Bonn's gesture as a "Cornerstone of the Inner Change of Germans." German Jews hailed the Chancellor's words as being indispensable for "cleansing the atmosphere" between Germans and Jews. Dr. Leo Baeck, president of the Reichsvertretung der deutschen Juden, an organization founded by German Jewry after the rise of Nazism, wrote to Dr. Adenauer saying that his commitment had created a basis for the necessary heart-to-heart talks between Jews and Germans.

The Israeli response was much more reserved. Ever since the

November 1949 statement by Adenauer, the Israelis had been debating their future policy toward Germany. They were not convinced of the sincerity of Adenauer's offer on moral grounds, and they saw virtually no sign of a German change of heart with respect to anti-Semitism. They felt that whatever Bonn offered or promised would be done only for the sake of political expediency, and many wanted no part of it. Nevertheless, Adenauer's speech made a considerable impression on a number of Israeli leaders. The first major breakthrough with the public-opinion makers came from the pen of Erich Winter, who recorded his impression of West Germany in the most popular Israeli daily, *Davar,* in an article that cast doubt on neither the sincerity of Adenauer's offer nor his motives.[70]

Since every third Israeli had experienced personally the horrors of Nazism, the very idea of direct talks with West Germany caused a deep crisis of conscience. But Ben-Gurion's government decided to push ahead.[71] From then on, things began to move. No formal talks were held immediately, but quiet, discreet, and mostly secret conversations among interested parties began to take place simultaneously in many parts of the world.

The man who broke the impasse on the Jewish side was Dr. Nahum Goldmann, president of the World Jewish Congress. Recognizing the temporary impossibility of direct contact between Israel and Germany, he suggested that Jewish world organizations act on behalf of Israel.[72]

Under his leadership, representatives of world Zionist and non-Zionist organizations, in a series of meetings in October 1951, considered the German offer.[73] Once the decision was made to deal with Adenauer, more than twenty Jewish organizations formed the Conference of Jewish Material Claims Against Germany (Claims Conference) to represent world Zionist and non-Zionist (but not anti-Zionist) Jewry in the forthcoming negotiations with the Germans. Dr. Goldmann was chosen chairman.[74] Despite his consummate diplomatic skill and dogged persistence in 1951 and 1952, Dr. Goldmann never pretended that he took the initiative in pushing through, so to speak, the collective claim against Germany. According to him, this honor belongs to Dr. Barou and no one else.[75]

Adenauer's offer and the decision of Ben-Gurion's government to accept it evoked as much soul-searching among Diaspora Jewry as among those in Israel. Many American, British, and South African

Zionist and non-Zionist Jews did not consider the forthcoming talks desirable. Men of stature, learning, vision, and religious conviction felt that it was morally wrong to do business with the Bonn government.[76]

The resistance was widespread, passionate, and protracted. Its principal spokesman was Dr. Joseph B. Schechtman of New York, chairman of the World Council of Herut-Hatzohar. He argued that Germany was morally "untouchable," unconditionally "traif," at least insofar as Jews were concerned, and thus not a fit partner to any international deliberations.[77] He pleaded that the "fundamental objective of the foreign policy of the Jewish people" should be "to establish the fact of Germany's moral and political uncleanliness."[78] Lack of organized contact with the Germans, he insisted, would demonstrate to the world Jewish aloofness and moral greatness; a nonfraternization policy would amount to "a permanent mute reproach and indictment."[79] A leading Mizrachi spokesman feared that direct contacts with the Germans "must be construed as a measure of forgiveness."[80] Dr. Schechtman also felt that negotiations with the Bonn government "would automatically erase the stigma of Germany's moral untouchability in international relations"; after all, how can you negotiate a settlement and still call your opposite number a murderer?[81]

The advocates of nonfraternization also quoted Abba Eban's remark "that the motives that prompted Dr. Adenauer to offer reparations were far from lofty."[82] The Chancellor's declaration of September 27, 1951, was downgraded as supposedly having been elicited by the American State Department "as one of the conditions to the full acceptance of West Germany in the concert of powers against further encroachment by the Communist axis."[83] A revisionist publication anticipated that Bonn's negotiators would make a generous long-term offer, which Dr. Hermann J. Abs (Germany's chief negotiator at the London Debt Conference) then would probably not pay.[84]

Dr. Schechtman also predicted that West Germany would pay "only a token amount"[85] and then cheat the Jews and Israelis of the balance. By entering into direct formal contacts with the Bonn government, he argued, and then breaking off talks because of inadequacy of the German offer, the "Jews would never again be in a position to recover their previous unassailable stand of moral indignation." [86] After all, the Germans had a long tradition of defaulting on international commitments, and there was absolutely no guarantee that "some future German government will not repudiate the debt." [87] Furthermore, opponents of a deal with Germany felt that to accept the proposed terms would make Israel a mere distributor of German-made goods.[88] Dr. Schechtman described the suggested payments-in-kind agreement as a sort of "economic vassalage" for Israel.[89]

The architects of an agreement with Germany treated opposition as mere emotionalism. They tended to minimize the depth and breadth of the furious debate in Jewish circles—to play down the "Remember what Amalek has done to you" attitude that was strong everywhere.[90] Dr. Nahum Goldmann, the principal advocate of direct negotiations with Bonn, argued that since the Nazis had looted Jewish property, it would be immoral for the Jews not to claim it back. By not doing so, the Jews would be, in fact, paying a premium to the murderers! [91] And since the Western Allies would not claim Jewish property from the government of West Germany, direct talks were inevitable. In trying to overcome the widespread opposition to direct negotiations with the Germans, Goldmann repeated again and again his argument that it would be immoral not to seek to recover the private and public Jewish property stolen by the Nazis. A quixotic negative attitude might be appealing, he felt, but in terms of human lives it was silly and morally unjustifiable.[92] Another Jewish writer said that in the forthcoming talks the Jews and Israelis would be compelled "to keep company with the German snake in order to salvage our possessions from its mouth." [93] Dr. Goldmann and his aides also countered the opposition argument that direct talks with the Germans would erase the stigma of Germany's moral untouchability in the international community by charging that "We are not dealing here with a *quid pro quo*. Nobody is saying to the Germans: You pay us; we forgive you. We are promising nothing; we are offering nothing. We are simply claiming what is ours, morally and legally." [94] The advocates of talks tended to minimize the purely moral problem by saying that the time was not ripe for solution, that only history could settle the spiritual aspect of the German debt to the Jewish people, but that heirless property belonged to the Jewish people.[95]

Dr. Goldmann's claim, that Jewish demands for restitution and compensation merely sought the return of what had been stolen, enjoyed considerable public support. "No matter what the Germans offer, they are not giving, but giving back," wrote one commentator in *Israel Speaks*.[96] *Congress Weekly* insisted that it would be utter folly to permit those who had killed and robbed Jews to retain possession of the stolen property.[97] Of course, it was generally understood and constantly reiterated that no indemnity could ever make good the loss of Jewish life and that the Nazi crime could not be expiated by any measure of material compensation. Nor did the advocates of direct talks take seriously the opposition's claim that West Germany would eventually default on the promise. One writer asserted that the Federal Republic must pay simply to show the world the difference between the Third and the Fourth Reich! [98]

As a final argument, Dr. Goldmann spoke convincingly of the dire situation of Israel's economy and claimed that German payments "should make Israel as economically independent as any state can hope to be in our interdependent world." [99] He also pointed to Israel's desperate housing situation, which could be changed by the delivery of thousands of German-made prefabricated houses.[100] Other writers substantiated these arguments by emphasizing that while German payments would expiate nothing, they would represent "a substantial contribution towards the consolidation of a sovereign Israeli State" [101] and would represent the economic salvation of Israel.[102] In fact, in the fall of 1951 Israel's shortage of foreign currency became alarming.[103]

5

Repressed Inflation in Israel: 1949–1951

What was Israel's economy like in the fall of 1951 and early 1952, on the threshold of the Wassenaar negotiations?

After proclaiming its independence, Israel initiated unrestricted immigration of Jews from all over the world. As soon as the shores of Israel were opened up, the waiting masses of Ashkenazim poured into the country in fantastic numbers. In the second half of 1948, immigrants from Europe entered the country at a rate of 13,000 per month. In 1949, about 20,000 entered every month. In 1950, Sephardic Jews from Iraq, Yemen, Tunisia, Morocco, and Algeria came to Israel at a rate of 13,000 a month. In the first half of 1951, the influx was again over 20,000 a month.

When the mass immigration ended in October 1951, almost 700,-000 immigrants had entered Israel.[1] Slightly less than one-half of all arrivals came from Eastern Europe, primarily Poland, Romania, and Bulgaria, while the rest came from Africa, the Middle East, and the Orient. By the end of 1951, almost half of Israel's population had come after 1948. This three-year wave of free immigration created very serious absorption problems and resulted in a great strain to the social system. The burst of indiscriminate admission brought to the country many people with no skills, for whom it was almost impossible to provide employment and housing. Moreover, a large number of the physically exhausted, the aged, and the chronically and mentally ill became public charges to the welfare institutions and the government.[2] At the end of 1947, there lived in the territory of what constituted pre-1967-war Israel 1.39 million inhabitants; of these, roughly 630,000 were Jews.[3] But since almost 700,000 Arabs left Israel during the hostilities in 1947 and 1948, the total population after 1947 declined; and it was only at the end of 1951 that Israel's population stood again at 1.4 million. By the end of 1964, over 2.5 million lived in Israel, of whom 286,385 were non-Jews. From 1948 to 1951, Israel's population increased 20.6 per cent a year.[4] From 1948 to 1964, a seventeen-year span, the average increase in population came to more than 6 per cent a year, one of the highest rates of population growth in the world in any comparable period.[5]

It is true that the Malthusian specter has haunted economists and statesmen for the last hundred and fifty years because population tends to double every twenty-four years, whereas the food supply grows much more slowly. But imagine the problem and all its corollaries for a population growing at Israel's rate! In 1949, for every 1,000 residents 266 immigrants and tourists came to settle in Israel; in 1950, the rate was 154 per thousand; and in 1951, it was 132 per thousand.[6] These were truly high rates of influx and much higher than those of any other country with mass immigration. In the United States, for example, during the peak of immigration in the nineteenth century the rate was only 16.1 immigrants per 1,000 residents, whereas in Israel the rate was more than ten times that figure.[7] One observer estimated that if Israel's ratio of immigration to total population were applicable to the United States, it would mean an influx of almost 38 million newcomers annually.[8]

The European Ashkenazim arrived in Israel with no possessions except some gold coins, some precious stones, and a few dollar bills, which they had managed to hide throughout the years in ghettos and concentration camps. Immigrants from Iraq and Egypt were better off, but those from Yemen and other Asiatic countries were desperately poor and mostly illiterate, and they bore the further stigma of differing in appearance and custom from the European immigrants. Once they were in the country, the government and the Jewish Agency provided them with the first necessities, including temporary quarters, until permanent housing and employment became available.

After the War of Liberation, Israel was surrounded, as she still is, by hostile Lebanon, Syria, Jordan, and Egypt. Since the Arabs signed only an armistice and no peace treaties, the Israelis found it difficult to believe that they would not attack to seek revenge for the humiliating defeat they suffered in 1948 and 1949. Even though the guns

were silent, fear of the Arabs was very much in the air, and the
survival of the state became the number one concern of the general
public. The necessities of being ready at a moment's notice, of
strengthening the borders, and of dispersing the growing population
produced an atmosphere of half-war, half-peace.[9] During the first
few years of Israel's existence, strategic considerations became "a
social virtue," and purely economic criteria in use of resources were
relegated to the background. Resources were commandeered by government and military officials; deficit financing was the order of the
day. The emphasis was on short-run solutions, on improvisation; a
long-term policy had to wait.

Direct Controls in Action

The policy of the "Ingathering of the Exiles" created an aggregate
demand that outstripped the country's economic capabilities, that is,
its short-run aggregate supply. Israel faced an enormous inflationary
gap, and the government had to decide either to let the market forces
generate enough forced saving and thus restore equilibrium, or to
control inflationary pressures by a system of direct controls. To cope,
the government had to convince the people to tighten their belts
and reduce their standard of living. In democratic countries such
measures are unpopular and difficult to implement because of the
powerful influence of pressure groups on the government. In Israel
open inflation was politically unacceptable because of the strong
egalitarian and collectivist orientation of the prevailing value system
in the government, the Histadrut, the universities, the kibbutzim,
and the political parties.

Experience with open inflation in industrially advanced countries
had demonstrated that it redistributed national incomes in favor
of profit-takers and hurt those with fixed incomes and wage earners.
At that time, Israel had a particularly strong bias toward building
an egalitarian workers' society. On the other hand, hyperinflation
in industrial countries leads to fast expansion and renovation of
industry. For instance, in Germany during the hyperinflation of
the 1920s, the flight out of the mark into real values resulted in the
very substantial growth of German industry.[10] At the same time,
however, hyperinflation broke the backbone of the German middle
classes, which later became the staunch supporters of the National
Socialists. Israel was not yet an industrial country, and the short-run

supply conditions were extremely inelastic. The Israeli government consequently assumed that open inflation would not result in rapid and substantial expansion of industrial capital. Above all, it was feared that the social consequences of rapid inflation would be very disturbing politically.[11] Therefore, Israel decided to repress the inflationary potential through price, wage, rent, and foreign-exchange controls, coupled with the rationing of goods and raw materials.[12]

In April 1949, the government set up a system of physical controls that virtually suspended the operations of the market forces.[13] Officially, these controls were designed to fight inflation by rolling back the wage-price spiral and by distributing equitably the scarce supplies of consumer goods.[14] Some observers felt, however, that direct controls were used to raise the internal value of the Israeli pound by bringing down prices and wages; others believed that the objective was the redistribution of the national income "in favor of the poorer classes." J. T. Shuval argued that direct controls aimed at three objectives: (1) to lower prices, (2) to save foreign currency by importing only essential supplies, and (3) to increase domestic production.[15] Patinkin claimed simply that direct controls attempted "to keep the cost of living down," [16] and D. Horowitz argued that in the early years of statehood "everything had to be done to equalize standards, that is, to carry out a leveling-up process." [17] Since the political objective of the Ingathering of the Exiles was paramount, the economic forces were artificially subordinated to that objective.[18]

Because of the early collectivist-egalitarian bent of the government, Israel introduced physical controls primarily for social reasons, such as the avoidance of starvation and social polarization, regardless of the economic consequences. The Ministry of Supply and Rationing was made responsible for their administration, and Dr. Dov Joseph, the hero of Jerusalem in the siege in 1948, was put in charge. His ministry consisted of four divisions: one was responsible for food purchases and rationing; another fixed and controlled prices; the materials and supplies section allocated raw materials and other inputs to the producers; and the inspection section was in charge of the enforcement of the entire gamut of controls.[19]

Repressed Inflation

Dr. Joseph's price-wage, rent, floorspace, and foreign-exchange controls, together with the rationing of many consumer goods and the priority system in the distribution of raw materials, subjected a large area of the economy to government regulation. Only the production and distribution of so-called "nonessential" goods remained free of government control. Such a system is called "a partially repressed inflation." [20]

In the controlled sector, a monetary income did not automatically entitle an Israeli who earned a pound to convert it into rationed consumer goods. He could purchase goods only if the currency was accompanied by rationing coupons or purchase permits. In theory, monetary income, insofar as it could be spent on legal purchases of rationed consumer goods, should have maintained a constant purchasing power, assuming that the cost of living remained stable. The income for which there were no rationing coupons could either be spent in the "free" markets or saved.

Direct controls, by themselves, do not eliminate excessive monetary demand, but merely prevent it from raising the price and wage levels. In an economy subject to direct controls, two types of monetary income exist side by side: income endowed with legal purchasing power and income rendered powerless for legal purchases because of lack of rationing documents. The difference between these incomes constitutes the monetary overhang, or waiting purchasing power.[21] The income levels, the comprehensiveness of the rationing system, the level of prices, the trend of the cost-of-living index, and the total currency supply—all determine the size of the waiting purchasing power.

The larger the sector of the economy subject to direct controls, the larger the waiting purchasing power and the stronger the tendency for the marginal value of incomes above the legal expenditure level to fall to zero. After all, what is the point of earning money that can scarcely be spent! [22] In such a situation, the declining productivity of labor, the widespread substitution of leisure for work, or illegal economic activity are likely to result in a falling Gross National Product. On the other hand, although a large uncontrolled sector is likely to preserve incentives to work, it will also undermine the controlled sector and thus lead eventually to a wage-price spiral.

In Israel, the uncontrolled market was a buffer that absorbed the excess purchasing power. In this "free" market the demand and supply forces determined the price for every commodity; here inflation was open, not repressed. From December 1948 to the end of

December 1951, the total currency supply increased from I£ 100.8
million to I£ 241.5 million.[23] The increase from December 1948 to
December 1949 was 39.1 per cent; during the next year, the increase
was 35.4 per cent; in 1951, the supply rose 27.2 per cent. At the annual
compounded rate, the growth of the total currency supply was 33.9
per cent.[24] From April 1949 to June 1950, the rate of increase in the
total currency supply was 48 per cent, while during the same period
the cost-of-living index was reduced by various means, mostly subsidies, to 14 per cent. Thus, the real value of Israeli currency grew
by 72 per cent.[25]

In the initial stages of repressed inflation, when nearly all Israelis
knew that the new country demanded sacrifices from everybody,
people were willing to tighten belts and live under "austerity." But
with the increase in the real value of the total currency supply and
the world-wide scramble for raw materials after the outbreak of
the Korean War in mid-1950, shortages on the official markets grew
more acute. Under those circumstances, the waiting purchasing
power spilled over into the "free" markets, eventually undermining
the controlled markets as well.[26]

Price Controls

Generally speaking, price-fixing for the purpose of repressing inflationary pressures calls for setting up so-called maximum prices,
that is, below-the-equilibrium prices. Without controls all prices are
likely to rise in the short run. Thus, avoidance or slowing down of
increases is the rationale of price-fixing. Price control aims at the
stabilization of three interrelated types of costs: the cost of living,
the cost of investment goods, and the cost of items responsible for
the cost push. The main elements of the cost of living are food,
clothing, rent, and fuel, all of which have to be controlled to bring
about stability. And because the prices of investment goods are
determined by wages and the costs of inputs, stability of the prices
of investment goods calls for control of such cost-push items as
wages, raw materials, and profit margins.

In Israel there were four types of ceiling prices: frozen prices,
pounds-and-prutoth prices, formula prices, and "regardless-of-cost"
prices. Since the very purpose of physical controls was to roll back
the cost-of-living index, Dr. Joseph's ministry pursued a price policy
that led to what might be called "regardless-of-cost" price ceilings.

It frequently ordered arbitrary price cuts for all items entering into the cost-of-living index, reducing the profit margins of manufacturers and distributors which seemed to be too high.[27] To wage a successful campaign against a rising cost-of-living index, Dr. Joseph's ministry pursued a policy of very low prices for foods and other necessities. It also used equalization funds and subsidies. Frequently, production costs were completely disregarded and the resulting "regardless-of-cost" ceiling prices were maintained by substantial subsidies to keep the producers in business. Since production costs differed from place to place, the Ministry of Supply operated a Special Fund to keep the price of a given commodity uniform throughout the country.

Dr. Joseph did not hesitate to use the Equalization Fund to reduce prices and pay subsidies for all items that entered the official cost-of-living index. It was his strong arm. All domestic raw materials—building materials, capital equipment, and all important consumer goods, such as shoes, furniture, and clothing—were subject to price-fixing. Even such services as shoemaking, tailoring, barbering, house-repairing, porterage, and laundering were price-fixed. All imported foodstuffs, agricultural products, and processed food items—more than 600 food commodities—were subject to ceiling prices.[28] These were fixed in cooperation with the producers' representatives.

Yet despite price cuts and money-wage reductions by the Histadrut on three occasions, Dr. Joseph's efforts to keep the cost-of-living index stable were only partially successful.[29] During their first year of operation, Dr. Joseph's price-stabilization efforts were supported by the public's general feelings of enthusiasm and self-sacrifice.[30] But in the summer of 1950, the outbreak of the Korean War had a number of repercussions in Israel. The world-wide scramble for raw materials with its inevitable sharp price increases forced the introduction of rationing of textiles and footwear on August 1, 1950.[31] The people began to lose faith in the ability of price controls to stem the tide of inflationary pressures, and from then on black markets flourished.

From March 1949 to June 1950, the cost-of-living index was reduced by different administrative means from 370 to 317, 14 per cent. By December, however, despite the massive efforts of Dr. Joseph to reduce the price of the official "consumer's basket," the cost-of-living index had risen to 324. In June 1951, it stood at 343, and by September it had risen to 383.[32]

The policy of pushing down the cost of living was not accompanied by drastic measures to siphon off the waiting purchasing power in the hands of the public. On the contrary, the total currency supply kept rising by some 30 per cent a year. This divergence between the downward tendency of the official cost-of-living index and the rising trend of the total currency supply meant that the real money supply was growing and wreaking havoc in the economy.[33]

In the second half of 1950 and throughout 1951, the official cost-of-living index did not reflect the sharp price increases of those daily necessities that could be bought only on the black market. For instance, in September 1951, the black-market-to-official-price ratio for fresh meat was 7.7; for eggs it was 3.2; for edible oils, 9.3; for sugar, 25.0; for rice, 10.0; and for potatoes, 5.7.[34]

From August 1950 on, the public lost confidence in the currency and began a "flight into goods." [35] Because of their war and postwar experiences, the immigrants from Central and Eastern Europe were very inflation-conscious, whereas the Sephardim from the Middle Eastern countries believed only in gold. Rumors of future shortages tended to aggravate the inflationary pressures.[36] By the fall of 1951 price control became a fiction, and black-market prices, market-determined prices, predominated. Price-fixing had failed to stem the tide of inflationary pressures.

Food Rationing

Food rationing is an integral part of any system of direct controls. Maximum ceilings on prices, rents, wages, and foreign exchange are, as a rule, designed to stabilize the cost of living. To make sure that the hundreds of thousands of immigrants living temporarily on the public dole would get a fair share of scarce supplies, rationing was inevitable. Without it, the necessities of life would be sold on a first-come, first-served basis, and to queue up for them people would have to abstain from work. Time spent in the food lines would be reflected in high rates of absenteeism and a declining G.N.P. On the other hand, people with good connections and high incomes would be able to buy scarce but price-fixed items under the counter. Thus the very system of maximum prices, without rationing, might have led to a system of discrimination against the poorer sections of the population. And, politically, with so many thousands of new immigrants, the Israeli government could ill afford to let that happen.

Israel's food rationing was based on a "linking system." In April 1949, every resident received a card that "linked" him to a particular store.[37] In June of the same year, the distribution of coupon books was started. The quantitative food ration was the predominant method. Dr. Joseph felt that the British "value system" or the U.S. "point system" would be administratively too cumbersome for Israel. For rationing purposes, all Israelis were classified into three categories: infants to the age of two years, children to the age of eighteen years, and adults.[38]

Except for bread, which could be purchased at very low prices, most foods were rationed. Yet despite an acute foreign-exchange shortage and irregularities in supplying all called-up rations, the Israeli population was well fed. Table 5-1 shows that from the beginning of rationing in 1949 through the 1952–1953 period the average daily caloric intake was about 2,600.

Most of these calories were obtained from legal purchases of rationed foods, although some came from nonrationed foods and the black market. Fortunately, the daily caloric intake was more than the minimum 2,400 calories recommended by the League of Nations. In 1959–1960, the caloric intake was only 6.2 per cent higher than

TABLE 5-1

AVERAGE DAILY FOOD INTAKE PER CAPITA

Year	Calories	Index	Fats per day (grams)	Index	Animal proteins per day (grams)	Index	Cereals and cereal products (index)
1949–50	2,610	100.0	73.9	100.0	32.2	100.0	100.0
1950–51	2,677	102.6	74.4	100.7	33.7	104.7	101.4
1951–52	2,706	103.7	68.2	92.3	26.2	81.4	111.8
1952–53	2,736	104.8	68.3	92.4	26.0	80.7	115.1
1953–54	2,849	109.2	75.3	101.9	27.6	85.7	116.2
1959–60	2,773	106.2	86.8	117.5	33.9	105.3	91.8

Source: F. Ginor, *Uses of Agricultural Surpluses* (Jerusalem: Bank of Israel, 1963), pp. 426–427, 430–431.

a decade earlier under rationing. Of course, caloric intake per day is not a sufficient measure of a diet's adequacy. Israeli rations were quite deficient in fats and animal proteins.[39] For instance, in 1959–1960, the daily fat consumption was 17.5 per cent above that of 1949–1950, and 27 per cent above that of 1951–1952. In 1951, the shortage of foreign exchange was responsible for the drastic cut in imports of edible oils and fats to 50 per cent of the previous years.[40] The consumption of animal proteins held up at the more than 30 grams per day level during the first two years of rationing, but again because of foreign-exchange difficulties it dropped by almost 20 per cent in 1951–1952 as compared to 1949–1950. The shortage of animal proteins was partially alleviated by the distribution of more vegetable protein. However, since bread remained free of rationing, people could eat more of it, and did. For instance, in 1949–1950 cereals constituted 48 per cent of the daily caloric intake; in 1952–1953 it rose to 53 per cent. A decade later, in 1959–1960, cereals constituted only 41 per cent of all calories consumed.

Table 5-2 shows that as long as the ration of meat, fish, sugar, and milk products remained low, the nominal per capita consumption of wheat continued to rise rapidly. In 1949–1950, per capita consumption of wheat was 120.4 kg., whereas in the next year it rose by almost 6 per cent. In 1952–1953 it rose by 13 per cent over the previous year. Not until 1953–1954 did per capita wheat consumption start to decline.

The high demand for bread was not due to human consumption

TABLE 5-2

CONSUMPTION OF WHEAT PER CAPITA

Year	Kg.	Index
1949–50	120.4	100.0
1950–51	127.5	105.9
1951–52	144.0	119.6
1952–53	148.0	122.9
1953–54	143.1	118.9
1959–60	114.5	95.1

Source: F. Ginor, *Uses of Agricultural Surpluses* (Jerusalem: Bank of Israel, 1963), p. 436.

alone. Because the price of bread was very low and it was not rationed, it was used as a "substitute fodder" for chickens, ducks, and rabbits.[41] Rubner notes, for instance, that in 1951–1952 the legal price of 1 kg. of chicken was four times that of bread, whereas the black-market price was twelve times greater.[42] Since sufficient quantities of feed grains were not available, farmers, kibbutzim, and individuals fed their animals the cheap bread. Animal proteins produced in this way were sold on the free market at very lucrative prices.

"Bread-conversion" is an excellent example of how maximum prices lead to incredible misallocation of resources. Even though Israel was importing roughly 70 per cent of all wheat either from the United States or Canada, a substantial portion of it was converted into animal protein and sold in illegal channels. Thus, officially allocated hard currency for supposedly indispensable imports was diverted to produce meat, poultry, and eggs. According to one observer, the bread-conversion practices used up 20 per cent of the total imports of wheat and flour at a cost of $3–$4 million a year.[43] Since per capita wheat consumption did not begin to decline until 1954, as much as $20 million was probably wasted in this way; on a yearly basis, bread-conversion used up 10 per cent of all Israeli export proceeds during the period of direct controls.

Similar misuse of bread has been repeatedly noted in the Soviet Union, especially during Khrushchev's rule in the early 1960s. Since the price of meats and poultry on the so-called farmer's markets remained high, Soviet citizens bought low-priced bread and fed it to the livestock. In the Soviet Union the courts considered these transgressions to be "economic misbehavior," and in especially gross cases of abuse sentenced the offenders to death. In Israel, because "economic misbehavior" is not a capital crime (although those caught feeding bread to cattle and chickens were punished), bread-conversion practices continued until market forces made them unprofitable.

Allocation of Raw Materials and Investment Goods

During the two world wars, all major belligerents established systems of priorities for the allocation of raw materials, semifabricates, and finished goods. Wartime priority ratings served two basic purposes: they aided producers in obtaining the necessary inputs from suppliers, and they enabled producers to plan and execute contracts in the order of indicated urgency. In wartime America, Germany, and Britain, preference ratings were given to the producers of tanks, planes, ships, and guns, all the way down to the subcontractors; and the flow of raw materials was determined by a priority system.[44] The system was designed to subordinate civilian to military demands. The quantities of vital raw materials that might be used for non-military production were limited. In the Soviet Union, for almost forty years the government has waged a policy of forced economic growth by a similar system of priorities; indeed, forced pace of growth was and still is looked upon as the magic key to the future. The goal of Stalinist industrialization, to be pursued at almost any cost, was to "overtake and surpass" the advanced capitalist countries, especially the United States.[45]

Direct controls, as a rule, are designed to cut down the propensity to consume and to release resources for a "hot war," or for an "investment war" as in the case of the Soviet Union. Had Israel intended to pursue the Soviet type of industrialization, it would have poured investment resources, extracted from the population by physical controls, into heavy industries such as steel, machine-making, and construction. This did not occur, however, because the Soviet kind of "forced-draft" industrialization, in the view of Horowitz, Governor of the Bank of Israel, "cannot be imposed except in a pre-democratic or totalitarian state by the most ruthless methods of repression. Any attempt to carry out the policy in a democratic society would inevitably induce the conclusion that, if capital formation is to be effected by coercion, a totalitarian regime would be preferable as being more efficient in that sort of operation." [46]

During the first three years of Israeli independence, heavy military expenditures, enormous absorption and integration costs, and outlays for economic development were inflationary because they generated money incomes but not readily available consumer goods. In addition, the Israelis were in a hurry and wanted to "telescope into 20 years a development that should normally take a century." [47] To cope with all these pressures, planning was inevitable.

The crucial factor in any program of economic development is the ability of the economy to release enough resources in the form of savings to permit a rapid rate of capital formation. Three types of saving can provide the means of industrialization: private domestic saving, government saving, and foreign saving. As a rule, investment activity depends on the level of national income and the existing capital stock. Economists differentiate between gross and net investment. The former refers to the amount of new plant and equipment created during a given year, plus additions to inventories. The latter refers to net additions to the capital stock, the gross investment minus the yearly wear and tear on plant and equipment, which is called depreciation.

The salient feature of Israel's investment activity was and still is its dependence not upon domestic annual saving, but on import surplus. From 1949 to 1951, Israel's gross investment approximated almost one-third of the G.N.P.[48] In 1949, gross domestic investment, in current prices, was I£ 76.5 million; calculated at a realistic exchange rate of $2.73 per I£, it came to $208.8 million.[49] In 1950, gross domestic investment was I£ 140.5 million, or $299.27 million, assuming a rate of exchange of $2.13. In 1951, gross investment was I£ 188.1 million, or $332.94 million, assuming again a "realistic" rate of exchange of $1.77.[50] Thus from 1949 through 1951, the value of gross investment came to $841.01 million.[51] The foregoing figures vary from author to author, depending upon the assumed value of the "realistic" exchange rate of dollar to pound.

Israel's investment funds during the 1949 to 1951 period came primarily from abroad in the form of a large import surplus. The dollar values of the import surplus for these years are not precise. According to Rubner, the import surplus in nominal dollars amounted to $824 million from 1949 to 1951; [52] according to Halevi and Klinov-Malul, it was $861 million,[53] and, according to S. Riemer, $960 million.[54] If we take the mean value of these figures, the import surplus amounted to $882 million.[55] The difference between this value of import surplus and the estimated $841 million value of gross investments is $40 million; but the difference between import surplus and *net* investments made in the three years of direct controls is more than $250 million.[56] An excess of import over the net or gross investment value meant that capital imports were used to finance consumption. Even though, during 1950 and 1951, saving in terms of percentage of G.N.P. was positive (1.5 per cent and 8.2 per cent, respectively),[57] direct controls did not generate investment funds. Most of the investments were financed from capital imports, while price controls and rationing of consumer goods raised the standard of living of the community at large.

Because of Israel's unprecedented rates of immigration, unique in the history of mankind, most of the investment resources were poured into housing and agriculture. According to Patinkin's calculations, investment in dwellings constituted 47.1 and 48.2 per cent of the gross capital formation in 1950 and 1951, respectively,[58] whereas gross investment in machinery and other equipment amounted to 18.0 and 16.2 per cent. In these same years, the investment in agriculture was also greater than that in machinery and equipment. The role of the government in financing this investment was large; its percentage of total gross domestic capital formation in 1950 was 61.1 per cent, and in 1951, 54.1 per cent.[59]

The official policy of "open doors" to all Jews was pursued along with "firm control on all major aspects of economic life." [60] A corollary was that incoming Jewish businessmen lacked organized support and had so many obstacles thrown in their path that some economists deplored the crippling of an "amazing fund of private initiative." [61]

Government officials decided what, how much, when, and where to produce and distribute. With the imposition of direct controls in April 1949, all domestic and imported raw materials were allocated by the Ministry of Supply and Rationing, which had three departments: heavy industries, light industries, and textiles.[62] All imported raw materials were allocated to plants within an industry on a fair share basis, as suggested by the producers' and trade associations. Needs were determined by the number of firms in an industry and the rate of their productivity in an administrative district. To prevent black marketeering, raw materials were allocated on a basis of "linking methods," that is, a firm's allotment of raw materials and semifabricates depended "upon the delivery of specified quantities of products." [63] These rules of thumb were frequently altered by shortages, political pressures, and the whim of bureaucrats.[64]

From mid-1949 to the end of July 1950, raw materials were controlled, but clothing and footwear remained unrationed. All government-approved producers of these consumer goods received purchase permits for raw materials, fuels, and necessary semifabricates, which could be bought at fixed prices when available. The firms' managements had to commit themselves to produce the standardized "austerity" clothing, footwear, and furniture, but as long as these items remained unrationed, they could use raw materials for other purposes as well. Since the raw material situation was "particularly grave," [65] producers usually sold some of their output in the black market and made windfall profits. Before the rationing of footwear and clothing, consumers bought these items on a first-come, first-served basis over the counter, or on an "asked-price" basis, which was illegal.

With the outbreak of the Korean War in June 1950 and the accompanying world-wide scramble for raw materials, Dr. Joseph felt that daily necessities should come under his control. Without warning, he introduced rationing of clothing and footwear on August 1, 1950.[66] This measure was extremely unpopular with both the general public and the business community. Merchants declared a general strike against the government, but Dr. Joseph prevailed and, as was not the case with food rationing, "points" were required for all legal purchases of footwear, cloth, knitwear, furniture, leather items, iron bedsteads, mattresses, hats, brooms, and even notebooks. Manufacturers and merchants of these goods received raw materials and supplies on the basis of the purchase permits and points turned in to the National Bank, which administered all "point" accounts. Special numbers of points were alloted to expectant mothers, ex-servicemen, newly married couples, and those who required work clothing and footwear. These points were distributed in the form of ration permits wherever the resident did not have ration books. Almost from the outset, however, clothing and footwear rationing was subverted by the sellers' resistance. Retailers withheld sales at legal prices, regardless of whether the buyer had points or special purchase permits. They concealed stocks in private homes and in remote warehouses.

Because of an acute shortage of hard currency, imports of raw materials were low. In the leather industry, for example, the supply of hides to "shoe factories was most unsatisfactory until December 1950." [67] The absence of stocks forced production to depend on domestic hides, which were hardly sufficient to provide footwear for even a month's supply. Not until March 1951 did the Ministry of Trade and Industry receive some good quality leather, enough for the production of better-grade footwear for six months. For another example, the manufacture of "utility" furniture had to be suspended in mid-1950 for lack of raw materials.[68] The bottleneck of foreign exchange, however, stymied all government efforts to keep the industrial wheels running.[69] Consequently, in addition to the official allocation of raw materials, the government introduced in the fall of 1949 an "imports without payment of foreign currency" scheme.[70] For these imports a firm needed a license but no allocation of foreign currency by the Ministry of Finance. As it turned out, most of these raw materials were used to produce luxury items which were sold on the "uncontrolled" markets. Thus, nonpayment imports helped to subvert the legal market, so that by the end of 1951 rampant black markets had become a way of life.[71]

The government's inability to control inflationary pressures led to a flight from currency into material assets. For example, as the official cost-of-living index fell and real daily earnings rose, Israelis had more money to spend, but the official allocation of consumer goods became smaller.[72] The "waiting purchasing" power spilled over into the black markets, and people bought anything they could. In such a spending-happy milieu, Israeli business turned to the production of "new," not previously produced, goods, most of which were luxury items of low use-value. Because of rising costs and the prevailing cost-plus methods for determining prices, business establishments easily obtained authorization for higher prices for many low-utility items. With such a distorted price-cost structure, it was lucrative to produce nonessential goods and suspend the production of forks, knives, pots, or electrical switches. For instance, one Israeli manufacturer stopped producing drinking glasses, which had to be sold at a low fixed price, and turned to fancy liqueur glasses, which could be marketed at profitable "free" prices.[73] As a result of this reorientation of production, the development of many branches of essential consumer goods was retarded.[74] In agriculture, economic rationalization imposed similar behavior on the kibbutzim. Because potatoes and vegetables fetched a low fixed price (they constituted part of the cost-of-living index), it was hardly profitable to grow them, and many kibbutzim turned instead to the cultivation of flowers, which were free of price controls.

Under the prevailing system of fixed prices, the self-interest of the business community was diametrically opposed to the common interest of the Israeli public. Thus, resources were wasted on a grand scale, and Israel's economy in 1950 and 1951 resembled what the late Swiss economist Wilhelm Röpke once called a "hair-oil, ash-tray, herb-tea economy." [75] Israel's economy suffered from disorders of economic metabolism, so to speak.

The flight from currency was manifested in other developments resulting from Israel's price-freeze policy. With the Israeli pound heavily overvalued, everybody sought foreign exchange, especially dollars. If foreign exchange could not be obtained legally, smuggling of capital was often resorted to.[76] Official allocations of hard currency for certain "indispensable" imports made them very cheap in terms of domestic currency. Imported foreign machinery and equipment, incidentally, were used to build many capital-intensive industrial facilities, while thousands of unemployed immigrants were searching in vain for jobs.

In the prevailing inflationary milieu, where the Israeli pound was no longer functioning as a "store of value," and where even its unit-of-account function was in jeopardy, a "getting out of money" philosophy led the business community to engage in feverish investment in plant, equipment, and inventories. Investment decisions were warped; they were made primarily to safeguard the working capital of the firm. Such investment became "a vehicle for flight from the currency." [77] Bureaucratic strangulation led eventually to almost complete repudiation of the entire gamut of direct controls by wholesale violations of it.[78]

Thus it is seen that the first three years of Israel's existence were extremely difficult. The government had to fight a war, cope with immense immigration, and develop the economy as well. The aim of direct controls "was not only to ensure a just distribution of essential commodities, but to fight inflation, by diverting inflationary sources from the field of consumption to the field of investment and production." [79] However, in the view of Israel's finance minister no progress was made "in the execution of this central aim." [80] A foreign expert also reported at the time that direct controls did not reduce "the proportion of private income devoted to consumer expenditures." [81]

The widespread prevalence of black markets,[82] cost-plus pricing policies, haphazard distribution of raw materials, the "flight out of money," and the highhanded bureaucratic manner in the allocation of the hard currency led to a considerable demoralization of Israeli society, which was reflected in low productivity of both men and machines. Since black market activity was not subject to capital punishment, many Israelis violated the price controls and allocation procedures. The temptation to break the law was great and many succumbed. It was demoralizing for the Yishuv and the immigrants alike to see how the initial enthusiasm, the feeling of a common heritage, and the sense of belonging were sapped by unscrupulous individuals who cared only for themselves. These persons engaged in frauds and forgeries, obtained or granted administrative favors, and grew fat and rich.[83] "Protektsia" established itself, and the general public soon learned who was part of the establishment and who wasn't. Honest, law-abiding firms suffered losses, and patriotic individuals eked out an existence on official allocations. Many of the immigrants felt isolated from the mainstream of Israel's life and believed that there was a marked difference between the "first Israel" and the "second Israel." [84]

In current prices, the G.N.P. in 1949 and 1950 increased, but because of the continued high influx of immigrants and the high investment for housing the "actual output of products and local services per capita diminished by an average of 18 per cent." [85] To get the economy moving again, to restore incentives, to introduce a better method of coordinating the aggregate demand and supply, and to let market forces introduce a modicum of economic efficiency, the Israeli government needed to institute major economic reforms.[86]

Foreign-Exchange Control

Israel took over from the Palestine government a well-developed system of foreign-exchange controls patterned after the British system. The term "foreign-exchange controls" refers to a "system of regulations designed to assure both that foreign exchange coming into the possession of residents of the controlling country is sold in official channels and that this exchange is used only for approved payments abroad." [87] In practical terms, an exporter may not spend export proceeds any way he wants. Foreign-exchange regulations stipulate that export proceeds must be surrendered for domestic currency at a prescribed rate of exchange either to the central bank or a ministry. The sole purpose of controls is to ration the available supply of foreign exchange according to some predetermined set of priorities.[88]

Under foreign-exchange controls, regulations are strict as to what constitute "frivolous," "permitted," and "indispensable" payments abroad. The items on the government's priority list receive foreign-exchange allocations first and on good terms, the lowest domestic currency price per unit of foreign currency. Only after the "indispensable" applications have been approved can those for the "less vital" imports be considered. The latter applications, if approved, buy foreign exchange on "expensive" terms, that is, high domestic currency price per unit of foreign currency. For instance, importers of such indispensable items as foodstuffs, raw materials, and machinery are permitted to acquire the necessary foreign exchange, let us say dollars, for very few units of domestic currency. But for such items as automobiles, importers are asked to pay a higher rate. Then, of course, black market rates prevail for unapproved transactions. Foreign-exchange controls alone cannot eliminate a balance-of-payments deficit; together with domestic price, wage, and rent controls combined with rationing, labor conscription, and housing controls, they may temporarily block the excess or waiting purchasing power.

In terms of foreign exchange, the Ingathering of Exiles turned out to be a very costly undertaking for Israel. It was estimated that $2,300 was spent on each new immigrant upon his arrival in Israel,[89] so that a total of close to $2 billion was required to cover the integration costs. The country had at that time hardly anything to export except citrus fruit and diamonds, yet it had to provide simultaneously for defense, absorption of hundreds of thousands of immigrants, and the financing of the economic development of a small and barren country. From its inception, Israel's imports of goods and services were larger than its exports. This excess is known as import surplus. In 1949, it was $220 million; in 1950, $282 million; and in 1951, $359 million.[90] During the three-year period of austerity, the surplus came to a total of $861 million. This deficit was financed by $345 million in unilateral transfers or gifts and $416 million in loans.

Short-term borrowing, as a percentage of import surplus, was quite substantial: [91] the short-term debts came to 10.9 per cent in 1949, 18.1 per cent in 1950, and 8.9 per cent in 1951, or roughly $106.5 million. According to an official source, however, between 1949 and 1951 "almost 40 per cent of the excess of imports was covered by loans—partly short-term and medium-term"; [92] that is, roughly $340 million of the above $860 million. The late Levi Eshkol, then Israel's finance minister, admitted that Israel was forced to borrow heavily because world Jewry did not contribute enough.[93] The shortage of foreign currency was so acute that the Israeli government had difficulty in paying for essential imports.[94] It was only after the Consolidation Loan in 1954 that Israel was freed "from repeated nightmares concerning the payment of short-term debts in foreign currency." [95] In 1953, the short-term indebtedness was $72.8 million, and by the end of 1954 it was reduced to $34 million.[96]

Since there were very few items to export, the ratio of exports to imports during the years of mass immigration was 11.3 per cent in 1949, 11.7 per cent in 1950, and 11.7 per cent in 1951.[97] From 1949 to 1951, finished consumer goods, raw materials, and fuel comprised more than 75 per cent of the total merchandise imports; the rest were investment goods imports.[98] In 1952, 45 per cent of all consumer goods were imported.[99] All sugar and almost all grains were imported during the early years of statehood.

In day-to-day operations, all applications for export and import licenses were addressed to the Ministry of Trade and Industry, Ministry of Agriculture, and Ministry of Religious Affairs. Upon receipt of the license and the endorsement by the foreign-currency control division of the Ministry of Finance, the importer could buy foreign exchange for Israeli currency at a prescribed price.[100] During the austerity period, December 1948 to September 1949, the official exchange rate for exports between the United States dollar and Israeli pound was $3/I£ 1, or I£ 0.333/$1; and from October 1949 to February 1952, it was I£ 0.357/$1.[101] The black market rate, however, was many times higher.[102] According to one Israeli observer, "the official exchange rates had become a fiction." [103] At the end of 1951, Israel's foreign-exchange reserves, its hard currency in other words, were virtually zero. In 1952, foreign-exchange reserves amounted to $16.5 million and were sufficient to finance Israel's indispensable imports for half a month.[104] The country lived virtually from ship-to-mouth.

Rent and Housing Controls

Control over housing and rents is integral to a system of direct controls. In general, rent control strives to protect tenants from rising housing costs in the same fashion that price controls attempt to prevent price increases of goods and services. But price controls alone do not guarantee that consumers will be able to obtain consumer goods at a fixed price; rationing is necessary for that. Similarly, because the fixing of rents does not guarantee housing to the tenant, housing controls are designed to assure some minimum of floorspace and protect tenants against eviction. The control of floorspace is as important in any effective system of rent control as rationing in price control.

During Israel's first three years of mass immigration, demand for housing far outran the available supply. Providing housing, or rather shelter, for the immigrants was accepted "as a public responsibility." [105] It was obvious to the government that the impoverished immigrants would be unable to pay for housing on a commercial basis. Therefore, since housing was one of the fundamental instruments of absorption, the Israeli government decided to provide public housing.

In 1948, the government took over the rent restriction laws that had been promulgated by the British in February 1940.[106] This legislation made it virtually impossible for a landlord to evict a tenant, except in a limited number of cases. The landlord was also prohibited from increasing the rent.[107] Tenants enjoyed almost absolute protection, although the rent restriction laws did provide that a tenant could be evicted for any of five reasons: [108]

(a) the tenant fails to pay the rent due;
(b) the tenant causes nuisance or annoyance and damages to property;
(c) the tenant sublets and makes unreasonable profits;
(d) the owner needs the apartment himself;
(e) the housing is slated to be demolished or reconstructed.

In 1940, the average rent for a room in a city was I£ 1.0 per month; at the end of 1951, the rent on prewar houses was still I£ 1.0 per month, even though the average worker earned roughly I£ 85 per month, as compared with average earnings of I£ 6.0 per month in 1940. In 1939, rent took from a quarter to a third of a worker's income, whereas in 1951 it was only 6 to 9 per cent.[109]

Under these circumstances the landlords of unfurnished prewar apartments were losing money and consequently kept their property in disrepair.[110] Since rent control laws applied only to unfurnished rooms or apartments, the landlords, as a rule, converted their rental property into furnished apartments with high rents by adding a chair. In terms of Israeli law a room consisted of an area not less than 6 and not more than 8 square meters. An entrance hall with an area of 8 square meters or more was counted as half a room.[111]

Because leased apartments were so scarce during the years of mass immigration, the practice of "key money" (dmay maphteach) came into use. One Israeli economist wrote that the "housing shortage was little short of a calamity, and the payment of 'key money' (lump sum down-payments to ensure right of tenancy) became an accepted institution in the teeth of rent controls." [112] Taking key money was not considered a criminal offense because rent control in the prevailing inflationary milieu "sharply cut the value of the older apartment houses for the owners, while, for the tenants the value of these same apartments zoomed." [113]

To lease a room the prospective tenant had to pay the lessor (in 1951) close to I£ 3,000 and thereafter pay the fixed rent. Since the government was anxious to keep down the cost of living and curry favor with the impecunious voters, it refused to change the outdated rent laws. The result was that "not a single house or flat was built in Israel during the first decade for letting." [114] During the years of mass influx "most public buildings for immigrants were wholly financed from public sources, and rented to immigrants at a fee which at best covered only maintenance costs." [115]

From 1949 to 1951, the population was increasing by more than 100,000 a year, and 30,000 new dwellings were necessary annually.[116] Incoming immigrants went to reception camps, where they were accommodated, fed, and provided with basic necessities by the Absorption Department of the Jewish Agency. In 1948, a "national company for immigrant housing," Amidar, was set up with the participation of the Jewish Agency, the Jewish National Fund, the government, and most of the major companies. Its objective was to build as much housing as cheaply as possible.[117]

At the end of April 1949, 60,000 immigrants lived in 24 camps; a year later, 95,000 lived in 35 camps.[118] While in the camps the immigrants were entitled to free room and board. But at the end of 1949, the Housing Department of the Ministry of Labor was set up to provide permanent housing for immigrants and to scatter the population throughout the country by building new towns, villages, and agricultural settlements. However, because of shortages of cement and other building materials as well as of skilled workers, permanent houses could not be built in sufficient numbers to accommodate all the newcomers. By the end of 1951, 20 per cent of the population of 1.4 million lived in wooden, tin, or canvas huts.[119] It was not until the end of 1952 that no one lived in tents any longer, though 190,000 were still housed in camps.[120] Unemployment was very widespread among the camp population, and many immigrants suffered from frustration, apathy, and despair.[121] In 1949, unemployment as a percentage of the labor force, including immigrants in camps, was 13.9 per cent; in 1950, it was 11.2 per cent; and in 1951, 8.1 per cent.[122]

In general, a system of direct controls implies wage controls and frequently labor conscription. Wage controls are designed to prevent a rise in personal incomes and to ward off a wage-price spiral. These controls are either of a general wage-freeze type or a commitment by the government, labor unions, and employers to preserve the existing wage levels.[123] Under the latter policy, labor unions promise to abstain from wage demands on condition that prices of foodstuffs, rents, and essential consumer goods will not rise. Under a system of direct controls, to make sure that manpower is available in needed quantities for priority industries, labor has in some instances been conscripted. Israel, however, had no labor conscription. Instead of a labor shortage, there was a labor surplus, with the basic problem at the time being how to find employment for idle hands. Moreover, during the austerity period the "price of labor was the only uncontrolled price." [124] Even though this period witnessed a remarkable compression of wage differentials because of the egalitarian wage philosophy of the Histadrut,[125] from 1949 to 1951 the daily nominal earnings of industrial workers rose substantially.[126]

Despite the various attempts to control the inflationary potential, by 1951 disillusionment with the system of direct controls had become general. Flourishing black markets led to the "disintegration of the system as a whole"; [127] and "the economic crisis in Israel became more acute." [128] Resources were wasted on a large scale; and foreign exchange reserves were nonexistent. By the end of 1951, "the economic situation was forbidding in the extreme." [129] Therefore, since the virtually unchecked course of open inflation was dangerous for the Ben-Gurion government, political self-preservation won out and a new economic policy was promulgated in early 1952. It undid what the Fabian trade unionists, Marxists, utopian socialists, and old-line Zionists had practiced for more than three years. Among other things, the new economic policy involved the devaluation of the Israeli pound and the scrapping of many of the direct controls. The market forces were given a new lease on life, and a period of economic consolidation could begin.

6

The Wassenaar Conference:
Negotiating a Debt of Honor

In 1951, parleying with the Germans was considered by most Jews and Israelis to be almost indecent, if not sacrilegious. The mere possibility of sitting with Germans around a conference table implied condoning the unforgettable suffering of the Jews at the hands of the Nazis. The memory of the extermination camps and the ruin and exile of relatives and friends was so fresh and strong that immediate contacts were deemed impossible. For 3,000 years the Jewish people had remembered the crimes committed against the early Israelites; for centuries Jews, remembering the Inquisition, had refused to set foot on Spanish soil. Now, to enter into formal negotiations with the Bonn government only five years after the Holocaust was inconceivable. But despite these anguishing questions, the scheduled conference day was approaching inexorably.

On December 6, 1951, Dr. Adenauer met secretly with Dr. Goldmann in London at Claridge's Hotel.[1] For Dr. Goldmann this meeting "was the most difficult emotionally and perhaps the most momentous politically."[2] He intended to persuade the chancellor to agree upon a billion dollars as a basis for negotiations, because only if this was acceptable would Ben-Gurion ask the Knesset to authorize formal negotiations with the Bonn government.[3] Dr. Goldmann was very much aware that he was requesting "something unusual, something that by conventional standards might be considered incorrect."[4] At the end of his twenty-five-minute presentation, Goldmann asked Dr. Adenauer's confirmation in writing that the material basis for the forthcoming talks be the Israeli note of March 12, 1951, which demanded a sum of $1.5 billion from Germany as a whole. According to Dr. Goldmann's account, the chancellor was visibly moved and he replied that his desire for restitution was sincere. In fact, he regarded this obligation as "a debt of honor for the new Germany." Furthermore, and this was most significant, he was prepared to approve the undertaking Dr. Goldmann requested on his own responsibility.[5] Indeed, Dr. Adenauer signed the requested letter that same day.[6]

Before entering into direct negotiations, however, Ben-Gurion needed the Knesset's permission. Accordingly, parliamentary discussion of Israel's claim against Germany was announced for January 7, 1952. And everyone knew that the Knesset's acceptance of Dr. Adenauer's invitation would mean that the government of Israel took official cognizance of the existence of the Bonn government.

The question of direct negotiations with the Bonn government was hotly debated in the press, because no political issue had ever aroused the Yishuv more. Feelings ran perfervidly against the talks.[7] The public at large was concerned lest Israeli-Jewish-German negotiations be viewed as a move to accept compensation for the mass murder of the Jews. Spokesmen of the extreme Left and Right were the most antagonistic. *Kol Ha'am,* the Israeli Communist paper, *Al Hamishmar,* the organ of the Mapam Party, and *Herut,* the publication named for that group, were outspoken in their opposition to direct contacts. The religious parties simply refused to condone parleying with a "nation of murderers."

Regardless of political affiliation, these publications spoke the heart and mind of the people. Only the Mapai press strongly pushed Ben-Gurion's line. Of course, the arguments of the Mapam Party, Israel's pro-Soviet labor party, were hollow. For, although that party fanned the flames of moral war between the Jewish and German peoples in the name of Jewish honor, certain of its members journeyed to East Berlin to apologize for the "reactionary" Jews.[8] To the Mapam people, West Germany represented merely a "continuation of Nazism."[9] The opposition of Herut came primarily from that group's strong convictions that Germany was an international pariah and that direct talks would probably erase the stigma of its moral untouchability. The Germans had not repented for their Nazi past, they argued, and the Bonn government should not be allowed to bring about West Germany's return to the community of nations.[10] So-called "blood money" pamphlets circulated widely; they were designed to strengthen the "we won't talk to Germany" groups.

Nor was Israel's merchant class much interested in receiving German capital goods. Substantial segments of the business community feared that a flood of German-made goods would undermine the prevailing seller's market. Private industry also opposed the agreement; they liked the existing protectionist policy which made it possible for them to make a comfortable profit.[11]

Ben-Gurion and his cabinet braced themselves for the confrontation with a hostile Knesset. Regardless of their personal feelings about the Germans, they were convinced that Israel as an independent state had to conduct its affairs according to normal standards of international relations. The economic situation was desperate and the government had the courage to say openly that emotions would not close the huge gap in the country's balance of payments.[12]

On the date set for parliamentary discussion of Israel's claim, well-organized opposition groups attempted to prevent the debate. More than 1,000 demonstrators converged on the old Knesset building on King George V Street, stoned its walls, smashed windows, and threw tear-gas bombs. A battle with the police raged for two hours, during which ninety-two policemen were injured and hundreds of demonstrators taken to the hospital.[13]

Within the Knesset hall, the debate took place in an atmosphere of violence unprecedented in Israel's parliamentary life.[14] But despite the clamor of the crowds, the wail of ambulance sirens, the explosion of gas grenades, and the volleys of rocks shattering windowpanes, the meeting continued. Ben-Gurion asked the Knesset for permission to begin formal talks with the government of West Germany. He had made up his mind about this inflammatory matter, and for him there was nothing morally wrong about claiming Jewish property. He reminded the members that if the request were not granted Israel would not be able to collect more than a billion dollars' worth of heirless Jewish property. "Let not the murderers of our people be also their inheritors!" he exclaimed.[15]

But the opposition felt differently. Before the parliamentary debate, Menahem Beigin, the leader of Herut, had called Ben-Gurion "that maniac who is now Prime Minister." [16] In voicing his opposition, Beigin made a highly emotional appeal and said that certain things *were* worse than death, such as direct talks with the Germans. "What price are we going to get for grandpa and grandma?" he challenged.[17] The Communists, for their part, insisted that the whole thing was a "trick by the Western powers designed to facilitate the grooming of West Germany as the spearhead of new hordes to attack Russia." [18]

During the Herut-led demonstrations outside the building, the members of the Knesset were forced to move from one side of the chamber to the other to avoid danger. A number of parliamentarians were struck by flying rocks and glass, but Ben-Gurion and his Mapai people held the line.

On the second day of the debate, the Knesset was cordoned off by rings of barbed wire, guarded by steel-helmeted police. The terror of the day before had been removed, and the debate proceeded under more normal conditions.

On Wednesday, January 9, the prime minister went on the radio to issue a strong warning to the dissenters and their leaders. Calling them a "gang of hooligans," he charged that it was unpatriotic to support the Herut-led terrorism.[19] Emotions were so frenzied that there was danger the country might be plunged into civil war.[20] At the end of the debate, in a dramatic roll call, the Knesset voted 61 to 50, with 5 abstentions and 4 absentees, in favor of Ben-Gurion's request. Mapam, Herut, General Zionists, and Communists voted en bloc against it.[21] The decision delegated full powers to act to the Knesset Foreign Affairs and Security Committee, where Ben-Gurion held a majority of eight of the fifteen members.

With this authority in hand, the government of Israel entered into discussions with the representatives of world Jewry to map a common strategy for the impending talks with the Germans. Dr. Goldmann called for another meeting of the Claims Conference in New York on January 20. He was appointed chairman of the executive committee to direct the negotiations. Other members of the executive committee were Jacob Blaustein of the American Jewish Committee, Frank Goldman of B'nai B'rith, Israel Goldstein of the American Jewish Congress, and Adolph Held of the Jewish Labor Committee.[22] Further discussions were held in February in Paris and New York.[23]

By the end of February, a spokesman for the Israeli Foreign Ministry announced that his government had officially accepted the West German invitation, and Dr. Goldmann transmitted to Adenauer word of the Knesset's readiness to undertake direct talks. On February 29, the chancellor asked his finance minister, Dr. Fritz Schäffer, to prepare for the forthcoming talks with Israel.[24]

Since the cabinet had assured the Knesset that no Israeli would enter the territory of the Federal Republic, and since no German could come to Israel to discuss the matter, the talks had to be held on neutral territory.[25] Accordingly, the negotiations got under way at Wassenaar, near The Hague, Netherlands, and continued, with some interruptions, from March 21 to August 27, 1952. They were marred by bitter controversy in Israel and Zionist circles all over the world, and by the hostility of the Arab states. To mislead opponents of the talks, the press created the false impression that they were being held in Brussels.

Three parties were represented at the conference table: the German delegation, led by Professor Franz Böhm; the Israeli delegation, headed by Dr. Felix Shinnar and Dr. Giora Josephthal; and the Claims Conference, represented by Moses A. Leavitt and Alex L. Easterman.[26] Adenauer's speech of September 27, 1951, provided one basis for negotiations—the German moral debt. The Israelis, for their part, were making a claim for the expense of integrating half a million *olim* (immigrants),[27] on the ground that the absorption of such an influx of diseased, impoverished, and broken people caused huge outlays for the newly constituted state. At the same time, the Claims Conference was asking for a payment of $500 million for the welfare and rehabilitation of Jewish victims residing outside the Federal Republic. The two claims came to $1.5 billion.

To substantiate their claim, Israel's representatives advanced three arguments. First, the total of 500,000 refugees was supported by a breakdown of figures on Jewish immigration from 1933 to 1951, giving annual numbers of influx and countries of origin. The German delegates had no reservations about accepting the figure itself. Second, and much more difficult, was the question of whether all immigrants to Israel had been forced to leave their native countries because of Nazi persecution. The record showed that immediately after their liberation by the Allied armed forces in the spring of 1945 many Jews had returned to their native countries, such as Poland, Hungary, Romania, and Czechoslovakia, but there had met such anti-Semitism that they decided to leave again. Jewish homes had often been taken over by Gentiles who were reluctant to move simply because "the Jew" had come back. Of the surviving Jewish firms and businesses, the machinery was worn out, the supplies gone, and the plants "nationalized" by the newly installed Soviet-type governments. The Israeli delegation pointed out the above sequence of events, and the Germans accepted the fact that the original Nazi persecution was responsible for the "second Jewish exodus." [28] The third argument dealt with resettlement and absorption costs.

Initially, the Israelis demanded $3,000 per immigrant, a figure the West Germans accepted with some slight modifications.[29] The mechanics of justifying the size of the Israeli claim was initially suggested by David Horowitz in 1951.[30] However, it should be kept in mind that the method of computation represented *only* a rational basis for a claim that was definitely outside the realm of mathematics.[31]

When the talks opened at Wassenaar, the first items of business were to determine the exact amount of the Israeli and Jewish demands, to state the German position on these demands, to settle certain technicalities and future procedures, and finally to gain some insight into the attitudes each side brought to the parley. The meetings took place in the most chilly diplomatic atmosphere imaginable. The delegates spoke mostly in English to avoid having to use German. Israeli and Jewish delegates took care to avoid public social contacts with their German counterparts. There were no handshakes in public; a simple nod passed for a greeting. For reasons of domestic politics, and for purely personal reasons, nothing but the utmost reserve was expected from the delegates representing world Jewry and the Israelis.

The first encounter on March 20, 1952, was highly dramatic, according to Josephthal.[32] Everyone rose when the Israelis came in. The opening statements were read standing by Gershon Avner and Professor Böhm. The German statement was to the point and, from the Israeli position, negative because (1) the London Debt Conference had fixed Bonn's foreign debts, (2) the Allies were managing the West German foreign exchange, and (3) the Federal Republic could pay only limited amounts.[33]

The initial Israeli reserve was soon softened by human imponderables. For instance, during the second meeting on March 24, Dr.

Otto Küster, deputy chairman of the German delegation, wrote a note to Dr. Shinnar, saying that his English had a trace of Swabian accent. He pushed this note across the table and back came a quick answer: "Yes," wrote Dr. Shinnar, "I was born in Stuttgart." It also turned out that the two had attended the same Gymnasium.[34] From that day on the negotiations were held in German.

During the second session, Dr. Shinnar presented the particulars of the Israeli demands, namely, the payment of $1 billion, one-third in hard currency and two-thirds in goods, over a period of five to six years.[35] The Germans accepted the obligation to make payment, in line with Adenauer's speech, but disagreed with the Israelis on the amount and the period of time. It was Professor Böhm's responsibility to translate Adenauer's pledge into practical measures. The West German finance minister, at that time Dr. Fritz Schäffer, repeatedly stressed his country's large financial commitments, as did Dr. Hermann J. Abs, a leading German banker and chairman of the London Debt Conference of 1952. In no time at all the "limited ability to pay" argument became a bone of contention among the three negotiating partners at Wassenaar.[36]

The two principal factors behind the German position of "limited ability to pay"—first expressed by Adenauer and later reiterated by his agents—were the country's incomplete economic recovery and its long-standing foreign debts. West Germany had unquestionably made great gains after the currency reform of 1948, but in 1952 the standard of living was still low compared with what it had been before the war and with the standard in most other Western countries. One particularly weighty reason for this comparatively slow recovery was the influx of more than eight million refugees and expellees. It is true that after recovery got under way the West German industrial capacity was larger than before 1939, but steel capacity was still the principal bottleneck. For, by the early 1950s the Western Allies continued to keep restrictions on certain strategic industries to prevent the Germans from rebuilding their war potential; for example, they were still forbidden to replace the dismantled steel mills.[37]

By the end of 1951, the first favorable balance of payments for goods and services had emerged. The surplus stood at only $160 million, but export developments augured well for 1952. Indeed, the 1952 surplus turned out to be $580 million.[38] However, there

were many strong claims against these surpluses, first and foremost
of which were the long-outstanding foreign debts. To regain their
credit on the international markets, the Germans had to settle these
obligations.

Thus the talks at Wassenaar were inseparable from those in
London at the Debt Conference, where Dr. Hermann J. Abs was
negotiating for the Bonn government the settlement of prewar
German debts.[39] Three days before Adenauer's formal invitation
to the Israelis on December 6, 1951, he had held last minute talks
with Dr. Abs to discuss Germany's outstanding debts and Bonn's
ability to pay. At that meeting Adenauer reportedly did not bring
up the matter of the invitation to Israel, but there is no doubt that
Abs knew about it. Abs insisted that the Federal Republic could
not incur any new obligations without informing her creditors and
gaining their concurrence. According to the head of the German
delegation, Professor Böhm,[40] Abs believed that such a warning
would prevent Adenauer from assuming any additional obligations,
such as those demanded by Israel. Supposedly, Abs first learned of
Adenauer's invitation from Moshe Keren, an Israeli diplomat, in
London on February 29, 1952.[41] Abs, feeling that this new turn contradicted all previous instructions, cabled Bonn for clarification and
new instructions. He was summoned to the capital on March 8, and
it was only then that he was officially informed of the forthcoming
talks in Holland. He wanted to resign at once, but was persuaded
by Dr. Adenauer to stay on. It was at this point that Professor Böhm
asked Dr. Walter Hallstein, an influential official of the German
Foreign Ministry, to inform the government of Israel that the talks
at The Hague must be coordinated with the London Debt Conference.

Dr. Abs' over-all objective in London was to find ways and means
to reduce Germany's total obligations in foreign exchange. At first
he took a rather inflexible attitude which he justified by saying that
Adenauer's willingness to incur the heavy new indebtedness to Israel
put him in a difficult position. How could he reconcile the desire
to scale down German foreign indebtedness with the Bonn government's willingness to incur new debts without precedent in international law? Abs argued that it was not realistic to ask former
creditors to cut down their claims and, at the same time, agree to
take on new, burdensome obligations, a situation that would amount

in effect to those creditors making payments to Israel. Because there was no basis for pressing the Israeli case before the World Court in The Hague, Abs tended to minimize Israel's claim. He insisted that the same bargaining rules adopted for the London Conference also be used at Wassenaar.[42]

Initially, Abs had many supporters, including Böhm, who agreed that even if Bonn assumed new foreign-exchange obligations, its ability to make good on such promises was highly doubtful. Germany's economic problems included a shortage of foreign exchange and an uncertain future in foreign trade. For these reasons, Bonn hinted, if Israel would agree to accept goods and not demand hard currency or gold, a satisfactory settlement might be arrived at quickly, although Abs disagreed. In the early stages of negotiations, however, Dr. Shinnar insisted on gold or hard currency, demands which Abs opposed strongly.[43] Since the London Debt Conference and the Wassenaar talks were interrelated, sharp differences arose almost at once among the German, Israeli, and Jewish delegations.[44]

These differences were not only much resented by the Jews in the Diaspora but they also caused much anguish among the Israelis.[45] In a March 1952 demonstration in Tel Aviv, some 40,000 people were reported to have protested against the direct talks with the Germans by raising their right arms en masse and taking the oath: "If I forget thee, O murdered Golah, let my right hand wither. I swear never to relent, never to rest until our six million murdered brethren have been avenged." [46] The early hopes and almost exaggerated self-confidence of the leaders of the Claims Conference and of Ben-Gurion's government were badly shattered. Five months earlier, the mayor of Tel Aviv, Israel Rokach, had been ready to proclaim a hunger strike if Ben-Gurion's government entered into direct negotiations with the West German government.[47] The feeling then against the talks had run so high that one Israeli writer, Leib Rochman, declared he would cease to say kaddish for his murdered father, mother, brothers, and sisters if they were held. Another Israeli writer, Dr. Dworetzki, threatened to ascend Mount Zion and commit suicide.[48]

It was in such an atmosphere of growing tension that Professor Böhm was instructed to suggest the sum $750 million, not as a firm offer, but as a tentative bargaining figure. The Israeli delegation objected strongly and pointed out that the chancellor's offer had nothing to do with the settlement of foreign debts. The costs of resettling the 500,000 refugees, they claimed, were not subject to bargaining. The Israelis demanded a firm offer, including details on the method of payment. Böhm's offer of $750 million was just "a trial balloon . . . worth nothing more than a phone number," according to one Israeli delegate.[49] As a result, the Israelis walked out of the conference on March 31, and the Germans left for Bonn the next day.[50] No quick compromise was in sight.[51]

In 1952, the balance of payments trends remained the Federal Republic's chief financial imponderable. The billion dollars which Chancellor Adenauer had accepted as West Germany's share in the negotiations was a gigantic sum, as Goldmann called it, and it was opposed by cabinet members, party leaders, bankers, and industrialists.[52] The problems created by the imposition of the fantastic 132 billion mark obligation by the Allied Reparations Commission in 1921 were still vividly remembered, and many responsible Germans were afraid that the Federal Republic would not be able to honor all its obligations without undermining the mark (DM).

The transfer problem simply haunted the Germans. If they failed to raise or earn the necessary foreign exchange, Bonn's credit standing could not be reestablished; without it the Federal Republic's economic recovery might be seriously endangered. For this reason, the Germans kept emphasizing that the London and Wassenaar talks had a natural financial connection.[53] This was the so-called "one pot theory." [54]

The Germans were aware that moral obligations were completely different from financial obligations, but Adenauer knew that if the Wassenaar talks failed the London talks would also collapse, and vice versa. Nevertheless, the Israeli delegates demanded priority consideration and rejected all references to the interdependence of the two conferences. They were afraid that since other German creditors were "getting about 40–50 per cent, we shall get about 300–350 million." [55] On the other hand, Abs, aware of Israel's extremely difficult foreign exchange situation, probably hoped to be able to settle for less than the amount the Israeli delegation demanded.[56]

With no compromise in sight, Böhm, who had returned to Wassenaar, went back to Bonn for the second time within the week.[57] The Germans were being put on the spot by the Israelis, who wanted to know exactly and officially how much Bonn was going to pay. Privately they knew "what the delegation here is recommending, but it is not clear whether the German treasury will accept such an obligation." [58] While in Bonn, Böhm met with Adenauer and Abs, who told him that the London debt talks had been put off to May 19. On April 7, back in Wassenaar, Böhm talked to the Israeli negotiators for two hours and offered them DM 3 billion instead of the 4.2 billion they had demanded. Adenauer had apparently authorized him to make this offer even though it had not been approved by the government. [59] On April 8, the Germans declared in writing that the London and Wassenaar talks were interconnected and that more concrete proposals could be made only within a month or so. [60] On April 10, the German delegates informed the Israelis that definite proposals would be made by mid-June. [61] On May 6, the Knesset decided to break off talks officially until the receipt of a binding offer. [62]

The collapse of the Wassenaar negotiations came as a bitter disappointment to Professor Böhm and his deputy, Dr. Küster. [63] Back in Bonn they used all their influence to mobilize public opinion and to test the sincerity of Dr. Adenauer's promise. They went to Dr. Schäffer, the finance minister, and asked for more money for Israel. His answer was a flat No. Additional spending would have to be paid for by either further taxation or the raising of a new loan. Deficit financing was out of the question. Bonn's Basic Law, paragraph 110, ruled out public deficits for the time being and, as the Federal Republic's first finance minister, he felt obliged to respect the new constitution both in letter and spirit. [64] Parsimony was the supreme virtue of Schäffer's fiscal policy and a balanced budget was to be the tangible manifestation of his wisdom. Schäffer felt that West Germany's credit standing depended not only upon the settlement of its external debts, but upon the stability of the Deutsche Mark as well. When the two negotiators asked whether, in a country with an annual budget of DM 2 billion, an additional DM 100 million could be made available for Israel, the answer was again No.

Küster thereupon offered his resignation and Böhm threatened to resign in protest against the government's equivocal attitude toward the specific promises of the chancellor's widely acclaimed September speech. [65] The two men felt that Abs' and Schäffer's attitudes would lead to nothing and insisted that the Jewish claims must be satisfied for moral, if for no other, reasons.

Although, officially, the Wassenaar talks were in suspension, they were continued on an *ad hoc* basis. Consternation over the dead-locked negotiations prevailed not only in Jewish and Israeli circles, but among many West Germans as well. Chancellor Adenauer knew that the impasse could be broken only by his direct intervention.[66] He did not want to create the impression that he had broken his word to Dr. Goldmann; indeed, Adenauer never hesitated or hedged "in carrying out his word to the last letter." [67] Almost all West German newspaper editors were also aware that the continued impasse at Wassenaar might eventually result in a heavy blow against the Federal Republic.[68] They urged the resumption of talks and settlement of the Israeli and Jewish material claims.

With this in mind, the chancellor invited Dr. Goldmann to his home for a meeting on April 20, 1952.[69] At that talk, Dr. Goldmann reminded Dr. Adenauer that agreement would be possible only if Bonn's payments to Israel and the Claims Conference were regarded as a debt of honor, one that could not be settled by financial horse-trading methods.[70] Only the day before, Dr. Abs had reminded Dr. Goldmann and Dr. Shinnar that the two conferences were interdependent.[71]

On April 23, Professor Böhm advised the chancellor that the Israeli demands were justified and should be met for the sake of West Germany's political future. The decision had to come from Bonn and as soon as possible.[72] Adenauer also recognized that political considerations were much more important than economic and financial ones.[73] Quite simply, he wanted and needed an understanding between West Germany and Israel. He also had to honor his word. The Israelis probably knew this, and they refused to take Abs seriously. In fact, on April 19, 1952, Dr. Josephthal wrote that the unofficial news from Bonn was pretty good.[74] The fact that the Israeli negotiators insisted that moral claims were not negotiable frightened the Germans, according to Dr. Josephthal, who was convinced that this was the best negotiating tactic, because otherwise the Germans might "have treated us like a commercial creditor." [75]

While the Wassenaar deadlock continued, American Jewish leaders conducted talks with U.S. government officials, Congressmen, and Senators, and even with the President himself. Of particular importance were the talks and subsequent exchange of letters between Jacob Blaustein, a wealthy American and the senior vice-president of the Claims Conference, and President Truman.[76] This influential chairman of the American Jewish Committee pleaded with the President for help to overcome the impasse at Wassenaar. As a non-Zionist but pro-Israel American Jew, Blaustein has served on many occasions as a catalyst, and whenever he talked to Presidents Roosevelt, Truman, Eisenhower, Kennedy, and Johnson, they listened to him. His influence with American presidents was always enormous, yet he avoided the limelight of noisy publicity. The State Department had supposedly asked the newspapers not to apply too much pressure on Adenauer's government.[77] Blaustein's words did not fall on deaf ears, and in a few short weeks President Truman and the U.S. High Commissioner in West Germany, John McCloy, and others had brought the negotiators back to the bargaining table in Wassenaar.[78]

These growing pressures led to the first direct confrontation between Dr. Abs and Dr. Shinnar at Arlington House, London, on May 19.[79] The day before this meeting, the London *Observer* had published a front-page article under the heading, "Israel Before Economic Collapse." Dr. Abs asked what kind of compromise could be worked out, hinting that he would be inclined to offer a sum up to DM 800 million instead of DM 4 billion.[80]

The Germans apparently felt that the Israelis "were so broke" that they would "khapp (grab) and accept anything." [81] Dr. Shinnar replied that on the matter of Israel's resettlement claim no compromise was possible. In his excitement, Dr. Shinnar exclaimed that if this generation did not collect the $1 billion, their children or even their grandchildren would.[82] Dr. Josephthal reported that the "talk between Shinnar and Abs ended in a row." [83] Jewish reaction to the unofficial proposal by Abs was extremely sharp. According to Dr. Goldmann, who wrote a long and strongly worded letter to the chancellor, Dr. Abs' offer was an insult to the Jewish conscience.[84] Upon receipt of this letter, Adenauer was quick to grasp that a continued impasse at Wassenaar would undo all his carefully laid groundwork for the restoration of German prestige. He had hoped that a large-scale material settlement with Israel and world Jewry would make West Germany more "acceptable" in international eyes. The hoped-for prestige, which the Bonn government so sorely needed, was evaporating. According to Shinnar, his sharp exchanges of May 19 with Abs made the latter realize for the first time that the Israelis would not horse-trade, no matter how precarious the economic situation of their young country.[85] The next day, Dr. Shinnar left for Paris to meet Israel's foreign minister, Moshe Sharett.[86]

On May 20, 1952, the Foreign Policy Committee of the Bundestag unanimously "adopted a resolution stressing that the claims of Israel and the Jewish people were of a moral nature and should be given precedence over the commercial claims under discussion in London." [87] The implication of this decision was that from now on Dr. Abs' talks in London would not be coordinated with those at Wassenaar, and the Israelis would not have to "queue up in London," as Sharett used to say, but instead would receive preferential treatment.

On or about the same date, the chancellor recalled Abs from London. Böhm's resignation was not yet effective, and the only way to induce him to stay on the job seemed to be to raise the German offer to Israel. Dr. Küster had already resigned. According to Goldmann, "in the history of diplomatic negotiations there have been few examples of government representatives dissociating themselves so openly from the viewpoint of their government and announcing their solidarity with the other side." [88] This stance was of inestimable moral value and should never be forgotten.

To assuage Böhm, the chancellor brought him together with Abs for a talk. A few days earlier Böhm and the chancellor had exchanged sharp words during which Böhm told Adenauer that the Israelis would probably accept an offer of DM 3 billion. But the chancellor had rejected this proposal until he could consult with Abs. When both men finally got together, Abs reported the intransigence of Shinnar, saying that Israel insisted on a settlement of DM 4.2 billion within 6 years, with 60 per cent of the sum to be paid in hard currency and 40 per cent in goods. To Abs the Israeli claim of DM 4.2 billion was as much out of the question as Böhm's personal proposal of DM 3 billion. Schäffer, the finance minister, had a figure of DM 2 billion in mind.[89]

Since the fear of another "transfer problem" had, from the very outset, stymied the Wassenaar talks, Böhm had asked Professor Fritz W. Meyer, an economist at the University of Bonn, to prepare a memorandum on the question of whether payments in kind would seriously impair Bonn's ability to discharge obligations arising out of the future Israel Agreement. Professor Wilhelm Röpke (Geneva) wrote a second memorandum on this question. Both scholars argued that payments in kind were not necessarily identical with payments in foreign exchange.[90] This view was also shared by Ludwig Erhard, then minister of economics, but Dr. Abs disagreed.[91]

To break the deadlock, Adenauer came to the conclusion that Böhm's proposal was fair and asked him to go to Paris and make his offer to Dr. Goldmann. Böhm agreed to do so, and both men met there on May 23.[92] On the same day, they held a second meeting, attended also by Dr. Shinnar, Dr. Josephthal, Dr. Barou, and Gershon Avner.[93] Böhm made it clear that he was not authorized to make any binding proposals; he merely wanted to sound out Israeli reaction. His offer was a sum of DM 3 billion, within a period of eight to twelve years, in German-made goods. Dr. Goldmann accepted the offer in principle, but he felt that Bonn should discharge this obligation in seven years and that at least one-third should be paid in foreign exchange.[94] The Israelis were determined not to resume talks at Wassenaar prior to receipt of a formal and firm offer from the government of the Federal Republic.[95]

On May 28, Adenauer met in Paris with Dr. Goldmann, but the chancellor could not offer anything concrete because his cabinet had not yet discussed Böhm's proposal.[96] The basic reason for this seeming procrastination was that during May the Contractual Agreement between the British, American, and French governments, on the one side, and the Bonn government was negotiated, and the chancellor had devoted most of his time to it. The British High Commissioner, for instance, reported that between "May 6th and May 22nd, 1952, we held eleven all-day meetings with the Chancellor." [97] The treaty was signed on May 25, and Dr. Goldmann observed that during this ceremony American Secretary of State Dean Acheson and British Foreign Minister Anthony Eden had a chance to talk to Dr. Adenauer about the stalled Wassenaar talks "and emphasize the unfortunate consequences their failure would have." [98] Neither Eden nor Acheson in their memoirs has mentioned exactly what was said on that occasion. Even though Adenauer could not give Goldmann anything official, the two men agreed to issue an optimistic communiqué to the press to the effect that the chancellor was determined to bring the Wassenaar talks to a speedy conclusion and that they would be resumed in the very near future.[99]

On June 1, Shinnar flew home to inform the Israeli government of the latest developments. Of course, he knew that Adenauer "was bent on putting into effect the proposals Professor Böhm had made with his knowledge."[100] The only real resistance came from Dr. Schäffer, his finance minister.[101] On June 8, Blankenhorn summoned Goldmann from New York to Bonn.[102] Shinnar arrived in Cologne on June 9 and that same evening he held preparatory talks with the Secretary of State, Dr. Hallstein, and Böhm.[103] Incidentally, Dr. Shinnar entered the territory of the Federal Republic of Germany secretly—a step he took with mixed emotions since Israelis were forbidden to go to that country.

The crucial talks took place on June 10 in Bonn when all major issues were resolved.[104] Dr. Shinnar, Dr. Goldmann, and Dr. Barou met twice that day with the German team consisting of Adenauer, Hallstein, Böhm, Abs, and Abraham Frowein, secretary of the German delegation at Wassenaar. The Germans agreed to pay between DM 3.4 and 3.5 billion; agreement was also reached on the annual payments, including the obligation to deliver goods in the amount of DM 400 millon before March 31, 1954.[105] However, the German delegation wanted fourteen years to pay while the Israelis were willing to grant at most ten years. The Germans prevailed. At the insistence of Dr. Abs, an *Absichtserklärung* (declaration of intent) was written into the Agreement, which suggested that a loan for the payment of the thirteenth and fourteenth installments be made.[106]

Two weeks earlier in Paris, Dr. Gershon Avner had told Böhm that Israel had no sterling balances to pay for indispensable oil imports.[107] The failure of Dr. Horowitz's mission to London in the spring of 1952 to obtain a £5 million loan placed Israel's oil imports in grave jeopardy. Dr. Shinnar knew that, without oil, Israel would have no water or electricity and very little production; it would mean economic near-paralysis of the hard-pressed country.[108] For this reason, he sought and obtained the so-called *Ölbrief* (oil letter) concession, which, in fact, meant that one-third of the entire sum would become available in sterling, enabling Israel to receive oil from Britain.

During the June 10 meetings, according to Shinnar, a new Abs emerged.[109] As long as the London and Wassenaar talks had to be coordinated, Abs saw his task as primarily to reestablish the Federal Republic's credit standing. When his instructions had been modified, he helped greatly to establish Bonn's moral credit.

The major stumbling block was the Claims Conference's initial request of $500 million for the victims of the Third Reich living outside Israel.[110] The German delegation adopted a negative attitude toward this request for various reasons, and Dr. Goldmann "stated categorically that even if an agreement were reached with Israel, I would not sign any settlement that did not somehow satisfy the demands of the Claims Conference." [111] Goldmann reported that "it took a lot of doing to persuade Hallstein and the others to agree to a payment of about five hundred million marks to the Claims Conference, on the condition that this obligation might also be discharged in the form of goods to be delivered to Israel, which would then reimburse the Claims Conference." [112]

On that same day, "Adenauer promised to recommend to the cabinet the Claims Conference demand for a half-billion marks." [113] Thus the second and most dramatic phase of the Wassenaar talks ended on a note of accord, although the Claims Conference made a substantial concession to the Germans. Dr. Josephthal recorded that the Israelis were "very satisfied" with the outcome; he added that "naturally we shall be criticized in Israel, but I think all serious-minded people will hail this settlement." [114] Dr. Goldmann also noted that his negotiating partners "were deeply moved" in the late evening of June 10.[115] On June 17, Adenauer presented his cabinet with the proposed terms of the Israel Agreement, which were quickly approved. On the same day he informed Dr. Goldmann about this turn of events.[116]

The actual resumption of negotiations on June 28 marked the third phase of this first formal Jewish-German confrontation after World War II. Since the substance of Adenauer's proposal had already been accepted, there remained only the working-out of technical details.

Two committees, one dealing with economic and the other with legal matters, went to work. The legal committee drew up the draft of the treaty, while the economic committee prepared the lists of commodities, quantities, and dates of delivery. In this final stage of negotiations, Dr. Goldmann agreed on "four hundred and fifty million marks for the Claims Conference and fifty million for non-Jewish victims." [117] As head of the Claims Conference delegation, he agreed to take a substantial cut from the original claim in exchange for Bonn's commitment to enact legislation for compensation of all Nazi victims in the nearest possible future. The Claims Conference's initial demand for the support and rehabilitation of the survivors of the Holocaust was reduced from $500 to $107 million. Dr. Goldmann had supposedly no authority to make this concession, and he was taken to task for it by his fellow negotiators of the Claims Conference at a meeting in London on July 7.[118] However, it was too late to reopen the bargaining process, although Blaustein tried valiantly but not too successfully to do so. The Shilumim Agreement was actually drawn up by Dr. Jacob Robinson, who at that time was in Wassenaar.[119] According to Josephthal, he "is a real authority on international law and helps us a great deal." [120] The talks all came to an end on August 27, 1952.

7

Ratification of the Luxemburg Treaty: A Stormy Maneuver

The signing of the various agreements known as the Luxemburg Treaty took place in the Luxemburg City Hall on September 10, 1952. It was the first official "amicable ceremony in almost two decades" [1] between Jews and Germans.

For the participating delegations, as well as for the news-hungry press correspondents, September 10 started very early. Utmost secrecy prevailed because Jewish terrorists stood ready to kill all who participated in negotiating this accord. Finance Minister Sharett and Böhm had escaped assassination during the Wassenaar period.[2] For this reason, selected newspapermen were summoned by a pre-arranged 7 A.M. phone call to a secret meeting place and from there were driven to the Luxemburg City Hall. It was a quiet ceremony. Scarcely a word was spoken as the German, Israeli, and Jewish delegates faced each other across a long table.[3] Chancellor Adenauer faced Finance Minister Sharett. To Adenauer's left sat Professor Böhm facing Drs. Shinnar and Josephthal, the two heads of the Israeli delegation. To Sharett's left was Dr. Goldmann, vis-à-vis Dr. Walter Hallstein. Dr. Adenauer signed first, then Sharett. When Goldmann's turn came, an unexpected hitch occurred. His fountain pen was dry. Hallstein offered him his pen, and Goldmann accepted it. Was that an omen? For a moment the Jewish delegates felt uneasy; the Germans were visibly embarrassed.[4] Sharett and Adenauer had signed what came to be known as the German-Israel (Israelvertag) or Shilumim Agreement.[5] Throughout the signing ceremony the atmosphere was extremely reserved. In winding up the Knesset debate in January 1952, Moshe Sharett had emphasized that German payments of integration costs would not entail either "recognition or conciliation." [6] There was no public handshaking. Hands were shaken later, after the delegates withdrew beyond the view of photographers into an adjoining room where the mood was one "of friendliness and mutual sympathy." [7]

Throughout the Wassenaar negotiations, the representatives of Israel and of the Claims Conference stressed that the "compensation sought was for *material losses* suffered by Nazi victims and was not in reparation for moral wrongs inflicted. *Those wrongs were irreparable in their totality, a viewpoint which the German government also acknowledged.*" [8] On this occasion, Finance Minister Sharett explained that the just-signed agreements were of great moral significance because they represented a precedent for voluntary reparations for the spoliation of property.[9] However, he also carefully stressed that this accord did not signify a healing of wounds inflicted by the Nazi exterminations. The Israeli and Jewish delegates felt that no material compensation could ever atone for the German moral guilt toward the Jews. Nevertheless, it clearly marked the beginning of a German-Jewish dialogue.

Throughout the world the signing of the Treaty of Luxemburg—which still required ratification by both governments—was received with neither jubilation nor approval. Hundreds of speeches against the acceptance of collective compensation (Shilumim Agreement) were made in Israel as well as in the United States. Newspaper articles and pamphlets urged all Jews to condemn them. Surely payment of this kind reminded people of the Teutonic *Wergeld,* the blood money which could atone for the most heinous crime. Opponents of the payments made some lurid calculations: DM 3,000 million paid for six million Jews killed. That meant DM 500 for every Jew murdered. "Jews are cheap," they protested.[10]

Others reminded American Jews that West Germany had committed itself to pay only 54.8 per cent of the original claim submitted by the government of Israel and the Claims Conference. Such a settlement was nothing to be proud of. The agreed-upon delivery schedule was the most "disastrous practical aspect of the entire scheme," the critics predicted. Adenauer was expected to remain in power only up to 1956. Thereafter, from 1957 to 1964, with seven or nine annual deliveries still due, West Germany would be governed by a new Nazi regime. With such a future in sight, Israel and world Jewry would soon discover that the golden prospects of German deliveries would turn out to be empty promises.[11]

Prime Minister Ben-Gurion and some of his ministers, on the other hand, were pleased with the Luxemburg Treaty. According to Dr. Goldmann, Ben-Gurion expressed these sentiments for what was achieved at Wassenaar: "You and I have had the good fortune to see two miracles come to pass, the creation of the State of Israel and the signing of the agreement with Germany. I was responsible for the first, you for the second. The only difference is that I always had faith in the first miracle, but I didn't believe in the second one until the very last minute." [12]

In West Germany, there was no enthusiastic mass approval, either. The treaty was not rejected; it was simply received with apathy. This notwithstanding the fact that, earlier, Kurt Schumacher, leader of the opposition, Carlo Schmidt, leading intellectual of the Social Democrats in the Bundestag, Rudolf Küstermeier, editor of the influential newspaper *Die Welt*, who spent twelve years in Hitler's concentration camps, Basilea Schlink, founder of the Ecumenical Sisterhood of Mary Darmstadt, Gertrud Luckner, Romano Guardini, Willy Brandt, and above all Erich Lüth had all been instrumental in generating strong support for the "We Ask Israel for Peace" action.[13] This action had been designed to demonstrate to the world that the Germans were ready to atone for atrocities committed in their name by Hitler's henchmen. Above all, responsible Germans wanted to counter the popular Jewish view that West Germany was "a nation of nihilists, sceptics, and cynics" and that "economic rehabilitation was not followed by an inner moral recuperation." [14] They wanted to show the Israelis and world Jewry that the Germans were ashamed of their Nazi past, that they had unfouled their nest, and that they wanted to express remorse for what happened to the Jews in the Third Reich.[15] Yet the "Peace with Israel Movement" remained a rather small-scale venture of responsible Germans, not a mass movement. Voluntary cash contributions to it amounted to less than DM 100,000, and this figure is probably a fair indicator of the prevalent German attitude that the "Jews were responsible for anti-Semitism." [16] The German will to make restitution was not very strong.[17]

Adenauer and the Treaty

The complete story of Adenauer's role in the moral rearmament of West Germany is not yet told, but the record contains some documentation and much speculation. Adenauer was well aware that Nazi atrocities had produced a lingering and understandable anti-German bias throughout the world. Hitler had violated the laws of international morality by practicing industrialized genocide, and Germany itself had come to be regarded as a felon among nations. National penitence, by paying moral reparations, was at least one possible way for the German people to work their way out of their pariah status. Adenauer also felt that, without reconciliation with the Jews, his new Germany would neither have a proper foundation nor experience a moral rejuvenation. As a charismatic leader, he was able to translate his vital convictions into policy. To do whatever he could to undo the Nazi past was his personal, heartfelt obligation. He was not afraid to use power to wipe out the Nazi misuse of it, to find an honorable solution.[18]

Chancellor Adenauer and his government rejected the concept of the "common guilt" of all Germans, but assumed moral and material responsibility for the suffering of the Jews at the hands of the exterminators of the Third Reich. The concept of collective guilt, such as the charge that all Jews are responsible for the death of Jesus Christ, is, of course, simply a manifestation of primitive mentality. In all democratic countries, where civil liberties exist *de facto* (not just in constitutions on paper), responsibility for any criminal act is attributed to those who committed it. It is impossible to blame all Russians for the slaughter of Stalin's victims, and it is equally impossible to implicate all Germans or, for that matter, all Christians for the Nazi genocide.[19] If the common guilt principle should be valid, then all retribution would have to be on a collective basis as well.

During the Wassenaar talks the German delegation stressed again and again that making material amends to the State of Israel was not a legal acknowledgment of a liability, because international law allowed no such obligation.[20] To make a beginning, to start with a clean slate, to extend a hand to the Jews and Israelis, this was the moral obligation that the Bundestag elevated to a contractual commitment.[21] The Luxemburg Treaty was signed to discharge what might be called the pressing moral duty of all responsible Germans.

It is this author's conviction that reconciliation with Israel was a deeply felt need for Adenauer. As a practicing Catholic and a highly self-disciplined Christian, he believed in God, sin, penitence, and atonement. The recent German past weighed heavily upon him and threatened the future. As a human being, Adenauer seems to have felt that the only way to escape feelings of guilt and worry about the future was through reparation—making up for the wrong done in the past—and firm resolution to avoid such sin in the future. He was a shrewd politician, and he confessed once that successful politics had to be simple.[22] He was also a highly paternal and patriarchal chancellor.[23] He liked to make "lonely decisions" and for advice he used to turn to very few individuals. For economic advice he went to the banker Robert Pferdemenges; for publicity expertise, to Ernst Bach; and for moral tutoring, to Cardinal Frings of Cologne.[24] Like Winston Churchill, he did not drift with time and events, and he had the good sense "of acting in the stream of history." [25] He admired and practiced decisiveness, resolution, and strength.[26]

The man in the street was probably sympathetic to Adenauer's cause, but grass-roots political support and action were not strong. The Federal Republic inherited the "political neutralism" of the Weimar Republic, and all important decisions were made by a small ruling elite. The average German felt that reparations for whatever reason was the affair of the government, which knew best. In Adenauer's "patriarchal-type democracy," from 60 to 70 per cent of all laws emanated from the government, not the Bundestag.[27] Consequently, most of the credit for the moral and political recovery of West Germany properly belongs to him. He took the initiative in starting the Wassenaar negotiations. The four agreements signed at Luxemburg in the fall of 1952 "cannot be considered by any stretch of imagination as having been either initiated or settled by orders or pressure from the Allied governments." [28] For him, the settlement of the Jewish material claims was much more a moral than a political question, although he never forgot the latter aspect.[29]

Only the small—but vocal—organized groups of the extreme Left and Right actively opposed the Luxemburg Treaty. *Der Ring,* the organ of the former internees and denazified Germans (Entnazifizierungsgeschädigter), was one of them. In West Berlin, *Nation Europa* was another. In November 1952, it printed a proclamation which said, among other things: *"Peace with Israel—Yes! Repara-*

tions to Israel—Never! Let us unite in our fight against reparations, which actually represent a Bolshevik-type Morgenthau Plan in disguise. Let us fight for German-Arab friendship." [30]

The East German authorities actually joined hands with the Neo-Nazis of West Germany. For the Communists, "making it good again" could have only one meaning, to eradicate fascism. Monetary payments, they claimed, could never do that.[31] West German Communist agitation against the Shilumim Agreement was not very effective.

The German middle class was silent and passive on the matter. Nazi-tainted lawyers, judges, bureaucrats, university professors, and officers were back on the job. Their true attitudes on Adenauer's policy of moral comeback were reflected in inconsequential daily talk. As the staunchest supporters of Nazism, the middle classes had suffered greatly under the Allied denazification procedures, but by 1952 most of them had been rehabilitated. The ratification debate gave them a chance to vent their past frustrations.

Some felt that the payment of DM 3,000 million was something like the Peterspfennig (Denarius S. Petri) which all Catholics had paid to the Pope for indulgences in the Middle Ages. Reparations money was some sort of down payment on the purchase of an *indulgentia* that would enable the Germans to remit at least part of the crime. Some may even have felt that the Jews or Zionists were running the world, and that the Germans were being forced to curry their favor. These feelings were never voiced openly, nor was much written about these attitudes, but they existed and persisted for anyone not willfully blind or deaf. It is possible, of course, that the Germans simply wanted to forget the Nazi past.[32] But it is also possible, or even probable, that they felt that "we can live without the favor of Israel." [33] In the fall of 1952, the Nazi, or rather Christian, legacy of Jew-baiting was still strongly ingrained in the minds of most war-generation Germans.

Chancellor Adenauer set the reconciliation with Israel and world Jewry as the most immediate and vital task of his government. He wanted to regain for the new Germany the confidence of the Western Allies and to win a place for it in the Western alliance against possible Soviet aggression.[34] As a demonstration to the world of his intentions, Adenauer insisted that the first international treaty to be signed by his government should bear witness to the moral comeback of the new, postwar Germany.[35] He signed the Luxemburg accord on September 10, 1952, at 8 A.M., two hours before he affixed his signature to the treaty for the European Coal and Steel Community.

Basic Provisions of the Israel Agreement

The Luxemburg Treaty consisted of four related but separate agreements. The first, between the State of Israel and the Federal Republic of Germany, was the Shilumim, or Israel agreement. Under its terms the Federal Republic committed itself to pay 3 billion Deutsche Marks to the State of Israel. The second, called Protocol No. 1, was an agreement with the Conference on Jewish Material Claims against Germany (generally known as the Claims Conference). By this pledge the Bonn government incurred the obligation to initiate new legislation for individual compensation to the victims of Nazi persecution. The third, called Protocol No. 2, was an agreement, signed by Adenauer for Germany and Goldmann for the Claims Conference, calling for the payment of DM 450 million to the Claims Conference for rehabilitation of Nazi victims.[36] The sum of DM 3.45 billion, roughly equivalent to $820 million at the prevailing exchange rate of DM 4.20 to the dollar, was to be paid to Israel. But DM 450 million (or $107 million) were to be transferred to the Claims Conference in New York.[37] This amount was to be applied to the work of Jewish relief organizations throughout the world. The fourth agreement provided that Israel undertake to refund to Germans the value of secular property, mostly that of the Knights Templar, located in Israel.[38] The exact period for the discharge of West German deliveries was not stated absolutely, but it was estimated to run between twelve and fourteen years.[39] However, there was a stipulation that the first complete payment be made between the date of ratification and March 31, 1953. In Germany, the agreement was signed into law on March 20, and Israel ratified it on March 22, 1953. DM 60 million were due the day the accord came into force, and the remaining DM 140 million of the first payment were to follow no later than March 31, 1953. The second payment year was to run from April 1, 1953, to March 31, 1954, when another DM 200 million were due. From then on, the payment year was to run from April to March 31 of the following year. Thus, the third payment year started on April 1, 1954, and for the next nine years the German Federal Republic was to pay DM 310 million. The final payment was to be DM 260 million.

Shortly after the treaty went into effect, some observers maintained the hope that the entire German material obligation toward Israel could be discharged by March 31, 1964.[40] However, this was not to be the case. The treaty contained an escape clause permitting the Bonn government to reduce payments due after April 1, 1954. Article 3 (a) (iii) stipulated that yearly installments might be reduced should the government of the Federal Republic of Germany be of the opinion that it could not comply with the terms of subparagraph (ii), which fixed nine annual installments of DM 310 million each. If the West German government decided to take advantage of this stipulation, the yearly payments might be reduced to DM 250 million, but no less than that.[41]

This is precisely what the Germans did. Article 4, however, permitted earlier and larger payments than those stipulated in Article 3. Whichever course of action the Bonn government took, according to the terms of the treaty, the yearly installments were due in equal amounts on the 15th of April and on the 15th of August of each year. These sums were to be paid into the account of the Israel Mission with the Bank Deutscher Länder, the West German central bank whose name was later changed to Deutsche Bundesbank. Bonn's obligation to Israel was spelled out in terms of goods and services, not foreign exchange, except for two yearly German payments of DM 75 million due in pounds sterling, so that Israel could pay for the oil delivered by the British company, Shell.[42] To assure equal treatment for Israel-bound deliveries, the shipments were to be considered exports under the provisions of Article 5 (a) of the agreement. All firms making deliveries to Israel were permitted to claim certain tax refunds, as provided in the Law of Preferential Tax Treatment for Export Stimulation of June 28, 1951.[43]

Article 6 and the Schedule contained a listing of all goods to be delivered. Commodities were divided into four groups; a fifth covered services such as shipping, insurance, and administration. The principal categories of commodities were ferrous and nonferrous metals, products of the steel and metal-working industries, chemicals, and agricultural products.

The first schedule, in other words the first consignment of goods selected by Israel, was applicable only until March 31, 1954. Thereafter, each subsequent delivery schedule was to be fixed by the Mixed Commission, and its composition was to be based on the schedule of the preceding year.

Article 10 contained an "escape clause" which enabled West Germany to cope with unforeseen developments that might adversely affect her ability to pay. In addition to reduced payments in special circumstances, West Germany could also, after consultation with Israel, temporarily suspend annual payments. These rights could be exercised only if "economic or financial capacity was negatively affected in a fundamental and lasting manner." [44] Should this occur, an Arbitration Commission was to determine what the Germans were to do. However, the treaty specifically provided that any suspension or reduction of annual payments should not reduce West Germany's total liability of DM 3.45 billion. In other words, in case of balance-of-payments difficulties, Germany was permitted to reduce temporarily only the next annual installment due, after an application had been made to the Arbitration Commission. Payments could be stopped only after an understanding had been reached by the two contracting parties or by decision of the Arbitration Commission.

Israel incurred three specific obligations. First, she was committed not to export Shilumim commodities to other countries unless such goods had undergone substantial transformation by industrial processes. The prohibition against re-export was designed to prevent Israel from reselling German-made products. However, Israel was permitted to import German raw materials and export them as finished articles. The agreement also stipulated that if the re-export provisions were violated, Israel would be "liable to a penalty equivalent in amount to the value of the commodities at the time when they were so exported." The penalty could be imposed by the Arbitration Commission, and any penalty so imposed was to be deducted from the next annual installment.[45] Second, Israel was prohibited from defraying "freight charges on the carriage of commodities beyond the German frontier, except where transport by sea is provided by German shipping companies." [46] Third, Israel committed herself to pay DM 450 million ($107 million) to the Claims Conference, representing twenty-three Jewish organizations, with headquarters in New York.

In general, all commercial transactions arising out of the Israel agreement were subject to the jurisdiction of German courts. Article

12 provided that, in case of disputes, the Israel Mission would act on behalf of the State of Israel. Since the latter made contracts with individual firms in West Germany, German courts held jurisdiction. This provision was especially important because at the time the Luxemburg Treaty was signed the two countries had no diplomatic relations. Ambassadors were first exchanged in the summer of 1965, only after West Germany had fully discharged her obligations toward Israel.

Four separate agencies were set up to implement the treaty. For instance, all disputes between the contracting parties were subject to arbitration. The agreement designated the Israel Mission for the government of Israel, and the Bundesstelle (officially, Bundesamt für gewerbliche Wirtschaft) for the government of the Federal Republic.[47]

The Israel Mission, located at Cologne, was the sole and exclusive purchaser of Shilumim commodities and services. It signed all contracts with German suppliers. It enjoyed diplomatic status, its members having broader and wider immunities and privileges than those usually accorded a trade mission. All senior officials of Israeli nationality were exempt from the jurisdiction of German courts, and no taxes were levied on the income, profits, and capital of the Israel Mission or its members.

The Bundesamt was located at Frankfurt am Main. Upon placing an order with a firm, the Israel Mission notified the Bundesamt and gave details about the type, quantity, prices, and terms of delivery of the commodities. This office then determined whether the orders placed were in conformity with the provisions of the Shilumim Agreement. It also saw to it that the appropriate tax provisions of Articles 5 and 6 were not violated. In addition, it approved the payment of invoices submitted.

The third agency, whose members were appointed by the two governments, was the Mixed Commission. Its function was to supervise the operation and implementation of the treaty. After March 31, 1954, it laid down the schedules of commodities and services for subsequent years.[48] This body had no power to adjudicate disputes.

The fourth agency was the Arbitration Commission. It consisted of two arbitrators and an umpire. Its principal function was to settle disputes between the contracting parties. This Commission was responsible not only for the Reparations Agreement, but also for

Protocol No. 2, which covered the payment of DM 450 million to the twenty-three Jewish organizations.[49]

The Shilumim Agreement was not intended to settle the individual claims of Israeli nationals for restitution of identifiable property or compensation for persecution by Nazis. Its purpose was to reimburse the State of Israel for the cost of integration and absorption of up-rooted and destitute Jewish refugees from Germany and German-occupied territories.

Ratification of the Treaty

The Luxemburg Treaty required the ratification of the Bundestag and the Bundesrat, which was to prove as stormy as the negotiations at Wassenaar. The trouble arose from the paradiplomatic activity of the Arabs, the opposition of Dr. Schäffer, Bonn's finance minister, and the possible breakup of the "restitution coalition" of the Social Democrats and Adenauer's Christian Democrats.[50]

The Arab League made no bones about the fact that, if the Luxemburg Treaty were ratified, they would impose a boycott against West Germany.[51] For their part, German businessmen at first paid little attention to the Arab threats. However, the German press, the business community, and probably the bureaucrats slowly began to turn to favoring the Arabs. For instance, a memorandum of the Arab Higher Committee for Palestine was widely circulated among German business groups. Numerous German-sponsored "Middle East Societies" distributed the memorandum, which claimed that the intended payments "for all losses of former German Jews" might be "helping an aggressor nation to build up her war potential for further aggression." [52] The League threatened that no Arab state would issue import licenses to German firms, arguing that Israel did not deserve any compensation payments because she had refused to do anything for the million Palestinian refugees who had been forced to flee without taking their property. The estimated Arab losses were said to be close to the fantastic sum of $100 billion!

Arab pressures gradually mounted. In early November 1952, the Saudi Arabian government instructed all West German firms to cease their operations because of the German-Israel agreement.[53] Some German newspapers showed sympathy for the Arab position. For example, one business-oriented publication reported that forthcoming German shipments of capital goods to Israel would certainly be to the disadvantage of all Arab states. It was also claimed that the Bonn government had not answered an important Arab query as to why Israel should receive all the goods agreed upon at Luxemburg, when many Jews had simply gone overseas and not become citizens of Israel.[54] Franz-Joseph Strauss, an important CDU politician and later West German Finance Minister, also published an article against the ratification of the treaty in early January 1953.[55]

For Adenauer, the ratification of the Luxemburg Treaty was of the greatest moral significance.[56] Regardless of what the various pressure groups did or said, he remained firm in his resolve.[57] Unfortunately, it took more than six months to ratify the treaty.

The agitation against ratification continued. Dr. Hjalmar Schacht, the former Nazi Minister of Economics, asserted that the Bonn government had signed the agreements under Allied pressure. Professor Böhm refuted this, pointing out that no West German agreement had been more unanimously endorsed by government, opposition, and all members of the coalition than the Luxemburg Treaty.[58] In the same vein, he denied that ratification would involve a violation of Arab-German friendship. He emphasized the moral aspects in his argument.[59]

While these pros and cons were being debated, the Jewish and Israeli press resented "the vague and meaningless promises of Adenauer." [60] Why the delay, many wondered? When will Adenauer get down to brass tacks? The Jews and Israelis were perplexed, to say the least. In addition, a few minor technicalities, such as the initial discriminatory shipping clause, slowed down the process of ratification. Dr. Shinnar reported at one point that it looked as if the Bundestag would not be able to ratify the treaty during the spring session and would have to postpone it.[61] Furthermore, the first Adenauer government's "four-year term of office was about to expire, and according to the constitution any matter not finally settled by the outgoing government would have to await its turn on the agenda of the new one." [62] Neither the chancellor, nor the Israeli government, nor the Claims Conference wanted that.

The Jewish and Israeli diplomatic reaction to the Arab challenge was subtle. They pointed out that what Arab threats of economic sanctions against German goods overlooked was the economic weakness of all the Arab states. How could an Arab state which depended on the German market impose a boycott against the buyer? It was a joke without substance. At the same time, the Israelis admitted that the forthcoming German deliveries of capital goods would be of tremendous importance in their economic development and that it was Israel's economic progress that the Arab states feared most.[63]

To assuage the Arabs, West Germany granted some Arab countries substantial sums for economic development.[64] According to some, the Arabs were bought off. The Arabs, in turn, claimed that the Germans had bought off the Jews. But, no matter what the terminology, the treasury of the Federal Republic was paying substantial sums to the treasuries of the various Arab states as well as to the Israelis.

On March 4, 1953, the chancellor spoke before the Bundestag and urged the ratification of the Luxemburg agreements for moral reasons.[65] The ratification, he said, would close the saddest chapter in German history. Even those who had committed no crime against the Jews must make a contribution to overcome the stigma attached to all Germans. The proposed deliveries to Israel were not really reparations, because Germany had never fought Israel. The delivery of German goods should be viewed as a compensation to the State of Israel for the cost of the absorption of many thousands of Jewish immigrants. To save foreign exchange most of the payments would be made in the form of goods. Finally, the moral commitment on the part of Bonn was so strong that "a moral obligation was elevated to legal obligation." Such was the masterly persuasion of the chancellor.

The decisive debate took place on March 18. Most of the cabinet members and members of the Bundestag, including the Social Democratic opposition, spoke overwhelmingly in favor of speedy ratification. Only the Communists and neo-Nazis opposed it. Deputy Müller, a Communist, termed the payment of DM 450 million to the Claims Conference, which he called a holding company for Zionist organizations, an outrage. In the name of *Wiedergutmachung*, Israeli industrialists would get all they needed to build up their basic industries. The real benefactors would be the industrialists of West Germany, Israel, and the United States. "After all," Müller exclaimed, "Americans have forced West Germany into signing this agreement. U.S. imperialists want to build up Israel's war potential so that she can become a bastion for further aggression in the Middle East." [66] The Communists took the position that they would support only individual compensation for damages suffered. The two major parties, Christian Democrats and Social Democrats, were in favor of ratification. Without the full and wholehearted support of Dr. Kurt Schumacher, the chief of the Social Democratic Party, it would have been difficult to obtain ratification of the Luxemburg Treaty.[67] The Bundestag approved the agreement on March 18, 1953. Excluding the Berlin representative, 239 deputies voted for the agreement, 35 voted against, and there were 86 abstentions.[68] Fritz Schäffer, the finance minister, opposed the agreement. He hoped he could convince the Cabinet as well, but was unable to do so.[69]

The Bundesrat ratified the agreements on March 20, after it was assured that the existing Israeli prohibition against German ships entering Israel's ports would be lifted.[70] Theodor Heuss, president of the Federal Republic, signed the law the same day. The Israeli government ratified the treaty on March 22. Five days later, the two parties exchanged the ratified documents in the Secretariat of the United Nations.[71]

So it was that the Bonn government formally extended a conciliatory hand toward the Jews. The leaders of West Germany knew only too well that material amends could never undo what had happened to the Jews at the hands of the Nazis in the Third Reich, but at least a beginning had been made in a large-scale gesture of restitution and good will in recognition of a moral obligation. The DM 3.45 billion was not exactly the billion dollars originally requested, "a large sum for Germany at that time," but it was close to it.[72]

For their part, the concerned Jews of the world and those in power in Israel saw not only the realistic value of accepting reparations and compensation from the Germans, but the moral and judicial imperatives as well.

Significance of the Luxemburg Treaty

In the field of international law the Luxemburg Treaty, especially the global compensation to the State of Israel, was probably the innovation of this century, a *res nova*, a *sui generis*.[73] To Dr. Goldmann, his ability to persuade the chancellor to pay global restitution was truly revolutionary.[74] In contrast to time-honored treaty-making practice, Bonn's government negotiated the Luxemburg treaties not only with the State of Israel but also with world Zionist and non-Zionist Jewish organizations.

To the traditional diplomat or historian, steeped in conventional theories of international law, the very concept that world Jewry could be made a party to an international treaty scarcely made sense. It did not make much sense to anti-Zionists either, because "Jewish people" as a homogeneous entity does not exist.[75] But conventional wisdom and the Zionist infighting with anti-Zionists could not change the outcast status of the newly established Federal Republic of Germany. Therefore, in order to rise out of its pariah ghetto, the Bonn government was determined to take a new approach toward the solution of the material claims against Germany.[76] Chancellor Adenauer knew that a stiff legalistic approach would not solve anything. Since it had been Hitler's plan to exterminate all Jews as a people, the chancellor felt obliged to pay compensation to every Jew, non-Israeli as well as Israeli, who had suffered at the hands of the Nazis.

With this in mind, the Bonn government recognized the representatives of both Zionist and non-Zionist world Jewry as partners to The Hague negotiations.[77] Professor Böhm has stated that this was done deliberately to do justice to all Jews wherever they live.[78] This recognition of private Jewish organizations conferred upon them a certain legal status, a departure in international relations worthy of note. Another innovation was that the agreement was concluded between two states which did not maintain diplomatic relations—and which for the time being did not contemplate establishing such relations. One of them had not legally existed as a state and the other had not been constituted in its present form when the events giving rise to the negotiations occurred. Thus the West German-Israel agreement was not properly a diplomatic treaty, nor was it a commercial accord in the accepted sense. Nevertheless, diplomatic representation was not deemed necessary for implementation of the accord.

The German-Israel, or Shilumim, Agreement has been popularly called a reparations agreement, but this label should be accepted with reservations. Reparations usually refer to "a levy on a defeated nation forcing it to pay some of the war costs of the winning countries." [79] In other words, victors impose and exact reparations from the vanquished by force. The element of brute force, however, was absent in the treaty-making negotiations at Wassenaar.[80] In point of fact, Israel's armed forces had never engaged the troops of the Federal Republic of Germany, and Bonn had agreed to incur material obligations toward Israel only as a successor state to the Third Reich. West Germany wanted to make material amends for the crimes perpetrated in the name of the German people by the Nazis.

Thus, while moral considerations probably provided the initial impetus, other motives were at work as well. To get back into the world community of nations, Bonn's political interests demanded that Germany make a settlement with the Jews and Israel. The Israeli government and many Jewish leaders in the Diaspora have acknowledged Adenauer's symbolic gestures of good will and the part they played in bettering Bonn's image in the Western world. But moral considerations apart, the Shilumim Agreement was *Realpolitik* par excellence. Shortly after the Luxemburg Treaty was signed, Dr. Goldmann visited the German chancellor. During an interview after the meeting he stressed the "great moral significance of the Luxemburg Treaty and the large amount of good will toward the Federal Republic that would result from it." [81] In another interview with representatives of Israel by a correspondent of the foremost German weekly, *Die Zeit,* the Israelis made the point that the various Luxemburg agreements were likely to create throughout the world a completely different and a much more favorable image of Germany.

For an individual Jew, the successful initiation of the "moral comeback" policy of West Germany did not mean anything; the very thought of contact with the Germans was repugnant. For the survivors of the death mills, all Germans were incurable moral lepers. All who lived through the Holocaust felt that no matter what Adenauer, Ben-Gurion, and Goldmann did or said, relations between Germans and Jews must remain artificial and superficial, at least in this generation. To them, the moral comeback was a fiction. The members of Israel's Cabinet were aware of the moral revulsion with which the nation viewed the Wassenaar negotiations in 1952. But Premier Ben-Gurion and his ministers also knew that respect for moral sentiments is one thing and the urgency and pressures of the realities of life are something else again.[82] For the Prime Minister, the Shilumim Agreement merely reimbursed the State of Israel for stolen Jewish goods. There was really nothing much to philosophize about, whether to "take or not take." According to the Torah, as quoted by Rabbi A. Bahod, ". . . he shall restore that which he took by robbery" (Lev. 5:23).[83] The restoration of sums owed to the former owners or their heirs had nothing to do with the problem of forgiveness. Only the victim can forgive. The robber must wait for that. This was exactly the line of reasoning that Dr. Goldmann relentlessly pursued.[84]

For most Germans, moral comeback was an affair of the government and, with few notable exceptions, they did not wish to be reminded of Nazi crimes. The "average" German felt that he had repented both individually and publicly and, by so doing, had accepted material responsibility for the past. The new generation of Germans, born in the 1930s, believed they should not be expected to live with a feeling of eternal shame for being German. In 1952, it was roughly estimated that the Luxemburg Treaty would cost the Federal Republic from 6 to 8 billion Deutsche Marks.[85] In 1968, however, Dr. Goldmann felt that the total sum would amount more nearly "to at least fifty to sixty billion marks, . . ." and "the bulk of this astronomical sum has gone to (the Jews)." [86]

The Federal Indemnification Law of 1953 enabled the former persecutees to claim compensation for loss of life, damages to body and health, including medical costs, reduction of income, loss of freedom, incarceration, arrest, property losses, capital losses, discriminatory taxes, impairment of economic and professional advancement, etc.[87] Chancellor Adenauer's government, while rejecting common guilt accepted the notion of common shame for the deeds of the Nazi government.

As the decade of the Sixties got under way and the West German balance of payments miracle continued to surprise the world, and as new categories of claims were made upon the Bonn government, the West Germans began to suspect that new indemnification claims were put forward simply because of the prevailing economic prosperity of the Federal Republic of Germany.[88] The responsible West German press made the point that the feeling of collective shame could not be expected to last forever and that it was time to wind up the moral comeback payments. The right-wing press, of course, had opposed this policy from the outset, and for years since has played up every single irregularity. Headlines like "Revenge Without End" or "Why Should West Germany Be An Atonement State?" or "What Is Our Hereditary Guilt?" were to be seen in various rightist publications. Schäffer and Rolf Dahlgrün, the two finance ministers, were also critical of the scope of the moral comeback payments. Schäffer had supposedly said that "our exorbitant payments, unprecedented in history, are neither honored nor acknowledged." [89] But regardless of these reservations and distortions, the various Bonn governments faithfully continued to fulfill the promises made at Luxemburg in 1952 "in full measure and beyond." [90]

In the history of international relations, the Luxemburg Treaty has no counterpart. It is an accord without precedent. It represents a symbol of hope to the entire world and a warning to all lawless and amoral totalitarian governments. To the Jews, the Shilumim Agreement and the Indemnification Law of 1953 meant that for the first time in two thousand years they had received material compensation for injuries inflicted upon them. These payments, however, did not necessarily mean the wiping clean of the slate containing the account outstanding between German and Jew. They merely reduced many Jewish reservations in dealing with the Germans. How could the Jewish moral claims fail to persist? Historically, the Jew does not forget the wrongs done to his people. Undoubtedly, future generations of Jews at the Wailing Wall and elsewhere, intoning prayers, will recall the German Holocaust even more fervently and indelibly than the crime of Amalek.

8

Implementing the Agreements:
How and What

By signing the three Luxemburg agreements in 1952, the Bonn government undertook to redress the material wrongs against the Jews by restitution, by personal indemnification, and by payment of a lump sum to Israel. Under the first agreement, Shilumim, the Bonn government agreed to pay DM 3 billion to the State of Israel. The second, Protocol No. 1, was Adenauer's pledge to initiate new legislation for individual compensation to all victims of Nazi persecution. The third, Protocol No. 2, called for the payment of DM 450 million to the Conference on Jewish Material Claims against Germany for rehabilitation work with Jews throughout the world.

The Shilumim Agreement did not settle the claims of individual Israeli citizens for personal indemnification. It was, rather, Bonn's payment of collective Jewish claims for heirless private and communal property and a compromise rationalization of the cost of resettlement and integration in Israel of refugee European Jews. By its terms, Israel would receive a total sum of DM 3.45 billion, from which it would reimburse the Claims Conference DM 450 million. West Germany committed itself to pay two-thirds of the entire sum in goods and one-third in foreign exchange.

For any country to make remittances to another state depends upon its ability to collect the necessary sums in domestic currency, and to convert or transfer those funds into foreign exchange. The first problem can be solved usually by taxation or domestic borrowing; the second depends upon the country's capacity to earn sufficient amounts of foreign exchange. Conversion of domestic into foreign currency constitutes the essence of the "transfer problem."

West Germany's discharge of its Luxemburg obligations took place amid unprecedented prosperity. At the London Debt Conference Dr. Abs had been afraid that the comeback of West German industry on the world market would be extremely difficult. Abs and other responsible individuals remembered the dreadful reparations experience of the 1920s and they were aware that remittances in gold or dollars could be made only by regularly "selling substantially more to the rest of the world than she [Germany] purchased from the rest of the world." [1] At the time of the Luxemburg agreements, nobody knew that West Germany was well on the way to becoming a country of persistent and huge trade and balance-of-payments surpluses. The propensity of the German people to accumulate dollars and gold eventually became embarrassing to the country which in 1945 had been seen as an outcast nation in ruins and without hope.

Economic Growth of West Germany, 1953–1966

By 1952, massive injections of Marshall Plan aid, together with hard work, a gift for improvisation, loyalty of workers to their plants, powerful incentives for employers as well as employees, achievement of a stable currency, and determined efforts to accomplish a revival of foreign trade—all of these factors had contributed to a considerable rise in the German standard of living.

This rapid economic recovery was singularly responsible for the great success of Adenauer's leadership at the polls on September 6, 1953.[2] West Germany was not yet sovereign, but the country was moving swiftly ahead, economically and politically. From 1955 to 1959, the Federal Republic went through another period of rapid economic growth that brought with it an even more amazing rise in the economic well-being of the population. The prevailing prosperity was largely responsible for the "enduring stability of political conditions in the Federal Republic"; [3] for continuously rising affluence tended to make people forget the war, the Allied bombing raids, and the humiliation of the defeat, postwar desolation, and denazification.

To comprehend the economic background in which the Bonn government discharged its Luxemburg obligations, it becomes necessary to examine a few select indicators, such as the growth of Gross

National Product, the rise in industrial production, the accumulation of gold reserves, and the level of employment.

The Rise in G.N.P.

Gross National Product is defined as the market value of all finished goods, in any given year, in a particular country. The barometer of a country's economic weather, G.N.P. is a measure of total production and of combined utilization of available resources. Economists distinguish between the G.N.P. in "current prices" and in "real" or "constant" prices. The first refers to the current market value of all finished goods, while the second, or "real" G.N.P., is a measure in constant prices as of some base year. Since there is constant change in the purchasing power of all currencies, G.N.P. in current prices may rise ten times in a given period, but if the general price level in the same period has also risen ten times, the real G.N.P. has remained constant. For this reason, in order to get a better measure of changes in the behavior of G.N.P., economists eliminate the effects of price increases or decreases by "deflating" or "inflating" the current G.N.P., with the help of a price index. That is, the G.N.P. in current prices is divided by the respective price indices for relevant years. The result is a G.N.P. in constant prices, which makes comparisons over a period of time more satisfactory than would the use of unadjusted figures.

Table 8-1 shows that, in 1953, West Germany's G.N.P. in both stable 1954 prices and in current prices was 147 billion marks, but in 1966 it stood at DM 481 billion in current prices and at DM 333 billion in 1954 prices. Thus, during the fourteen-year period when the Shilumim payments were being made, the G.N.P. of the Federal Republic grew at the average rate of 6 per cent per year.[4] In 1952, when the Luxemburg Treaty was signed, the economic forecast for West Germany was poor.[5] It was a year when the economy turned from a seller's into a buyers' market.[6]

Despite the solid achievement of economic reconstruction during the years 1948 to 1952, the per capita G.N.P. in 1952 was 6 per cent below the 1938 level, while neighboring countries enjoyed a comparatively higher standard of living than before the war.[7] The prewar years, of course, had been serious depression years in Britain and throughout most of Europe.

TABLE 8-1

GROWTH OF WEST GERMANY'S GROSS NATIONAL PRODUCT [a]

Year	G.N.P. in current prices (billion DM) rounded to nearest million	G.N.P. at 1954 constant prices (billion DM) rounded to nearest million	Growth rates of real G.N.P.[b]	Growth rates of per capita G.N.P.[c]
1952	137	136	—	—
1953	147	147	8.1%	7.0%
1954	158	158	7.4%	6.3%
1955	180	177	12.0%	10.9%
1956	199	189	6.8%	5.7%
1957	216	200	5.8%	4.7%
1958	232	207	3.5%	2.4%
1959	251	221	6.8%	5.7%
1960 [d]	297	255	15.3%	14.2%
1961	326	269	5.5%	4.4%
1962	354	280	4.1%	3.0%
1963	378	289	3.2%	2.1%
1964	414	308	6.6%	5.5%
1965	453	326	5.8%	4.7%
1966	481	333	2.1%	1.0%

[a] West Germany, Statistisches Bundesamt, *Statistisches Jahrbuch für die Bundesrepublik Deutschland,* 1968 (Stuttgart: W. Kohlhammer Verlag, 1968), p. 494 (hereafter *Statistisches Jahrbuch*).

[b] Calculated as: $\dfrac{Y_t - Y_{t-1}}{Y_{t-1}} \times 100$, where Y_t denotes the base year and Y_{t-1} the previous year.

[c] Calculated as $51{,}350(r)^{14} = 59{,}638$, where 51,350 and 59,638 are the yearly average populations. $r = 1.1$ per cent. During 1950–60, the compound annual percentage change of West Germany's population was also 1.1 per cent: see A. Maddison, *Economic Growth in the West* (New York: Twentieth Century Fund, 1964), p. 29.

[d] From 1953 to 1960, the figures did not include West Berlin or the Saar region; after 1960, both territories were included. Thus, without Berlin and the Saar, the G.N.P., in current prices for 1960, was DM 280 billion, and in constant prices, DM 240 billion; the growth rate of real G.N.P. was 8.6 per cent.

Again examining Table 8-1, the figures indicate that the real G.N.P. showed an 8.1 per cent growth rate and the per capita G.N.P. one of 7.0 per cent. In 1954, expansion continued and prices started to move up slightly.[8] The real G.N.P. rose by 7.4 per cent. In 1955, the West German economy entered into a phase of full employment, and in some fields of definite overemployment.[9] The prevailing economic vigor was reflected in the 12 per cent rate of growth for the real G.N.P. and almost 11 per cent on a per capita basis. In 1956, full employment continued, but bottlenecks in labor made it difficult to expand output at former rates.[10] Therefore, in the second half of 1956 there was some slack in the economy; for the year as a whole, the real G.N.P. growth rate was 6.8 per cent. The first months of 1957 were marked by some caution, in view of the expanding productive capacity, but in general the economy continued to push forward rapidly,[11] chalking up a 5.8 per cent increase in the real G.N.P. 1958 was significant for four reasons: first, the economic upswing was then ten years old; second, West Germany "came nearer than in any previous year to the famous 'magic triangle' of monetary and economic objectives—optimum employment, price stability, and equilibrium of the balance of payments"; [12] third, the Deutsche Mark became fully convertible; [13] and, fourth, after the almost feverish activity of the former years, the real growth rate of the G.N.P. sagged to 3.5 per cent.[14] Thus, 1958 was a year of relative stability.

However, the recovery came sooner than expected. From mid-1959 on, the economy entered what the Deutsche Bundesbank called "a somewhat undesirable boom," [15] with the main impetus for the expansion of industrial production coming from abroad. The recorded rate of unemployment was less than 1 per cent, so that labor became the most inhibiting factor in the economy, and the country experienced "absolute labor shortages." [16] Increased productivity or the importation of foreign labor were the only ways to expand output. Both were used, and the real G.N.P. rose by 6.8 per cent. When the superboom continued into 1960, signs of "internal overstrain," such as steep increases in production costs and lengthening of delivery periods, were in strong evidence.[17] From 1950 to 1960, the real G.N.P. more than doubled. In 1961, despite continuous full employment and upward price trends, there was a slight relaxation in contrast to the feverish economic activity in 1959 and 1960.[18]

The Deutsche Mark was re-evaluated upward by 5 per cent on March 6, 1961, which made West German goods more expensive abroad and foreign goods less expensive in the Federal Republic.[19] For that year, the real G.N.P. grew at a rate of 5.5 per cent. Boom conditions, with overfull employment, and rising prices and wage costs per unit of production proceeded almost unabated in 1962, although pressures on profit margins considerably reduced the entrepreneurial propensity to invest.[20] As a result of these contradictory tendencies, the real G.N.P. grew only 4.1 per cent. The year 1963 was marked by a vigorous rise in foreign demand for German capital goods. In the first part of the year the economy in a few industries even had some excess capacity.[21] The real G.N.P. grew at a moderate 3.2 per cent for the whole year. In 1964, the country experienced its fourth economic boom since the currency reform of 1948; the boom continued until mid-1966, and the economy was characterized by a full utilization of existing industrial capacity and an improbable 0.4 per cent of unemployment.[22]

In 1964, the real G.N.P. growth rate was 6.6 per cent, and in 1965, 5.8 per cent. It was only in 1966, with a substantial slackening of investment demand and a serious government crisis, that the specter of a sharp recession started to haunt businessmen, workers, and government officials.[23] Under these conditions of uncertainty, the real G.N.P. crawled upward at a mere 2.1 per cent.

Per capita G.N.P., in current price, more than doubled between 1950 and 1960, rising from DM 2,087 to DM 5,362, and reached DM 8,060 in 1966. In the fourteen-year period under investigation, the per capita growth rate fluctuated between 1 per cent in the recession year of 1966 and 10.9 per cent in 1955. For the entire period, the per capita G.N.P. grew 4.9 per cent a year.[24]

The Index of Total Production

While the real G.N.P. from 1953 to 1966 grew at the average annual rate of 6 per cent, the money G.N.P. from 1951 to 1955 rose by 7 per cent, which the *London Economist* described as a "fantastically durable rate." [25] This remarkable economic achievement has puzzled many economists, who have offered a long and varied list of explanations of what made Germany's high average growth rates possible. German and Swiss economists of the "Freiburg School" have claimed that the reason was the absence of direct controls and the maintenance of vigorous competition and good markets.[26] The "unswerving dedication of the German authorities to the goal of monetary discipline," [27] along with a fiscal policy which encouraged accelerated depreciation of plants and equipment and reinvestment of profits, are other factors suggested.[28] The insistence of the first finance minister of West Germany, Dr. Fritz Schäffer, on parsimony and the stability of the mark during his term in office, is a possible reason.[29] The active role of the government in fostering rapid capital formation is another explanation.[30] Then, from 1950 to 1960, West Germany's total domestic fixed investment absorbed 21.9 per cent of the G.N.P. (at factor cost), and this achievement was possible because of low private consumption expenditure and low nonproductive investment.[31] Out of the total fixed investment, additions to machinery and equipment were particularly large, a fact which accounts for the great upsurge in output per man-hour.[32] Proverbial German industriousness is also offered as a partial explanation of the country's postwar growth.[33] Responsible labor union leadership, which never lost sight of the heavy dependence of the country upon exports, is another possible cause.[34] A historic piece of luck in being able to export modern capital equipment of the right kind, at the right time, and at competitive prices is still another hypothesis.[35] Finally, the elastic labor supply is offered as an answer.[36]

Whatever the interpretation preferred by individuals, one thing is certain: there is no single explanation for the spectacular economic rise of West Germany in the 1950s and 1960s.

Of course, economists have known for a long time that countries which have been ravaged by long and destructive wars seem to behave according to the principle that "the farther you fall, the higher you bounce." [37] The "catch-up" motivation for investment in postwar years also accounts to a great extent for some of the feverish economic activity. This almost inevitable phenomenon was dealt with by John Stuart Mill, who explained that capital is always used up faster during war than in peacetime; when peace comes, obsolete capital equipment is replaced by better and more modern machines.[38]

Once German economic recovery was under way, the growth in industrial production was almost dizzying at first. From 1953 to 1966, the index of total production rose from 67 to 161, an increase of almost two and a half times,[39] or, at the annual compound rate, 7 per cent.[40] For the decade 1950–1960, the annual growth rate of total output was 7.6 per cent, while from 1956 to 1961 it was 5.9 per cent.[41] Within this picture, the automotive, electrical equipment, and electronics industries grew almost twice as fast as industry as a whole, while textile production lagged considerably.[42]

Low Rate of Unemployment

While over the fourteen-year period the real G.N.P. grew at an average annual rate of 6 per cent or 4.9 per cent per capita, total production rose at an annual rate of 7 per cent. Without an adequate labor force, and above all without modern and responsible labor union leadership, West Germany's economic rise would hardly have been possible. For this reason, some writers have preferred to speak of the German "labor miracle." [43]

Because German labor unions were re-created from scratch in 1945, they did not suffer a hangover from nineteenth-century labor ideology, and consequently were, and have remained, flexible.[44] For instance, if the demand in a particular plant rose above its existing capacity, new labor-saving machinery or other necessary improvements were introduced at once, as a matter of course. During this process, the skilled manpower that was eliminated was automatically re-allocated to different jobs, almost without union interference. Strikes in tight labor markets would not improve matters—something recognized in Germany by both labor union leadership and joint works councils.

In addition, the expansion of industry has not been blocked by shortages of skilled labor, because German industry has developed a training system that turns out nearly half a million skilled workers annually. To become a skilled member of the labor force, an apprentice must pass examinations and obtain a certificate of proficiency, a document held in esteem by labor unions. When certain jobs are "de-skilled," the change merely affects the training schedules for new workers, not workers who already have earned a certificate.

Given the institutional manpower peculiarities of postwar Germany, Table 8-2, which shows the unemployment ratio, may prove useful. In 1953, when West Germany started to make deliveries to Israel, the unemployment rate was 7.5 per cent, with very heavy

TABLE 8-2

UNEMPLOYMENT IN WEST GERMANY, 1952–1966

Year	Unemployment (per cent)	Year	Unemployment (per cent)
1952	8.4	1960	1.3
1953	7.5	1961	0.8
1954	7.0	1962	0.7
1955	5.1	1963	0.8
1956	4.0	1964	0.7
1957	3.7	1965	0.7
1958	3.7	1966	0.7
1959	2.6		

Source: W. Vogt, *Die Wachstumszyklen der westdeutschen Wirtschaft* (Tübingen: J. C. B. Mohr, 1968), p. 16. See also West Germany, Presse- und Informationsamt der Bundesregierung, *Regierung Adenauer, 1949–1963* (Bonn: 1963), p. 697.

pockets of unemployment in Bavaria, Lower Saxony, and Schleswig-Holstein. At the end of 1952, these areas accounted for 56 per cent of all unemployment.[45] Parenthetically, unemployment was particularly heavy among refugees and expellees. By 1955, however, the rate of unemployment was down to 5.1 per cent.

With full employment, there were definite labor shortages.[46] By 1959, the recorded rate of unemployment fell to 2.6 per cent.[47] During this period of full employment, workers were offered noncontractual wage increases, and the number of vacancies remained five times as great as the number of unemployed.[48] It was at this point that German firms began to install labor-saving equipment and to import workers. In 1961, 550,000 foreigners worked in West Germany,[49] and total wages and salaries paid per employed person rose by over 10 per cent;[50] the year before, the increase had come to 9 per cent. Another by-product of the extremely tight labor market was the emergence of labor hoarding. Certain firms kept men on their payrolls even though the workers were superfluous, because they feared that laid-off workers would not be replaceable when needed. This led to costly hoarding of labor, which, in turn, checked the growth of productivity.[51]

By 1962, the labor shortage had reached extreme proportions. The

service industries felt the pinch acutely. A side effect was a decrease
in personal performance resulting from a declining zeal to work.
One manifestation was increased absenteeism.[52] In 1963 and 1964,
very tight labor markets continued and hundreds of thousands of
Italians, Greeks, Serbs, Spaniards, Turks, and Portuguese migrated
to West Germany. In 1966, the total of immigrant workers reached
1.24 million; they constituted 5.7 per cent of all wage and salary
earners.[53]

While the rate of unemployment fell from 7.5 per cent in 1953
to 3.7 per cent in 1957, the number of employed wage and salary
earners rose by two and a half million. In 1958, the unemployment
rate was 3.7 per cent, in 1959 2.6 per cent. In 1966 it remained at
less than one per cent for the sixth year in a row. From 1953 to 1966,
the number of employed wage and salary earners rose by six million,
truly a remarkable achievement!

Before 1959, the high level of employment was achieved not by
any artificial stimulation of demand, but by continued government
emphasis on providing powerful monetary incentives for both producers and consumers. As long as additional labor could be obtained,
the cost-of-living index was marked by considerable stability.[54] From
1953 to 1958 (the first six years of the Shilumim Agreement) the
cost-of-living index rose nine points, or 1.5 per cent a year. During
the same period, the price index of machinery and equipment rose
11 per cent.[55] The years before 1959 were also characterized by considerable wage restraint on the part of the German labor union
leaders. Knowing that the well-being of the workers was inextricably
tied up with export markets, they did not press for "all-you-can-get
wages." [56]

It was only in 1961, when manpower resources, especially skilled
labor, were virtually exhausted that the wage-price spiral got under
way. In that year, the cost-of-living index rose 2.6 per cent, while
the wage costs per unit of production jumped 6.2 per cent.[57]

Thus, from 1960 on, West Germany's chief domestic problem was
how to cope with inflation. Up to that year, the cost-of-living index
had risen by 1.5 per cent a year—a rate of inflation that does not
warp economic behavior because the monetary unit continues to
discharge its simultaneous functions as a store of value, a unit of
account, and a medium of exchange. But when the cost-of-living
index rises by more than 2 per cent a year, consumers as well as

producers anticipate further price-wage increases and their economic behavior usually becomes quite speculative, which makes sustained economic growth impossible. The West German achievement in the face of less than 1 per cent of unemployment for six years was remarkable, indeed unique in history, because in other countries, where considerable unemployment existed, the rate of inflation was greater.[58]

The Growth of Exports

According to H. C. Wallich, preoccupation (almost to the point of obsession) with exports was the sacred cow of the West German economic policy.[59] Throughout the 1950s and 1960s, the Federal Republic had an active commodity account, as shown in Table 8-3. Over the fourteen-year period of Shilumim payments, the average surplus in the commodity account was DM 5.1 billion marks. This gives rise to the question: What accounts for the German *export-freudigkeit* (literally, export-pleasure), as one expert called it? [60] In this period, exports grew at an annual rate of 13 per cent,[61] and imports at 11 per cent.[62] Many reasons have been offered to explain the perennial surpluses in the commodity account: inflationary

TABLE 8-3

GROWTH OF GERMAN COMMODITY SURPLUSES
(billions of DM) [a]

1953	+2.5	1960	+5.2
1954	+2.7	1961	+6.6
1955	+1.2	1962	+3.5
1956	+2.9	1963	+6.0
1957	+4.3	1964	+6.1
1958	+5.9	1965	+1.2
1959	+5.4	1966	+8.0

Source: *Statistisches Jahrbuch 1968*, p. 275.

[a] The values of imports are reckoned c.i.f. at the German frontier, i.e., including the costs of freight and insurance, while export values are f.o.b. If, however, exports and imports had been f.o.b., the export surplus would have been greater; but then freight and insurance costs would appear in the service account: see *Report of the Deutsche Bundesbank for the Year 1963*, p. 75.

trends abroad,[63] strong foreign demand for German investment goods,[64] undervaluation of the mark,[65] and other reasons.[66]

Merchandise transactions constitute only one item in the total export-import exchange program in a given period, which enables a country to earn, let us say, American dollars. For example, when West Germans sold Volkswagens in New York, the exporting firms either augmented their dollar balances in American banks or changed dollar proceeds into Deutsche Marks at home. In addition, West Germans could earn foreign currency by transporting commodities and passengers in their merchant ships. West Germans could also, in a sense, "export" scenery by attracting American tourists to their country. Tourism is always an excellent source of foreign currency; when Americans visit the Federal Republic, they usually exchange dollars for Deutsche Marks. Still another way for West Germany to obtain dollars would be through outright grants from the U.S. government for some purpose, such as resisting Communism, let us say. This type of transaction is called a unilateral transfer. The merchandise and service accounts together are called the current account, which shows the country's current earnings and expenditure status. If West Germany showed an import surplus on current account, then West Germans could export long-term or short-term promises to pay (IOUs) to the United States and receive in return American dollars. Such transactions are usually recorded in the capital account. Still another way would be to export gold and receive dollars. The sum total of payments of a given country to others, and by others to that country, is referred to as that country's balance of international payments. Current receipts (credits) always equal current obligations (debits), because what a country exports (commodities, services, or gold) should equal what it imports, plus or minus its foreign claims or indebtedness.

Thus, a country can offset an import surplus by: (1) borrowing long-term capital abroad, (2) unilateral transfers, (3) reducing investment abroad, (4) exporting gold holdings, and (5) using short-term credits.[67] From 1953 to 1966, the West German commodity account recorded a surplus in every single year. Since the export of commodities is undertaken for profit, a persistent surplus in the merchandise account automatically means that these autonomous transactions were profitable.[68]

In addition to earnings from commodity exports, shipping, and the like, services rendered to American troops contributed heavily to German foreign exchange earnings. From 1953 to 1964, West Germany had a favorable balance of transactions in commodities and services, and it was only in 1965 that a small deficit, in the amount of DM 46 million, was recorded.[69] This persistent export surplus of goods and services could have been offset by the export of long-term or short-term capital, building up investments abroad, the import of gold, or giving grants or nonreturnable donations to other nations.

Even though West Germany chose the last alternative and made large-scale unilateral transfers,[70] its balance of payments remained in persistent favorable disequilibrium. Capital funds, instead of flowing out of West Germany, flowed into the country, as a result of which the nation's monetary reserves and accumulation of gold increased uninterrupted, as can be seen from Table 8-4.

The stupendous growth of West Germany's gold reserves and the continuous influx of foreign exchange also increased the domestic currency supply, because exporters converted their dollar receipts into Mark balances. Had this process gone unchecked, West Germany might have suffered from what became known as "imported inflation." [71] To counter any inflationary consequences of the favor-

TABLE 8-4

WEST GERMAN GOLD AND TOTAL MONETARY RESERVES
(billions of DM)

Year	Gold holdings	Total monetary reserves (net)	Year	Gold holdings	Total monetary reserves (net)
1953	1,367	8,158	1960	12,479	31,628
1954	2,628	10,930	1961	14,654	28,281
1955	3,862	12,781	1962	14,716	27,729
1956	6,275	17,795	1963	15,374	30,301
1957	10,674	22,917	1964	16,992	30,313
1958	11,085	26,105	1965	17,639	28,807
1959	11,077	23,621	1966	17,167	29,837

SOURCE: *Report of the Deutsche Bundesbank for the year 1966*, p. 164.

able merchandise export balances, the influx of foreign exchange was neutralized by means of domestic credit deflation.[72]

The first minister of finance, Dr. Fritz Schäffer, preached and practiced the philosophy of balanced budgets in poor years and budget surpluses in good years. He ended the fiscal year 1952–1953 with a surplus in the federal budget of DM 1.05 billion.[73] This, incidentally, was the year when the outlook for West German exports had been deemed pessimistic.[74] By 1957, Dr. Schäffer's parsimony manifested itself in the accumulation of DM 7 billion of unspent federal funds.[75] Nevertheless, the restraint of domestic demand by credit deflation and the sterilization of budget surpluses were constantly threatened by the booming export business.

In an open economy, exports constitute (in addition to consumption expenditures, investment spending, and government outlays) the fourth element of the aggregate demand. An autonomous increase in exports, like an increase in autonomous domestic spending, results in multiple "respending rounds," which raise the level of national income in a multiple of the increase in exports. Such foreign-induced "injections" into the domestic-income stream produce magnifying effects on national income and employment. The continuous growth in the commodity exports of West Germany represented a series of extra additions to the aggregate demand, thus increasing national income and employment.[76]

No matter how impressive the accruals of gold and other hard currencies by West Germany, it is well to keep in mind that they were not caused solely by the surpluses in the commodity and service accounts. Foreign exchange kept on pouring into the country because of its higher interest rate and the persistence of rumors of an upward adjustment of the Deutsche Mark.[77] To discourage the influx of foreign capital, the Bundesbank reduced the interest rate to 3 per cent, which was the same level "as the discount rate of the Federal Reserve Banks in the United States; and . . . lower than that in all other industrial countries, except Switzerland. . . ."[78] By 1963, the Bundesbank reported that "everything ought to be done which might turn away foreign capital."[79] However, as can be seen from Table 8-4, West Germany's gold and foreign exchange holdings continued to grow up to 1965, yet this development was not regarded as dangerous by government authorities.[80] In fact, although there were chronic surpluses in the commodity account, those in charge refused to "inflate" the Deutsche Mark so as to catch up with inflation abroad.[81]

At the time Chancellor Adenauer signed the Luxemburg Treaty in 1952, the Federal Republic had patched up and, to a great extent, rebuilt its industrial plant. Yet per capita income was still below the 1938 level. More than one-third of its people lived in sub-standard housing. One-fifth of the population consisted of refugees and expellees, who were bitter and, in some cases, hopeless. The immediate economic future was clouded by uncertainty, even pessimism. At the time nobody could foresee the spectacular growth that was about to ensue. West Germany would grow rich and fat, but before that happy condition was even indicated its leaders had decided to make collective amends to Israel, as well as to pay individual compensation to all who had suffered during the Third Reich. And they had done so at a time when the new nation was still poor.

The Legal Framework for Implementation: The Yearly Protocols

The Luxemburg Treaty, signed on September 10, 1952, came into force on March 20, 1953, and the first payment of DM 200 million was due during the budget year 1952–1953, which ended March 31, 1953.[82] By March 31, 1954, another DM 200 million was to be paid to the government of Israel. Thereafter, the yearly installments were to vary between DM 250 and 310 million, and it was assumed that the higher rate would be paid. However, the Federal Republic could unilaterally reduce the sum to DM 250 million if it wished. For this reason, the entire obligation could be discharged in from twelve to fourteen years. One of the peculiarities of this agreement was that the government of Israel was to receive a fixed sum without any interest, although the total of DM 3.45 billion was a liability of the federal government of Germany.

If the going interest rate is 6 per cent a year, then the value of one Deutsche Mark is 94 pfennigs a year later.[83] At the prevailing interest rate of 6 per cent, one mark to be received in fourteen years was equivalent to .442 pfennigs in 1953. The other way around, .442 pfennigs invested in 1953 at 6 per cent would have grown into one Deutsche Mark in fourteen years with interest compounded annually. On the other hand, for the Israeli government the interest-free obligation of DM 3.45 billion meant that every mark due in 1953 was not allowed to grow to DM 2.26 in the fourteen-year period. Had West Germany committed itself to pay interest on the DM 3.45 billion, at a rate (r) of 6 per cent, then the principal (A) of DM 3.45 billion, after fourteen years would have grown into DM 7.8 billion, according to the pattern of the formula already in use.[84]

As soon as the Israel agreement came into force, the two contracting parties set up the Mixed Commission as the principal agency of implementation. It held the responsibility to determine the yearly delivery schedules, to decide on possible re-exports to third countries by Israel of German goods, to settle purchases of non-German origin, and to cope with other difficulties that might arise.

The German delegation consisted of representatives from the Bundesbank, and the ministries of economics, foreign affairs, labor, food and agriculture, finance, justice, and transportation. This broad representation was necessary to facilitate coping quickly with the varied and changing tasks. Its Israeli counterpart also represented all major sections of the government, including the Special Ministerial Committee which supervised the Shilumim payments.

The Mixed Commission met for the first time on May 18, 1953, and talks continued to June 16. On that date the first protocol was signed. It contained detailed regulations for the day-to-day implementation of the Agreement. These regulations were issued as *Runderlass Aussenwirtschaft* Nr. 51/53.[85] Subsequent implementation changes, amendments, and innovations were to be decided upon by the Mixed Commission and written into the yearly protocols.[86] The yearly protocols were signed after the Israelis and Germans had agreed on a number of broad categories of goods from which the Israelis could choose in each budget year. During the first few years of the Shilumim Agreement, the Mixed Commission adhered strictly to the commodity breakdown of Article 6 (d) of the original Schedule, according to which Israel was permitted to order DM 26.5 million from Commodity Group I (ferrous and nonferrous metals), DM 45.0 million from Group II (investment products), DM 35.0 million from Group III (products of the chemical industry), DM 3.5 million from Group IV (agricultural products), and DM 15.0 million from Group V (services), or a total of DM 125 million.[87] The remaining DM 75 million was to be paid in foreign exchange for the import of oil to Israel.

Israel soon found that year-to-year ordering was too restrictive. But by 1955 the initial schedule was revised, and Dr. Shinnar, the head of the Israel Mission, was permitted to order greater amounts of capital goods than provided for in the initial agreement.[88] The procedure was simple and flexible (the Israel Mission was the sole agency authorized to place orders with German firms, like any foreign buyer, while the Bundesamt für gewerbliche Wirtschaft, located in Frankfurt am Main, served as the supervisory agency): (1) The Israel Mission placed all orders on forms containing information on prices, terms of delivery, the budgetary allocation to be used for the particular order, the commodity type, name of the foreign trade bank, and the date of delivery. (2) This order form went to the Bundesamt for checking; it was then returned to the Israel Mission with the so-called Feststellungsvermerk (approval of the order and guarantee of payment). (3) With this in hand, the Israel Mission could place the orders with German firms. (4) The producer's bill, accompanied by proof that the commodity ordered was either of West German or West Berlin origin, went to the Bundesamt, via the Israel Mission. (5) The Bundesamt rechecked all entries and, if in order, returned the forms to the Mission with authorization for payment. (6) The Israel Mission then instructed the foreign trade bank to make payment. (7) Once payment was completed, the bank sent the seventh copy of the order to the Bundesamt.[89] This legal-administrative framework was spelled out in the regulations forming part of the first protocol. To husband foreign exchange and to stretch the funds as far as possible, the Germans had succeeded in including as part of the first protocol that employment of business agents by the Israel Mission was prohibited; in addition, goods of non-German origin could be ordered only in exceptional circumstances. Furthermore, freight costs could be defrayed from Shilumim funds only if German bottoms were used.

By the terms of the Agreement, the Federal Republic was to deliver DM 3.45 billion in goods, not outright foreign exchange, except for the payment for oil imports in pound sterling. At the conclusion of the Shilumim Agreement, DM 1.05 billion were paid in pounds sterling, one-third of the total.[90] The changing requirements of the rapidly transforming economy of Israel were reflected in the various protocols. Since these documents are still secret, their contents can be only briefly summarized from secondary and tertiary sources.[91] Two protocols (Nos. 2 and 3) were signed in 1954, on March 4 and August 5, respectively. The second permitted the Israelis to shift funds from one group of commodities to another within prescribed limits. It also allowed them to place advance orders for 1955 with manufacturers without asking for any additional funds. The Mission had to find sources of credit for interim financing.

The third protocol dealt with the temporary shifting of DM 55 million from the arrears of 1952 and 1953 to purchase urgently needed agricultural goods of non-German origin.[92] Some of the underdeveloped countries had accumulated large debts vis-à-vis West Germany, and these claims were used to pay for Israeli needs of rubber from Indonesia, hides from Argentina, sugar from Poland, and wheat from Turkey. It was also agreed that German shipping companies would carry 42.5 per cent of all freight in 1954, and 50 per cent in subsequent years.

The difficulty with the purchase system was that, at first, Dr. Shinnar could order nothing above the yearly quota. He was afraid that German funds would be dribbled away on items of little importance to the build-up of Israel's infrastructure or industry. Hence, as early as 1953, Dr. Shinnar wanted to write orders on account of future years, but without actually asking the Finanzministerium to make the sums available ahead of time.[93] This procedure was formalized in 1955 when two protocols were signed: No. 4 on February 17 and No. 5 on July 22. Accordingly, Israel was again permitted to buy agricultural products and raw materials of non-German origin, and to place some advance orders without asking for additional funds. From April 1, 1955, to March 31, 1956, Bonn would pay DM 75 million in sterling for British oil deliveries to Israel and DM 175 million in goods. For the first time there were substantial deviations from the original schedule, and the Israelis could order the following amounts: from Group II, DM 64 million, an increase of 42 per cent; from Group III, DM 40 million, an increase of 14 per cent; from Group IV, DM 12 million, an increase of more than 300 per cent, primarily for the purchase of raw materials; from Group V, DM 18 million, an increase of 20 per cent.[94]

The fifth protocol was a major breakthrough for Israel. After two years of experimentation, the Israeli government decided to utilize the Shilumim funds to accelerate its long-term growth. The Mission at Cologne submitted to the Mixed Commission a request for eleven industrial projects as well as plans for the expansion of the Israeli merchant fleet. The Israelis asked for permission to place advance orders of DM 280 million. The ordered items were to be delivered from 1956 to 1959, with payments to be made up to 1962 from the yearly installments due. The interest charges for the financing of these facilities by the banks and private firms was to be paid from Shilumim funds. This package request was approved by the Mixed Commission and became the celebrated "Investment Protocol." The Israelis had to find their own sources for the interim financing. The most important projects of this program were copperworks at Timna in the southern Negev, roughly at the point where King Solomon smelted copper; construction of a pig-iron plant; purchase of merchant and passenger ships; expansion of the railway network, including signaling equipment, Diesel cars, and railway coaches; purchase of pipe and pumping stations for the irrigation of part of the Negev desert; equipment for the expanding chemical industry; additional electrical power stations; and construction of a pipeline from Haifa to Tel Aviv.

The sixth protocol, signed on March 14, 1956, determined deliveries for the budget year 1956–1957.[95] The new delivery schedule made further changes in deference to Israeli wishes. For instance, the Mixed Commission permitted Israel an increase in goods from Group I from DM 41 million to DM 44 million. From Group II, the limit was raised from DM 64 million to DM 73.5 million, thus enabling Israel to order more investment goods. The purchases for Group III were lowered from DM 40 million to DM 35.0 million, as were the orders from Groups IV and V. The reductions in the two latter categories were from DM 12 million to DM 7.5 million and from DM 18 million to DM 15.0 million, respectively.[96] This protocol was a milestone because from here on the pattern of Israeli orders did not change. Year after year, the *Bundesanzeiger* recorded that the Federal Government made available DM 250 million to the Israeli Mission and that the 1956 delivery schedule remained unchanged.[97] By 1962, however, commodities worth DM 2.95 billion had been delivered to Israel, and for the next three years the Israelis merely received what had been ordered in prior years.[98]

Protocol No. 11, of June 20, 1960, was of some importance because it authorized changes in German foreign trade regulations. After that, Shilumim funds could be used to pay for services of business agents abroad and for German technicians to install and service industrial facilities in Israel. Costs of construction and repairs had to come from the development budget, not from the Shilumim funds, however. The permission to employ business agents was designed to develop closer contacts, on a purely commercial basis, between German sellers and Israeli buyers.

Protocol No. 12, of August 9, 1960, determined the disposition of the remaining Shilumim funds. The Israel Mission was again permitted to place advance orders and to pay for them from yearly installments.

The thirteenth to the eighteenth (and last) protocols made no changes in the composition of the deliveries. From 1961 on, the protocol-signing ceremony was a mere formality. By March 16, 1965, the date of the last protocol, 95 per cent of the total sum due had already been delivered to Israel (actually before the end of 1962).[99] Thus, there was a favorable difference between the nominal and actual implementation of the Shilumim Agreement.

The Yearly Allocations from the Federal Budget

Article 3 of the Agreement stipulated that the Federal Republic of Germany would discharge its obligation to Israel through yearly allocations from the budget. The Israelis had hoped to receive an annual appropriation of DM 310 million, but in 1954 Finance Minister Schäffer reduced this sum to the lowest permissible amount, DM 250 million.[100] This change, of course, meant that it would take fifteen years to discharge the obligation of DM 3.45 billion. With two payments of DM 200 million, prior to April 1, 1954, and twelve payments of DM 250 million, from April 1, 1954, to March 31, 1967, the total would come to DM 3.4 billion. The last DM 50 million would then have to be paid in the budget year extending from April 1, 1966, to March 31, 1967, fifteen years in all.[101]

What prompted the finance minister to act this way is hard to say. Well-known for his tight-fisted finance, he apparently felt that parsimony was absolutely necessary and that he could not spare more than DM 250 million a year. Yet, how is this to be reconciled with the fact that he finished the fiscal year 1952–1953 with a surplus of

DM 800 million,[102] and that the years 1953 and 1954 also showed substantial surpluses?[103] These surpluses augured well for the Shilumim Agreement because they demonstrated that the Bonn government had the funds to pay German manufacturers for Israel's orders without either resorting to printing money or going into debt. Moreover, from 1953 on, West Germany's commodity surpluses were growing at a surprisingly vigorous rate.

Politically, Dr. Schäffer's decision may have been a move to serve notice to the Allies and free-spending German politicians that without new taxes no additional funds would be available. Psychologically, however, it was a blunder of great magnitude. Public-opinion makers in the United States, Britain, and Israel suspected that the Germans were beginning to play tricks and that sooner or later they would find a way to repudiate what they had solemnly promised at Luxemburg. Economically, it was a mistake, too, because it not only prolonged the implementation period but also put more pressure on the economy, since a sizable portion of the orders were written when the country was operating under conditions of full employment. Had the finance minister been operating in the red, the Treasury could have used its credit-drawing rights at the Bundesbank in the amount of DM 1.5 billion a year and easily could have paid the full amount of DM 310 million annually. With the prevailing excess capacity in industry and heavy rate of unemployment (especially in the so-called "poverty pockets" along the eastern border), the extra DM 60 million of government expenditure a year could have provided extra jobs. However, as cannot be emphasized too strongly, throughout the 1950s the economic policy-makers in West Germany were much more concerned with how to increase the supply of goods, create incentives for labor and business, and safeguard the stability of the currency. Full employment, as an objective, did not enjoy the highest priority.

The appropriated sums were administered by the Ministry of Finance and credited to the account of the Israel Mission at the Deutsche Bundesbank. Legally, these sums were due annually on April 15 and August 15. The Agreement, formally terminated on March 31, 1966, was paid off in full in the course of the fourteen fiscal years of its implementation, as shown on Table 8-5.

Analysis of Table 8-5 reveals that the three data columns show different entries for most years, except from 1962 to 1965. All un-

TABLE 8-5

ANNUAL PAYMENTS

Fiscal year	Federal budget data [a]	Deutsche Bundesbank data [b]	Ebeling's Entwurf data [c]
1952–53	DM 80,005,000		
1953–54	DM 237,863,000	DM 268,000,000	DM 317,867,269.28
1954–55	DM 331,221,000	DM 354,000,000	DM 331,221,314.13
1955–56	DM 250,180,000	DM 267,000,000	DM 250,180,458.83
1956–57	DM 250,000,000	DM 245,000,000	DM 249,552,443.97
1957–58	DM 246,656,000	DM 225,000,000	DM 246,656,037.08
1958–59	DM 253,000,000	DM 261,000,000	DM 253,086,035.26
1959–60	DM 251,436,000	DM 266,000,000	DM 251,436,441.45
1960–61	DM 244,884,000	DM 259,000,000	DM 250,000,000.00
1961–62	DM 255,116,000	DM 255,000,000	DM 250,000,000.00
1962–63	DM 250,000,000	DM 250,000,000	DM 250,000,000.00
1963–64	DM 250,000,000	DM 250,000,000	DM 250,000,000.00
1964–65	DM 250,000,000	DM 250,000,000	DM 250,000,000.00
1965–66	DM 300,000,000	DM 300,000,000	DM 300,000,000.00
	DM 3,449,705,000	DM 3,450,000,000	DM 3,450,000,000.00

[a] *Bundeshaushaltsplan für das Rechnungsjahr 1954 (and 1955, 1956, 1957, 1958, 1959, 1960, 1961, 1962, 1963, 1964, 1965).*

[b] Deutsche Bundesbank.

[c] Bundesamt für gewerbliche Wirtschaft, *Die Durchführung des Abkommens vom 10. September zwischen der Bundesrepublik Deutschland und dem Staate Israel in den Jahren 1952–1962*, p. 63. For the final four sets of figures (fiscal 1962–63 on) see J. Ebeling, *Entwurf zu einem Abschlussbericht bzw. Ergänzungsbericht zu dem im Jahre 1962 seitens des Bundesamtes für gewerbliche Wirtschaft erstatteten Bericht aus Anlass des 10. Jahrestages der Unterzeichnung des Abkommens vom 10.9.1952 zwischen der Bundesrepublik und dem Staate Israel*, p. 7 (hereafter cited as *Ebeling's Entwurf*).

spent balances in any particular fiscal year could be carried over for future use by the Israel Mission. The fiscal year 1952–1953 ended on March 31, 1953, and the Bonn government was required to make the first payment before that date. It did; so that on March 24, 1953, the Israel Mission paid the first DM 70 million to the British-owned Shell Company for delivery of oil to Israel.[104] It took time, of course, for Israel to come up with a reasonably acceptable plan for an effective utilization of the Shilumim funds.

Officially, it took fourteen fiscal years to pay off the sum of DM 3.45 billion. Yet there is evidence to suggest that Bonn actually discharged its collective obligation toward Israel in a considerably shorter period. What does the record show?

The West German budgets and the official West German report on the implementation of the Israel Agreement show that the Israel Mission paid to the West German finance ministry, commercial banks, and private firms and corporations more than DM 14 million in interest charges.[105] In 1954, interest charges were DM 250,000; by 1959, they had risen to more than half a million DM; and by 1960, to DM 1.4 million. For the fiscal year 1965–1966, more than DM 2.6 million were so spent.[106] All interest costs were defrayed from the Group V allocations, which were not controlled by the Bundesamt für gewerbliche Wirtschaft.[107]

The ticklish question is: Why did the Israelis pay interest at all? Had not the Bonn government solemnly promised Israel DM 3.45 billion as a global compensation for material damages? They not only had, but they were most eager to discharge this obligation honorably, hoping that these "moral reparations" would both help Israel to consolidate its economy and improve Bonn's image abroad. How, then, is it possible to reconcile Bonn's collecting interest from Israel on account of prepaying the yearly allocations, while at the same time refusing to pay interest on the entire DM 3.45 billion obligation?

The Israelis wanted to collect the sum due as quickly as possible for a number of reasons. For example, during the first couple of years after the ratification of the Agreement, the Jews in the Diaspora and many Israelis doubted seriously the integrity of Bonn's promise to deliver goods. Although Dr. Shinnar apparently never took these prophets of doom seriously,[108] this pessimistic outlook caused the Israelis to place a few rather hasty orders with West German shipyards for ships as well as a controversial floating dock, which would make possible repairs to ships of 7,500 tons in Haifa. New ships, as a rule, possess international liquidity; that is, they can be sold quickly and at a good price. Furthermore, by ordering ships, the Israelis hoped to tie the hands of the German government, since the delivery period for a ship usually stretches across years.[109]

Expected future price rises were another consideration. The Agreement did not provide for the stability of the Deutsche Mark, so if prices rose by 10 per cent during the period of implementation, the Israeli government stood to lose that much.[110] Thus, to prevent the evaporation of Israel's purchasing power through a future inflation in the Federal Republic, a speedy ordering of goods seemed indicated.

Chronic stopgap conditions in Israel also threatened the DM 3.45 billion. Some Israeli leaders feared that, for reasons of political expediency, a "muddling through" utilization of the funds would simply "eat them up . . . without preparing the economy to stand on its own feet." [111] Hillel Dan, first director of the Shilumim Corporation of Tel Aviv, was very much afraid of just such a possibility. For this reason, he asked Dr. S. Trone, one-time chief engineer for the General Electric Company, to prepare a long-term plan utilizing Shilumim funds for the development of Israel's infrastructure.[112] However, Dr. Trone's report, which recommended the development of utilities, transportation, and electricity and water resources, was largely ignored by the government of Israel.[113] Director Dan complained that government orders for capital goods "were slow in coming," and stated that he wanted to use the incoming funds for the development of electricity, communications, irrigation, and shipping, a lasting monument in Israel to the Jewish suffering in the Diaspora.[114] He argued that the only proper use of these funds was one contributing to an "industrial revolution in Israel." [115] In 1953, a parallel argument said, Israeli purchases were "dictated more by the immediate needs of the economy rather than by the requirements of an over-all long-term development." [116] Without such a plan, a writer in *The Israel Economist* wondered "whether the government will prove alive to the opportunity or whether the Reparation funds, too, will be expended disproportionately on goods destined for current consumption." [117]

The breakthrough came in 1955, when the Israel Mission submitted for the approval of the Mixed Commission an investment program of DM 280 million. It was only then that Dr. Shinnar could coordinate a purchase schedule as a vital part of Israel's long-term development program. Hillel Dan was dismissed from his post as head of the Shilumim Corporation in 1955,[118] but not before he had prevented certain Israeli politicians from dribbling away the DM 3.45 billion for purposes of producing political dividends.

Speedier fulfillment of the Shilumim Agreement for any or all of these reasons did not imply a violation of its terms. True, accelerated implementation was not written into the Agreement, *expressis verbis,* but it was in strict conformity with Article 4, which stipulated that the Federal Republic of Germany "will endeavour, by increasing the annual installments, to pay the sum payable in pursuance of Article 1 of the present Agreement, *within a period of time shorter than that which would result from all or any of the provisions of Article 3, paragraph (a).*" The flexible interpretation of Article 4 thus enabled both parties to implement the Agreement to their mutual advantage,[119] and the Bonn government to give favorable consideration to most Israeli requests.

The Arab press, unfortunately, asserted repeatedly that substantial sums, over and above the Agreement, were paid to Israel. Their charges were eagerly picked up by the East German press and right-wing critics in the Federal Republic. Because newspaper controversy inflamed minds, regardless of the evidence, the German government decided to release very little information on the matter in order to avoid battles in the press.

What specific form did these accelerated payments take? How were they handled administratively? How costly did they turn out to be for Israel? Documented information on these subjects is still scant. Personal interviews with Israeli and German government officials and Dr. Shinnar's memoirs constitute the few known available sources of information. The facts show that four types of speed-up arrangements emerged: *"Vorgriff,"* prefinancing, interim financing, and loans.

The German term *Vorgriff* (literally, anticipation) was used to designate the pre-ordering of goods from future allocations of annual receipts. This technique enabled the Israel Mission to place binding orders with German firms for many expensive projects, to be paid for in future years as the installments fell due, without asking the West German Ministry of Finance for the funds in advance. The first major *Vorgriff* took place in 1955, when Dr. Shinnar was given permission to place orders for investment goods and ships for delivery from 1956 through 1959.[120] The total cost of this package deal came to DM 280 million. More precisely, the Israel Mission placed bids, to be financed by the Shilumim funds, for eleven industrial projects deemed of crucial importance for the development of Israel's economy.

The techniques of prefinancing (*Vorfinanzierung*) were numerous. For example, the Finance Ministry would deposit the entire annual payment, or a portion, to the credit of the Israel Mission at the Bundesbank in January, instead of on the statutory dates of April 15 and August 15. For such favors, the ministry earned interest ranging from 2 per cent to $3\frac{1}{4}$ per cent, per annum. Or, the Finance Ministry would make available to the Israel Mission on April 15 and August 15 DM 37.5 million, deposited in an English bank, regardless of whether the oil had been delivered or not. The Germans were required to pay for the oil only after the presentation of invoices. Because the advance payments were made, however, the Israelis had additional foreign exchange at their disposal, and the Finance Ministry again earned interest income. Again, according to a mid-1955 ruling of the Mixed Commission, the Finance Ministry was to make payments quarterly. If a particular bill had to be paid in the preceding quarter, the Finance Ministry would advance the money and charge the Israel Mission an agreed-upon interest. It was stipulated, however, that manipulation of the funds due should never exceed the yearly installment of DM 250 million.[121]

Interim financing (*Zwischenfinanzierung*) was used to pay for large items. For example, once a particular order was approved by the Bundesamt, a down payment of 20 per cent usually was required. Another 20 per cent was due at an agreed time, and the balance at the time of delivery. Many Israeli purchases were financed by private German banks, such as the Sol Oppenheim Jr. & Cie. Bank of Cologne. In 1955, Finance Minister Schäffer gave the Israel Mission an interim credit of DM 40 million for one year at a very low interest rate.[122] Interest payments on all interim financing were met from Group V funds.

Last, and most important, in the loan type of speed-up arrangement was the DM 450 million put up by the Deutsche Bank in 1958 to pay the last two installments ahead of time.[123] The story of this transaction goes back to early 1958, when Dr. Shinnar flew to the United States, hoping to be able to arrange a loan to enable the German government to speed up the implementation of the Shilumim program. This possibility was within the letter and spirit of the Agreement of 1952, Article 4 (b), which stated that if the Federal Republic obtained "an external loan or any other financial relief from external sources in a currency generally and freely convertible and destined exclusively for the purpose of financing the obligation undertaken in Article 1, the entire proceeds of such a loan or relief shall be used for such purpose, and shall be applied to the last annual installment payable under the present Agreement." Dr. Shinnar came back with a promise from the Bank of America that such a loan could be arranged.[124]

For the Bonn government, with gold and foreign exchange balances piling up embarrassingly, it was out of the question that West Germans should borrow abroad. But after secret negotiations, Dr. Hermann J. Abs, president of the Deutsche Bank and Dr. Shinnar's adversary in 1952, granted the Israel Mission a loan of DM 450 million at the prevailing long-term interest rate of 6 per cent per annum. Abs' bank received as collateral a promise to pay out of future Shilumim payments by the Finance Ministry. On the surface, this transaction appeared to be *"bombensicher"* (absolutely safe). Yet many serious objections were raised against it and only those who negotiated it know how hard it was to arrange. Dr. Shinnar, head of the Israel Mission, admitted that, in his view, no other banker in the world would have given him this loan.[125] The statement was the supreme compliment to Dr. Abs from a high-ranking Israeli. It was also one way to express gratitude for all the good will manifested by numerous responsible Germans in all walks of life, who did their best to pay off the monstrous material mortgage of the Nazi years. Again, it must be recalled, the two parties knew that only the material part of this mortgage could be settled. But this material settlement, so it was hoped, would lead to an Israeli-German dialogue. What, then, were the arguments against this transaction, when on the surface it looked so safe, with the Finance Ministry still committed to pay DM 250 million for a number of years and the Deutsche Bank holding a first claim on them?

Despite their defeat during the 1956 Sinai campaign, the Arabs, and especially Egypt's President Nasser, continued to proclaim to the world that Israel was doomed and that one day all the Jews would be pushed into the sea.[126] In the Western world nobody really took these threats seriously, but a banker cannot have enough security. Since the Shilumim Agreement was a political, not an economic, document, Dr. Abs had to keep in mind some of the implications of the Arab threats. For instance, had Egypt's threat materialized, the Bonn government would presumably no longer have had to pay Israel, since that nation would have ceased to exist. In that eventuality, had he granted the DM 450 million, he would never have collected a penny of it (especially since this transaction was not insured by the Hermes Corporation, which specializes in taking over some of the risks of German exporters). Another threat that faced Dr. Abs was the possibility that the Finance Ministry, for whatever reason, would not pay all or a portion of the outstanding Shilumim obligations. Undoubtedly he could have sued the Finance Ministry, but such action would have unquestionably been difficult, costly, and time-consuming.[127]

The principal objection to this transaction was much simpler and had to do, primarily, with the operations of a commercial bank. As such, the Deutsche Bank was concerned with profitability and liquidity. Profitability can frequently be attained at the expense of illiquidity, and excess liquidity can cost or even impair profitability. Discounting all the political risks, the DM 450 million loan, at the prevailing long-term rate of interest, was obviously a profitable transaction, so that little objection could be made to it on that score. What was more difficult to rationalize were two liquidity aspects of the transaction. First, the loans of the Deutsche Bank were normally granted for no longer than four years. But in this case, the first maturity date was set at almost three and a half years after the loan was negotiated, and the last payment was due on August 15, 1965. In total, the Israel Mission committed itself to repay the entire loan in eight equal maturities of DM 62.5 million, which meant that the loan was extended over just about twice the normal repayment period.[128] The second liquidity factor was that in 1958 the size of this loan amounted to roughly one-sixth of all Deutsche Bank loans outstanding! This put the Israel Mission in the position of being the most important debtor of the Deutsche Bank. Thus, it was probably for reasons of bank liquidity, as well as the desire not to arouse the Arabs, that this transaction was kept secret for such a long time.

In the end, however, everything turned out well. Dr. Abs' bank made money, and the Israelis took possession of goods sooner and at better prices than would otherwise have been possible. The Finance Ministry continued to make the yearly installments available to the Israel Mission on January 1, instead of April 15 and August 15, and with these funds Dr. Shinnar was able to pay off portions of the Deutsche Bank loan. Funds from the Treasury, at 2 to 2½ per cent interest, were much cheaper than funds from the Deutsche Bank at 6 per cent. The actual quarter-by-quarter payments show that from

1962 on the Israel Mission paid off bills for orders placed in prior years, which indicates that, after 1961, few orders were placed by the Israelis within the framework of the Shilumim Agreement.[129]

Deliveries of Goods and Services

In the course of fourteen years, West Germany delivered goods and services worth DM 2.4 billion and paid in pounds sterling for British deliveries of oil to Israel DM 1.05 billion.[130] The various goods were bought in accordance with certain specifications and were divided into various categories. A breakdown of what was bought, under the various categories, is shown in Table 8-6.

Of a total of some DM 391 million spent on Group I purchases, 70 per cent went for structural bars, large pipes, sheet plates, and steel strip. By the end of 1957, the Israelis had received 150,000 tons of structural steel, 512,000 tons of bulk steel, 160 kilometers' length of steel rails, and 110,000 tons of irrigation pipe—with a total value of DM 258 million.[131] Orders for these items were particularly heavy because of the rapid pace of Israel's industrialization. New industrial plants, pumping stations, irrigation networks, roads, and improvements in the entire communications network came in rapid succession. As shown in Table 8-6, 11.5 per cent went for goods of the iron- and steel-producing industry.[132]

During the first few years of the Agreement, in addition to building materials, the Israelis also ordered large quantities of industrial and agricultural raw materials. For instance, in 1954 and 1955 the acute shortage of raw materials in Israel frequently made continuous operations in certain industries impossible. To ameliorate these conditions, the Israel Mission ordered substantial amounts of raw rubber, raw hides, thread, and wood, as well as wheat and sugar.

The lion's share, 55 per cent, of all orders was written for Group II capital goods, which consisted of machinery, ships, turbines, and precision instruments. One-quarter of all purchases in this category, a sum of DM 586 million, was spent on ships. Israel acquired a total of fifty-nine vessels of different types and one floating dock. To achieve this, thirteen German shipyards delivered forty-one freighters, four tankers, two passenger ships for the Mediterranean service and two for the trans-Atlantic runs to the Americas, eight fishing cutters, two customs cruisers, and the aforementioned floating dock.[133]

TABLE 8-6

ORDERS FOR GOODS AND SERVICES PLACED BY THE ISRAEL MISSION,
1953–1965

	In 1,000 DM	Per cent
Group I: Steel, Ferrous and Nonferrous Metals		
Goods of the iron- and steel-producing industry	274,292	11.5
Products of the foundry industry	20,814	0.8
Drawn and cold-rolled iron and steel products	28,866	1.2
Products of the nonferrous metal industry	66,815	2.8
	390,787	16.3
Group II: Steel and Metal-Processing Industries		
Machine-building	315,385	13.2
Motor vehicle industry	24,582	1.0
Steel construction	129,949	5.4
Ship-building	585,572	24.4
Electrical equipment industry	223,125	9.3
Precision industry/optical instruments	20,321	0.9
Iron, steel, and tin goods	27,501	1.1
	1,326,944	55.3
Group III: Chemical and Other Industries		
Rubber, asbestos	18,106	0.7
Chemical and pharmaceutical products	159,629	6.7
Textiles	74,766	3.1
Wood-working industry	35,766	1.5
Leather	12,583	0.5
Stones and earths	13,877	0.6
Ceramics and glass products	14,000	0.6
Mineral-oil industry and mining	8,198	0.3
	336,925	14.0
Group IV: Agricultural Products	91,217	3.8
Group V: Services (insurance, freight, etc.)	254,127	10.6
Total, Groups I–V	2,400,000	100.0
Oil Deliveries from Great Britain	1,050,000	
Total, all orders from the Israel Mission	3,450,000	

Source: J. Ebeling, *Bericht über die Durchführung des Abkommens zwischen der Bundesrepublik Deutschland und dem Staate Israel vom 10. September 1952* (Bonn: Bundesminister für Wirtschaft, 1966), p. 26.

By 1957, the Israelis had completed the basic structures and buildings and were in need of the tools and machinery to equip them. From that year on, orders of this nature were written on a large scale.[134] For instance, in Group II, almost DM 316 million worth of orders were placed with German machine-building industries. In the machinery category, the Israelis received textile machinery, motors, lathes, equipment for the chemical industry, wood-working equipment, road-building machinery, locomotives, pumps, agricultural machinery, equipment for sugar factories, and office equipment.

Third place within Group II went to the electrical equipment industry. With the rapid industrialization of the country, new sources of power became indispensable for further progress. To effect the necessary growth, the Israelis ordered and the Germans delivered five power stations, which raised the electricity generating output of Israel from 175,000 kW to 635,000 kW, almost a fourfold increase. In addition to the delivery of complete power-generating plants, the Germans provided thousands of meters (hundreds of miles) of cable and power lines, modern teletype equipment for the Israeli Post Office, and electromedical equipment for hospitals. Because of these deliveries, telephone and telegraph services were greatly improved. For instance, long-distance dialing equipment was made automatic and large modern teleprinters were installed. The total spent for these purchases was DM 223 million.

The German members of the Mixed Commission were appreciative of the rapid growth of the Israeli economy. They therefore lent a sympathetic ear to the growing requests for more investment goods and approved the increase in these orders as well as the corresponding reductions in Groups III and IV.

For agricultural products in Group IV, a total of DM 91 million, or 3.8 per cent of the total commodity purchases, was spent. Delivery of wood, primarily for railroad ties and telephone poles, and pulp for the paper-making industry accounted for DM 36 million. DM 13 million was spent for non-German rawhides, while DM 14 million went for the purchase of stones for furnace construction.

The outlay for Group V, covering services such as interest payments, transportation costs of shipments made in German bottoms, insurance costs, and administrative expenses, on the average came to DM 15 million a year. These expenditures were not subject to supervision by the Bundesamt. Instead, Dr. Shinnar, on behalf of the Israel Mission, spent these sums as he saw fit.

An interesting development in this category was the substantial increase in expenditures from roughly DM 15 million a year earlier to DM 21.5 million in 1961, and to DM 54.7 million in 1965. Why was there such a substantial increase at the very end of the Shilumim Agreement? For the answer, another review must be made of the terms of the 1952 Luxemburg Treaty, by which the Government of Israel incurred the obligation to refund the value of certain property belonging to specified religious organizations, and to make payments for damages which resulted from the fighting in 1948. For instance, the International Union of Lutherans in Geneva, the Archbishopric of Cologne, and the owners of property belonging to the members of the Order of St. John of Jerusalem—the Knights Templar—were the principal claimants.[135] For a long time, the parties involved could not agree on the value of the property. Professor Max Sörensen, a Danish international lawyer, was asked to mediate. On the basis of his recommendations, the sum of DM 54 million was agreed upon.[136] Since most of the Templars were living in Australia, the Bonn government signed a special agreement to settle this outstanding obligation.[137] Israel's perennial shortage of foreign exchange was probably responsible for the tardy discharge of this obligation, and it finally took some pressure on the part of the German officials to convince the Israelis that it was high time to make settlement. The total of DM 62.3 million was distributed as follows: [138]

The International Union of Lutherans of Geneva	DM	3,585,000
The Archbishopric of Cologne	DM	500,000
Compensation for the secular property of the members of the Order of St. John of Jerusalem	DM	54,000,000
plus payments to the Jewish organization in West Germany by request of the Claims Conference	DM	4,200,000
	DM	62,285,000

The obligation of DM 75 million in pounds sterling for British deliveries of oil to Israel was written into the Shilumim Agreement by letters Nos. 4A and 4B.[139] In total, the Israelis received DM 1,050 million for such oil deliveries. These amounts were usually deposited at some London bank. In that fashion, the steadily growing demand for oil, at least for the time being, could be satisfied. For fourteen years, German payments covered roughly 28 per cent of Israel's consumption of oil and oil products. Upon the termination of Shilumim payments, Israel had to spend export proceeds for gasoline imports.

In addition to making collective compensation to the government of Israel, the Bonn government also began to make individual compensation payments in accordance with Protocol No. 1. The total payments to Israel's government and its citizens from 1953 to the end of 1965, the sum of DM 7,758 million, are broken down in Table 8-7.

TABLE 8-7

WEST GERMAN PAYMENTS TO ISRAEL
SHILUMIM AGREEMENT AND INDIVIDUAL COMPENSATION
(millions of DM) [a]

Year	Shilumim Agreement	Individual compensation	Total to Israel	Total of all "moral reparation" payments
1953	268	0	268	268
1954	354	39	393	508
1955	267	88	355	617
1956	245	172	417	924
1957	225	296	521	1,396
1958	261	314	575	1,505
1959	266	367	633	1,738
1960	259	480	739	2,259
1961	255	496	751	2,750
1962	250	557	807	2,740
1963	250	593	843	2,530
1964	250	494	744	2,104
1965	300	422	722	2,223
1953–1965	3,450	4,318	7,768 [b]	21,562

Source: Deutsche Bundesbank.

[a] The Annual Reports of the Bank of Israel show variations in the figures for individual years, but totals do not differ significantly. The discrepancy is due in part to the release of blocked marks in 1953 and 1954, and in part to "prepayment" techniques for goods and services used by the Bundesfinanzministerium. For this reason, the nominal DM 250 million figures shown for the years 1962–1964 are not meaningful. By 1962, almost 95 per cent of the total payment value was already in Israel.

[b] From 1956 to 1966, West Germany spent $7.1 billion on foreign aid, which equals DM 28.4 billion.

As can be seen, the payments for individual compensation were larger than for the collective Shilumim compensation, the subject of this volume. But individual compensation brought a large influx of West German marks that contributed so substantially to the economic transformation of Israel, a development germane to the subject at hand. For West Germany, its government's commitment to pay for the material damages suffered by the Jews at the hands of the Nazi government had two effects: economic and political. The economic effects touched such variables as Gross National Product, employment, and exports, while the political effect was the emergence of a better public image of West Germany abroad.

9

The Impact on West Germany

The Shilumim Agreement had both an economic and a political impact on West Germany. The consequences of the thousands of large and small orders were felt in several sectors of the economy; and the faithful, quiet, and smooth discharge of all the obligations arising out of the Luxemburg Treaty contributed to a more acceptable image for Bonn in the Western world during the 1950s and 1960s.

In 1952, during the Wassenaar negotiations, most European and American economists expected hard times ahead, especially after the end of the Korean conflict. No one could foresee that the under-developed two-thirds of the world would wake up and embrace the creed of economic progress through change. The Germans themselves looked toward the future pessimistically. They were primarily concerned with achieving the ability to discharge and service foreign debts and earn enough foreign exchange to pay for indispensable imports. Talk of a future export boom of machinery and capital goods was simply discounted.

In 1953 West Germany had both idle and insufficient capacities in many sectors of its economy. Millions of bitter and unemployed expellees and refugees crowded into camps in the depressed areas near the border of East Germany. The specter of unprecedented large-scale unemployment haunted economists and politicians alike. Fearing the worst, some German delegates at Wassenaar probably felt that the Shilumim Agreement could be used indirectly as a small-scale public works program to take up the slack in industry and to reduce the level of unemployment. After all, two-thirds of the

DM 3.45 billion was to be paid in goods, and payments in kind, under conditions of industrial under-utilization and involuntarily idle manpower, made sense. Moreover, payments in kind were likely to prevent dissipation of precious gold and dollar reserves.[1]

The Shilumim Agreement was unique,[2] and unique events and phenomena in the course of time constitute material for the economic historian. In the view of Joseph A. Schumpeter, the great Austrian economist of the twentieth century, economics deals essentially with unique processes in historic time, and the proper understanding of economic phenomena of any epoch, including our own, calls for both a command of factual knowledge and an adequate historical sense, that is, a sense of the spirit of the times. He admonished economists to pay more attention to the *Zeitgeist*, to acquire more historical experience, in order to avoid blunders in economic analysis.[3]

An economic historian evaluating the Shilumim Agreement must ask: How representative? How often? How long? How large? [4] The question "How representative?" has already been answered. No nation had ever made payments to another for material damages on a collective basis. The question "How often?" has also been answered. Collective compensation and individual indemnification for material damages was a singular event. These payments should not be confused with restitution of identifiable property to former owners, a practice of long standing.

The question "How long?" has two parts. The Shilumim obligation has been discharged in full. Nominally it ran for fourteen years, but actually the DM 3.45 billion was paid in twelve years. Individual compensation payments still continue and, according to some estimates, by 1975 the total cost of the Luxemburg Treaty will have been DM 46 billion, and by 2000 over DM 62 billion.[5] By the end of 1966, DM 23.2 billion [6] had been transferred abroad and DM 8.1 billion [7] paid to German residents for material damages. The question "How large?" can best be answered by relating the Shilumim outlays to the G.N.P. and to the size of the Federal Budget,[8] as shown in Table 9-1.

A country's ability to make payments abroad in gold or universally accepted currency depends upon its capacity to raise extra tax or other revenues domestically, and to convert domestic funds into foreign currency. The first is a fiscal problem, whereas the second is a balance-of-payments adjustment problem.[9] Two-thirds of the

DM 3.45 billion Shilumim obligation was discharged in German-made goods and one-third (DM 1.05 billion) in pounds sterling for British-delivered oil. Thus, the real transfer, or balance-of-payments adjustment problem, was very minor. Had the West German government not paid for the oil, it would have been by-passed completely.

The real burden of the Shilumim payments manifested itself in the reduction of current domestic consumption and of investment out of Gross National Product. Each year the Bonn government had to raise the extra sums to pay for the Shilumim goods. But because of the rapid rise of West Germany's G.N.P., the resulting *real burden* was light, not heavy, as column 5 of Table 9-1 shows. In 1953, Shilumim's cost was less than one-fifth of 1 per cent of the G.N.P.; in 1954 it rose to slightly over one-fifth of 1 per cent. From 1955 to 1959, it was one-tenth of 1 per cent, and thereafter, less than one-tenth of 1 per cent.[10] Column 6 shows the proportion of Federal expenditures made for Shilumim goods. This was 1.35 per cent in 1953, 1.69 per cent in 1954, 1.19 per cent in 1955, and under 1 per cent thereafter.

In addition to paying for the Shilumim Agreement, in 1954 West Germany started to *transfer* funds abroad in lump sums and in monthly payments to individual victims of the Nazi regime. These payments were made directly in the form of foreign exchange. For example, in 1954 West Germany transferred abroad a total of DM 508 million, 77 per cent of which went to Israel. In 1955, as column 7 shows, Israel received DM 355 million of foreign exchange from Bonn's treasury: 88 million in foreign exchange, 75 million in sterling for British-delivered oil, and 192 million in goods. In 1957 individual compensation payments exceeded Shilumim payments, and they continued to do so by a considerable margin until 1965. Column 8 shows that both kinds of payments to Israel constituted almost one-quarter of 1 per cent of West Germany's G.N.P. in 1954, 1957, 1958, and 1960, and exactly one-quarter of 1 per cent in 1959. In 1963 these outlays still claimed more than one-fifth of 1 per cent of the G.N.P., and in 1965 they amounted to 0.15 of 1 per cent. The same payments, shown in column 9 as a percentage of the yearly expenditures of the Bonn treasury, came to 1.87 per cent in 1953, reached the peak of 2.44 per cent in 1960, and declined to 1.12 per cent in 1965. From 1953 to 1965, Israel received DM 3.45 billion from the Shilumim Agreement and DM 4.3 billion from the individual compensation payments.

(1) Year	(2) West German G.N.P. current prices (billions of DM)	(3) Federal expendi- tures (billions of DM)	(4) Shilumim (millions of DM)	(5) Shilumim as per- centage of G.N.P. (4):(2)	(6) Shilumim as per- centage of federal expendi- tures (4):(3)
1952	137	20.4	—	—	—
1953	147	19.7	268	0.18	1.35
1954	158	21.0	354	0.22	1.69
1955	180	22.4	267	0.14	1.19
1956	199	27.7	245	0.12	0.88
1957	216	31.5	225	0.10	0.71
1958	232	33.4	261	0.11	0.78
1959	251	36.5	266	0.10	0.72
1960	297	31.2	259	0.08	0.85
1961	326	45.0	255	0.07	0.56
1962	354	49.9	250	0.07	0.50
1963	378	54.4	250	0.06	0.45
1964	414	57.8	250	0.06	0.43
1965	453	64.2	300	0.06	0.46
1966	481	67.3	—	—	—

Source: Deutsche Bundesbank data and author's calculations.

Columns 10, 11, and 12 show the amounts transferred abroad for *Wiedergutmachung* purposes, which totaled DM 21.5 billion. In 1953 moral reparation payments represented one-third of 1 per cent of the G.N.P. and claimed 2.42 per cent of the federal expenditures. In 1957 and 1958 they constituted 0.64 of 1 per cent of the G.N.P., and the respective shares of the federal expenditures were 4.43 and 4.50 per cent. In 1960 almost 7.5 per cent of Bonn's expenditures

9-1

MORAL REPARATIONS

(7) Total payments to Israel (millions of DM)	(8) Total payments to Israel as percentage of G.N.P. (7):(2)	(9) Total payments to Israel as percentage of federal expenditures (7):(3)	(10) Total moral reparation payments abroad (millions of DM)	(11) Total moral reparation payments abroad as percentage of G.N.P. (10):(2)	(12) Total moral reparation payments abroad as percentage of federal expenditures (10):(3)
—	—	—	—	—	—
—	—	—	—	—	—
393	0.24	1.87	508	0.32	2.42
355	0.19	1.58	617	0.34	2.75
417	0.20	1.50	924	0.46	3.34
521	0.24	1.65	1,396	0.64	4.43
575	0.24	1.72	1,505	0.64	4.50
633	0.25	1.73	1,738	0.69	4.75
739	0.24	2.44	2,259	0.76	7.48
751	0.23	1.66	2,750	0.84	6.11
807	0.22	1.61	2,740	0.77	5.49
843	0.22	1.55	2,530	0.66	4.65
744	0.17	1.28	2,104	0.50	3.64
722	0.15	1.12	2,223	0.49	3.46
419	0.08	0.61	1,653	0.30	2.45

went for external *Wiedergutmachung* purposes. After 1961 these expenditures declined from 6.11 per cent in that year to 3.46 per cent in 1965. Compared with the burden of Soviet-imposed reparations on Finland after World War II (in 1945, for example, reparation payments constituted 7.6 per cent of the Net National Product and 20.9 per cent of state expenditures), West Germany's moral reparations were not heavy.[11] Although Bonn's reparations were not proportional to Finland's, it should be kept in mind that in addition to the DM 23.2 billion West Germany transferred abroad between 1953 and 1966, an extra DM 8.1 billion was paid in individual compensation to German residents.[12] Further, the Bonn government has paid DM 1 billion in global compensation to twelve countries for material losses sustained by their citizens.[13]

Adenauer's policy of external *Wiedergutmachung* would have been politically impossible without large-scale compensation to millions of Germans who had lost property during World War II. The Law of Emergency Aid of 1949 introduced a 3 per cent levy on all physical property, based on the value of the property as of June 21, 1948.[14] Between 1949 and 1952, while this law was on the books, DM 6.2 billion was collected and used for immediate relief. The Equalization of Losses Law of 1952 imposed a 50 per cent levy on physical property as assessed on June 21, 1948, and 100 per cent on all inflation and currency reform windfalls of debtors.[15] This levy, which will be paid quarterly up to March 31, 1979, is expected to raise more than DM 88 billion.[16] By the end of 1961 DM 42.3 billion had been paid to nine different categories of recipients.[17] By the end of 1966 DM 59.1 billion had been paid.[18] In 1953, for instance, 6.3 per cent of all federal expenditures was budgeted for this purpose; [19] in 1955 these expenditures were 7.7 per cent.[20] In 1962, 4.9 per cent of the total federal expenditures was so used,[21] and in 1965 the percentage was 3.4.[22]

From 1948 to 1962, DM 289 billion were paid for the consequences of the lost war.[23] Of this sum, 7 per cent went for *Wiedergutmachung*, or moral reparations.[24] Even though 7 per cent seems to be a small sum, from the standpoint of domestic politics it was a heavy burden. After all, payments from the Equalization of Losses fund went to millions of voting Germans, while the billions that were transferred abroad went to a relatively small number of people. Nevertheless, every chancellor of the Federal Republic of Germany has defended and continued these payments. They have been made for moral as well as political reasons, and no matter how strong the pressures to end or reduce them, they have been continued. The Bonn government thus deserves credit for its external *Wiedergutmachung*, for making payments that heretofore have been unknown in the annals of mankind.

Whereas the economic historian is concerned with Shilumim's uniqueness, the economist wants to know how Israel's DM 2.4 billion worth of orders of various goods affected West Germany's employment, G.N.P., industrial production, and foreign trade. He can use two methodological approaches to determine those effects: input-output analysis and multiplier analysis.

The input-output table is a shorthand quantitative presentation of an economy which shows the interdependence of its different branches.[25] Changes in the output of one industry will have some impact on all sectors of the economy. If the shipbuilding industry, for example, wants to increase its output by 10 per cent, it will require larger inputs from all other industries which supply it. This means that the output of these suppliers will also have to rise. But since they will want to produce more, the suppliers, in turn, will require larger inputs from other industries. Thus there will be seemingly infinite rounds of adjustments, assuming no bottlenecks. In conditions of general equilibrium, each sector of the economy would produce only that number of its products required by all other branches, and none would remain unsold. This method is not useful for our purposes here, however, because the Shilumim goods produced in the course of a decade represented only a minuscule fraction of the outputs of various industries, with the exception of shipbuilding.

Because Israel's orders for Shilumim-financed goods served as "injections," so to speak, into the West German economy, the multiplier analysis method can perhaps best reveal some of their effects on the utilization of West Germany's industrial capacity and on employment.

In traditional macro-economic theory a given level of national income is explained in terms of consumption, private investment, government spending, and net exports. When conditions of under-employment exist, with involuntarily idle manpower and excess industrial capacity, aggregate supply exceeds aggregate demand and the economy suffers from a deflationary gap. The chief cause of idle resources is too low a level of planned private investment and government purchases. One of the basic remedies for closing the gap is an increase in autonomous investment, an expenditure independent of expenditures in other sectors of the economy. An autonomous increase in government expenditures will increase the Gross National Product by a multiple of the change in such expenditures.[26] It omits domestic governmental transactions. The government spends large sums on such matters as military forces, education, and the upkeep and building of roads. These payments inevitably affect employment, industrial production, and national income. In the economist's jargon, government expenditure policy, taxation, and the management of public debt to keep an economy fully employed is called fiscal policy. Government expenditures, like private investment, represent an "injection" into the income stream, and taxes act as a "leakage" from the income stream. If under-utilization of industrial plant and idle manpower are to be overcome, the government has to embark on a "stabilization policy."

The difficult decision is always how much government spending and what tax rates are necessary to achieve the desired increase in national income. No matter which option is chosen, the autonomous increase in government expenditure triggers the multiplier process, which then raises the level of national income in the multiple of the change in government outlay. Every additional dollar the government spends enters the income stream. However, if the finance minister insists on a balanced budget and collects an extra dollar to match the extra outlays, private spending is not reduced by a full dollar, because part of that extra dollar would have gone into savings. The expansionist effect of the dollar spent by the government, for whatever purpose, exceeds the depressing effect of the dollar taxed, thus making a net addition to total spending and raising the equilibrium level of the Gross National Product. This relationship is called "the balanced budget theorem." It is true, of course, that this theorem assumes constant propensities to invest and consume and disregards other possible shifts in the behavior of firms; it is therefore not possible to assert that a balanced increase of z dollars in the government budget will increase G.N.P. by exactly z dollars, but there is no doubt that the G.N.P. will expand.

Shilumim Orders and German Industry

The fear of a recession, a shortage of dollars, and idle manpower were responsible for Bonn's insistence at Wassenaar that the Shilumim payments be made in kind and not in dollars, gold, or Swiss francs. The West German position was that payments in kind were not necessarily identical with payments in convertible currencies, because even though certain types of goods would not be exported at all, they could prudently be included among the categories that Israel had to take. This attitude was made explicit in Article 6 of the Shilumim Agreement, which prescribed the specific commodities, and in what amounts, the Israel Mission had to order annually. The Germans anticipated that the orders would serve as injections and benefit various industries, particularly those in the depressed areas, which included, in the early 1950s, West Berlin, the former Navy shipyards at Wilhelmshaven, and twenty-six towns and eighty-two rural districts in the areas bordering East Germany.[27]

From 1953 to 1965, Dr. Shinnar's Israel Mission placed 50,165 orders with the Bundesamt für gewerbliche Wirtschaft, made 29,647 alteration requests, and cancelled 753 orders. The year-by-year placement of orders was as follows:

TABLE 9-2

SHILUMIM ORDERS

Year	Orders	Alterations	Cancellations
1953	3,095	—	—
1954	8,357	5,440	89
1955	5,628	4,060	174
1956	6,845	3,598	104
1957	6,538	4,019	61
1958	8,457	4,422	95
1959	5,125	3,064	55
1960	2,542	2,060	37
1961	2,752	1,774	27
1962	515	888	42
1963	221	227	48
1964	90	70	1

Source: J. Ebeling, *Bericht über die Durchführung des Abkommens zwischen der Bundesrepublik Deutschland und dem Staate Israel vom 10 September 1952* (Bonn: Bundesminister für Wirtschaft, 1966), p. 20.

Israeli orders went to 4,570 firms, including those of West Berlin; their value varied from a minimum of DM 100 to DM 25 million. More than 3,000 orders were placed in 1953, and by 1954 this number had almost tripled. During the succeeding two years more than

12,000 orders were placed; and by the end of 1956, 48 per cent of all orders had been made. From 1957 to 1961, there were an additional 25,414 orders, more than 8,000 in 1958 alone, the year when Dr. Shinnar successfully negotiated the difficult DM 450 million loan with the Deutsche Bank. To ascertain whether these Shilumim-financed "injections" produced additional employment by means of the multiplier process, we must list the rates of capacity utilization in selected branches of the West German economy.[28]

Table 9-3 shows that the index of capacity utilization of total industry was 89.0 in 1953 and 94.5 in 1965. We have seen how the West German economy went through periods of revitalization from mid-1948 to the end of 1951, of normalization from 1952 to roughly 1957, and of overemployment beginning in 1957–1958.[29] During revitalization and normalization, the shortage of investment funds was the principal bottleneck to economic expansion, and unemployment was still quite substantial.[30] Throughout the fourteen-year period, with the exception of 1958 when the total index dipped a fraction below 90 per cent, German industry continued to operate at very high rates of capacity utilization. The economy continued to grow vigorously, occasionally entering into export-led booms such as those of 1955 and 1961. During boom years the machine-making and electrotechnical industries were utilized at 100 per cent. In 1960, the iron-working, chemical, and textile industries also achieved 100 per cent utilization.

The record of the shipbuilding industry, however, was quite uneven. During the first and second Shilumim years, 1953 and 1954, considerable under-utilization of shipyards existed. In 1953 more than one-quarter of all shipyards were idle, whereas in 1954 the excess capacity was close to 13 per cent. After the two boom years of 1957 and 1958, when 100 per cent capacity operations prevailed, West German shipyards suffered hardships.

By 1957 the rate of unemployment had dropped below 4 per cent, and labor shortages plagued the economy for many years to come.[31] Yet the purpose of Article 6 had been to create additional employment, especially in the depressed areas. And in 1951 and 1952 it made good economic sense because of stagnation and large-scale unemployment. However, in 1954 West Germany's finance minister, Fritz Schäffer, cut the yearly payments to DM 250 million and thus slowed down the entire implementation program. The bulk of Israeli orders

Table 9-3

Index of Utilization of Capacity, West Germany, Selected Industries

Industry	1953	1954	1955	1956	1957	1958	1959	1960	1961	1962	1963	1964	1965
Total industry	89.0	92.4	97.0	96.4	93.9	89.9	92.1	98.1	96.8	94.4	92.5	95.6	94.5
Iron-working	85.1	87.4	97.8	96.8	93.4	78.5	85.7	100.0	95.2	89.3	82.1	92.2	88.2
Machine-building	88.2	90.6	100.0	99.1	93.8	90.5	90.2	98.2	100.0	94.4	88.6	93.2	96.0
Ship-building	73.2	86.7	95.5	98.3	100.0	100.0	88.0	88.8	89.6	89.4	85.8	92.2	94.4
Electro-technical	78.8	89.9	100.0	97.1	92.5	87.6	90.1	97.9	100.0	93.5	88.6	91.1	95.5
Chemicals	89.3	94.7	97.2	94.4	94.3	90.3	95.6	100.0	95.1	95.1	95.6	97.2	95.5
Textiles	92.0	94.4	97.1	100.0	99.9	92.4	95.3	100.0	97.0	98.0	97.8	97.4	96.6

were placed after 1956, when serious labor shortages existed and machine-making industries were operating at near capacity. Seen this way, the Shilumim purchases added fuel to the fire of an already overheated economy. Israel wanted and got a vast array of capital and investment goods, but was not interested in labor-intensive goods which could have been produced easily in the depressed areas. In fact the distribution of the Shilumim orders shows that depressed areas benefited much less than originally hoped.

The lion's share of the Shilumim goods originated either in the highly industrialized Ruhr Valley or in Hamburg and not in the depressed areas. The Ruhr Valley produced more than 50 per cent of the goods, while overpopulated Schleswig-Holstein and Bavaria, with substantial pockets of unemployed refugees, produced only 4.3 per cent and 5.1 per cent, respectively. Thus, Article 6, for a number of reasons, did not generate additional employment in de-

TABLE 9-4

DISTRIBUTION OF SHILUMIM ORDERS BY AREA [a]

State	Amount (DM 1,000)	Percentage
Nordrhein-Westphalia	576,534	32.4
Hamburg	345,989	19.4
Baden-Württemberg	187,309	10.5
Lower Saxony	145,492	8.2
Hessen	97,444	5.5
Bremen	92,864	5.2
Bayern	91,442	5.1
West Berlin	83,605	4.7
Rheinland-Pfalz	82,378	4.6
Schleswig-Holstein	76,439	4.3
Saarland (since 1959)	1,712	0.1
TOTAL	1,787,208	100.0

Source: Bundesamt für gewerbliche Wirtschaft, *Die Durchführung des Abkommens vom 10 September 1952 zwischen der Bundesrepublik Deutschland und dem Staate Israel in den Jahren 1952–1962* (Frankfurt a/M.: 1962), p. 59 (mimeo).

[a] Up to March 31, 1962.

pressed areas. Full employment, unprecedented prosperity, and acute labor shortages came only in 1957, after which the formerly depressed areas became sources of labor for the industrialized Ruhr Valley. Although it is true that the number of Shilumim orders that went to labor surplus areas was low, the figures should be viewed with reservation because the West German Central Statistical Office recorded exported goods according to the location of a company's main office and not according to the location of actual production. For this reason, the thousands of subcontractors who did some work in assembling Shilumim goods did not appear in the official statistics. Yet many were located in depressed areas.[32]

West Berlin, because of its territorial isolation from the rest of the Federal Republic and its heavy unemployment and underemployment, enjoyed preferential treatment in the allocation of some Shilumim orders. Although Berlin lacks heavy industries, it has been traditionally a center of high-quality, labor-intensive products, especially in electronics and communications, and in electricity-generating and railroad-signaling equipment. In 1955, for instance, the Israel Mission asked one firm there to produce an entire electrical generating facility with a total value of DM 80 million.[33] This order kept that firm going for a number of years. Thus, although according to Table 9-4 West Berlin's official share in the total production of Shilumim goods was only 4.7 per cent, actually it was considerably higher because of a substantial amount of subcontracting, especially in shipbuilding. Many Shilumim ships obtained thousands of items from West Berlin. But again, since the subcontracting work is not reflected in official statistics, the share appears lower than it actually was. Precisely what Shilumim production contributed to improving the city's employment is difficult to say, but it was undoubtedly substantial.

The West German Shipbuilding Industry

Of the DM 2.4 billion spent by the Israel Mission, almost 25 per cent went for ships. To assess to what extent these purchases helped to improve the capacity utilization of West German shipyards, we shall first examine briefly the operations of this industry from 1953 to 1965.

Before the war Germany had an efficient shipbuilding industry with a yearly capacity of 500,000 gross registered tons.[34] But wartime destruction and postwar reparation removals left it a shambles. Not until 1949 was West Germany again allowed to build ships of a pre-scribed size. In 1950 its shipbuilding capacity was one-quarter of that in 1939; it stood at 350,000 gross registered tons in 1951,[35] the year all restrictions on West German shipbuilding were removed.[36] From 1953 to 1965, merchant vessels launched by the Federal Republic totaled 13.5 million gross registered tons.[37] By the end of 1962 Israel had ordered 49 vessels, with a total of 450,000 tons,[38] which repre-sented 3.5 per cent of all merchant vessels launched by Germany. The Israel Mission had placed two large orders for ships: from 1953 through 1955, Dr. Shinnar asked for bids on 18 vessels, and in Octo-ber 1956 32 ships were ordered.[39] Israel's decision to go ahead with these purchases was based primarily on security considerations, on national pride in seeing the Star of David on ships plying the oceans, and on the lack of other projects for the utilization of Shilumim funds.

In 1953, when German shipyards were operating at only 73.2 per cent of capacity, the Israeli order for 3 ships with a total gross ton-nage of 14,000 was probably much appreciated.[40] The Korean War boom was over and many ships were idle, as were the yards. The West German situation was particularly critical because British shipbuilders were offering better terms. In 1954 the Israelis placed another order for 11 ships with a total gross tonnage of 58,656,[41] and took possession of 6 ships. In 1955 West German shipyards operated at 95.5 per cent of capacity, and in 1956, because of the Suez crisis, at almost 100 per cent, a situation that lasted through 1958. In the fall of 1956, when Dr. Shinnar ordered 32 additional ships, the costs were 15 to 20 per cent higher than they would have been in Japan or France, because German shipyards were flooded with orders.[42] Not until 1959 was there considerable world-wide under-utilization of shipyards, which resulted in almost cutthroat competition.[43]

After 1958 when medium and smaller shipyards had difficulty in keeping fully employed, they turned more and more to repair work instead of building new vessels.[44] Although these yards obtained a few new construction orders from public authorities in 1960, there was anxiety about the future.[45] In 1961 continued sluggishness of international seaborne shipping and a 5 per cent revaluation of the Deutsche Mark made it more difficult for German yards to compete effectively with foreign yards.[46] After the end of the Suez crisis, the experts spoke of stagnation in the shipping industry.[47] Thus, despite the continued vigor in almost all branches of German industry during the fourteen-year period, shipbuilding was a notable exception. Certain cities threatened to become distressed areas. In Hamburg, for example, shipyards employed more people than any other industry,[48] that is, one-seventh of all industrial workers, and for every shipyard worker two others were employed in the various supply industries. Most of these subcontracting industries (*Zulieferindustrie*) were located outside of Hamburg. In other port cities the situation was even more critical. In Emden, 77 per cent of the total work force was employed in shipyards; in Bremerhaven, almost 50 per cent; and in Kiel, Lübeck, Flensburg, and Cuxhaven, between 25 and 40 per cent.[49] Thus, the 49 Shilumim-financed seagoing vessels, the 8 fishing vessels, and the 2 customs cruisers did contribute to fuller utilization of the yards. The first orders placed in 1953 were very welcome and had favorable effects both in the yards and in the supply industries. The orders placed at the height of the Suez crisis in 1956 were on top of an already heavy backlog, but with the onset of world-wide shipping stagnation in 1958 they enabled the yards to keep operations at higher levels of capacity than otherwise would have been possible. Consequently even the second batch of orders for ships had a beneficial employment effect, although it cannot be calculated exactly. In summary, it is probably fair to say that the Shilumim-financed ship purchases served to some extent as a government-financed public works program, even if the total of DM 586 million spent was small in relation to the entire production of the shipbuilding industry over the fourteen-year period. From 1953 to the end of 1962 the value of the total output of West German shipyards was DM 20.2 billion, of which the Shilumim share was 2.9 per cent.[50]

To build and to equip 49 seagoing vessels required vast amounts of supplies from hundreds of firms in different industries. Moreover, the extra costs meant extra profits, and extra employment as well. Shipyards depend heavily upon other industries because the building of a ship requires, among other things, steel, machinery, propellers, turbines, navigational gear, coffee cups, furniture, and linens. German officials, in acquiescing to the Israeli request for 49 ships, were well aware of this interdependence between shipyards and suppliers. By permitting Israel to order ships, they created extra business—and not just for shipbuilders alone.[51]

Some General Economic Effects of the Shilumim Purchases

The Israelis spent DM 2.05 billion for goods in Groups I, II, and III, while in Group IV, agricultural products, and Group V, services, they claimed DM 345 million, for a total of DM 2.4 billion.[52] After deducting DM 0.6 billion spent on ships, DM 1.5 billion was left for steel products, machinery, and equipment. Across a busy decade for West Germany, this sum was minuscule indeed, and its economic impact small. Had the Federal Republic suffered from severe under-employment, these extra purchases would have been a stimulant. But Shilumim goods, 80 per cent of which were capital goods, repre-sented extra demand in an overheated economy. The West German government might have done better to transfer the amounts owed to Israel in 1957, let us say, in foreign exchange. At that time West Germany had plentiful gold and dollar reserves, and the transfer could have been accomplished painlessly.

The Shilumim Agreement was implemented without fanfare and without headlines. The Bundesamt staff of some ten officials in Frankfurt am Main worked efficiently with the Israel Mission of Cologne. The cooperation was mutual because purposeful alloca-tion of the available funds was a common objective. Again and again Dr. Shinnar praised the "correct" attitude of the German officials vis-à-vis the Israelis and their requests.[53] A high official in Bonn's Finance Ministry summed up his impressions by saying, "Oh, we disagreed on many things more than once, but we never became disagreeable!" [54] Dr. Hans A. Goers, chairman of the Mixed Commis-sion, stated that he had clashed with Dr. Shinnar not more than twice.[55] Mutual good will infused the spirit as well as the letter of the Shilumim Agreement. The German officials did not harass the Israelis with picayune administrative red tape, but instead permitted the pre-ordering of goods on account for future years, agreed to prefinance Israeli purchases, and finally guaranteed the DM 450 million loan that made it possible to conclude the Agreement sooner. The Shilumim funds enabled Israeli planners to accelerate the economic development of their country. The certainty that DM 250 million would be available annually for investment goods gave the Finance Ministry a breathing spell from the perennial fear of a hard-currency shortage.[56] Moreover, speedier implementation of the Agree-ment enabled the Israelis to order goods at lower prices. The growth of purely commercial trade was the inevitable result of the economic relations that commenced with Shilumim. From 1953 to 1965 West Germany imported DM 1.1 billion worth of goods from Israel and exported DM 1.26 billion worth, in addition to Shilumim goods.[57] In the spring of 1966, after the Shilumim Agreement was discharged in full, the Bonn government began giving Israel economic aid, which is likely to strengthen further the commercial ties between the two countries.

The world's press, of course, traced the progress of the Shilumim Agreement.[58] According to one British observer, it was "perhaps the finest feather in the Bonn Government's cap from the point of view of public opinion in the Western world." [59] After the first five years, it was reported that German deliveries were of "great benefit to the Israeli economy." [60] By the end of 1962, after ten years, Bonn's meticulous discharge of its obligations had contributed considerably to improved relations between the governments of Israel and West Germany.[61] Israel, of course, would have survived without German-made goods, but the steady flow of capital equipment accelerated considerably the pace of economic development, and Israel's government gave proper credit to the Bonn government for "having faithfully carried out its commitments to pay reparations." [62] In 1965, it was reported that $600 million out of $850 million of the Shilumim funds were spent upon the development of the country.[63] *The New York Times* even said that the Shilumim deliveries became "a principal foundation of Israel's economic growth." [64]

The Political Impact of Bonn's Moral Reparations

In the spring of 1966 the Shilumim Agreement was finally and meticulously fulfilled. Individual compensation payments continued, and the governments of Israel and the Federal Republic were negotiating a new agreement to enable Israel honorably to receive German economic aid in the future. These achievements bore witness to the seriousness of the Bonn government's intention to earn its way into the community of democratic nations. No foreign government and no judicial authority could legally force the Bonn government to recognize the Jewish moral claims against Germany. In 1969 Dr. Goldmann wrote that during the Wassenaar talks there "was no basis in international law for the collective Jewish claims," and the fact that Adenauer's government was persuaded to recognize and satisfy them by material means "was a triumph of momentous significance." [65]

What was the impact of these moral reparations payments? (Bonn's commitment to pay the State of Israel DM 3.45 billion can hardly be called conventional reparations.[66] Moral or conscience reparations is more appropriate.) Did they improve the image of West Germany in Israel, in the United States, in England, at the governmental level? How did Bonn's "moral comeback policy" affect the individual Jew in the Diaspora and in Israel? More to the point, how do the survivors of Auschwitz look upon West Germany and the Germans today? Further, how do Germans young and old look upon the Jew today? And how was Germany's "moral comeback" reflected in the mass media, literature, and press in the Diaspora and in Israel?

It would take another volume to answer all of these questions in detail. Yet, in assessing the impact of the Shilumim Agreement it is necessary to look for clues to political and diplomatic benefits to the West German government. All things considered, apart from the moral requirements, Adenauer needed a better international image for the Federal Republic. Thus, his policy of launching the "moral comeback" was also motivated by the necessities of *Realpolitik*.

The first attempt to evaluate the political impact of the German *Wiedergutmachung* policy, of moral reparations in general, and of Shilumim in particular was made at the Fifth Plenary Assembly of the World Jewish Congress, held in Brussels in August 1966.[67] It was the first intellectual confrontation of the Jews, the Israelis, and the Germans after the Holocaust on the question of German-Jewish relations. Dr. Goldmann, then president of the World Jewish Congress and the driving intellectual force in organizing this German-Jewish debate, stated in his introductory remarks that the relations between the Germans and the Jews were still "the most complex and important problems of the Jewish generation of today." [68] Since it was unrealistic and impractical to ignore Germany, he advocated that Jews seek coexistence in this generation with the Germans.[69] The intellectual exploration of this difficult coexistence, he reiterated, had nothing to do with the *questions of forgiveness, reconciliation, or an attempt to forget the past*.[70] He also declared that the Jews had a right to be oversensitive on this subject, not the Germans.[71]

Three member-groups of the World Jewish Congress, Herut-Hatzor, Achdut Haavoda-Poale-Zion, and Mapam, refused to participate in the debate, but they submitted statements of opposition to this item on the agenda.[72] Mr. Isaac Remba, representing the right-wing Herut party, wrote that *all* Germans were responsible for the murder of one-third of all Jews, and many of the murderers were still at large. His view was that the Shilumim payments and individual compensation were no great favors, that the Germans were merely returning a minuscule part of what they had robbed,[73] and that in this generation no reconciliation between the Germans and Jews was possible. Mr. Abraham Schenkar, of the Achdut Haavoda-Poale-Zion, opposed the meeting because it contained "the seeds of appeasement." [74] It was morally wrong to give the West Germans the *hechsher* (stamp of approval, used to indicate that food is kosher) they so badly needed. The statement of the left-wing Mapam stressed that the time for German-Jewish dialogue had not yet arrived and that any German-Jewish debate would be interpreted "as the beginning of reconciliation." [75]

Of those who did participate, the principal speaker from the Israeli side was Professor Gershom Sholem of Hebrew University, Jerusalem. Professor Salo W. Baron of Columbia University, and Dr. Joachim Prinz of New York City, represented Jewry in the Diaspora. Dr. Eugen Gerstenmaier, then speaker of the German Bundestag, Golo Mann, professor of history, the philosopher Karl Jaspers, and Dr. Hendryk G. van Dam, the Jewish representative of West Germany, spoke for the German side in this debate.

Professor Sholem, in a moving address, touched upon many sensitive areas that still mar individual German-Jewish relationships.[76] For many Israelis, the German people represented a "hopeless case," and they doubted that the Germans would ever turn over a new leaf and abandon their deep-seated anti-Semitism. A new working relationship between Jews and Germans could emerge by quiet work, based on respect, honesty, open minds, and, above all, good will.[77]

Professor Mann, a German himself, felt that he could never fully trust the Germans, not even as human beings, because the shadows of Auschwitz and Treblinka were still upon us.[78] Anyone who had gone through the 1930s and 1940s would "remain in the innermost of his soul a sad man until he dies." [79]

For the well-known philosopher Karl Jaspers, who could not attend in person but sent a message, the Nazi genocide would "remain associated with the very idea of Germans, just as pyramids of skulls evoke the name of the Mongols." [80] Whether an individual German had been an active murderer or a passive onlooker, the Germans should never forget that by preferring to stay alive, by being quiet or indifferent, their being alive constituted their "grievous fault." And even though most Germans were not guilty of genocide, all Germans bore a moral and political responsibility for the deeds of the government of the Third Reich, which they chose in 1933.[81] Jaspers believed that there must be no eternal enmity between Jews and Germans; only those who had survived the Holocaust could forgive. But who could forgive the murder of the millions of Jews? Only the victims themselves, according to Jaspers, and no one could speak for them. Thus, the only kind of reconciliation possible was through material amends to the State of Israel and individual compensation. Such acts did not constitute reconciliation, forgiveness, or forgetting. He praised Chancellor Adenauer for his "political good sense" and his "understanding for Jewish unforgiveness" in signing the Luxemburg Treaty in 1952, but he deplored some of the excesses of sterile nationalism on both sides. Jaspers found it impossible to speak of Jews and Germans as a collective entity; therefore, the problem of Jewish-German relations was for the moment insoluble, though not hopeless.[82]

Dr. Gerstenmeier felt that the Nazi genocide had left an indelible curse on all Germans.[83] The purpose of the debate, "Germans and Jews: Unsolved Problem," had nothing to do with reconciliation or cleansing the slate. Rather, Dr. Goldmann had put this item on the agenda to show the Germans that, at the end of the Shilumim payments, German-Jewish relations had still not been solved and that vigilance against the rise of extremists was called for.

The debate was widely reported in the press, but most Israelis and probably most of the Diaspora Jewry were against it. Earlier, in May 1966, ex-Chancellor Adenauer had gone to Israel at the invitation of the government.[84] He was deeply impressed by Israel's achievements and recorded in his memoirs that he ". . . encountered little hatred or animosity." [85] He was made an Honorary Fellow of the Weizmann Institute; and he was feasted, welcomed, and appreciated almost everywhere, except for one incident at a dinner party at the home of Prime Minister Levi Eshkol. Eshkol said that the Jewish people were still looking for ". . . testimony that Germany recognized the burden of the past and sought a new path for herself in the community of nations." [86] Adenauer felt that these remarks were insulting, and in his reply said that the Jewish people should at least appreciate the Bonn government's material compensation payments and good will.[87] He admonished that ". . . nichts Gutes daraus entstehen kann, wenn man uns die Annerkennung verweigert," [88] and refused to raise his glass in answer to Eshkol's toast to German-Israel understanding.[89]

At the end of Shilumim, Adenauer knew that reconciliation between the Germans and Jews could not be expected in the near future. And so did Dr. Goldmann. As long as hundreds of thousands of Jews still carried concentration camp numbers tattooed on their arms, the very thought of face-to-face contact with the Germans was repulsive. To the survivors of the Holocaust, all Germans were moral lepers. Formal and correct relations between Bonn and Jerusalem made a useful fiction, but on the person-to-person level, especially for the older Jews and Israelis, the Germans were still rabid nationalists, militarists, and anti-Semites. Thus it was, three weeks after the Brussels debate, during the Jewish Agency Executive's nine-day plenary meeting in Jerusalem, that Dr. Goldmann was subjected to a sharp attack for his views on Germany.[90] The representatives of the Executive probably spoke the mind of the Jewish people: "Goldmann, it was still too early to talk to the Germans!" In October 1966, Dr. Goldmann summed up his impressions of the Brussels debate by saying that, despite the noisy opposition from the extreme left and right, the German-Jewish dialogue was useful and that it would pave the way for the establishment of a normal coexistence between the Jews and Germans.[91] For the Germans, the road to acceptance would be long and fraught with difficulties, and they would have to be patient.

The Image of West Germans in the Diaspora

In the spring of 1945, after the end of hostilities in Europe, a noted German philosopher confided to his diary that anti-Germanism together with anti-Semitism were the two basic "frames of mind" (*Grundstimmung*) in the world.[92] Germanophobia was a fact of life, and the mass media in the Western, as well as the Communist, world were anti-German.

In America the historical image of Germany during this century has been changing radically almost from decade to decade. Before World War I Americans had a veritable love for Germany and admired its culture, learning, and technology; thousands upon thousands of young Americans went to study in Germany.[93] During World War I, however, the image of the Hun replaced all that had been admired before 1914. With the advent of the Third Reich, the stereotypes of World War I re-emerged; and during World War II, the *furor teutonicus* became the symbol of supreme evil. As soon as the first survivors of the Nazi death mills told what had happened during the Holocaust, how the Germans practiced industrialized genocide, the revulsion against and hatred of everything German was complete and almost universal.

But the Cold War, especially after the Marshall Plan got under way, placed the western parts of Germany on the side of the United States, and no matter what appeared in the mass media or in literature a new successor-state, the Federal Republic, emerged from the smoldering ruins of the Third Reich. It eventually became an ally of the United States and was subject to what one German historian called far-reaching "Westernization" (*Verwestlichung*).[94] The eastern part of Germany, on the other hand, was transformed into a Soviet style country, and it underwent "Easternization."

Designed to create a better public and published image of the Federal Republic, the successful and quiet discharge of the Shilumim Agreement and the continuation of individual compensation payments considerably improved West Germany's image in America, at least in government councils. Similarly, the Israeli government and world Jewish organizations acknowledged Adenauer's symbolic gestures of good will. There is no question that two decades of moral reparations have led to the emergence of a much-improved image of West Germany on the governmental and administrative levels. And in that sense, Adenauer's and his successors' moral comeback policy received the "hechscher" of the Western world.

How did Americans, in city, suburb, and countryside, view Germany in the spring of 1966? Generalizations are never satisfactory, but they are useful in that they reflect to some extent the speech, thought, and feelings of many men and women. Since the end of World War II, millions of American soldiers have been stationed on West German soil, and many millions more of American tourists have visited the country for shorter or longer periods. For these reasons alone, the Federal Republic is familiar country to Americans. They generally respect and admire Germany's enormously successful economic comeback and the resurgence of its shattered cities. West Germany is *the* military prop of the NATO alliance, and the Washington-Bonn political axis is firm. In the United States, the almost universal acceptance of the Volkswagen reflects the popularity of German-made products.

On the other hand, published opinion in the United States about West Germany is still contradictory, fuzzy, and negative. Why? According to one interpretation, the American masses are really not all that concerned with West Germany. They take it or leave it alone, so to speak. Another reason may be that four relatively small groups interested in things German are Germanophobic: American Jews, Americans of eastern European descent, academicians (especially at the leading universities in the Northeast), and certain circles within the federal government.[95] In the American mass media West Germany is still suspect, and the stereotyped view of *furor teutonicus* is very much in evidence. The popular image portrayed is one of Germans as cruel aggressors, incapable of ever becoming true democrats.[96] It is still popular to be afraid of Germany and to see Germans as incorrigible.[97]

Throughout the 1950s and 1960s numerous widely read American books dealt with many German topics from an anti-German point of view. As a popular historical account, nothing matched William L. Shirer's *The Rise and Fall of the Third Reich* (1960). Most reviewers acclaimed it as a great historical work. Shirer's working hypothesis was that the Third Reich was a natural outcome of the unique pattern of German culture. He stressed the collective responsibility of all Germans for the rise of Nazism. According to Shirer, Germans nearly always prefer order to freedom and put obedience above individual conscience. More than one million copies of his book have been sold in America, and in the 1970s paperback editions are still on sale in almost every supermarket. It has influenced young and old, students and teachers alike, and Shirer's view that only Germany's historical and cultural heritage could have made Nazism possible will be heard for a long time to come. Despite its popularity this work has been criticized on four accounts: its somewhat simplified conception of German history, its lack of objectivity, its author's failure to acquaint himself with the nature of industrialized totalitarianism, and its dated scholarship.[98] And in many of the numerous books dealing with politics and history that came after Shirer, the central theme was that the Federal Republic of Germany was the moral descendant of the Third Reich.[99]

The revival of Nazism in the Federal Republic of Germany seems to be an *idée fixe* of American journalism, film, and television. Except for Chancellor Adenauer, Germans are seen as being unable to become good democrats.[100] In 1969 it was reported in the West German weekly *Der Volkswirt* that, according to Mr. Erwin Single, the editor of the German-language *New Yorker Staatszeitung und Herold,* CBS permitted week after week the presentation of Germans as spies, mad scientists, puffed-up blockheads, sadists, and other unpleasant figures.[101] The appearance of old movies on television—especially the heavy-handed, anti-German wartime dramas—is still frequent. Such reruns are cheap inputs that earn money for the TV stations. Although there is no malice intended in showing them, their effect may nevertheless be cumulative upon the subconscious mind, and therefore upon the formation of attitudes. In the fall of 1965 the *Frankfurter Allgemeine Zeitung* also quoted the *New Yorker Staatszeitung und Herold* which protested against the presentation on American TV of the entire German nation as a collection of subhumans and idiots.[102] In many American homes, viewers are thoroughly familiar with such widely serialized shows as *Hogan's Heroes* and *Combat,* in which Germans are depicted as stupid, repulsive, obedient, and always arrogant aggressors.[103]

The British mass media have exhibited similar attitudes toward Germans.[104] One Englishman felt that the British "popular press . . . had proved itself both unable and unwilling to free itself from the clutches of war-time propaganda," and ". . . news of positive trends [was] neglected."[105]

Needless to say, the Holocaust and the industrially perfect assembly-line murder of millions of Jews cannot and should not be forgotten. The Nazi legacy is still a terrible burden, and neither the West German government nor the Germans themselves can expect quick improvement of the German image even after a quarter century of good behavior.[106] Even the massive payments in the form of moral reparations—costly cosmetics as one writer called the Luxemburg Treaty payments—cannot quickly and effectively improve the image of Germans abroad.[107]

The year after the discharge of the Shilumim Agreement saw the eruption of the June 1967 war between Israel and Arab states. The United States and the Federal Republic of Germany maintained a "hands-off" policy in that conflict to prevent its escalation. In the United States the majority of the non-Jews seemed, relatively speaking, not very much concerned about the outcome of the war, and there was a remarkable silence and indifference in the churches.[108]

In contrast to American apathy, a spontaneous feeling of sympathy and desire for action in support of Israel broke out throughout West Germany, a reaction that took Israel by surprise. The West Germans collected funds, bought Israel bonds, prayed for Israel's victory, volunteered for all kinds of civilian service in Israel, donated blood, offered homes for Israeli children, collected medical supplies, marched and declared to the world that "There can be no neutrality against injustice" and that "It is our moral obligation to support Israel." [109] It should be noted that all these declarations of solidarity with Israel were made at a time when Israel's government stood alone, before its spectacular victory, defying the inaction of the United Nations.

The Israelis were ready to fend for themselves, but the moral support of West Germany was the least expected and probably the most appreciated. The German mass media spoke in clear language: Israel's existence is in danger and world public opinion cannot permit and should not tolerate another "Munich Fiasco." [110] The Israeli ambassador to West Germany, Asher Ben-Natan, made no bones about the fact that the moral mass support of the West Germans during the June 1967 conflict led to the emergence of a new element in relations between Israel and West Germany. Above all, from then on, correct relations between Bonn and Jerusalem led to better relations in general at the grass-roots level.[111] West Germany had also become a very important arms supplier to Israel at a time when virtually all other countries maintained an arms embargo.[112]

In summary, in 1953 Adenauer's "moral comeback" policy had been an affair of the government. Most Germans over thirty did not want to be reminded of Nazi crimes because, after the long war, near-starvation, chaos, and suffering, they were primarily concerned with the material aspects of life and living. They accepted the government's decision to settle Israel's collective claim as well as to pay individual compensation. They yearned to be considered just normal people, like Frenchmen, Italians, and Englishmen.[113] The Bonn government signed the Luxemburg Treaty voluntarily; it was not a legal obligation and could not have been binding in any court in the world. At the same time, the Shilumim policy meant a deliberate destruction of Arab good will. Despite the furor in the Western press in 1964 and 1969, when the West German parliament's discussion of the statute of limitations and the prosecution of Nazi crimes destroyed much hard-won diplomatic porcelain, the *Wiedergutmachung* payments were continued. And if the payments were so unpopular, why was this never successfully exploited by right-wing parties, which even today are splinter groups without any representatives in the Federal parliament? The drastic change in Israeli attitudes toward West Germany and Germans has demonstrated that the "moral comeback" is probably not a fiction any more in that country. And the Luxemburg Treaty of 1952 to a large extent paved the way.

10

Shilumim Funds:
Monument or Current Expense?

Considering Israel's difficult economic situation, there was some fear that the government would use up a considerable portion of the DM 3.45 billion for current needs. A number of Israelis felt that nc matter how pressing the import requirements of the moment, the Shilumim funds should be invested primarily in developing the country's infrastructure so as to bring it closer to economic independence. Since the sum of DM 3.45 billion represented material compensation for Jewish suffering in the Diaspora, they believed there could be no more appropriate or lasting monument for future generations.

Dr. Solomon Trone's Plan

The first plan for the utilization of the Shilumim funds was prepared in mid-1952 by Dr. Solomon Trone, an American General Electric Corporation engineer. Dr. Trone came to Israel in the second half of 1951 at the invitation of Hillel Dan, managing director of Solel Boneh, an important part of the producers' section of the Histadrut.[1]

Israel's finance minister, Eliezer Kaplan, had asked Dr. Trone to prepare a ten-year development plan on the assumption that $615 million from Germany, $181 million from other countries, and I£ 825 million would be available.[2] When the plan was almost ready, the cochairmen of Israel's delegation at Wassenaar, Dr. F. E. Shinnar and Dr. G. Josephthal, informed Dr. Trone that only $339 million of the German $615 million and $94 million from other countries would be forthcoming.[3] Dr. Trone rewrote the plan accordingly.

Dr. Trone, a development planner with many years' experience in the Soviet Union, Korea, China, and India, was an advocate of a market-oriented economy and preferred private and corporate initiative to government regulation. He and Hillel Dan worked closely in preparing the details. Both agreed that the government should plan the development of Israel's transportation, electricity, irrigation, water resources, and part of its natural resources.[4] They differed, however, on some important matters: Trone suggested that the entire Shilumim amount be spent on infrastructure, whereas Dan preferred to develop the heavy and basic industries; Trone also felt that the responsibility for developing the steel, copper, kaolin, and potash industries should be left to private enterprise, whereas Dan wanted the government to do the job because he felt that Israel could not afford to wait upon private initiative. Eventually the two clashed bitterly, and Dr. Trone left Israel in anger.[5] But despite their disagreements, both Trone and Dan believed that under no circumstances should the Shilumim funds be used "to cover immediate pressing needs." [6]

Trone pleaded for the establishment of a Ministerial Committee on German Payments to insure that industrial development was not jeopardized by shortsightedness. He saw the prevailing economic situation in Israel as characterized by "lack of coordination, multiplicity of planning organs, shortage of raw materials and of spare parts, lack of managerial and administrative skills, etc." [7]

Dr. Trone proposed (1) the dissolution of all independent planning organizations in the various ministries; (2) the creation of a small planning body of economists and technicians, selected only for their experience, ability, and knowledge; and (3) an integrated development plan to be worked out by this body in collaboration with the Cabinet.[8] He declared that competence in execution and the power to act were indispensable for getting results. Trone indicated that qualified men were available but were often found in the wrong chairs.[9] To him, planning the future of Israel's industrial development meant only one thing: "replacement of industrial chaos by industrial order." [10]

Since spending several hundred million dollars on German goods and capital equipment within a relatively short time was likely to require a substantial administrative effort, he urged the creation of "one single authority where all dealings connected with German Payments will be concentrated." [11] This authority would prepare all lists of requirements, including specifications for machinery and equipment. He recommended that one technical and economic office, located in Israel, should write specifications for all goods to be ordered, while another office, located in West Germany, should be in charge of placing bids and orders. The two offices should maintain close liaison.

When Dr. Trone's report was submitted, the Government had not prepared "a basic overall program for the use of Reparation funds." [12] But the prevailing attitudes were not conducive to such planning; hardly anyone believed that the West German government would actually make the promised deliveries. Many argued that even if the Bonn government honored its commitment, Israel should not accept German-paid oil and goods.

What Is Infrastructure?

Development projects like Dr. Trone's are what economists call investments in infrastructure. Sometimes called social overhead capital, infrastructure is "generally divided into economic investment which is needed to enable other production for the market to take place, and purely social capital, which improves well-being directly." [13] Economic investment comprises the transportation network, irrigation facilities, communications systems, the gas and electricity generating and transmitting network, ports, government buildings, police and fire protection, and sewers; this aggregate is known as the material or physical infrastructure. [14] The purely social overhead capital "includes the plant and equipment required for shelter, education, and public health." [15] The availability of material infrastructure facilitates directly and indirectly the structural transformation of a country, for it serves as a foundation upon which primary, secondary, and tertiary industries can be mounted. By itself it does not produce any consumer goods, but without it "directly productive activities" would hardly be possible. [16]

A vital part of the stock of material infrastructure is human capital, or human infrastructure. [17] The general level of education, specialization, and skills, the degree of motivation, organizational and business talent, and the quality of values are a few of its salient components which, in the final analysis, constitute the developmental potential of a country.[18] Recent work has confirmed the crucial importance of nonmaterial investment in economic development.[19] In the case of the United States, for instance, "the largest fraction of the rate of growth of income should be attributed to education and the growth of knowledge and know-how. . . ." [20] Educational expenditures contribute to productivity by raising the quality of human capital, and it is only fair to note that without elimination of the "master bottleneck," the shortage of competent teachers in secondary education, economic growth is practically impossible.[21]

Still another integral part of the social overhead capital is the institutional infrastructure,[22] which consists of the legal framework—mores, habits, property rights, contracts, inheritance laws, law enforcement, and status. If, for example, the prevailing modes of behavior of individuals, groups, and institutions, as influenced by ethnic, religious, linguistic, and other cultural traits, result in discrimination against individuals or groups, then the institutional infrastructure does not integrate properly, which is to say that it does not provide equal treatment for all and thus impedes the structural transformation needed for economic growth. Such institutional shackles perpetuate backwardness.[23] This infrastructure, sometimes called the social infrastructure, is by no means a well-defined concept, because the boundaries between human infrastructure and institutional infrastructure are by no means clear.[24]

A brief survey of the literature indicates the significance of infrastructure, especially material infrastructure, for economic development. For instance, W. W. Rostow asserts that without infrastructure (he calls it social capital), consisting of transportation, communications, energy-producing facilities, and an innovation-minded society, there would be no economic take-off into steady growth.[25] Another writer stresses that without infrastructure a country cannot overcome the economic dualism of backwardness. Investment in infrastructure, however, makes it possible both to raise output and to bring about social and institutional transformation.[26] The late J. Stohler argued that properly planned infrastructure investments assure society of "the technically greatest increase in well-being." [27] Since these investments do not pay for themselves, the government must finance them. Private return on such investment is low, but social gains are high. It is impossible to say exactly how much infrastructure is needed to make a country viable in these terms, but the amount is large.

From the very beginning of the colonization of the Holy Land, Jewish settlers either by intuition or design stressed development of the infrastructure.[28] Early Zionists hoped by so doing they would be able to transform the neglected province of the Turkish Empire into "an outpost of Western civilization." [29] This outpost, so they hoped, would eventually become an independent Jewish state. Therefore, Jewish immigrants built roads, set up agricultural settlements, established schools, reclaimed land, and drained the malaria-infested swamps. The Jewish idea "of agricultural settlement as national overhead investment was foreign to the point of view of many of the mandatory government economists." [30]

To improve and preserve human infrastructure, the early settlers developed proper disposal of sewage. Traditionally, both human and animal waste flowed through village ditches, and trachoma, a contagious inflammation of the eye closely related to the absence of hygienic surroundings, was pandemic. The pioneers also tried to utilize the waters of the Sea of Galilee and the Jordan River for irrigation. Since life itself depended on the availability of water, irrigation became a major concern of Jewish settlers and Zionist planners.[31]

By the time Israel emerged as an independent state, it already had many of the characteristics of a European country. For more than fifty years Zionist-inspired settlers had been laying foundations for the hoped-for Jewish state. Most of this activity was directed toward building infrastructure. Physical infrastructure was slowly created by constructing roads, irrigation ditches, and canals; human infrastructure was partly shaped and molded by the inculcation in the settlers of the virtues of manual labor and of the aspiration to be farmers and soldiers.[32] Many of the *olim* of the *aliyas* came from middle-class backgrounds and were well-educated youngsters. The institutional infrastructure, in turn, was a by-product of the utopian socialism and the collective action of many Jewish organizations both abroad and in Palestine. The Jews had their own defense forces, administration, medical services, religious institutions, welfare organizations, the Histadrut, and financial intermediates which poured funds into the colonization of Palestine. Incidentally, in the 1930s a large-scale influx of well-to-do German immigrants brought to Palestine not only money but many skills.[33] From 1933 to 1939 the almost 9 million pounds sterling (more than $40 million) transferred from the Third Reich by the Havarah Company helped to accelerate the build-up of the infrastructure for all the Yishuv living in Palestine at that time.[34]

After the departure of the British administration in 1948, Israel could take over the existing physical infrastructure because the new country had skilled manpower and engineers to operate the irrigation systems and to keep the communications lines open. Moreover, the human infrastructure, consisting of the skills, general education, specialization, and rational and technological attitudes of the people, did not crumble with the departure of the British administrators. The Jews could fill all the posts left vacant; in fact, one writer observes that at the time of its establishment Israel was endowed with an "exceptional quality of human resources." [35] He goes on to say that "in 1948 the educational level of the Jewish population in Israel was close to the highest in the world." [36] Similarly, the institutional infrastructure remained virtually intact, so that the government of Israel, although plagued by many problems, could proceed to absorb immigrants, fight a war, and launch the industrialization of the country.

Hillel Dan at the Helm of the Shilumim Corporation

Once the Shilumim Agreement was ratified in March 1953, Hillel Dan was asked by Levi Eshkol, then finance minister, to head the Shilumim project. Dan agreed to take the job, provided the funds would be used exclusively for economic development and not for current consumption. He also explicitly requested that other ministries, foreign or domestic economic experts, and politicians not be permitted to interfere with the activities of the Shilumim Corporation.[37]

Dan, a highly successful pioneer businessman, was aware that experts knew the facts and had a remarkable propensity to argue and weigh all the pros and cons. What he questioned, and he made no bones about it, was the ability of the experts to apply their knowledge properly to Israel. Because the young country's case was unique, he felt that the pioneers' experience and intuition would be a better guide to spending Shilumim funds than the momentary considerations of the politician or the moot deliberations of the intellectuals. Dan's reservations and conditions were not acceptable to Pinhas Sapir, then general director of the Finance Ministry, who felt that the government should have the final say.

The impasse was resolved only after a conference at Ben-Gurion's home, where Pinhas Lavon pleaded Dan's cause, and Moshe Sharett, unable to stay until the end of the conference, left Dan a note saying, "Take the job. It is important; you are the man who can make something out of it." [38]

Dan accepted and became the first director of the Shilumim or Reparations Company, whose purpose was to establish a Development Corporation to create new chemical industries, expand the electrical generating capacity, develop mining and water resources, modernize roads, railways, and ports, and build up the merchant marine. To synchronize these manifold activities, the boards of directors of the Shilumim and Development corporations were to be identical. The Development Corporation was to be under the supervision of the Council of Ministers and headed jointly by Dan and Sapir.[39]

The Shilumim Corporation in Action

The prevailing taboos tended to denigrate everything related to the Shilumim Agreement. Most Israelis and most Jews in the Diaspora doubted the sincerity of the West German government to make good on the Luxemburg promise. The survivors of the German concentration camps eyed Bonn with hostility, suspicion, and mistrust. It was fashionable to argue that since the wicked Germans had not paid reparations in the 1920s, why should they become so "Christian" all of a sudden? "Just wait," the argument went, "and they will find a way to renege." The public-opinion makers throughout the Western world echoed and popularized these views. Despite the gloomy outlook, Dr. Shinnar, Dan, Dr. Goldmann, and a few Israeli officials with close contacts in Bonn remained undaunted. Their good common sense told them that Bonn was ready and willing to discharge fully the Luxemburg Treaty.[40]

As agitation against Shilumim continued and the press fired frequent broadsides, Dan found that running the Shilumim Corporation, located in Tel Aviv, was a hazardous exercise. To put it mildly, the public disregarded it and the government gave it little encouragement, save for Finance Minister Levi Eshkol, who saw it as a source of long-term economic growth and possible political dividends as well. In the beginning, however, Dan had to pay the salaries of Shilumim Corporation employees, including his own, from the treasury of Solel Boneh, the construction arm of Histadrut. He also tapped Solel Boneh funds to pay for the corporation's first building.[41]

The organizational structure of the Shilumim Corporation was shaped by trial and error. Initially it had four departments, dealing with purchasing, finance and accounting, coordination, and technical matters.[42] Nominally, all purchases had to be approved by a subcommittee consisting of D. Horowitz, P. Sapir, S. Lipschitz, M. Z. Susayeff, H. Dan, and G. Josephthal.[43] However, the decision on what to buy, for the time being, was vested with the corporation.[44] The over-all philosophy for placing orders in Cologne was "Don't buy anything in West Germany you can produce in Israel."

By mid-1953, no plan had "yet been approved to ensure that the promises will be carried out," that is, one ". . . using German reparations for the development of the country." [45] Six months after the ratification of the Shilumim Agreement, *The Israel Economist* wrote that ". . . up to now purchases have been dictated more by the immediate needs of the economy rather than by the requirements of an over-all development plan." [46] Dr. S. Moses, the venerated first comptroller of the State of Israel, also wrote that at the end of 1953 ". . . the shortage of foreign currency may frequently compel the Government to draw on Reparation funds for covering current needs of particular urgency, but it is nevertheless necessary to make sure that the largest possible proportion of the Reparations are applied to the consolidation of Israel's economy." [47] During 1953 and 1954, raw materials and agricultural products worth DM 30 million were imported through the auspices of Shilumim.[48]

From the very outset, cooperation between Hillel Dan and the various government agencies, in particular with the Foreign Currency Division of the Finance Ministry, was fraught with difficulties.[49] Dan complained publicly ". . . nobody listens to me. . . ." [50] The Shilumim Corporation was at loggerheads with the ministerial subcommittee that was supposed to approve the corporation's orders.[51] A half year later, *The Jerusalem Post* observed that "A cloak-and-dagger atmosphere reigns in its [Shilumim's] offices." [52] Dan wanted to make large-scale purchases or preorder goods and equipment as quickly as possible, but in 1953 the officials in the Foreign Currency Division took their time and scrutinized every application for foreign exchange allocation. The two agencies clashed sharply and often.

Dan was not satisfied with the slow pace and speeded up the buying program to take full advantage of the available Deutsche Marks. He simply placed orders in West Germany in amounts that exceeded the corporation's foreign exchange quota by "more than 40 per cent." [53] Dan had seized the initiative, and the participation of the Foreign Currency Division was reduced "to formal approval of import licenses ex post facto." [54]

Dan's philosophy on the use of the available funds was simple: "Don't eat them up! Develop Israel's infrastructure and a few heavy industries!" He aimed at bringing Israel closer to economic independence. He knew that Shilumim funds presented a unique opportunity for the young country to lay a solid foundation upon which to erect primary, secondary, and tertiary industries. Also, the prevailing eleemosynary nature of Israel carried with it a measure of political dependence, and he wanted to change it.[55]

Nevertheless, Dan's hands were tied, not only in Israel but also in West Germany, because the Shilumim funds were available not in foreign exchange but in German goods, subdivided into many precise categories. He could order, year by year, only a certain percentage of a particular category of goods; he also had to take certain commodities which he really did not want. In 1953 and 1954, West German officials adhered strictly to the prescribed commodity schedules.

Dr. Trone's plan was never approved by the government, and at first Dan ordered ships, investment goods, raw materials, and foodstuffs on an *ad hoc* basis. By November 1, 1954, fully 25 per cent of the entire Shilumim amount due had been spent.[56] However, Dan's goal was to channel most of the funds into economic development projects, that is, into infrastructure. His counterpart in West Germany, Dr. Shinnar, head of the purchasing mission in Cologne, was in agreement with that course of action.[57]

In 1953, a special economic advisory staff was created, headed by the American economists Oscar Gass and Bernard Bell, for the judicious utilization of available funds.[58] Gass drew up a realistic import plan for 1954 with a total outlay of $250 million a year, and he urged the government to channel more funds into industrial and basic development.[59] Gass's committee also rewrote the original Trone plan.[60] However, and this is quite interesting, Shilumim funds were not included in Israel's foreign currency budget.[61]

In June 1953, Dan submitted his own four-year plan, quite similar to Dr. Trone's of mid-1952. It called for an outlay of $283 million in foreign exchange and I£ 245 million in domestic currency.[62] $138 million would be used for capital equipment, heavy machinery, and ships, and $59 million for items from all other groups prescribed by the Shilumim Agreement.[63] Dan's main concern was what he called basic development. He wanted to increase rapidly and substantially the country's electrical generating capacity, to modernize and develop Israel's railroads, to expand the ports of Haifa and Jaffa, to increase the irrigated area, and to accelerate the exploitation of the minerals of the Negev desert.[64]

Dan's plan was by no means accepted quickly or endorsed enthusiastically by his colleagues. According to Dan, Sapir opposed everything he proposed. Sapir was dead set against the acquisition of ships. (Incidentally, Dr. Trone had not recommended the purchase of ships from West Germany, except for two tankers of 15,000 tons each needed for security.[65]) Horowitz, now governor of the Bank of Israel, and Josephthal, head of the Absorption Department of the Jewish Agency, also opposed ordering ships. A widespread press campaign was launched against Dan's merchant marine building plan; he was supported only by the Defense Ministry.[66] Despite such massive resistance, Dan's plan was given grudging approval.

To overcome the widespread suspicion that the Bonn government would not honor its DM 3.45 billion pledge, Dan proceeded to order goods and capital equipment in such a way as to make West German industry a "co-interested party of the Shilumim Agreement." [67] He wanted to accomplish this by preordering as much in the way of capital goods as possible and by compelling German producers to coordinate their production schedules with Israel's long-term orders. Even though the Shilumim Agreement did not provide explicitly for credit, Dan and Dr. Shinnar had already explored that possibility in 1953 and obtained almost all they asked for. One of the reasons, among others, Dan decided to order twelve ships and a floating dock was precisely to tie the hands of the German government.

Dan flew to Cologne often, supervising closely the activities of the purchasing mission, as did the state comptroller, to prevent corruption and "undue influence." At the end of 1953, Dr. Moses reported that Dr. Shinnar "represents the Mission before the German institutions with dignity and success. As a result of these positive factors, the first stage of operations may be regarded as a gratifying achievement." [68] Dan put the Shilumim Corporation into the take-off stage despite numerous obstacles. By the end of 1955, Shilumim funds had undeniably become an important fact of the country's economic life. In 1953, for instance, Shilumim imports accounted for 11.2 per cent of all imports; in 1954 they came to 23 per cent; and in 1955, 22.1 per cent. [69]

Despite his success, political developments eventually brought Dan's chairmanship of the Shilumim Corporation to an end. He had remained at the helm of Solel Boneh, used its funds to pay Shilumim Corporation expenses, and brought with him a number of Solel Boneh officials. When even the most stubborn sceptics of the "blood money reparations" stripe realized that Bonn was paying punctually and honorably, a clamor reverberated throughout the country.

Dan's deprecators claimed that he exploited the Shilumim Corporation to build up the industrial empire of Solel Boneh. The slogan, "Dan gives too much to Solel Boneh," was already on many lips in the fall of 1954. According to Dan's autobiography, his political opponents were all out to "get him." [70] As one of the foremost of Israel's self-made industrial captains, a man who had built up Solel Boneh from nothing, he had his detractors in all walks of public life. He ran Solel Boneh with an iron hand and used his economic power and administrative skill the way he deemed best. His economic philosophy was "What is good for Solel Boneh is equally good for Israel." He believed that the new country needed all the material infrastructure and heavy industries it could get, and the quicker the better. [71]

As the political pressure mounted, Prime Minister Moshe Sharett gave Dan an ultimatum: "Leave the Board of Governors of Solel Boneh or leave the Shilumim Corporation." [72] He was officially accused of having misused his position as director of the Shilumim Corporation to discriminate against the various Histadrut business interests to the advantage of Solel Boneh.[73] Dan denied these charges and went back to Solel Boneh. Sapir became his successor. During Dan's tenure goods and equipment worth almost DM 1 billion had been ordered, and he was absolutely convinced Bonn would discharge its commitment in full. His departure ended the extreme centralization of the Shilumim expenditures.

With Sapir running things, the role of the various government agencies in determining orders increased, while that of the Shilumim Corporation declined.[74] From 1955 on, the ministerial subcommittee, headed by D. Horowitz, took over. The new criteria were: (1) to increase Israel's production; (2) to diversify industry and reduce imports; (3) to develop new industries, such as steel production and mining; and (4) to receive in the shortest possible time all of the Shilumim funds.[75] Once the ministerial subcommittee decided how much to allocate for each of these purposes, the Shilumim Corporation asked the respective recipients to prepare a justification for their requests. The following information was required: (1) What would this investment project contribute to the G.N.P.? (2) What would be the contribution to employment and balance of payments? (3) How much hard currency would this purchase from Germany save? In addition, the industrial users were asked to submit their balance sheets, income statements, etc. The Technical Department then determined whether the requested equipment would really do the job. The Israelis were very much aware that the purchase of industrial equipment required elaborate specifications. Technical changes and new designs necessitated continuous changes in specifications. Without such scrutiny Israel would have lost much valuable DM currency. If the project was approved, the buyer was asked for the name of a West German producer he would like to deal with. He was requested to submit more than one bid to avoid possible kickbacks. For large and complicated projects, the buyer was requested to send a specialist to the producer to check the suitability of the equipment.[76]

For these reasons, the Technical Department standardized purchases as much as possible. To improve matters further, the Technical Department manager was appointed to the planning committee of the Ministry of Commerce, which was responsible for the preparation of lists of industrial projects.[77] Using these lists, the Ministry of Commerce prepared the estimates of total requirements and sent them to the Shilumim Corporation, which in turn prepared a list of goods and equipment to be ordered. The Ministry of Commerce insisted on centralized purchases because of better discounts and lower transportation costs and insurance rates, as well as to avoid possible corruption.

When Shilumim goods arrived in Israel, buyers paid for them in local currency. The exchange rate was set by the ministerial economic committee at $1 or DM 4.2 to I£ 1.800.[78] Sales proceeds accrued to the Treasury which channeled them into the development budget.[79] The exchange rate was realistic, unlike the rate of $2.80 to the Israeli pound which prevailed from 1949 to 1951, and made foreign-made goods a virtual gift to Israeli importers. In 1953, roughly I£ 62 million were needed to pay for Shilumim imports.[80] However, because of the tight money policy, shipping, railways, mining, and export industries were hard put to find the local currency to pay for them. Shilumim goods could have been sold on credit. But in that case the development budget would lose operating funds and the government would have to cut its operations drastically. Otherwise, resort to the printing press was inevitable. Or the banking system could lower the liquidity ratio and provide the necessary credits. Eventually monetary stringency eased and the necessary local currency was provided. Thus in 1953–1954 German counterpart funds financed 30 per cent of the expenditure for the development budget;[81] in 1958–1959, 18 per cent was so financed, and in 1960–1961, 16 per cent.[82] From 1953 through 1964, Shilumim counterpart funds accounted for 9.7 per cent of Israel's gross investments.[83]

Purchasing Mission in Cologne

Once the approved lists were transmitted to Dr. Shinnar's office, the purchasing mission asked for bids from German producers. These were usually followed up by negotiations designed to cut the prices of the components. As a rule, Israeli customers decided what to buy and where. Since Shilumim purchases were exports from the standpoint of German law, producers were asked to deduct the 7 per cent export premium from the agreed-upon price.[84] The mission also received a three-year guarantee instead of the usual one-year guarantee. For most installment purchases it managed to obtain a reduction in the down payment of from 30 per cent to 10 per cent. All told, an estimated $5 million was obtained in discounts during the implementation of the Shilumim Agreement.

The staff of the purchasing mission—an excellent team—worked slowly, carefully, and efficiently; [85] it did not rush things through, and its slow response was the only major criticism Israeli buyers made against it. For five years, the purchasing mission, to conserve funds, used no purchasing agents, only service agents. Dr. Shinnar felt that the use of service agents would be indispensable for the proper installation and running-in of the German-made equipment.[86]

In 1955, the Israeli government invited German experts and craftsmen to install the German-delivered equipment.[87] Such a step, which was extremely daring because of the strong anti-German sentiment in Israel, was of the utmost importance. Without proper technical skills and knowledge of the machinery-operating procedures, and lacking experience, the Israelis might have ruined many a machine at the very start. That is precisely what had happened in Indonesia and the Philippines, where the governments refused to admit Japanese engineers with the result that a great deal of the Japanese-delivered equipment was ruined by incompetent usage. Even though the very word "Germany" was still charged with emotion, Israel decided to use West German industrial experts to install and initially supervise the equipment until Israeli technicians had familiarized themselves with it.

Only in 1958 did the Knesset's monetary committee permit the employment of purchasing agents as well.[88] In addition to placing orders, the purchasing mission of Cologne arranged transportation, insurance, and other necessary services. According to the Luxemburg agreement, the goods were to be transported half in Israeli and half in German bottoms. As a recognized large buyer, the Shilumim Corporation was entitled to a 10 per cent discount from the Maritime Conference, which governs transportation rates for all large buyers; yet it got 15 per cent from the very outset. In addition, German and Israeli shipping companies gave the Shilumim Corporation an unofficial special 2½ per cent discount.[89] These were remarkable cost-saving devices.

What has been frequently overlooked, however, was the rapid qualitative improvement of Israel's infrastructure made possible by the Shilumim Agreement. For instance, Haifa, Israel's only deep-water port at that time, had been classified Number 4, the lowest possible, by the Maritime Conference. In shipping circles Haifa had a bad reputation that caused high insurance premiums for all cargoes bound there. During the years of mass immigration such "an alarming amount of pilferage and damage due to careless operation occurred," that the shipping firms took countermeasures.[90] After conditions improved, the Maritime Conference upgraded Haifa to Number 3, which meant lower shipping rates. For the purpose of transporting Shilumim-financed goods from West Germany, the Shilumim Corporation negotiated a special agreement with the Maritime Conference enabling the purchasing mission to ship goods as if they were bound to a port in the Number 2 category; such reclassification meant savings of $1.20 per ton shipped. The total estimated savings on transportation fees came to more than I£ 5 million.[91] Had decentralized shipping been practiced, transportation expenses would have been roughly 20 per cent higher. Another cost-saving device was insurance. The necessary coverage on goods was handled by a pool of German and Israeli insurance companies, 70 per cent German and 30 per cent Israeli. By such practices, an estimated saving of 20 per cent on insurance premiums was achieved.

From 1953 to 1955, the Germans insisted that the Israelis order goods from all specified categories in the amount of yearly allocations, with no exceptions.[92] In 1955, however, in the Fifth Protocol, signed on February 22, Dr. Shinnar submitted to the Mixed Commission a request for eleven industrial projects and asked for permission to place advance orders totaling DM 280 million. Thus, after two years of experimentation the Shilumim funds were integrated into the over-all planning of Israel's economic development. Despite this eventual integration, the utilization of Shilumim funds was still hampered, according to an official Israeli study, by lack of entrepreneurs in Israel, lack of projects, and the fear of the Israeli business community of losing commercial ties with friendly countries.[93] What was actually bought and why will be analyzed in the next chapter.

11

Shilumim Deliveries: Breaking the Bottlenecks

In the early 1950s Israel's economic structure was blemished by bottlenecks, shortage of foreign exchange, and poor coordination of demand and supply. But each year, Shilumim provided a small but certain amount of foreign-made goods and supplies. With this certainty in hand, Israeli economic planners could make small but strategically significant investments, otherwise not feasible, which frequently resulted in spectacular increases in the productive capacities of various industries.

Ships

From its inception the State of Israel has been surrounded by hostile countries bent on its destruction. Its only friendly frontier is that of the Mediterranean Sea, which provides the major avenue for keeping trade lines open. Thus from the conventional, nonnuclear strategic point of view an adequate merchant marine is vital to Israel, both militarily and economically.

In May 1948, Israel's sea power was extremely weak and vulnerable, consisting of only four ships with 6,000 gross registered tons.[1] A year later, only 4 per cent of its total sea-borne trade was carried in Israeli bottoms. Although the government subsidized the growth of the merchant marine, the cost of expanding and operating it was staggering for several reasons: prohibitive construction prices, high operating costs, a very high pay scale for native seamen, shortage of qualified personnel, lack of profitable two-way traffic due to the small volume of export trade, and inaccessibility of the neighboring Arab ports. In 1952 the Israeli merchant marine still employed more than two hundred foreign sailors; it was not until 1956 that Israelis manned all their ships.

Thus it is not surprising that one-quarter of all Shilumim funds spent on goods and services went for West German ships valued at more than DM 585 million.[2] In all, 59 vessels were acquired with a total of 450,000 gross registered tons (GRT). Of these, 41 were freighters, 4 were tankers, 8 were fishing vessels, 2 were customs cruisers, and 4 were passenger ships—2 for service in the Mediterranean, and 2 for the American trade. The GRT of the individual vessels is shown in the Table on page 232.

It was Hillel Dan who, while at the helm of Shilumim, pushed hard for rapid expansion of Israel's merchant fleet. He was strongly supported by the military and the ZIM Navigation Company. Policymakers in the shipping company, many of them former Mossad officials, justified the acquisition of as many ships as possible on the grounds of national security. They felt that Israel needed ships in the event of a recurrence of the conditions that had brought thousands of illegal immigrants to Palestine in Mossad ships. Furthermore, because Israel was a melting pot for Jews, largely artisans and merchants from some seventy countries, out of whom it was striving to forge a normal nation, they felt that normalization would not be complete without Jewish sailors as well. The prospect of Israeli ships, the Star of David ensign proudly amast, on the high seas and in the busy ports of the world, was exhilarating, and clearly played a role in the ship-buying program.

Also, ships were valuable objects possessing international liquidity, and could easily be sold if it turned out that Israel did not need them after all. Furthermore, ordering them was one way to get the Germans to pay. Since the ZIM Company wanted ships and the Histadrut owned 50 per cent of ZIM, Dan probably was kindly disposed toward their request. Another consideration was that ships could earn money, including foreign currency, from the moment they were delivered,[4] whereas other equipment ordered from Germany required buildings, roads, and other preparations which sometimes cost more than double the specific investment. The hope existed, too, of tapping a larger share of the citrus-carrying trade.[5] At

Vessels Acquired Through Shilumim Funds

Passenger Ships	GRT	*Freighters* (cont.)	GRT
1. S.S. Israel	7,000	24. M.S. Galila	4,345
2. S.S. Zion	7,000	25. M.S. Kedma	4,345
3. S.S. Theodor Herzl	9,000	26. M.S. Yarder	4,400
4. S.S. Jerusalem	8,800	27. M.S. Kineret	4,400
		28. M.S. Amal	4,200
Tankers		29. M.S. Atid	4,200
1. M.T. Topaz	24,000	30. M.S. Akko	2,400
2. M.T. Har Sinai	22,000	31. M.S. Kesarya	2,400
3. M.T. Fabio	19,200	32. M.S. Ashdod	2,400
4. S.T. Haifa	18,500	33. M.S. Pal Yam	1,500
		34. M.S. Palmah	1,500
Freighters		35. M.S. Ashkelon	876
1. M.S. En Gedi	22,000	36. M.S. Atlit	876
2. M.S. Timna	22,000	37. M.S. Lakhish	750
3. M.S. Massada	22,000	38. M.S. Tsefat	750
4. M.S. Elat	22,000	39. M.S. Galgas	700
5. M.S. Har Kanaan	14,750	40. M.S. Har Ramon	240,000 cbf
6. M.S. Har Tabor	14,750	41. M.S. Har Gilad	240,000 cbf
7. M.S. Har Carmel	14,750		
8. M.S. Har Gilboa	14,750	*Fishing Vessels*	
9. M.S. Ampal	14,500	1. Doar	
10. M.S. Negba	14,500	2. Ophir	
11. M.S. Deganya	10,300	3. Carmel	
12. M.S. Beer Sheva	10,300	4. Saar	
13. M.S. Gedera	10,300	5. Neve Yam	
14. M.S. Tveriah	10,300	6. Dror	
15. M.S. Dagan	7,000	7. Lamerchaw	
16. M.S. Tapuz	7,000	8. Nitzan	
17. M.S. Alan	7,185		
18. M.S. Eshel	7,185	*Customs Cruisers*	
19. M.S. Shikma	7,185	1. Yarkon-Echad	
20. M.S. Shomron	6,960	2. Yarden	
21. M.S. Netanya	5,600		
22. M.S. Naharia	5,600	*Floating Dock*	7,500 tons
23. M.S. Yehuda	5,012		

that time, Israel's ships carried only 20 per cent of the citrus crop. At the same time, world trade was expanding,[6] expected to double in 20 years, and Israeli shipping circles felt that the country should share in those profits.[7]

In the final analysis, however, national security was Dan's main reason for ordering a large number of ships; he wanted to be sure that Israel could always maintain its sea-borne traffic.[8] No doubt he spoke the minds of most Israelis who feared the unreliability of the gentile world and felt that extra ships would provide extra safeguards for the young country. Those who objected strongly to the acquisition of ships cited the possibility of future losses. However, according to Dr. N. Wydra, general manager of ZIM, his company was "ripe for expansion and we knew what we wanted." [9] Since national interests were at stake, ships were bought.

In contrast to the way all other Israeli purchases were made in West Germany, the ZIM Company ordered the vessels directly from the shipyards. Apparently, ZIM officials did not like to work with Dr. Shinnar's purchasing mission; they also wanted luxuries and insisted on very high quality. (Incidentally, it was State Comptroller Moses who advised the Shilumim Corporation that ZIM should be allowed to acquire what they stipulated, provided the Ministry of Transportation approved.[10])

The ships were ordered in four stages: in 1953, only 3 cargo ships were ordered for delivery in 1954 and 1955; [11] in 1954, 9 vessels were ordered, to enter service from 1955 to 1957; in 1955–1956, 6 ships were ordered; and in 1956, a total of 19 vessels, 17 merchantmen and 2 tankers were ordered, to be delivered from 1958 to 1961. Thus ZIM ordered and took possession of 37 different vessels from the German shipyards.[12] For each ship, three contracts were signed: (1) between the Israel purchasing mission and the shipyard; (2) between the Shilumim Corporation and the ZIM Company; and (3) between the ZIM Company and the government of Israel.

This extensive ship-buying program in which Israel acquired 49 vessels was designed both to renovate and expand Israel's merchant fleet.[13] Renovation aimed at replacing old, slow, and expensive vessels by new ships specially built for Israel's maritime needs. This stage was completed in 1956.[14] In 1953, when the first Shilumim ships were ordered, the average age of the Israel merchant fleet was 21 years; by the end of the renovation stage, it had been reduced to 15 years.[15]

The expansion stage was marked by the acquisition of a number of tankers and freighters and by a sale of a number of old cargo ships. By the end of the program, Israel had acquired 450,000 gross tons built in thirteen West German shipyards. In the process, the average age of Israel's fleet was reduced from 15 years in 1956 to 11 in 1957; [16] it became, in fact, one of the most modern fleets in the world. This transformation became even more evident by the end of 1960, when only 7.7 per cent of the dry cargo fleet was over 10 years old, compared with 41.2 per cent in 1956.[17] Only 3 per cent was still over 20 years old, as against 18 per cent in 1956. As a result, the weighted average age of the entire dry cargo fleet was "only 4.4 years at the end of 1960." [18] By the end of 1964, the total gross registered tonnage of Israel's merchant fleet was 968,119 tons, and the fleet's average age was 5.4 years.[19]

Thus Shilumim contributed substantially to the modernization, quality, and expansion of Israel's merchant fleet. The stage was set for considerable cost reduction and greater efficiency, provided the maritime labor unions stopped asking for "all you can get wages" from ZIM. Unfortunately, this was not the case.

The acquisition of so many ships in less than a decade was not achieved without occasional setbacks, however. In 1965, the state comptroller noted that many of the ships were ordered "hastily, without sufficient preparation as to technical details." [20] It was not unusual, either during construction or shortly after delivery, for a vessel to require costly change orders or even basic design changes. For instance, air conditioning was installed in the liners *Theodor Herzl* and *Jerusalem* only after the two ships had already plied the high seas. Such oversights in specifications were costly and forced crews into long periods of idleness, which, in turn, were reflected in the red ink of ZIM's income statement. Moreover, the ZIM management was slow to inform the German shipyards about observed deficiencies within the agreed-upon period, after which repairs were not performed free of charge.

Israel's emphasis on speedy implementation of Shilumim also turned out to be costly at times. In the early 1950s, German shipyards were eager for business and their construction prices were low by international standards. The index of ship prices in West German shipyards developed as follows: [21]

1952—100	1956—126	1958—138
1955—115	1957—133	

Thus, when the Israelis ordered 32 ships in October 1956, construction costs were more than 25 per cent above those of 1952; in fact, they were at their peak, so the Israelis paid from 15 to 20 per cent more than the vessels would have cost in France or Japan. However, this order was the special so-called "ship project," and nothing much could be done about it. But if the Israelis had not been in such a hurry they would have been able to take advantage of the lower construction costs resulting from the general world-wide shipping crisis. In 1958, when the crisis worsened because of the slowdown of economic activity in the United States, a large number of ships of all flags were idle. Shipping rates also declined, and many Israeli ships were laid up.[22] Subsequently, Dr. Shinnar cut the orders by some 50,000 gross tons but the Israelis still paid through the nose for their vessels,[23] and the high prices later affected ZIM's finances negatively. Critics charged that the accelerated ship-acquisition program also cost dear in terms of credit and interest charges. But the average interest paid was 5 per cent,[24] and since it was incurred to accelerate this program, the over-all cost was not high at all.[25]

Could Israel have used the available West German funds better than for buying 59 vessels and a floating dock? The answer is obviously yes, if one judges the past by the criteria of the present. However, to pass historical judgment on these past events requires an honest appreciation of the conditions prevailing in Israel during the 1950s. Unquestionably the Shilumim-financed fleet-renovating and fleet-building policy was controversial.[26] The Mossad generation never forgot the security importance of water-borne communications, and the cost of maintaining national "shipping lines had more than a purely commercial significance to the economy of the country." [27] For this reason, national security took precedence over careful cost analysis. Purely commercial considerations and the principle of a reasonable return on capital invested were relegated to the background, at least for a while. That noneconomic considerations won out over economic criteria can be attributed to the principle that, in policy making economics, the politician and not the ivory-tower purist or the penny-wise economist has the last word.

At the end of the Shilumim Agreement Israel had a sizable and very modern fleet.[28] The ships were ordered in rapid succession and "without due market research, which resulted in some vessels starting to lose money as soon as they left the shipyards." [29] Since renovation and expansion of the fleet were the main objectives, Dr. Shinnar did not have to concern himself with the future profitability of the shipping companies. His task was simply to take possession as quickly as possible of all that was due to Israel. The four Shilumim-financed passenger ships, *Israel, Zion, Theodor Herzl,* and *Jerusalem,* fared particularly poorly and, while plying the high seas under the Israeli flag, ran up enormous deficits. By 1970 all of these ships had been sold, the sole survivor of the passenger fleet being the *S.S. Moledet* (not a Shilumim acquisition), whose fate is uncertain.

The reasons for the sad plight of the passenger fleet were many. One was that after the mid-1950s "the number of passengers travelling by sea declined relatively to that of air travellers." [30] The average annual decline was estimated at 3 per cent on transatlantic runs. Since world travel was growing rapidly, requiring more planes and ships, air and sea traffic were considered to be complementary. In mid-1957, *The Israel Economist* enumerated all the advantages that would accrue to the country by having an efficient passenger fleet.[31] However, the amply justified acquisition of liners turned out to be a costly affair. In no time at all, they became handsome, elegant, floating white elephants, costing the Israeli treasury millions in subsidies each year.

Other important reasons for the inefficiency of the Israeli liners were the high cost of wages, the work methods, and the demands of the Seaman's Union.[32] Because the job-oriented Seaman's Union made it impossible to trim the oversized staff, Israeli liners were very expensive to run. Furthermore, the ZIM Company suffered from top-heavy senior management, the former Mossad officials, for in Israel top-echelon executives are well-protected by the "first-in, last-out principle"; [33] the longer one's seniority, the more secure one is in one's job, regardless of whether the job is done well or the color of the company's ink.

Interestingly, what probably doomed the graceful and plush liner *Shalom* (a non-Shilumim ship) was religious politics. When many of the well-to-do voyagers did not particularly care to eat kosher food all the time, those who adhered strictly to religious dietary laws strongly objected. Arguments and threats of boycotts and excommunications frequently arose at sea among the passengers in the dining rooms of *Shalom*.[34] It was reported that since many people "do not choose ships as battlegrounds . . . the *Shalom* became the ship to stay away from if it was going to involve taking sides in a matter of religious politics." [35] The unresolved "kosher kitchen" issue undoubtedly harmed all Israeli liners.

From 1953 to 1964, the Shilumim-financed ship purchases amounted to $137.3 million out of a total of $751.3 million; German-built and Bonn-paid ships constituted 56.3 per cent of all ships acquired.[36] The modern Israeli merchant fleet's cargo vessels had a very high average carrying capacity (which is the product of dead-weight tonnage multiplied by speed). Nevertheless, shipping profits were low because of the high costs of wages and social benefits for the seamen [37] and the great difference between the physical quantities of imports and exports.[38] In fact, Israeli vessels frequently had to travel the seas empty-bottomed.

Yet, one of the reasons for the acquisition of so many ships so burdensome to the Israeli treasury had been the lack of other proper investment projects in the early 1950s. Dan admitted as much in his memoirs, for who in the early 1950s really believed that the Bonn government would honor its pledge in full? [39] Dan's fear was that the perennial lack of foreign exchange might prevent Israel from allocating the Shilumim funds for basic development. The acquisition of ships did not require the creation of expensive infrastructure, characterized by capital : output ratios in the order of 15 : 1. And since the gestation period for ships was virtually nil, they could be integrated into the economy at once.

The contribution of shipping to Israel's national income and employment turned out to be very small. In 1958 and 1959, shipping accounted for only *one* per cent of national income and only *one* per cent of the total number of persons employed.[40] And yet it received the lion's share of the Shilumim funds. The decision to acquire ships had been based primarily on strategic and political considerations. Though economic aspects unquestionably figured in the decision,

those who made it felt that in this case the virtues of economic cal-
culus could wait.

The Soviet Union in the 1930s built steel plants and created
machine-making industries, regardless of their heavy cost, and it was
not until the 1960s that they turned their attention to the problem
of efficiency. Similarly, after twenty years of consolidation and rapid
economic growth, the Israelis are now making efforts to raise the
efficiency of their economy. The standards of economic efficiency
have changed over the two decades of independence, but in fairness
to the men who disposed of the Shilumim funds we should recognize
and appreciate the qualitative upgrading of the economy brought
about by the fleet renovation and expansion in the 1950s and early
1960s.

Equipment for the Electricity Industry

The acquisition of ships took 24.4 per cent of the total sum spent
on the five categories of goods and services (DM 2.4 billion),[41] or 16
per cent of the total Shilumim payments of DM 3.45 billion.[42] Since
the Shilumim Corporation strove to channel the available funds into
basic development projects, such as transportation, the generating
and transmitting of electricity, the communications network, and
mining, Dr. Shinnar's goal was to obtain as many capital goods as
possible. Slightly less than 10 per cent, or DM 223 million, of all
purchases went toward the electricity generating and transmitting
network.[43]

A well-developed electricity network is an indispensable part of a
country's material infrastructure, for in many ways it is the foundation upon which almost all primary, secondary, and tertiary economic
activity is mounted. After the establishment of the State of Israel, the
Palestine Electric Corporation generated practically all of the country's supply, except for the 5 per cent generated by the British-owned
Jerusalem Corporation.[44] The Palestine Electric Corporation operated two plants, one in Haifa and the other in Tel Aviv, with a
total generating capacity of 99,000 kwh, the Tel Aviv plant producing one-third of this total.[45]

In 1949 the country's electricity generating capacity was already
inadequate, and an American industrial expert estimated that by
1952 the "rapidly growing demand for electrical energy may become

critical." [46] Obviously, additional electricity generating capacity had to be ordered as soon as possible, but the shortage of hard currency made this difficult. The supply of electricity was so inadequate that as of May 15, 1949, Israelis were forbidden to use electric stoves, irons, and cooking utensils from 7:30 A.M. to 11:00 A.M., and industry was without current from 12:00 noon to 1:00 P.M.[47]

Although a modest expansion program raised the generating capacity to 126,000 kwh by the end of 1952,[48] the need to achieve economic transformation of the country made rapid expansion of the electricity generating capacity imperative. However, the almost complete lack of hard currency reserves in 1952 jeopardized this expansion.

The big question was who would pay not only for the generating equipment but also for the oil to operate it. Since the Shilumim funds were to be used "mainly for development purposes," [49] Israel was able to solve both of these problems without much ado. In Israel the generating of electricity depended upon the availability of foreign oil, that is, generators and oil were complementary goods. At the time of the Wassenaar negotiations, Israel's shortage of foreign exchange was acute and it was unable to get long-term loans, a situation that threatened suspension of oil deliveries, particularly from British companies. Fortunately, West Germany was persuaded, in mid-1952, to make an exception to the "goods only" provision of the future Shilumim Agreement and provide foreign exchange in the form of pounds sterling to pay for oil deliveries to Israel during fiscal 1952–1953. This manner of payments for oil deliveries was maintained even after 1953, and in total the Germans paid DM 1,050 million for Israel's oil.

In 1952, Israel still had not prepared a general plan for the electrification of the country.[50] Dr. Trone's original report suggested two programs for expansion: the first aimed at 800,000 kwh generating capacity by the end of 1962, and the second, reduced program, proposed a generating capacity of 600,000 kwh also by the end of 1962.[51] He recommended, too, that Israel buy the big 50,000 kwh units in the United States and the 10,000 kwh units in West Germany. He wanted the entire distribution equipment ordered from Germany, since its quality equaled that made in the United States.[52] In view of the prevailing acute power shortage, Dr. Trone urged the installation of at least two 50,000 kwh units within one year. He was afraid that otherwise the power shortage would retard industrial development and irrigation, and curtail the supply of electricity to homes.

Under scarcity conditions there was a general tendency to seek independence from the Palestine Electric Corporation. Mekoroth Water Company, for example, wanted to install Diesel-driven pumps in its Yakon stations; several kibbutzim and moshavim had their own generating stations; and a number of municipalities wanted their own power reserves for water supply. Because people were not confident that the Palestine Electric Corporation could provide enough power at reasonable rates, they tended to shift for themselves. These scattered, small sources of power were expensive, and they wasted precious foreign exchange.

When Dr. Trone's recommendations were incorporated into Dan's proposals, electrical equipment became top-priority items on the shopping lists of the Israel Mission in Cologne. The growing volume of industrial production, the expansion of the irrigation system, and the increased number of households, all called for rapid expansion of the power supply. Thus, as early as 1953, the first orders were placed for electricity generating equipment with a total of 40,000 kwh to be used for two stations of 20,000 kwh each.[53] For security reasons, the new stations were dispersed geographically, although concentration might have led to lower production costs.[54] In 1957, German-produced electrical equipment boosted the electricity generating capacity by 20,000 kwh in the Tel Aviv area, and by 50,000 kwh in Ashdod. The total generating capacity of the Palestine Electric Corporation reached 250,000 kwh, apart from the 9,000 kwh capacity of the Jerusalem plant,[55] and by the end of 1958 it had risen to 366,000 kilowatts. Thus, in the three years from 1956 through 1958 this capacity had risen by 62 per cent.[56]

Apart from expansion of the generating capacity, considerable extension of the transmission and distribution network proceeded. The length of low-tension cables, which transmit electricity to consumers, grew by 11 per cent, and the length of high-tension cables, which conduct power over long distances, grew by 12 per cent. Substantial purchases of transformers, high-tension equipment, cables, and power-correcting generators significantly reduced losses of transmission both at power and transformer stations. This qualitative improvement of the transmission and distribution network accounts for the fact that, in 1956, for instance, the rate of consumption of electricity increased more than the rate of output. The rate of loss was 16.6 per cent of output in 1954, 16.7 per cent in 1955, and 15.2 per cent in 1956.[57]

The almost insatiable demand for electricity led to the ordering of a complete power station at Haifa, including two 75,000 kw turbo-generators. A repeat order was placed in West Germany for an identical power station to be constructed in Ashdod. Since the time lag between orders and the beginning of operations is four to five years, investment in this field has to be planned well in advance to prevent delays in expansion of capacity that would impair the efficient utilization of industrial investments.[58]

As Israeli industrial development gathered momentum, coordination between projected industrial and electricity capacities became necessary. As a rule, generating capacity of power stations has to be adjusted to the annual peak load (at midday during the summer months), with an additional reserve equal in size to the largest operating unit.[59] It was estimated in 1957 that by 1961 it would be necessary to double generating capacity; and industrial users would require 75 per cent of this increase. Economic planners and the general public remembered well the great power shortages of 1951, which stifled economic growth.

From the very beginning of the Shilumim operation, particularly while Hillel Dan was in charge, concentrated efforts were made to raise electricity generating capacity rapidly. In time, Israel acquired five power plants from West Germany, enabling capacity to grow from 175,000 kwh in 1953 to 720,000 in 1964.[60] The locations of Israel's power plants were determined by three factors: the availability of cooling water, easy access to oil, and present and future consumer needs. With the gradual development of the Negev desert, the new Ashdod plants by 1962 accounted for 27 per cent of the total generating capacity; Haifa's share was 42 per cent, and that of Tel Aviv, 31 per cent. By 1965, Ashdod's share had climbed to 42 per cent, while that of Haifa dropped to 33 per cent and Tel Aviv's to 25 per cent.[61] Ashdod's power is used primarily for irrigation; Tel Aviv's for households; Haifa's primarily for industry. To be precise, in 1962, 37 per cent of all power was used by industry, 26 per cent for irrigation, and 37 per cent for all other purposes combined.[62]

Israel's electricity consumption has been doubling every four years, whereas in other industrial countries doubling takes place every decade.[63] From 1948 to the end of 1962, the number of consumers quadrupled and the annual sales of electricity increased more than eightfold.[64] In terms of per capita consumption of electricity, at the end of 1961 Israel's figure stood at 1,250 kilowatt hours, approximating that of Italy, Denmark, and the Netherlands.[65] In general, the Middle East's electricity output has been among the lowest in the world despite substantial progress from the mid-1950s to the mid-1960s. For example, in 1963 the per capita output for the entire Middle East was 157 kwh compared with 1,320 kwh for Israel.[66] Israel's figure, in turn, was one-fourth the per capita output in the United States. While Israel's per capita electricity output is very respectable, at the end of 1962 15 per cent of all households still lacked electricity, whereas in Western Europe only 1 per cent did not have it.[67]

The installation of the five German-made power plants substantially raised Israel's generating capacity and provided the badly needed reserve capacity. Purchases of equipment also considerably renovated the stock of existing power plants. For example, at the end of 1962 almost 80 per cent of the electricity producing equipment of the Israel Electric Corporation was less than ten years old.[68] Rapid increases in the electricity supply and considerable qualitative improvements of the entire electricity sector "were due in large part to the equipment purchased under the Reparations Agreement." [69]

Because Israel is a small country, highly concentrated operations using large 75,000 kwh generators, high load factors, and modern transmission lines and transformers substantially increased the efficiency of this industry. But above all, the modernization of the power plants meant considerable savings in fuel consumption per unit of electricity produced. Whereas in 1948 one ton of oil produced roughly 2,500 kilowatt hours, in 1965 it produced more than 4,000 kilowatt hours, an increase of 60 per cent.[70]

Of course, making such large purchases inevitably gave rise to some problems. Until 1953 Israel had bought all its electrical equipment in the United States,[71] and the subsequent switchover to German-made equipment was difficult for Israeli technicians used to the American-made machinery. But now, since maintenance costs for the German equipment turned out to be much higher than for the American,[72] the Israel Electric Company buys the necessary equipment in the United States.

On the whole, the Shilumim purchases enabled Israel to expand its electricity generating capacity when the country was very short of hard currency and "other sources of foreign exchange were virtually exhausted." [73] Because most of the equipment could not have been produced in Israel at that time, without Shilumim these investments would have been either reduced in scope or postponed and the growth of Israel's industry and agriculture slowed down.[74] Shilumim not only quintupled Israel's electricity generating capacity, but paid DM 1,050 million for deliveries of British oil as well.[75] Since one-third of the imported oil was used to generate electricity,[76] and Shilumim paid for 28 per cent of all oil imports,[77] the total outlay on this complementary purchase amounted to DM 1,273 million, or 37 per cent of the entire DM 3.45 billion.

Equipment for Israel's Railways

Without an adequate transportation system, economic development is virtually impossible. Mountains, deserts, rivers, jungles, distance itself, impede the movement of goods and people, so that exchanges are restricted to local markets, which are narrow and offer little scope for specialization. Without specialization production costs remain high. To unite the many local markets into a national market, an adequate transportation system—railroads, canals, and roads—is a prime necessity.

In 1952, Dr. Trone's report on the use of Shilumim funds stressed the need not only for the build-up of Israel's electricity generating capacity but also for the expansion and qualitative upgrading of the entire railroad system.[78] He noted that the life of a bus or a truck is one-third that of railway rolling stock and that railway operating costs were considerably lower than those of buses, especially for fuel and spare parts. Consequently, he suggested the introduction of electric trains for suburban passenger traffic, and Diesel or steam engines for the proposed Negev line.[79] He admonished the economic planners to locate new industrial plants so that rail sidings and feeder lines could be arranged easily, and he deplored that this aspect of industrial planning had been neglected in the past. To increase the cargo volume shipped by rail, Dr. Trone called for considerable qualitative improvement of Israel's railroads. For instance, he wanted to speed up the turnover time of a box car from the 1952 average of 12 days to 5 days. That improvement could be achieved by providing open and closed storage facilities at all railway stations and by installing certain handling equipment. For the future transport of Negev potash and phosphates, he recommended the building of ropeways: potash from Sodom to Mamshit, phosphates from Machtesh to Mamshit. These would then move from Mamshit by rail via Beersheba to the new southern port, Ashdod.

The total investment needed for railway development was estimated at $44 million and I£ 18 million in local currency.[80] From 1954 to 1962, Israel Railways received German-made equipment amounting to $12.7 million (more than DM 50 million) from the Shilumim funds.[81] For the new track to Beersheba only German-made rails were used, and half of the Jerusalem-Tel Aviv line was replaced with German rails. In the marshaling yards, Shilumim-financed shunting engines increased the turnover considerably. Four hundred new boxcars were acquired, ranging from 25 to 50 tons capacity, which raised substantially the over-all cargo-carrying capacity. In 1962, the railways carried two and a half times more cargo than in 1953.[82]

Of particular significance was the electrical signaling and coordinating equipment installed in 1958.[83] Since Israeli railroads are single-track, the installation of such equipment along the Tel Aviv-Haifa line made express trains possible for the first time. This innovation not only permitted a larger number of cars on each train but it improved safety as well.[84] The installation of the Automatic Block System and centralized traffic control set the stage for considerable improvements in efficiency.[85] However, not all Shilumim-financed acquisitions were proper and successful. For instance, the twelve self-propelled railcars acquired in 1955 turned out to be unsuitable because of difficulties with traction power and hydraulic transmission. High operating and maintenance costs led to their demise in 1959.[86]

In addition to boxcars and self-propelled cars, Israel Railways also acquired a number of passenger cars, which replaced the forty-year-old coaches. The resulting improvement in passenger service led to only a slight increase in the number of passengers traveling by rail. In 1959 the increase was 3 per cent, "slightly more than the average annual increase during the last three years, but still not exceeding the rate of growth of the population."[87] Many of these cars are still in operation today. In 1962 50 per cent of the railway passenger-carrying capacity consisted of the Shilumim-financed coaches.

Even though Israel is a small country where short hauls predominate and trucks have an edge over railroads, the expansion and modernization of railways linked up Israel's empty South with the North, that is, with Haifa. By 1963, potash, phosphates, citrus fruit, and grain went north by rail, and in the opposite direction the rails moved supplies and equipment, into the Negev desert.[88]

In spite of the substantial qualitative upgrading of Israel Railways through Shilumim acquisitions, annual operating deficits not only continued but mounted. There were many reasons, but for the record a few in passing were stiff competition from trucks,[89] a very high labor component per unit of output, artificially low tariffs granted for such export items as citrus and minerals, and fare concessions to certain categories of passengers.

Nor was the thorough modernization of the railways accompanied by an improvement in operating costs. Because Histadrut officials virtually forbade the dismissal of displaced workers, they had to be retained. As early as 1956, the Bank of Israel reported that "the operational changes in the railways make it imperative to find a solution to the problem of rationalization. Otherwise, the railways will not be able to continue reducing their costs through the use of the modern equipment which has been put at their disposal with this very end in view." [90] Apart from these institutional difficulties, Mr. M. Savidor, general manager of the Israel Railways, observed in 1962 that "in general we are very satisfied with the quality of the German goods." He felt that "the busy cargo and passenger traffic, the modernity of their rail system, the comfortable journey by rail, all these were introduced with Reparations goods." He termed these innovations "a revolution" which is still incomplete because 70 per cent of Israel's "rolling stock is antiquated and most of our lines are equipped with 40 year old rails and nineteenth century signaling installations." [91] Mr. Savidor's impressive comment should not be overlooked in evaluating Shilumim's contribution to Israel's material infrastructure.

Telecommunications Equipment from Shilumim Funds

Although ships, electricity generating and transmitting equipment, and railway rolling stock and signaling devices considerably improved the operating capacity of these sectors of Israel's material infrastructure, the most remarkable qualitative improvement was in the field of telecommunications. Six million dollars (DM 25 million) was spent on modernizing the country's communications network.[92] Many Israelis still remember vividly the long hours it took to get a phone call through from Jerusalem to Haifa in the early 1950s. Without Shilumim-financed equipment the ease and convenience which were taken for granted at the end of 1962 would not have been possible.[93]

In 1952, Dr. Trone observed that "an extensive telephone network is not only a necessity for the business and administrative life of a country, but has considerable cultural value, and makes for closer contact between remote farms and cities." [94] He urged the introduction of fully automatic communications between the different districts and cities by underground cable, open wire, and radiophone connections. Such an expansion program, serving a population of 2.5 million, by 1962 would have provided 7.2 phones per 100 inhabitants, as compared with roughly 2.1 per 100 in 1952. Dr. Trone hoped that by 1962 Israel's level of telecommunications would be on a par with Western European countries.

Therefore, in 1953 officials of the Ministry of Posts went on a mission to West Germany to purchase underground cable, radio-telephone equipment, and related communications gear. Cables were needed to expand the lines from Jerusalem, Tel Aviv, Haifa, Afula, and Beersheba. A radiotelephone network was essential for the opening of the Negev desert, and telex stations were needed in Jerusalem, Tel Aviv, Haifa, Tiberias, and Beersheba.[95]

The first stage of this program, with an expenditure of $3.5 million, was completed by 1957. Through the acquisition of carrier equipment and the extension of intercity cables, much speedier service was possible. The time when you had "to wait several hours before getting your party" in calling long distance became a thing of the past.[96] Since it was not feasible to lay cables underground to the widely scattered settlements in the Negev, a central station was established to which they were connected by German-made wireless equipment. Installation of telex stations in Jerusalem, Haifa, Tel Aviv, and Beersheba also made written telephone calls possible within the country, as well as outside to the United States, Italy, England, and France. The quality of the German telecommunications equipment was satisfactory, according to the official Bank of Israel report.[97] However, the shortage of telephones persists to this very day.

Equipment for Haifa

Prior to the opening of Eilat and Ashdod, Haifa was Israel's only significant port. By 1952 it was obvious that with the growth of the economy Haifa would require extensive modernization and expansion. Without improvements, Haifa could become a bottleneck in the country's economy. To forestall such a possibility, Dr. Trone recommended extending the Kishon Canal so that bulk goods could be loaded and unloaded without intermediate transport; and he stressed the need for additional harbor stores, sheds, and open dumps. He also suggested the acquisition of modern floating equipment such as cranes, pontoons, launches, and tugs, as well as mobile and fixed cranes, fork lifts, and tractors.[98] Since Haifa was originally built as a protective harbor for the British Navy on the Levantine coast, in 1949 it had very few quays.[99] The port was large but not properly equipped for efficient operations.

The first major Shilumim-financed addition to Haifa's port was a 7,500-ton floating dock, which Hillel Dan ordered in 1953.[100] This order caused a storm of controversy in Israel. Dan's motive for ordering it was his desire to upgrade the quality of Haifa's port equipment, including ship-repair facilities, and to speed up the implementation of the Shilumim program.[101] Since the treasury had to pay from $500,000 to $1,000,000 a year for repairs to Israeli ships in foreign shipyards, it was hoped that the floating dock would save foreign exchange and provide employment for an extra three hundred workers.[102] Another reason may have been the absence of other good investment projects at that time.[103] When the floating dock arrived in Haifa in November 1954, Amos Landmann, the general manager of the port, refused permission for it to enter the harbor.[104] Eventually, however, it was incorporated into the port's over-all equipment, but for the first months it remained idle.[105] Later it turned out to be difficult to operate it efficiently.[106]

In addition to the floating dock, Haifa bought a 25-ton-capacity floating crane, which filled the efficiency gap between its 100-ton Samson crane and one of 15-ton capacity. To modernize the port along the lines suggested by Dr. Trone, Haifa also acquired, through the auspices of Shilumim, fourteen portal cranes, devices mounted on rails that make them mobile anywhere along the port's main quay, greatly increasing the port's cargo-handling capacity. Shilumim funds also provided the port with a dredge with a daily capacity of 200 tons. Before this acquisition, the existing dredge could handle only 25 tons a day.

DM 6 million were spent for the handling equipment and DM 8 million for the floating dock.[107] After this modest expenditure for modernization, Haifa's main port, along with the expanded auxiliary harbor of Kishon, was considered in the early 1960s to be quite well-equipped.[108] The port's expansion and modernization led to the continual upgrading of Haifa's international classification from #4 to #3 to #2, which meant lower cargo shipping rates and cheaper insurance premiums,[109] and a considerable saving of hard currency for the Israeli treasury.

Equipment for the Negev Minerals

Israel lacks any such industrial raw materials as coal, metallic ores, timber, and cheap sources of power. However, the Negev, an area of well over half the pre-1967-war territory, contains large deposits of potash rock, phosphates, ceramic clays, bromides, and copper.[110] The Dead Sea is particularly well endowed with chemical salts, and it has been estimated that it contains the following minerals in metric tons: [111]

Potassium chloride	2.0 billion tons
Sodium chloride	11.9 " "
Calcium chloride	6.0 " "
Magnesium chloride	22.0 " "
Magnesium bromide	980.0 million "

Along with the build-up of the country's material infrastructure, another major objective of Shilumim was the expansion of basic industries, one of which was development of the Negev's natural resources. A broader industrial base was indispensable if the country were to be brought closer to economic independence. Accordingly, the Shilumim Corporation allocated DM 72 million worth of equipment for the exploitation and development of Israel's natural resources.[112] DM 42 million were for the utilization of the Negev's resources, and DM 30 million for the purchase of irrigation pipes.[113]

The exploitation of the vast mineral wealth of the Dead Sea began in 1930 with the launching of the Palestine Potash Company, but the War of Independence brought its operations to a standstill. The northern plant was destroyed, while the southern part remained under the control of Israel's armed forces until 1949, when it was returned to the company.[114] It was idle until 1952, when the company's assets were taken over by the Dead Sea Works, Ltd., in which the government controlled 51 per cent of the stock. With the opening of the highway to Sodom in mid-1953, the first steps could be taken to reopen the southern plant.[115]

Israel's Dead Sea industry extracts potash by a unique production process based exclusively on solar evaporation. The costs of producing the various chemical salts are low and require no imported raw materials of any kind. The major obstacle to profitable exploitation was inadequate and costly transportation. Since chemical salts are heavy minerals, as a rule they are transported by railway in most countries. In Israel, however, in the absence of a rail link, salts have been transported by truck. In 1952, the transport of bulk goods by rail cost around 16 mills per ton/kilometer, while similar bulk goods by truck averaged 40 mills.[116] Thus road haulage per ton/kilometer was two and a half times the cost of rail freight; at the same time hard currency requirements for spare parts, gasoline, and oil were much higher. The average distance from the central Negev to the port of shipment (Haifa) was 300 kilometers (188 miles), and I£ 7.200 per ton could have been saved if minerals were hauled by rail.[117] In mid-1955, it cost an average of I£ 10 to haul phosphate rock and potash from the Negev to Haifa. With such domestic transportation costs, Israel's mineral industry was not competitive.[118] In 1956, the vast potash deposits were still not competitive on the world markets because of the unsolved transportation problems.[119] Dead Sea industry received only DM 2 million from Shilumim.[120]

In addition to the huge mineral deposits in the Dead Sea area, a careful geological survey in the southern Negev, around Timna, sixteen miles north of Eilat, uncovered the presence of 100,000 tons of copper ore, with additional deposits of up to 1.2 million tons as a possibility.[121] Since the concentration of available copper in the ore was normal, from 1.5 to 2 per cent, and the prevailing world price for copper ranged from $500 to $700 a ton, speedy exploitation of these deposits was in order. The major problems were how to connect Timna with the developed parts of Israel, how to provide the necessary sweet water supply, and how to extract copper in the most efficient way.

It was proposed that a plant be built to yield up to 5,000 tons of copper a year, the necessary equipment to come from Shilumim funds.[122] The Timna Copper Works, operated by Israel Mining Industries, was a high-priority development project in the early 1950s because Israel hoped that copper exports would become substantial earners of hard currency. By the end of 1956 construction was about 60 per cent completed, and about 90 per cent of the Shilumim equipment had arrived.[123] The value of this German-made equipment was $3.5 million, or DM 15 million.[124] It supposedly consisted of the most modern equipment available,[125] but the equipment had been ordered too hastily, and most of it was either nonfunctional or of poor quality.[126] After the necessary replacements were made, copper exports from 1960 to 1964 amounted to $18 million, 70 per cent of which was value-added.[127] This plant became one of the major contributors to Israel's supply of hard currency.

Negev Phosphates Ltd., located at Oron, forty-four miles south of Beersheba, also benefited from Shilumim by receiving five different types of German-made equipment. In 1953–1954, the first year of operation, its output was roughly 32,000 tons of raw phosphate with a 26 per cent phosphoric acid content.[128] The phosphate deposits were huge but difficult to utilize because the total absence of water made it impossible to develop an inexpensive beneficiation process.[129] The Oron plant was about thirty miles away from the irrigation system and ten miles from the local well. The available ore "was amenable to a dry process which yielded a usable concentrate assaying about 28.5 pct P_2O_5; but phosphate recovery was low." [130] The concentrate was sent 140 miles north to Haifa for further processing into superphosphate.[131] Unfortunately its grade was not up to the quality requirements of European and Far Eastern customers. Therefore, to tap these markets it was absolutely necessary to bring water to the plant and develop new technology in the form of the so-called flotation method.[132]

The Shilumim Corporation thereupon acquired the much publicized 38 per cent P_2O_5 calcining kiln.[133] The collection system which returns the valuable dust created in the process back into production also came from Shilumim. For almost six years the Negev Phosphates plant in Oron, its mines, and the beneficiation plant ran on electricity generated by its own power plant. The power plant then obtained two generators from Shilumim which added 1,300 horsepower to its electricity power supply. After they were connected to the national grid, these generators provided welcome reserve capacity.[134] The Oron plant also acquired through Shilumim three excavators and one low loader as well as one-third of its repair and maintenance equipment. Even though the total investment in this plant was small, Shilumim provided vital machinery and equipment at a time when foreign exchange was scarce, and provided impetus for the development and exploitation of the available natural resources.

Since the raw phosphates were sent to Haifa for processing into superphosphates, a simultaneous expansion of the facility there was necessary. Thus, Fertilizers and Chemicals Ltd. in Haifa received DM 12 million for such equipment as water-wash towers, dry-ice compressors, and spherical storage vessels for ammonia.[135]

In economic development, complementarity of all factors of production is of utmost importance. A complete plant without access roads is virtually useless, and the other way around. One hand washes the other, says a European proverb, and the acquisition of different types of Shilumim equipment for the exploitation of minerals was obviously done with these considerations in mind.

The government launched a major water resources project in 1952. Because industrial progress depended upon the availability of water, especially in the Negev, it was decided to transport water from the Yarkon River to the Negev in giant pipes 2.25 meters in diameter.[136] This project required 70,000 tons of steel a year and was completed in 1955. It entailed construction of a pipeline that ran 130 kilometers from Tel Aviv into the northern sections of the Negev.[137] The second major project drew water from the Sea of Galilee, 150 kilometers in pipes 2.5 meters in diameter, to the Yarkon. During 1957 and 1958, the Shilumim Corporation ordered almost DM 21 million worth of large main conduits from West Germany.[138] Israel's water economy, in both planning and execution, have been called a modern sensation.[139] Here again, a small amount of Shilumim funds accelerated the build-up of the country's physical infrastructure. The Mekoroth

Water Company received other equipment as well, and in 1965 8 per cent of its total assets came from the Shilumim Corporation.[140] The Shilumim Corporation thus spent DM 2.03 billion to build up the country's material infrastructure. For electricity generating and transmitting equipment and the oil to operate it, DM 1.27 billion was spent. Ships claimed DM 585 million, while the equipment for Israel's railways, telecommunications, development of natural resources, and some heavy earth-moving equipment required DM 174 million. The transportation costs of goods to Israel, insurance, interest charges, and administrative expenses claimed another DM 254 million.[141] This left a little over DM 1 billion for other purchases, such as raw materials, agricultural products, and the industrial equipment for Acco's steel plant, textile industry, and food-processing industries.

During the first Shilumim year in 1953–1954, Israel's economy suffered from considerable under-utilization of existing plant and equipment because of inadequate raw material imports.[142] In fact, the raw material shortage was so widespread that the "lack of imported raw materials threatened large sections of local industry with standstill." [143] Another source reported that foreign raw materials were "sadly lacking." [144] In 1954, the same situation prevailed.[145]

To alleviate the shortage, Hillel Dan proceeded to order raw materials, and by the end of 1953, $40.9 million worth of iron and structural steel had been imported; by the end of 1954, another $82.3 million of raw materials had arrived.[146] These imports constituted, in part, 220,000 tons of iron; 52,000 tons of fertilizers; 15,000 tons of lumber and wood products; 20,000 tons of rubber, textiles, and chemicals; 44,000 tons of wheat; 30,000 tons of miscellaneous food products; and 33,000 tons of equipment: [147] a total of 460,000 tons.[148]

Why did Hillel Dan commit so much of Shilumim funds for raw materials? Hadn't he stressed repeatedly the need for basic development, for building up the country's material infrastructure? Did he and his successors not strive to prevent dissipation of Shilumim on current needs? During the first few years, the Israelis had to adhere to the prescribed purchase schedules, and some items were acquired which could have been dispensed with. However, in 1953, Israel's foreign exchange reserves were desperately low; in fact, there was not nearly enough to pay for one month's imports.[149] At that time the country also suffered from heavy short-term indebtedness, and raw materials had to be imported frequently at higher than world prices.[150] Israël was a marginal buyer and took whatever it could get.

In total, Shilumim purchases of all forms of steel and iron products amounted to DM 391 million.[151] Raw material purchases came to DM 337 million, and agricultural imports DM 91.2 million. All told, DM 819 million were spent on raw materials. Did these imports constitute waste? Were these funds frittered away? Could they not have been used better by investing in material infrastructure?

To appreciate their significance, it is necessary to keep in mind that all factors of production have three characteristics: substitutability, complementarity, and specificity.[152] They are substitutable within a range, but are by no means perfect substitutes. Manpower can be substituted for machines, and vice versa, but machines can never eliminate workers completely. Complementarity means that industrial equipment requires the cooperation of other factors of production. A machine by itself cannot produce anything. It needs workers and raw materials. Specificity means that machinery has a very restricted applicability in the production process. It is either employed in the production of a part of a particular good, or it remains idle.

In this context, Shilumim-financed raw material imports not only refilled the empty bins and industrial pipelines, but also restored complementarity among the existing factors of production. Greater availability of raw materials also gave wider scope to the specificity of available industrial equipment and manpower. Working machinery, plants, and utilized manpower were the tangible results of the large-scale infusion of raw materials. It should be kept in mind that Israel's export industries exist mainly on imported raw materials. For example, for every dollar earned in exports, Israel had to import two dollars worth of raw materials.[153] Thus, while the Shilumim raw material imports lacked the spectacularity of Israel's development projects, they helped to alleviate some of the metabolic disorders of the economy caused by foreign exchange shortages. Above all, the huge steel and iron imports were used to erect structures for a number of future plants, which were to be equipped with German-made machinery.

It is known that DM 316 million was spent on textile machinery, chemical equipment, motors, metal-working machinery, cranes, pumps, equipment for sugar-producing factories, and office and construction equipment.[154] Some of these acquisitions went into the material infrastructure, as discussed above, but DM 267.5 million was allocated for the development and renovation of industry.[155] More than 1,300 firms acquired German-made equipment under the auspices of Shilumim. The lion's share went to the metals industry, which received DM 67 million, or 28.2 per cent of the total. The "Steel Town," near Acco, received over one-half of that sum. DM 56 million, or 23.1 per cent, went for the expansion and renovation of the textile industry. DM 40 million, or 16.6 per cent, was channeled into the food-processing industry, primarily into the sugar factories, and DM 22 million, or 12.5 per cent, was allocated to the chemical industry. The rest, in small amounts, went to other processing industries.[156]

The initial proposal to erect "Steel Town" near Acco was hotly debated in the press and government councils.[157] It was one of Hillel Dan's pet ideas and comprised a substantial complex of iron and steel facilities that would eventually produce 90,000 tons of pig iron, 118,000 tons of steel billets, and 100,000 tons of rolled steel products per annum.[158] The complex would cost I£ 121 million, more than half of which would have to be in foreign exchange.[159] Because of extremely high production costs, the entire "Steel Town" project was thought to be "of a highly marginal, if not submarginal character" by Israeli experts.[160] They warned that the project would consume millions of dollars of foreign exchange and require millions of pounds in subsidies.[161] One Israeli economist dubbed the project: "Israel's chief exhibition piece." [162] However, work went on, and by 1962 some I£ 50 million had been invested and I£ 15.5 million worth of equipment had come from Shilumim funds.[163] The rolling mill and Siemens-Martin furnaces came from West Germany, and the first smelting furnaces went into operation in 1956.[164] In 1958 the rolling mill was started up.[165] By 1960, the output of the "Steel Town" plant was roughly one-third of what had been hoped for and it employed 940 workers. It was a heavy money-loser and the Treasury poured in millions in subsidies to keep it going.[166]

In terms of profit and loss, such investments make no sense. However, Shilumim funds that went into "Steel Town" plants do not necessarily represent waste in socio-economic terms. The decision to make the investment was based on strategic and political considerations, matters removed from the more narrow framework of the economist. Thus, it was reported in early 1955 that because Israel is surrounded by enemies "it is highly undesirable that Israel should be completely dependent on importing the products of these industries in the event of war." [167] Because of compelling military considerations, the proposed "Steel Town" project made good sense. In the 1950s, industrial planning gave the "greatest emphasis to social, political and military factors rather than to purely economic factors." [168] And as long as the Middle East is the powder keg and Israel remains on a war footing, strategic considerations will remain paramount.

The second major claimant of Shilumim funds spent on industrial renovation and expansion was the textile industry.[169] Some 166 textile plants received German-made equipment of a total value of DM 56 million. For many years the textile industry enjoyed strong government support because, being labor-intensive, it provides many jobs, uses domestically raised cotton, and has the highest value added in industry.[170] Before 1953, Israel's spinning mills were equipped with obsolete machinery and no foreign exchange was available for newer equipment. Shilumim funds increased their productive capacity as well as the quality of output.[171] In addition, cotton weaving looms, machinery for yarn preparation, and finishing equipment were acquired. It was estimated that Shilumim enabled Israel to raise the productive capacity of the textile industry threefold or fourfold.[172]

The food industry received DM 40 million, and 93 firms were able to acquire German-made equipment. Two sugar plants, at Afula and Kiryat Gat, were built and equipped with Shilumim equipment.[173] The chemical industry got DM 22 million and the other branches were given small amounts.[174]

In sum, Shilumim made spectacular additions to the country's material infrastructure. It refilled the empty industrial pipelines, and provided equipment for some 1,300 plants. Shilumim assured extra foreign exchange when it was extremely scarce. It is not possible to say what exactly Shilumim's contribution to Israel's economic development was, because in economic development many factors remain unmeasurable and their impact becomes evident only much later. However, the foregoing concrete listing of some of the major items acquired bear clear testimony to the net addition to Israel's resources. Small investments, at strategic places, frequently broke critical bottlenecks in important sectors of the economy.

12

Economic Challenge for a Small Nation

By the spring of 1966 the Shilumim Agreement was fulfilled. There were no noisy protests and mass demonstrations such as marked its inception in 1952. There was only the most fleeting debate, with the publication of the official Bank of Israel report, *Hashilumim Vehashpaatam al Hameshek Haisrael*. The popular feeling throughout the land seemed to be: "You government people accomplished little with the German reparations money." [1] In the Diaspora, as late as 1969, Dr. Goldmann wrote, ". . . many Jews found it very difficult to recognize its positive side [Luxemburg Agreement]." [2] Two years earlier, Dr. Shinnar had said there was no need either to inflate or to minimize the impact of Shilumim on the economy of Israel. [3] The critics of Shilumim still claimed that it had been dead wrong to accept DM 3.45 billion in blood money, that it was a tiny fraction of what the Germans had stolen from the Jews, and that it was simply a return of Jewish property anyhow. Individual compensation payments did not represent any favors to either Israelis or Jews, so that there was no need to say thank you to anybody. [4]

The *Hashilumim* report, written by F. Ginor and Y. Tischler, reveals that from 1953 to 1964 Shilumim receipts represented 24 per cent of all unilateral transfers, 26 per cent of all capital transfers. [5] These receipts were particularly significant in 1955, when Shilumim funds accounted for 40 per cent of *net* unilateral transfers. [6] During the acute foreign exchange shortage in 1953, Shilumim underwrote 11.2 per cent of total imports and 15.6 per cent of the trade deficit; [7] in 1954 the corresponding figures were 21.2 and 33.1 per cent. In 1955 Shilumim imports were 19.8 per cent of total imports, and a year later 14.6 per cent. By 1960 the Shilumim share had fallen to

10.9 per cent, and in 1961, 10.5 per cent. By 1962, however, Shilumim represented only 4.6 per cent, and in 1964 1.5 per cent.

During these years Shilumim also financed a considerable proportion of the country's investment from counterpart funds. In the budget year 1953–1954, for example, one-quarter of the development budget came from Shilumim counterpart funds. During the next budget year, 47 per cent of the development budget came from this source. Thereafter, the percentage declined, but for the period as a whole (1953–1954 to 1965–1966), 20 per cent of the development budget was obtained from these counterpart funds.[8] Thus Shilumim was ". . . considered as one of the pillars of our economy." [9] From the beginning Shilumim represented an assured source of foreign exchange and foreign-made goods.[10] From 1953 to 1964, it financed 9.3 per cent of the foreign trade gap, accounted for 9.7 per cent of Israel's gross investments, and amounted to 2.5 per cent of the economy's total resources.[11]

The Jerusalem Post's summary of the *Hashilumim* study popularized the least important aspects of the Shilumim Agreement. It stated that without Shilumim ". . . our economy would have been much more efficient and less dependent upon foreign aid"; and concluded ". . . there is no doubt that with Reparations completed we are now better off. But would we not have been sounder and healthier without them?" [12] To balance the score, an editorial in the same issue reminded the readers that individual compensation payments and Shilumim had ". . . played a large part in the life of the individual recipient and equally in that of development in general in Israel." [13]

Dr. Shinnar's reaction, in a letter to *The Jerusalem Post,* was restrained but sharp. He disagreed with those who minimized Shilumim's impact on Israel's economy and who professed that the country would have been sounder and healthier without it. However, he did agree that Shilumim ". . . prolonged Israel's dependence on capital import." [14] But he also called attention to the fact that "Shilumim increased investments and helped the growth of the National Product." To Dr. Shinnar's mind, Shilumim helped build a sound basis for a healthy economy.

On April 29 the controversy was renewed with the argument that Shilumim "had only a marginal impact on Israel's economy." [15] The writer went on to say that without Shilumim Israel would have had less inflation. One reader claimed that "it was morally and economically wrong to request or accept reparations and that we would today be much nearer to economic self-sufficiency and its correlated political and military freedom of action, had we chosen the harder and more honorable course of standing on our own feet and living within—not beyond—our means." [16] However, another reader was startled by Israel's claim that without Shilumim "we would have achieved the same, or even sounder results." The writer termed it "a speculation in retrospect," and recalled "how the austerity regime could not be maintained longer than two or three years, and how it had to give way to the free market prematurely because the population refused to put up further with the hardships of everyday life, while the black market flourished in any case." [17] These sample letters reflected the smoldering public disagreement over Shilumim.

An English synopsis of the *Hashilumim* report,[18] written for a different audience and published in May, flatly rejected the critics' claim that the "golden rain" of reparations had spoilt the people, inflated aggregate demand, detracted from the efficiency of the economy, and led to rash spending. It recalled Israel's extremely difficult foreign exchange position in the early 1950s, and argued that "it is almost inconceivable that the economy could have proceeded smoothly towards a period of expansion without the flow of Reparation funds and other unilateral transfers. The public would probably not have been willing to continue the austerity phase for another lengthy period in order to devote maximum local resources to investment." It concluded that Shilumim had contributed to development "at a higher level of production, consumption and efficiency and a faster pace of economic growth than would have been possible without them. Israel's industry, transport system, electricity network and merchant fleet all owe much to Reparation funds. Without them, industrialization may have been delayed for another decade!" Dr. Shinnar also felt that Shilumim funds had helped particularly to overcome the take-off difficulties (*Anfangsschwierigkeiten*) of the economy of Israel.[19]

How to Evaluate Shilumim

No single criterion can be used to evaluate the effects of additional resources on the various branches of industry or on the economy as a whole. A number of factors ultimately determine to what extent the economy benefits from any particular extra investment or import surplus. But extra resources do have effects on the total output, employment, the balance of payments, price levels, and efficiency.[20]

Economists usually consider additional resources at the margin in terms of their effect on consumption, investment, and exports. Seldom do they ask why and whence these additional resources came. So, in order to assess their marginal as well as their political or social impact on a particular economy, one can analyze the elasticities of substitution among different sources of funds. For instance, if I need a loan and cannot get it from Bank X, I can probably get it from Bank Y; here, the two sources of funds are perfect substitutes. But if I do not get a research grant from the Ford Foundation, it is not at all certain I will get it from the National Science Foundation or the Social Science Research Council. Similarly, if Israel had not received almost $800 million or its equivalent from West Germany, it is not at all certain that the young state could have obtained the same volume of resources from other sources, let alone on the same terms provided by the Bonn government. In that sense then, we must also pay attention to why and whence the funds came.

An interesting methodology to measure the impact of additional resources on an economy was used in 1961 by Dr. Fanny Ginor, an economic adviser of the Bank of Israel.[21] She proposed first, in terms of aggregates, to measure the over-all contribution of extra resources, be they American grants-in-aid, Zionist gifts, or West German Shilumim, to investments, imports, consumption, and employment, and second, to determine their contribution to specific imports and specific investment projects. The assumption in both approaches is that imports and investments financed by, let us say, the Shilumim Agreement, would not have been equaled in its absence. Here the impact is evaluated at the margin in terms of the effect of extra resources on such measurable aggregates as consumption, investment, and total output.

Dr. Ginor calls this approach the "maximum effect" principle. It implies that without Shilumim funds total imports and investments would have been less by the *entire* amount of DM 3.45 billion. However, this "maximalist" assumption can be challenged on the grounds that because, since 1954, for example, gifts from abroad have been "used to build up reserves and reduce short-term debt, it was unrealistic to assume that the absence of reparations would have meant an equivalent decrease in imports." [22]

Because numerous reservations can be made against the "maximum effect" principle, Dr. Ginor substitutes the "minimum effect" principle. Here, alternative sources of hard currency, or their equivalents, would have left investments and imports at exactly the same value levels as they were with, let us say, the Shilumim funds. But this view implies that all sources of foreign funds are perfect substitutes, which is unrealistic. Moreover, since two-thirds of Shilumim funds were in German-made goods, the structure of Israel's output, investments, and consumption had to be different than it would have been had the West German government paid the entire DM 3.45 billion in foreign exchange. As it was, two additional factors further reduced the real value of the DM 3.45 billion: first, West German limitations on the annual spending schedule constrained Israel's time preference; and second, German insistence on tie-ins limited Israel's choice of goods as well as its ability to shop on the best market.

Israel Without Shilumim: Some Possible Alternatives

What might Israel have done to substitute for Shilumim funds? The *Hashilumim* report considers five alternatives: reducing imports; generating additional domestic resources; borrowing more heavily abroad; attracting more foreign investments; and obtaining more unilateral transfers, such as gifts from United Jewish Appeal and grants from the U.S. government.[23]

An evaluation of these alternatives suggests that although it would have been possible to replace most of the Shilumim funds, Israel's economic development would have been slowed down.[24] With domestic saving very low, it is probable that the high investment demand would have been met through an open inflation.[25] And this very likely would have led to the downfall of the Mapai government. In sum, had there been no Shilumim, asserts the *Hashilumim* report, there would have been a change in economic policy.[26] Economic controls very likely would have lasted much longer.[27] On the other hand, Shilumim's critics were probably right that, in the absence of Shilumim, direct controls would have been scrapped sooner. For example, one reason for the sudden slowdown of economic liberalization was the assured source of foreign supplies which enabled the Israeli government to continue "without material changes in the present economic setup." [28]

Israel's Economic Growth Rates, 1953–1966

The rate of Israel's growth has been quite remarkable, and the results truly impressive. Its Gross National Product, in real terms, rose annually from 1950 to 1967 at 9.3 per cent, or 3.4 per cent per capita; [29] by subperiods, the G.N.P. rose 12.1 per cent during 1950–1954; 10.1 per cent annually from 1955 to 1959; and 9.5 per cent annually from 1960 to 1964.[30] These rates of growth are very respectable by international standards.

The engine of economic growth and development is capital formation, which enables an economy to expand its material, human, and institutional infrastructure as well as industry and agriculture. Investment funds can come from the private sector, the government, or foreign countries. The salient feature of Israel's capital formation is that from 1949 to the present day, most of its investment funds have come from abroad. Professor D. Patinkin observed in this connection that during the first decade of the country's independence ". . . the import surplus was more than enough to finance net domestic capital formation; that is, in other words, domestic savings were not only a source of financing the investment program, but were probably even negative." [31] Other scholars stated that "Investment in Israel did not depend only, or even mainly, on saving but on the import surplus"; [32] in other words, the steady high level of investment was made possible by large and continuous import surpluses.

From 1949 to 1965, the import surplus was $6 billion, 70 per cent of which was financed through unilateral transfers, in other words, by gifts from American Jewry, U.S. government grants, and West German Shilumim and restitution payments.[33] For a slightly different period, 1950–1967, the import surplus was $6.4 billion, and the total net capital influx was $7.4 billion, which enabled "the financing of the import surplus and the accumulation of foreign currency balances which reached $845 million at the end of 1967." [34] Of this sum, $4.9 billion came from grants and $2.5 billion from loans and investments.[35] Of the $4.9 billion in grants, $775 million came from Shilumim and $1.2 billion from personal restitution; [36] *thus almost*

$2 billion or 40 per cent of all grants came from West German com-
mitments made at Luxemburg in 1952. From still another perspective, Shilumim funds accounted for 22.4 per cent of all grants received from 1953 to 1964 and represented 78.1 per cent of all capital
influx.[37]

Some critics have claimed that the "golden rain of grants" led to
widespread misdirection of resources. In 1953, for instance, Dr.
Landauer wrote *"das viele Auslandsgeld ruiniert uns."* [38] Others, like
D. Cohen, charged that foreign funds have been used "extensively to
bolster the high public and private consumption and also to finance
questionable investments both in inefficient public ventures and in
private 'approved enterprise' with low added value." [39] According to
Cohen, these funds were used to finance imports "below the effective
rate of exchange and exports above it," [40] to subsidize the high level
of disguised unemployment, especially in public services, as well as
many inefficient agricultural settlements, to support manufacture of
noncompetitive goods, and to finance costly public housing.[41]

To be sure, public financing of investment has been and still is
heavy. In 1954, for instance, 74 per cent of total investment was
publicly financed; in 1958 and 1959, 54 per cent was so financed.[42]
From 1960 to 1966, the share of publicly financed investments had
declined to 43 per cent.[43] The public sector consists of corporations
where more than 50 per cent of the outstanding stock is owned either
by the central government, local authorities, or such national institutions as the Jewish Agency or the Jewish National Fund.[44] The share
of housing in the total fixed investment was particularly heavy. For
instance, from 1950 to 1954 it was 41 per cent of total investment;
from 1955 to 1959, 34 per cent, and from 1960 to 1965, 33 per cent.[45]
It was probably the highest in the world.

Yet to absorb the masses of immigrants, to protect against the
strident and continuous military threats to the very existence of
Israel, to develop the scant resources of the country, required huge
outlays. Without proper roads and communications networks, the
size of the internal market could hardly grow. Power and water were
essential before economic development could even begin. It is inconceivable that investments in the material, human, and institutional
infrastructure could have been undertaken by the private sector.
Private enterprise exists to make money, not to spend it on sewage
treatment or other worthy general social purposes. However, some-

body must do something about eliminating disease, pollution control, slum clearance, hygiene, and education, because the social benefits of these projects are large. And these tasks fall properly on the shoulders of the government; indeed, Adam Smith sanctioned government intervention in the field of "public goods" almost two centuries ago. The government of Israel did assume the responsibility for projects benefiting the general social and public weal.

As soon as Shilumim funds became available, *The Israel Economist* declared that, after mass immigration and physical controls, the country "can make up for past errors and lay foundations for our economic independence." [46] Israel's heavy and persistent trade deficit made it an economically dependent country. Year after year, the country used more resources than it produced, and had to depend on outside help to make ends meet; in fact, Israel has been called a supported or an eleemosynary society.[47] According to Patinkin, its recurrent trade deficit ". . . represents the major failure of Israel's economic policy." [48] Economic independence has been the subject of many debates, but its attainment still eludes Israel.[49] It was about 1956 that Israel's infrastructure was well enough along to allow for concentration on the beginning of industrial development.[50] However, it was not until 1954 that the government recognized that the country's agricultural development was limited by the lack of water and arable land. Thereafter, the specific economic objectives of development were (1) provision of jobs for those who could not be absorbed by agriculture; (2) industrialization through import-substitution; and (3) an absolute need to increase industrial exports.[51]

At the same time that the Israeli government was building its material infrastructure, the country was suffering from a "brain drain," a flight of intellectual capital, which in many ways is governed by the laws that control the flight of physical or material capital. From 1948 to 1966, it was estimated that a total of 164,500 persons holding Israeli citizenship left the country for new horizons.[52] This means that one of every 16 persons, or 5.3 per cent of all immigrants to Israel, left the country.[53] Of course, many have returned and many others reside abroad temporarily.[54]

In addition to the bracing efforts of building up the country's infrastructure, material, human, and institutional, the government never lost sight of Israel's need to be prepared militarily. Israel is probably the only small country that has never relied on the forces of the United Nations or any large Western power for protection or for the actual defense of its borders. But the victories of Israel's arms in 1948–1949, 1956, and 1967 have exacted an awesome price in domestic resources. Keeping the country prepared militarily has heavily drained its foreign exchange holdings. For instance, from 1948 to 1956 "in foreign currency alone an average of some $70,000,000 was expended each year" on arms; 10 per cent or even more of the G.N.P. was spent on defense.[55] Since then it has been probably twice as much per year, and peace still eludes the Middle East.

To assure survival and to increase its bargaining position in the struggle for sources of conventional weapons, Israel commenced work on atomic weapons. As a result, in the mid-1960s Israel emerged as the sixth nuclear power, after the United States, the Soviet Union, the United Kingdom, France, and China. According to one report, Israel most likely has six A-bombs of the Hiroshima type, sufficient to destroy the major cities of the neighboring Arab states.[56] Israel also has the requisite delivery systems: A-4 Skyhawk jets, F-4 Phantom jets, and MD 660 rockets, able and readily available to drop the bombs where needed. Of course, this report was denied in *The Jerusalem Post* as "speculative, unauthorized and unfounded" one week later. But this denial was not that Israel does not have the bomb, only that "Israel will not be the first to introduce nuclear weapons into the Middle East." [57]

The real question is whether possession of atomic weapons will markedly improve Israel's security in the aftermath of the June war of 1967.[58] In the long run probably it will not, because the country is small and it will not have "any second-strike capacity in an atomic war with Egypt." [59] However, in the short run, possession of operational nuclear weapons gives Israel an excellent bargaining position for conventional weapons from the Western powers. The late Levi Eshkol is reputed to have told President Lyndon Johnson that Israel would not expand its nuclear capability "if the United States made direct sales to Israel of conventional arms equal in quality to those Nasser was getting from Moscow." [60] It was this bargaining tool that enabled Israel to obtain the 50 F-4 Phantom jets; previously most of its conventional weapons had come from France or West Germany.

Israel is indeed a unique country. It has a European standard of living, a well-developed material infrastructure, an excellent human infrastructure, and a unique institutional infrastructure. No other country, per capita, has ever received more outside assistance than Israel, yet its trade deficit has been large and persistent. The country's military burden is very heavy, both in terms of domestic resources and requirements of foreign exchange. It is a nuclear power. And, despite its delicate foreign exchange position, Israel has been in the foreign aid business since 1954,[61] with a small, but extensive and very effective, program, which has earned the country much good will and reputation except in the Arab countries.[62]

Thus, as a nuclear power and as a country giving foreign aid to some ninety countries, Israel is a developed nation. On the other hand, the inability to pay its way on current account means that it needs tremendous quantities of outside help. Israel's economic policy has always aimed at building and maintaining a progressive economy in agriculture, industry, tourism, and science, while at the same time preserving a suitable standard of living. Neither at the end of Shilumim nor in the early 1970s has Israel been able to strike a balance between economic growth and the standard of living.

Progress in the welfare of the population has been to a considerable extent mined from the development of the country and the achievement of a posture in trade balance. From 1958 to 1964 Israel's G.N.P. grew on the average from 10 to 11 per cent, and the per capita G.N.P. about 6 per cent.[63] It is important to keep in mind, however, that rapid growth of the G.N.P. does not automatically mean salability of the output. As one writer put it, ". . . an economy's mere physical ability to pump out an ever greater quantity of goods and services will be of little use in increasing growth if the output is not fully salable, both domestically and internationally." [64] West Germany, for example, has not chalked up such impressive growth rates as Israel, but its export record in the 1950s and 1960s has been the envy of the world. One reason for this success was that, for a long time, the export business was more profitable than domestic sales.[65] Israel, on the other hand, did not successfully restrict domestic demand, and inflation continued year by year.[66] Continuously rising domestic price levels tend to make sales in the home market more attractive than sales abroad; and as one writer noted, "the shift from export activity to production for the home market will be intensified to the extent that rises in domestic costs make it unprofitable to dispose of stock abroad at going world prices." [67] Inflation thus stimulates consumption and penalizes exports and savings.[68]

Despite rapid growth of the domestic product, continuous industrial diversification, and impressive gains in merchandise exports, Israel's industrial products, by and large, are still not competitive on the world markets.[69] In 1965, after a decade of intense effort at diversification and the creation of many plants for import-substitute products, citrus fruit and polished diamonds still accounted "for at least half of total merchandise exports." [70] This high degree of export concentration shows clearly where Israel's competitive edge on the world's markets lies. It has been said repeatedly that Israel's stupendous economic growth has resulted from the availability and successful assimilation of billions in gifts from world Jewry, the American government, Shilumim, and German compensation payments.[71] From 1949 to 1965, world Jewry provided 59.2 per cent of all unilateral transfers (gifts) and long-term capital as a percentage of import surplus.[72] The share of the United States was 12.2 per cent, and West Germany accounted for 28.9 per cent. In 1960, however, West Germany's share was 51.5 per cent, and in 1963 41.4 per cent.

In Israel all realists believe in miracles. In fact, according to Dr. Goldmann, Prime Minister Ben-Gurion told him after signing the Luxemburg Treaty: "You and I have had the good fortune to see two miracles come to pass, the creation of the State of Israel and the signing of the agreement with Germany. I was responsible for the first, you for the second. The only difference is that I always had faith in the first miracle, but I didn't believe in the second one until the very last minute." [73] At the end of Shilumim, however, many worried about what would happen ". . . when the Israeli balance of payments loses the support of the influx of German marks through reparations." [74]

Even though Shilumim funds were used to build up infrastructure and diversify industry, Israel has not been able to stop inflation and expand its exports rapidly enough to reduce its excessive reliance on foreign gifts. The list of analyses of the major faults of Israel's economy is long.[75] One of the major reasons for economic disappointments has been the "half-war, half-peace" milieu, which led to "heroic" attitudes toward economic questions, with the virtues of economic calculations of profit and loss generally condemned as cowardice, and terms like "profitable," "effect on balance of payments," and "economically viable" generally regarded as dirty words.[76] But as long as Israel is not able to make peace with its Arab neighbors, strategic considerations are of paramount importance and the economy cannot be left to economists alone.

The intriguing question at the end of this study is what will happen to Israel's economic development should peace come and past sources of unilateral transfers dry up? Any projection is necessarily clouded by political, social, and economic imponderables, but as a small country Israel suffers from certain debilities of smallness.

At the end of Shilumim, Israel's territory comprised almost 8,000 square miles (21,000 square kilometers) with a population of 2.5 million. It was a small country. The years after World War II witnessed the emergence of a few score new, independent and economically backward, but mostly small and very small countries. In 1967, for instance, 134 sovereign states and 32 nonsovereign countries made up our planet.[77] Eighty-five of the sovereign states had a population of less than ten million, and sixty-four countries had less than five million. In the early 1960s, out of 112 countries and territories classified as underdeveloped by the United Nations, no fewer than ninety-one had a population of less than fifteen million and sixty-one had less than five million.[78] In mid-1969, a UN study reported that there were ninety-six "vest-pocket" countries, "mini-states," or "see-throughs," with populations under one million, which are already sovereign or moving toward independence.[79]

Israel is a small country, but what exactly is a small country? What characteristics make generalizations possible? Is smallness determined by territory, population, or both? Experts differ,[80] but there is some agreement on the principal economic characteristics. In population, small countries range from 1 to 30 million, and in territory from 10,000 to 20,000 square miles of usable land. Excluded are such microstates as Malta, Monaco, Andorra, San Marino, and the island-state of Nauru, with its population of only 3,000. For our purposes, William G. Demas' upper limits—less than 5 million people and from 10,000 to 20,000 square miles of arable land—will be used because they more closely approximate Israel's size.

All small nations have common economic characteristics and certain disadvantages of smallness.[81] These, in turn, impose constraints on their economic growth, the efficiency of their economic activity, and their international trade.[82] They possess fewer natural resources than large countries, and their mineral wealth is "likely to be less varied and less abundant." [83] Their "economic structure . . . is typically less diversified than that of larger units." [84] This means that small nations must concentrate their economic activity in only a few sectors. Thus, the resources in a small country "are likely to be highly skewed," [85] whereas their aggregate domestic demand is likely to be highly diversified. And resource skewness compels them to exchange their few resources for a wide assortment of imports. Israel has no appreciable natural resources, except the Dead Sea minerals, that could be exploited economically at the present time.

The second salient characteristic concerns the effect of a small population on national economic efficiency. The market size is "probably too small to get all the technical economies available." [86] According to Demas, this is especially disturbing for a very small country, which he defines as one with less than 3 million people, because "its very small absolute size of population imposes sharp limits on the extent to which it can economically produce inter-mediate and capital goods for the home market." [87] For instance, small countries do not usually possess aircraft, automobile, engineer-ing, or machine-tool industries; as a result, they must import almost all such goods. Except for defense-related capital-goods production, Israel has no capital-goods industries to speak of.

A third economic characteristic is that a skewed resource pattern, potentially prohibitive production costs for industries using advanced technology, and little diversity of industrial activity compel small countries to overspecialize in a few products; they develop what Professor Kuznets has called a "few loci of comparative advantage." [88] Switzerland, for instance, is famous for its watches, and Denmark and New Zealand for their high quality agricultural commodities. Switzerland's highly developed industry and Denmark's and New Zealand's highly developed agriculture have enabled these nations to establish themselves on the world markets despite their size. Israel has citrus fruit and diamonds.

The point to keep in mind is that all small nations must export to live. This necessity is reflected in the foreign trade statistics of small countries, which show a high ratio of trade volume (exports and imports) to Gross Domestic Product. The high ratio reflects the degree of all small countries' dependence upon foreign markets.[89] Small and underdeveloped countries frequently have only two or three export commodities. For example, in El Salvador, Nicaragua, Costa Rica, Honduras, and Guatemala, coffee, bananas, and cotton account for 75 per cent of total exports.[90] In 1949, citrus fruit and polished diamonds accounted for 80 per cent of Israel's total merchandise exports, and in 1965 these same products still accounted for at least half of total merchandise exports.[91]

This pattern for small and underdeveloped countries still prevails. It means, in fact, that self-determination does not necessarily follow with political independence, and that all small countries, especially if they happen to be economically backward, are actually dependent countries. The "domination effect" of large countries can be somewhat mitigated only for the highly industrialized small nations that sell in markets where the demand for their products enjoys wide acceptance. However, for most nonindustrialized small nations the "domination effect" or "dependence status" is a fact of life because they have little to sell and the range of "alternative markets for the exports" is limited.[92] Mrs. Joan Robinson observed in this connection that "a large nation, with a large internal market within the orbit of its political control, has important economic advantages over a small one. The small nation has to weigh the prospects of gain from specialization against the security of home production for home consumption, while the large nation can enjoy a great deal of both." [93] Specialization without the underpinning of a large domestic market tends to impose upon small countries "penalties of specialization" because of the great risks associated with foreign trade.[94]

Manifestations of a Dependent Economy

The foregoing suggests that all small countries are dependent economies by definition. But what is a more precise definition of a "dependent economy"? For a meaningful generalization we must seek empirically testable relations. What factors and relationships can be singled out that would hold true under different circumstances in space and time? Although many variables are difficult to detect and escape measurement, the following "dependence indicators," all of which are quantitative, have been suggested by one scholar: [95] (1) a high ratio of the value of a nation's external trade to Gross Domestic Product; (2) a high ratio of "essentials" to total imports; (3) heavy foreign indebtedness; (4) urgent needs for foreign capital funds; (5) necessity to import foreign know-how and skilled workers. These dependence indicators could also apply to some large countries, especially when they are in the early stages of structural transformation, but in small countries these economic disabilities are magnified.

Although there are five dependence indicators that apply to Israel, we shall stress only the particularly important ones, namely the "high ratio of 'essentials' to total imports," and "heavy foreign indebtedness." All small countries have a highly skewed resource pattern and a limited domestic market for capital goods. The size of the home market particularly constrains the operations of heavy equipment and machine-making industries. Because these industries require large-scale plants for efficient production, mass production is not economically feasible in a small country unless it can rely on assured foreign markets. Thus, by and large, observes one writer, "the small countries do not possess the large-scale industries which require large markets for support." [96] Another writer speaks in this connection, of the "sub-optimal nature of too small an economy." [97] Still another economist has demonstrated that even with high per capita incomes, the smallness of a country severely limits the extent to which it can efficiently produce intermediate and capital goods.[98] That is, "the limited size of their home markets excludes small countries from some industries in which optimum efficiency is attained only in very large scale production." [99] On the other hand, a small domestic market has little or no effect on the service sector, agriculture, and the production of most consumer goods.[100]

The poor and small countries with only one or two export commodities find it particularly difficult to earn enough hard currency to pay for the indispensable imports. All disturbances to trade affect small countries in a decidedly unfavorable way; the man on the street knows that when big countries sneeze, it is the small countries that catch pneumonia. Their economic dependence is characterized by a marked difficulty in gaining access to foreign markets. Small poor countries must always fear the possible danger of substitution of their exports by some synthetic. Moreover, prices of essential imports may also change, that is, the terms of trade may become less favorable. Thus, small countries are extremely vulnerable; they are dependent nations, par excellence. In 1953 Levi Eshkol estimated that Israel would need at least $250 million annually to cover the essential imports. At that time, Israel's exports earned only a fifth of that sum.[101] At the end of Shilumim in 1965, Israel's exports covered 59.0 per cent of imports.[102]

The other important dependence indicator refers to heavy foreign indebtedness, that is, to an excess of external liabilities over external assets. Despite the fact that almost all small poor countries export only a few primary commodities, the export sector accounts for a large percentage of their national income. The world prices of primary commodities, be they minerals, oil, or agricultural staples, fluctuate substantially, continuously, and notoriously; consequently, the instability of hard currency earnings affects profoundly, and mostly negatively, domestic savings, investments, and national output. Since, as a rule, small underdeveloped nations are deficit countries on foreign account, it is virtually impossible to insulate them against the wide fluctuations of foreign exchange earnings. The best way out is to supplement domestic resources by borrowing abroad or by asking for developmental assistance in the affluent capitals of the world. Because most low-income countries do not have access to the capital markets proper,[103] they must borrow either on a short-term or medium-term basis. Indications are that the world's poor, large and small, are plunging deeper and deeper into debt.

How much foreign indebtedness can an underdeveloped country properly service? The old-fashioned golden rule was that "debt service should not exceed 10 per cent of external earnings." [104] That is, the relative burden of foreign indebtedness, as measured by "the ratio of service payments to external receipts," [105] should not be greater than 10 per cent. The debt-service burden for many underdeveloped countries, however, exceeds this conventional limit. The trend to international indebtedness among the developing countries is growing. For example, the average annual debt service of one hundred underdeveloped nations grew from 3 per cent of external earnings in 1956 to 7 per cent in 1962, and then to almost 10 per cent in 1968.[106] These figures refer only to interest charges on the foreign-held debt, excluding dividend and amortization payments. One writer has observed that "taking the developing countries as a unit, the debt service is on the average about 12 per cent of their yearly export earnings and showing a steady upward trend." [107] Israel's external debt on July 31, 1964, was $1 billion and to service it required 18 per cent of Israel's current export earnings.[108]

Thus, growing indebtedness poses particularly serious problems for the future of the small poor nations. A heavier foreign-debt burden means that a growing proportion of hard currency export earnings are unavailable for the importation of capital goods. While the large but presently still poor countries can develop their own capital goods industries and thus become less dependent, the small countries, as suboptimal economies, will have to import capital goods as long as they exist.

The point to keep in mind is that a skewed resource pattern and potentially prohibitive production costs for industries using advanced technology compel small countries to overspecialize in a few products. All small nations must export to live, which is to say to pay for the indispensable imports. They cannot industrialize like India or Brazil by developing their own capital-goods industries, but must finance industrialization through exports.[109]

Seen in this context, when peace in the Middle East finally comes, Israel will not be able to escape the strictures of smallness and it will have to pay attention to the time-tested economic verities, which for a variety of reasons it has disregarded in the past. Then it will cease to be an atypical small country. The days of the "heroic" two decades of independence will be a memory, when Ben-Gurion, Sharett, Dan, Sapir, Eshkol, Kaplan, Moses, Shinnar, and other olim built the infrastructure and set up noneconomic industries for strategic reasons.

Appendix A

World Jewish Congress
Political Department

55, New Cavendish Street,
London, W.1.

COPY

The Rt. Hon. Lord Henderson,
Under Secretary of State for Foreign Affairs,
Foreign Office,
Whitehall,
London, S.W.1.

25th July, 1950.

My Lord,

I have the honour, on behalf of the World Jewish Congress, representing Jewish communities and organisations in over 60 countries, to submit that the following considerations with regard to Jewish claims on Germany may be taken into account in the present Allied discussions on the German Occupation Statute.

The World Jewish Congress requests that in the revised Occupation Statute or in any other international instrument relating to the future Government of Germany, provision may be made to safeguard the rights inherent in, or arising out of those claims.

The Jewish claims on Germany are based on the fact that the German people is bound to accept responsibility for the acts of the legally constituted Government of the German Third Reich which ruthlessly massacred nearly six million Jews in Europe for reasons only of their race and religion, confiscated and otherwise wrongfully deprived the Jews

of Europe of properties and assets of incalculable value and destroyed
the institutional, cultural and religious life in every Jewish community
in the countries under German occupation before and during the Second
World War.

It is necessary to recall that the Nazi Government came to power
with the consent, and by the act, of the constitutionally elected representatives of the German people. On 24th March, 1933, the German
Reichstag by a four-fifth majority of its members, 447 against 92, voted
for the Bill which authorized Hitler to abolish all German laws and to
introduce new ones at his discretion. That Bill was not forced upon the
other parties by a majority consisting of members of the Nazi party,
nor, at that time, had the Nazi party gained the power to adopt totalitarian methods. By that fateful vote, Nazi rule became legalised and
legitimate, and parliamentary authority was given, consciously and
deliberately, to make wrong right and lawlessness lawful. In the case of
the Jews, the consequences of this act of the German parliament were
made known in advance to all Germans and were, therefore, constitutionally sanctioned by the German people. The redress of the wrongs to
the Jewish people, thus legally authorised, becomes the responsibility of
the German people, and thereby, of the present German Government.
The President and the Chancellor of the West German Federal Republic
have stated that their Government is desirous of redressing the wrongs
done to the Jews. While the sincerity of these declarations is not questioned, they only state a general principle but offer no practical remedies.

The World Jewish Congress summarises in the following points some
of those measures which the German Government should be obliged to
carry out in fulfilment of the rightful claims of the Jews.

1. *Official publication on persecution*

While the leaders of the present West German Government recognise the wrongs done to the Jews, they will be unable to do justice so
long as German public opinion does not accept the facts of the heinous
crimes committed by the Nazi Government in the name of the German
people. Five years after the end of the war and notwithstanding the
efforts made by the Allied Powers, a great part of the German people
is, or pretends to be largely unaware of the scope of the calamity
inflicted by the Nazi Government upon the Jewish people all over
Europe, and believes all reports of the persecutory measures including
the murder of millions of Jews in the gas chambers of the Nazi concentration camps, as Allied and Jewish propaganda. Unfortunately,
the failure of denazification and the cessation of war crimes trials by
Allied tribunals have been a factor in the German people's failure to

appreciate the appalling crimes committed, in their name, against the Jews of Europe. One alarming consequence has been the re-emergence of reactionary elements in Germany which again propound and disseminate the noxious doctrines of anti-Semitism which constituted one of the foremost weapons of Adolf Hitler in his pursuit of political power.

The German Government, in pursuance of its duty of eradicating the evil doctrines of Nazism and of impressing the German people with a sense of responsibility for the iniquities of the Third Reich, should undertake the obligation to explain to the German people, in an officially compiled publication, the facts of the mass exterminations, the robberies and persecution inflicted upon European Jewry by the Nazi regime, in order that there should be no room for doubt in German minds that these crimes actually were committed and that there is justice in asking Germany to satisfy Jewish claims, resulting from the Third Reich's war on the Jews. This obligation should be included in any new instrument of agreement between the Allied Powers and the German Federal Republic.

2. *Incitement to race hatred*

The Government of the Third Reich inaugurated and put into execution in Germany and throughout the world an anti-Semitic movement which poisoned the minds of millions of people in Germany and abroad. This movement was the one of the chief means employed to destroy democratic Government in Germany. It is, therefore, in the words of para. 3 of the present Occupation Statute, "essential to preserve democratic Government in Germany" that incitement to race hatred should be made a severely punishable crime by German law. It is important, particularly, that Germany should follow the recommendation of Article 7 of the Universal Declaration of Human Rights that "all are entitled to equal protection against any discrimination in violation of this Declaration, and against any incitement to such discrimination." It is urged, therefore, that, firstly, the Allied Powers should retain their authority under para. 3 of the present Occupation Statute and have the power to advise the German Government to enact legislation in the direction stated, and, secondly, that the German Government should undertake an obligation to enact legislation making incitement to race hatred a severely punishable crime.

3. *Re-education*

Hitler and the Nazi Government poisoned the minds of German youth through indoctrination with teachings of which chauvinism and

anti-Semitism were a particularly important feature. That these teachings have produced effects which have not yet been removed is shown
by the numerous acts of desecration of Jewish cemeteries committed by
German youths since the end of the war. The re-education of German
youth on the lines of democratic ideas is, therefore, vital in the interests
of Germany herself, in order, in the words of para. 3 of the present
Occupation Statute, "to preserve democratic Government in Germany." It is considered imperative that this, also, should be retained,
as a matter reserved to Allied control, in any revised Occupation Statute, and that, in consultation with Allied authority, the German Government should undertake to enact measures for the revision of school
and other text books, as well as for the screening of teachers in German
educational institutions, with a view of eradicating chauvinist and anti-
Semitic teachings and to prevent any revival of discrimination and race
or religious hatred.

4. *Crimes against humanity*

   The transfer to the German authorities of jurisdiction in relation to
trials of Germans accused of war crimes and of crimes against humanity has not proved effective. Large numbers of persons chargeable with
such crimes have not been brought to justice, and experience has shown
the necessity of including in any new agreement between the Allied
Powers and the German Federal Republic an obligation by the German Government to fulfil its undertaking to bring to justice those
accused of war crimes and crimes against humanity, by a speedy and
effective procedure, and that pending trials should be expedited. Moreover, the German Government should be obliged to undertake that,
in such trials, the principles laid down in the Four Power Agreement
on Procedure against Major War Criminals, and governing the International Military Tribunal at Nuremberg, shall be applied.

   Although the laws of humanity are legal rules in harmony with the
principles recognised by all civilised nations (Article 38(c) of the Statute
of the International Court of Justice) and although these laws were
recognised in Article 152 of the German Constitution of Weimar,
and by Article 1 (2) and by Article 25 of the Basic Law of Western
Germany, recent judgments by German tribunals in cases of persons
charged with crimes against humanity have shown a tendency to over-
ride or ignore these international rules and to rely upon the existing
German law which provides a facile escape for those accused of these
crimes. There has been an increasing tendency on the part of German
tribunals trying cases of crimes against humanity, to accept the defence
of "superior orders" or of "Notstand." This defence plea has been

rejected by the International Military Tribunal at Nuremberg and by other Allied tribunals, judging cases of persons accused of crimes against humanity. Should the plea of "superior orders" and "Not-stand" be accepted in future trials of German war criminals, it is unlikely that any German will suffer punishment either in particular crimes or in relation to the mass murder of many hundreds of thousands of Jews in the gas chambers of the Nazi concentration camps, and by other means.

It is submitted that in any new instrument between the Allied Powers and the German Federal Republic, the German Government should accept unequivocally the principle adopted by all civilised nations that crimes against the laws of humanity are punishable, and should undertake to enact legislation to the effect that in charges of crimes against humanity the defence of "superior orders" or "Not-stand" is not admissible.

It is urged also that the powers reserved to the Allied authority under para. 2 (i) of the present Occupation Statute should be retained and that any revised contractual instrument between the Allied Powers and Western Germany should provide that no amnesty, pardon or release in relation to sentences for crimes against humanity will be granted by the German authorities without the consent of the Occupation authorities in respect of sentences imposed by German as well as Allied tribunals.

5. *Restitution*

The measures promulgated by the Allied authorities in Germany since the end of the war to restore to the rightful owners or their successors properties and assets confiscated and otherwise wrongfully appropriated by reason of the oppressive enactments of the Third Reich directed against Jews have either not yet been fully carried out or have proved defective by reason of inadequate procedure. Although implementation of restitution measures has been entrusted to German agencies and courts, restitution, a reserved matter under para. 2(b) of the present Occupation Statute, is the direct responsibility of the Occupying Powers. Processing of the claims has not yet progressed to any great extent and will require to be continued for several years to come. The Germans have shown reluctance in implementing the existing Allied enactments in respect of restitution and they have shown little, if any, desire to introduce the further legislation required to give full effect to the accepted principle of restitution. In addition, the existing restitution legislation has provoked obstruction on the part of the Germans illegally in possession of property belonging to victims of persecution. There is danger that the existing laxity on the part of German authorities and the pressure exercised upon them by groups directly involved are likely to result in a serious curtailment of the implementation of the restitution measures in existence if and when Allied control is suspended or relaxed.

It is essential, therefore, that restitution remain a matter of Allied concern within the terms of any revised Occupation Statute. It is urged also that, in any new instrument between the Allied Powers and the German Federal Republic, the German Government should undertake to respect and to implement the restitution legislation enacted by the Allied Powers and that the procedure for implementation should be speeded up and improved in order that the properties of the victims of Nazi persecution should be restored to the legitimate owners, without delay and without undue cost to them.

6. *Compensation*

Legislation designed to restore to the true owners the properties of victims of Nazi persecution covers an important part of the economic losses suffered by them. Such legislation cannot, by virtue of its limited nature, make good the damage and injury by way of loss of life, health, liberty and possessions no longer recoverable. These losses, so far as their material consequences are concerned, must be made good by adequate measures for payment of compensation. Last year a General Claims Law was enacted in the U.S. Zone of Germany, and legislation providing for partial compensation mainly in respect of deprivation of liberty, is in operation in the British Zone, while laws not yet in force have been adopted in the Laender of the French Zone.

Moreover, the existing legislation is inadequate in application and inefficient in procedure. The basis upon which the legislation had been enacted is that compensation is payable only to those victims of racial and religious discrimination who were resident in Germany on a particular date; in the American Zone the date is 1st January, 1947, in the British Zone, 1st January, 1948, while in Hamburg the date is even as late as 1st January, 1949. These dates are arbitrary and have the effect of debarring from legitimate compensation many thousands of Jewish and other victims of the Third Reich who suffered injury and damage through imprisonment in concentration camps, and through the various other measures of persecution inflicted upon them by the Nazi regime. To limit and even to abrogate the just rights of these victims by fixing a terminal date of residence in Germany is unreasonable and unjust. No such limitation was fixed by the Nazi Government in pursuing and executing the measures of persecution. The determining factor in the payment of compensation should be the fact and the extent of the damage inflicted, irrespective of whether the victim was in Germany. Few of the surviving victims of the Nazi regime can ever be adequately compensated for the losses and injuries they suffered through persecution; to submit them to a residence test in Germany is to deprive them of common justice.

It is submitted, therefore, that under any revised Occupation Statute the matter of compensation should be reserved to Allied control, and that any new instrument between the Allied Powers and the German Federal Republic should contain a provision obliging the German Government to adopt for the whole of Western Germany a General Claims Law of compensation for the victims of Nazi persecution irrespective of their presence in Germany or not, and without relation to the date of such residence.

7. *Position of absentees*

In consequence of the persecutory acts of the Nazi Government there are in Germany to-day only about 25,000 Jews, compared with 580,000 in 1933. The problems of restitution and compensation must, therefore, be considered largely from the viewpoint of owners of property and claimants now living in foreign countries. It has to be emphasised that as far as restitutable property is concerned, "foreign" ownership did not come about by someone abroad acquiring property in Germany, with full knowledge of the risks involved. It was the result of the forced emigration of the owners who at the time of acquisition were residents of Germany and were, in most cases, citizens thereof. It is submitted that any new settlement with Germany would be incomplete, if, in respect to restitution, no guarantees were included therein to guard against the possibility of discriminatory treatment by German authorities to the disadvantage of the absent owners of these assets, whether as regards taxes or other levies or the holding and administering of such property. Furthermore, having been forced to leave Germany, many owners are not in a position to maintain the ownership or, for reasons of currency regulations or otherwise, to administer their holdings to their legitimate benefit. It is therefore urged that these persecutees be given the possibility of liquidating their assets on reasonable conditions with the right to transfer the equivalent received to their present residence, whenever they desire. In addition, since all the owners of these assets were victims of Nazi persecution, who were either expelled from the country or otherwise excluded from active participation in the public life of Germany and deprived of all rights of citizenship, their properties ought not to be subjected to any taxes or levies imposed upon the general population in order to remedy the financial consequences of the war waged by Germans or its aftermath (inflation, reparations, occupation costs, etc.).

Compensation payments also, if made in local currency, would be of little advantage to beneficiaries living abroad, unless there is adequate machinery to enable them to use these payments in the country of their present residence.

It is submitted, therefore, that the German Republic should be obliged to facilitate such transfers within reasonable limits.

8. *Collective Jewish claims against Germany*

Even if the before-mentioned measures of individual restitution or compensation were to be fully implemented, only a comparatively small number of Jewish victims of Nazi persecution—those who resided or had property in Germany or happened to be liberated on German soil—would receive partial indemnification; but not more than a fraction of the losses inflicted upon the Jewish people by the Germans during the era of Nazi domination of the European Continent would thus be made good. No one can bring back to life the six million Jewish men, women and children who were starved, tortured, shot or gassed to death by the orders of the Third Reich. Nor is it possible to resurrect the flourishing Jewish communities of Europe which were irretrievably destroyed by the cruelly calculated destructive measures of the Germans. Irreparable harm was done by these inhumanly criminal acts, perpetrated in ruthless compliance with "superior orders," to the surviving members of these Jewish communities and to the Jewish people as a whole which has severely suffered biologically, culturally and spiritually as a result of the barbarities of the German Nazi regime.

These crimes have created a responsibility on the part of the German people, which the German Government must discharge on a collective basis, as a measure of indemnification to the Jewish people. The German Federal Republic should, therefore, assume an obligation in an instrument of agreement with the Allied Powers, to indemnify the Jewish people by material compensation in goods, services or otherwise, commensurate with its share of responsibility for the German State as a whole. These payments should be made available to and utilised by responsible Jewish organisations in their efforts to rebuild the remnants of the destroyed Jewish communities in the countries where the survivors of the Nazi anti-Jewish persecution have found refuge in a new homeland.

In determining the extent of collective indemnification, regard should be had to the Paris Agreement on Reparations of December

1945. Under Article 8 of that Agreement, a small fund of German foreign assets in neutral countries was set aside for the benefit of non-repatriable victims of Nazi aggression. This was done in recognition of the fact that certain categories of victims of Nazism would not benefit from the reparations paid by Germany to the Allied Nations under the Reparations Plan. At that time it may have appeared that the number of such victims was comparatively small, since it was intended to cover the pitifully small number of survivors of the concentration camps in Germany who did not desire to return to their countries of residence where all their kith and kin had been slaughtered and where the poisonous anti-Semitism instilled by the Germans still permeated these countries. Since then, however, the number of Jews who, for these reasons, could not remain in their homelands has increased greatly. Jewish communities all over the world have been making the greatest sacrifices to provide for the present needs of these uprooted persons as well as for their re-settlement and rehabilitation. This task will continue for years to come and will require very considerable funds. Justice demands that this burden be shared by Germany and that the Federal Republic be made to assume a clear and unequivocal obligation to this effect.

9. *International supervision of burial places of victims of persecution*

There are throughout Germany a number of burial sites containing the mass graves and places of interment of those who perished as a result of Nazi persecution. In a number of such areas, such as Bergen Belsen, Ravensbrueck and Dachau, the large majority of persons buried were Jews; but in Bergen Belsen alone, the number of Jews buried in the mass graves is estimated to be 40,000.

Article 29 of the Geneva Convention does not apply to the care and maintenance of these burial places of victims of persecution. The men, women and children interred in them did not die as soldiers in battle. They were not war casualties in the accepted sense of the term. They did not die as political prisoners. They were the victims of the Nazi plan of mass extermination of civilian populations. They were murdered by brutalities and deliberately executed.

It is considered vital that, with the reduction and eventual withdrawal of Allied control in Germany, proper provision should be made for the protection and maintenance of these burial sites. Reference has already been made to the numerous desecrations of Jewish cemeteries in Germany since the end of the war, and these lend emphasis to the view that these places of interment of victims of Nazi persecution, cannot and ought not be left only to German care and maintenance.

The World Jewish Congress requests that the burial places throughout Germany, where the hundreds of thousands of the murdered victims of Nazi brutality are interred, should be placed under international supervision, in perpetuity, and that their care should be entrusted to an international consortium of the Governments to whose nationality the victims belonged; that such an international body should include the Government of Israel; and that the World Jewish Congress, representing Jewish communities and organisations outside Israel, should be associated with it. The World Jewish Congress urges that provision to this effect should be incorporated in any agreement between the Allied Powers and the German Federal Republic.

I am, My Lord,

Yours faithfully,

(Signed)   A. L. EASTERMAN

A. L. Easterman,
Political Secretary

An identical copy of this communication was sent to:

His Excellency Monsieur Rene Massigly,
Ambassador of France,
French Embassy,
58, Knightsbridge,
London, S.W.1.

Appendix B

World Jewish Congress
Political Department

55, New Cavendish Street,
London, W.1.

From: A. L. Easterman

STRICTLY CONFIDENTIAL
LIMITED DISTRIBUTION

GERMANY

Note of conversation with *Lord Henderson,*
Under-Secretary of State for Foreign Affairs,
(accompanied by Mr. Wilson), at the Foreign
Office, London, on Thursday, January 11, 1951,
from 11 a.m. to 12.45 p.m.

IMPENDING
SOVEREIGNTY

Mr. Easterman told Lord Henderson that, as public reports and other information reaching us indicated an imminent change in Western Germany's political status and the consequent withdrawal of Western Allied authority in Germany, this was a particularly important moment to discuss with him, as representative of the British Government, the major problems in which the Jewish people were concerned with regard to Germany.

This might well be the last opportunity available to us to seek the aid of the Western Allied Powers in securing from the Germans the rights and claims which had, during and since the end of the war, been put forward frequently by the World Jewish Congress. We had hoped that these rights and claims would have been in large measure fulfilled by this time, but, while there had been understanding by the Western Allies of the Jewish position and a certain amount of assistance in particular matters, we could not say, to our regret, that we had obtained anything like satisfaction. Indeed, now on the eve of Germany's reinstatement as a sovereign State, we were bound to say that our claims had remained unsatisfied. Accordingly, the purpose of this meeting was, in a sense, a final appeal to the British Government and for that matter to its Allies, to see that justice should be done to the Jewish people who had suffered so much at the hands of Germany.

To clear the way for a discussion of the problems themselves, Mr. Easterman asked Lord Henderson if he would tell him if we were right in assuming that West Germany's restoration as a sovereign State was imminent, if Allied control was coming to an end, and if so, when this was likely to materialise.

Lord Henderson said that it was right to assume that we were at "the penultimate stage" in relation to recognition of Western Germany as an independent sovereign State. He was not in a position to give, and no one could state, a precise date or even time when this would occur. It might be months, and he would not care even to suggest the number. The work of the Tripartite International Allied Study Group which had been examining the Occupation Statute, was not yet completed, and the work done in New York was not yet finalised. In his opinion, having regard to the general situation, the sooner Germany became a sovereign State, the better. The present dubious position was bad for Germany, as well as for the Western Allies, and undesirable in relation to the international situation.

JEWISH
CLAIMS

With regard to the Jewish claims, *Lord Henderson* said that, as he had told me on previous occasions, he not only understood the Jewish position and attitude with regard to Germany, but he had the fullest possible sympathy for the causes and impulses which governed it. He would say, as he had said before, that there was justice in the Jewish claims that Germany should redress the wrongs which the Hitler regime had inflicted upon the Jews. He and his predecessors had understood this and had done their best to satisfy these claims insofar as it was possible and practicable. They had been bound to base their efforts on what was possible and practicable and to consider the fulfillment of claims in the light of Germany's ability to fulfill them. He had consistently pursued the line of endeavouring to secure what was the maximum possible on the various claims that had been put forward. His attitude had always been positive, and he had put his views strongly.

TREATY OR AGREEMENT

Mr. Easterman enquired whether there was to be a Treaty between the Western Allies and the Federal German Republic.

Lord Henderson said that in according sovereign status to Germany, there would be a new contractual relationship between the Western Allies and Germany. He could not say whether this would take the form of a Treaty but he could say that the contractual relationship would contain the maximum sovereign rights for Western Germany.

Mr. Easterman said that the form of this contractual relationship was important because a Treaty between equals would preclude the continuance of any form of Allied control and authority, whereas something less than a Treaty could provide the possibility of the maintenance of Allied control. This was particularly important in relation to Jewish claims against Germany, because an integral part of our representations was that Allied supervision and control would secure the implementation of German obligations.

Lord Henderson replied that a grant of maximum sovereign rights to Western Germany implied the reduction of allied authority to the barest minimum.

Mr. Easterman then proceeded to a detailed discussion of the specific matters which were put forward in his letter to Lord Henderson of 25th July, 1950, and to which he had replied in his letter of 20th September, 1950.

RESTITUTION

On the subject of restitution, *Mr. Easterman* called attention to Lord Henderson's statement that "we have taken note of your views that restitution should remain a reserved subject in any revision of the German Statute, and the German Federal Government should undertake to respect and implement the Allied legislation in this field", and enquired what were the prospects of restitution remaining a reserved matter in the light of the impending grant of "maximum sovereign rights" to Western Germany.

*GENERAL
CLAIMS
LAW*

Lord Henderson said that he had always held and pressed the view that Germany should fulfil its obligations to the victims of Nazi persecution. It was his determination to see that this was carried out. As he had already informed Mr. Easterman on previous occasions, the British Government, through the High Commissioner in Germany, had advised the German Federal Republic in Bonn to enact a General Claims Law governing the matters in which we were concerned. He asked Mr. Wilson what the present position was.

Mr. Wilson said that he had from Germany that very morning a communication which was of a confidential character. At Lord Henderson's request and on Mr. Easterman's assurance that the matter would be treated confidentially, Mr. Wilson said that a General Claims Law had now been drafted by the Federal Government and the text was being forwarded to the Foreign Office.

Lord Henderson said that this draft Law would be carefully examined and the various points which we had raised would be fully taken into account, although he would not wish to be understood as saying that our views would necessarily be adopted in their entirety.

Mr. Easterman, in expressing appreciation of this confidential information, asked if it would be possible for us to be given the opportunity to examine the draft Law, with the view of suggesting amendments or improvements. *Lord Henderson* said that, while there was difficulty in such an unusual procedure, he would consider whether we could not be given a sight of those parts of the draft Law which related specifically to matters in which we were concerned.

COMPEN-SATION

Mr. Easterman then referred to the question of compensation to victims of Nazi persecution and to the unsatisfactory character of the existing legislation in Germany. The most serious objection was the arbitrarily fixed dates for residence in Germany as a qualification for compensation. The fact was that many thousands of such victims who had suffered damage by reason of Nazi persecution were either not in Germany on these dates, or had been compelled to leave before them. This manifest injustice was illustrated vividly by the case of Austrian Jews who had suffered at the hands of the Germans. The Austrian Government declined to compensate these people on the ground that they were not persecuted by Austria. If their claims for compensation were denied through a residence in Germany qualification, they had no means of securing their just right to be compensated.

Lord Henderson said that this was a new point worth consideration, and he would have it examined.

IMPLE-MENTING GERMAN LEGISLATION

Mr. Easterman, referring to the implementation of legislation regarding restitution, compensation and similar matters, enquired how the rights under this legislation could be guaranteed if Allied authority or control were either reduced to the minimum or eliminated by virtue of the new contractual relationship between the Western Allies and Western Germany. He suggested it was possible that, having enacted such legislation, the present German Government or a successor might, at some stage, either abrogate the legislation or render it inoperative for one reason or another.

Lord Henderson said that there was no reason to think that the German Government would not respect its obligations, especially those voluntarily undertaken. In the case of a successor Government, it was the normal practice that a Government did not abrogate the legislation of its predecessor. Besides, in the event of a Treaty or similar contractual relationship between States, there was always recourse to the International Court by one of the contracting States.

Mr. Easterman suggested that there was a difference between the rights of individuals, who did not have the right of recourse to an International Court, and those of States which had.

Lord Henderson replied that claimants could always, as was the custom, obtain the intervention of their Government on their behalf.

Mr. Easterman answered that, while this would be true in the case of citizens of one of the contracting parties, it would at least be more difficult in the case of claimants who were citizens of countries not party to the contractual relationship.

Mr. Easterman suggested that a Mixed Tribunal be set up, composed of representatives of the contracting Powers, and that beneficiaries of German legislation could appeal to this Tribunal for redress of grievances. There were precedents for such a Mixed Tribunal which would maintain the possibility of international supervision of the fulfilment of Germany's obligations to the victims of Nazi persecution.

Lord Henderson said that the suggestion would be carefully considered.

COLLECTIVE
INDEMNITY

Mr. Easterman dealt at some length with the right of the Jewish people to receive a collective German indemnity for the wrongs done to the Jewish people by the Government of the Third Reich and for which, in our opinion, neither the German Government nor the German people could divest themselves of responsibility. He referred to Lord Henderson's letter of September 20, stating that "in our view such proposals would have to come in the first place from the Germans themselves. To attempt to impose a measure of indemnification to the Jewish people would not, I am afraid, be practically possible and it would only stir up anti-Jewish feeling in Germany". With regard to the first point, we had no confidence that any such proposal would come from the Germans themselves.

Dr. Adenauer's offer of 10 million Marks, or about 2 Marks per murdered Jew, was regarded by the Jewish people as an insult. In any case, both the circumstances and the manner of this "offer" did nothing to reduce, if it did not in fact intensify Jewish bitterness against the Germans. With regard to the second point, one had to accept the difficulty, in the present political situation and having regard to the international conflict, of imposing on the Germans indemnification to the Jewish people. This did not, however, eliminate the duty of the Germans to assume responsibility and to make some real attempt to indemnify the Jewish people in some practical manner commensurate with the wrongs inflicted upon the Jews.

The Jewish people would have better understood the real position about "practicability" if Dr. Adenauer had, in the Bonn Parliament, said in the first instance to the German people, "a great crime has been committed against the Jews which we must understand and for which we must accept responsibility", and on the other hand to the Jews, "we recognise our responsibility for the crimes done to you, but we are unfortunately not in a position to offer you compensation in any way proportionate to the losses and the injuries you have sustained. But we are anxious to do everything we can". While accepting the difficulty of an imposed indemnity, there was still the time and the opportunity for the Western democratic Allies to use their influence to persuade and even to convince the Germans that they had a great moral duty towards the Jewish people, and that this recognition on their part should be accompanied by a practical token of compensation commensurate with the losses of the Jewish people. The British Government, with its long tradition of the observance of moral principles in politics, could play a particular part, at this last moment, in giving advice to and even exercising influence upon the Germans in this regard, and to advise the German Government that its observance of moral principles was an integral, if not the most important element in Germany's re-admission to the Family of Nations.

Lord Henderson said that he not only understood the emotions of the Jewish people in relation to Germany, but he fully sympathised with them. About the justice of Jewish claims there could be no question. The matter was, however, and unfortunately, a severely practical one. No amount of compensation could recompense the Jews for the human losses they had sustained, and any adequate indemnification was beyond the means of the German Government. He believed Dr. Adenauer to have been sincere in his offer, and he (Lord Henderson) thought it was a pity that the Jewish people had not considered this gesture as a starting point for discussion of an amount which, though it could never be adequate, could still have been regarded as a recognition of a desire on Germany's part to redress the wrongs done to the Jews. He referred to the Israel Government's refusal to end the state of war with Germany, and thought this was inconsistent with the expectation that Germany should make a payment by way of indemnification. On the question of the amount, Lord Henderson enquired what would be regarded as acceptable to the Jewish people.

Mr. Easterman replied that, as Lord Henderson himself had said, it was not possible to estimate any sum which could possibly represent the Jewish losses at the hands of the German Third Reich. Short of this (and speaking entirely for himself), Mr. Easterman would estimate an acceptable offer by the German Government to be £500,000,000.

Lord Henderson said that this was a figure beyond the capacity of Germany to pay, and any such sum could not, in any case, be paid except over a long period.

Mr. Easterman answered that it was not for him to express an opinion about this but, having been asked the question as to what would be considered an acceptable payment by way of indemnification, his reply was £500,000,000 and, no doubt, arrangements could be made regarding the method and time of payment. In answer to Lord Henderson's enquiry as to whom an indemnity could be paid, Mr. Easterman said that part of such a payment would obviously have to be made to the Government of Israel and part to a consortium of international Jewish organisations engaged in the work of Jewish rehabilitation and of providing for the survivors of the victims of Hitler.

Mr. Easterman concluded by addressing a most earnest and emphatic request that the British Government should take the initiative, especially at this crucial moment of the impending re-admission of Germany to the Family of Nations, to use the whole weight of their influence, backed by the great moral traditions of British politics, to impress upon the German Government the necessity of marking a restoration to sovereignty by expressing in a tangible and appropriate form its recognition of its moral duty and responsibility to compensate the Jewish people for the crimes committed against them.

Lord Henderson said that the views expressed and the suggestions made would receive most careful consideration.

15th January, 1951.

The foregoing documents are reprinted with the permission of Mr. A. L. Easterman.

Notes

Chapter 1

1. Many scholars have dismissed Nazi ideology as too vague, too contradictory, and too demagogic. It was more a movement than a doctrine, or a mystique for action, see J. Nyomarkay, *Charisma and Factionalism in the Nazi Party* (Minneapolis: University of Minnesota Press, 1967), pp. 17–25.

2. E. Nolte, *Three Faces of Fascism* (New York: Holt, Rinehart and Winston, 1966), pp. 282–285.

3. A. Höft, *Rassenkunde, Rassenpflege und Erblehre als völkische Lebenskunde* (Osterwieck und Berlin: Verlag A. W. Zickfeldt, 1938), pp. 147–149, 173–177. See also J. R. Bengtson, *Nazi War Aims* (Rock Island, Ill.: Augustana College Library, 1962), p. 115.

4. J. Isaac, *The Teaching of Contempt: Christian Roots of Anti-Semitism* (New York: 1964), p. 24.

5. Of the enormous literature on the Christian roots of anti-Semitism, the following works are representative: J. Parkes, *The Conflict of the Church and the Synagogue* (New York: The World Publishing Company, 1961); M. Hay, *The Foot of Pride: The Pressure of Christendom on the People of Israel of 1900 Years* (Boston: The Beacon Press, 1950); E. H. Flannery, *The Anguish of the Jews* (New York: The Macmillan Co., 1965); A. R. Eckardt, *Elder and Younger Brothers: The Encounter of Jews and Christians* (New York: Charles Scribner's Sons, 1967); W. P. Eckert and E. L. Ehrlich, *Judenhass-Schuld der Christen? Versuch eines Gesprächs* (Essen, H. Driewer Verlag, 1964); W. D. Marsch and K. Thieme, *Christen und Juden* (Göttingen: Vandenhoeck & Ruprecht, 1961); and H. Andics, *Der ewige Jude: Ursachen und Geschichte des Antisemitismus* (Vienna: Molden, 1965).

6. M. I. Dimont, *Jews, God and History* (New York: New American Library, 1962), pp. 144–156.

7. R. Hilberg, *The Destruction of the European Jews* (Chicago: Quadrangle Books, 1961), p. 5.

8. For a summary of the various elements of the German Volkish ideology, see G. L. Mosse, *The Crisis of German Ideology* (New York: Grosset and Dunlap, 1964), pp. 88–107.

9. F. Böhm, "Antisemitismus," in *Franz Böhm: Reden und Schriften* (Karlsruhe: Verlag C. F. Müller, 1960), pp. 251–253; E. Oestermann, "Antisemitischer Nationalismus und nationales Judentum," *Politische Studien,* 12 (1961), 575–590; and H. M. Klinkenberg, "Zwischen Liberalismus und Nationalsozialismus," in K. Schilling, ed., *Monumenta Judaica* (Cologne: 1963), p. 327.

10. P. Pulzer, *The Rise of Political Anti-Semitism in Germany and Austria* (New York: John Wiley & Sons, 1964), pp. 49–59.

11. H. Arendt, *The Origins of Totalitarianism,* New Edition (New York: Harcourt, Brace and World, 1966), pp. 170–175. See also J. Barzun, *Race: A Study in Superstition* (New York: Harper Torchbooks, 1965), pp. 50–77.

12. G. L. Mosse, *op. cit.,* p. 91.

13. E. H. Flannery, *op. cit.,* p. 180. See also N. Levin, *The Holocaust* (New York: Thomas Y. Crowell Co., 1968), p. 13; and M. I. Dimont, *op. cit.,* pp. 320–321.

14. E. Davidson, *The Trial of the Germans* (New York: The Macmillan Co., 1966), p. 41, and E. Nolte, *op. cit.,* pp. 50–51.

15. For a most thorough analysis of this work, see Norman Cohn, *Warrant for Genocide* (London: Eyre & Spottiswoode, 1967).

16. M. Samuel, *Blood Accusation—The Strange History of the Beiliss Case* (New York: Alfred A. Knopf, 1967).

17. N. Levin, *op. cit.,* p. 19. See also H. Arendt, *op. cit.,* pp. 100–101, 354–361.

18. A. Rosenberg, *Der Mythus des 20. Jahrhunderts* (Munich: Hoheneichen-Verlag, 1937).

19. M. J. Thornton, *Nazism, 1918–45* (Oxford: Pergamon Press, 1966), p. 3.

20. A. Rosenberg, *Der staatsfeindliche Zionismus* (Munich: Zentralverlag der NSDAP, 1943).

21. L. Poliakov and Josef Wulf, *Das Dritte Reich und seiner Denker* (Berlin: Verlags GmbH, 1959).

22. H. Mau and H. Krausnick, *German History, 1933–1945* (London: Oswald Wolff, 1962), pp. 34–36. See also W. Anger, *Das Dritte Reich in Dokumenten* (Frankfurt a/M.: Europäische Verlagsanstalt, 1957), p. 27,

and A. Gerschenkron, *Bread and Democracy in Germany* (Berkeley: University of California Press, 1943), pp. 151–153.

23. K. D. Bracher, W. Sauer, G. Schulz, *Die nazionalsozialistische Machtergreifung* (Cologne and Opladen: Westdeutscher Verlag, 1962), pp. 169–205; and an older work by F. Neumann, *Behemoth* (New York: Oxford University Press, 1942). See also H. Buchheim, *Das Dritte Reich* (Munich: Kösel-Verlag, 1958), pp. 50–51.

24. E. Davidson, *op. cit.,* pp. 99–143.

25. W. Treue, *Deutsche Geschichte* (Stuttgart: A. Kröner Verlag, 1965), pp. 733–734.

26. J. A. Schumpeter, *History of Economic Analysis* (New York: Oxford University Press, 1954), p. 21.

27. D. Schoenbaum, *Hitler's Social Revolution: Class and Status in Nazi Germany 1933–1939* (Garden City, N.Y.: Anchor Books, 1967), pp. 113–151.

28. For a typical account of Nazi property rights and qualifications, see H. Hunke, *Grundsätze der deutschen Volks- und Wehrwirtschaft* (Berlin: Hande & Spenersche Buchhandlung, 1938), pp. 78–81. For a recent work, see H. Genschel, *Die Verdrängung der Juden aus der Wirtschaft im Dritten Reich* (Göttingen: Musterschmidt Verlag, 1966), pp. 294–298.

29. E. Davidson, *op. cit.,* pp. 222–256, and D. Schoenbaum, *loc. cit.*

30. W. Treue, ed., *Deutschland in der Weltwirtschaftskrise in Augenzeugenberichten* (Berlin: Deutsche Buch-Gemeinschaft, 1967).

31. For the most thorough and comprehensive discussion, see A. Schweitzer, *Big Business in the Third Reich* (Bloomington: Indiana University Press, 1964), p. 253. See also R. Erbe, *Die nazionalsozialistische Wirtschaftspolitik 1933–1939 im Lichte der modernen Theorie* (Zürich: Polygraphischer Verlag, 1958).

32. A. Schweitzer, *op. cit.,* p. 467.

33. W. Anger, *op. cit.,* p. 29, and D. Schoenbaum, *op. cit.,* p. 86.

34. A. Schweitzer, *op. cit.,* p. 367.

35. For a fuller discussion see O. Nathan, *The Nazi Economic System* (Durham, N.C.: Duke University Press, 1944), pp. 19–21; L. Hamburger, *How Nazi Germany Has Controlled Business* (Washington, D.C.: Brookings Institution, 1943), pp. 10–11.

36. G. Stolper, K. Häuser, K. Borchardt, *The German Economy, 1870 to the Present* (New York: Harcourt, Brace and World, 1967), pp. 134–137, 139–142.

37. A. Schweitzer, *op. cit.,* pp. 451, 455.

38. G. W. F. Hallgarten, *Hitler, Reichswehr und Industrie* (Frankfurt a/M.: Europäische Verlagsanstalt, 1955). For an opposite view, stressing

the impotence of German industry under political interference, see H. E. Kannapin, *Wirtschaft unter Zwang* (Cologne: Deutscher Industrieverlag, 1966).

39. B. Klein, *Germany's Economic Preparations for War* (Cambridge, Mass.: Harvard University Press, 1959), p. 76.

40. H. Buchheim, *op. cit.*, p. 43. See also E. Davidson, *op. cit.*, pp. 7–9.

41. J. Robinson, *And the Crooked Shall Be Made Straight* (New York: The Macmillan Co, 1965), pp. 99–100.

42. H. Mommsen, "Der nazi Polizeistaat und die Judenverfolgung vor 1939," *Vierteljahreshefte für Zeitgeschichte,* 10 (1961), 68–87, and Anonymous, "Das Reichsministerium des Inneren und die Judengesetzgebung," *Vierteljahreshefte für Zeitgeschichte,* 9 (1961), 262–313.

43. For a listing of some of these popular myths, see J. Robinson, *op. cit.*, p. 91. For an excellent refutation of the "stab in the back" myth, see D. Horn, *War, Mutiny and Revolution in the German Navy: The World War I Diary of Seaman Richard Stumpf* (New Brunswick, N.J.: Rutgers University Press, 1967), which shows how hunger transformed German civilians and fighting men from ardent supporters of the Kaiser into reluctant supporters of the 1918 revolution that overthrew the monarchy.

44. W. Anger, *op. cit.*, p. 55.

45. For a juxtaposition of the canonical and Nazi anti-Jewish measures, see R. Hilberg, *op. cit.*, pp. 5–6, and A. R. Eckardt, *op. cit.*, pp. 7–16.

46. E. Nolte, *op. cit.*, pp. 376–379.

47. L. Poliakov and Josef Wulf, *Das Dritte Reich und seine Diener* (Berlin: Verlags GmbH, 1957), and E. Kogon, *Der SS-Staat* (Frankfurt a/M.: Europäische Verlagsanstalt, 1947).

48. On the unwillingness to receive Jewish refugees see G. Hausner, *Justice in Jerusalem* (New York: Harper & Row, 1966), pp. 226–261; A. D. Morse, *While Six Million Died: A Chronicle of American Apathy* (New York: Random House, 1968); and H. Habe, *The Mission* (New York: Coward McCann, 1966).

49. Among others, see M. Zelzer, *Weg und Schicksal der Stuttgarter Juden* (Stuttgart: E. Klett Verlag, 1964); Hannover Presseamt, *Leben und Schicksal* (Hanover: 1963); Z. Asaria, ed., *Die Juden in Köln* (Cologne: Verlag J. P. Bachen, 1959); Kommission zur Erforschung der Geschichte der Frankfurter Juden, *Dokumente zur Geschichte der Frankfurter Juden, 1939–1945* (Frankfurt a/M.: W. Kramer, 1963); H. Franke, *Geschichte und Schicksal der Juden in Heilbronn* (Heilbronn: Stadtarchiv, 1963); H. Lamm, *Von Juden in München* (Munich: Ner-Tamid Verlag, 1959).

50. H. Kamen, *The Spanish Inquisition* (New York: New American Library, 1966).

51. A. Bein, "Der jüdische Parasit," *Vierteljahreshefte für Zeitge-schichte*, 13 (1965), 121–149. In the 1920s and early 1930s, one of the more favored hate songs was:

> Der Jude nahm uns Silber, Gold und Speck,
> Uns Deutschen liess er diesen Dreck.
>
> [The Jew took our silver, gold, and bacon,
> And for us, Germans, he left this dirt.]

(The dirt referred to was the worthless paper currency at the end of the hyperinflation in 1923.)

52. F. Böhm, *op. cit.*, pp. 241–242.

53. For a brief discussion of rampant anti-Semitism in Germany, see W. H. Chamberlin, *The German Phoenix* (New York: Duell, Sloan & Pearce, 1963), p. 24.

54. The early works by G. Reitlinger, L. Poliakov and J. Wulf, and R. Hilberg based primarily on captured official German documents, were incomplete and one-sided. The Yad Vashem series on the Holocaust, utilizing Yiddish, Polish, Hungarian, Romanian, Russian, Lithuanian, and Hebrew sources, has added much detail. *And the Crooked Shall Be Made Straight* (New York: The Macmillan Co., 1965), by a well-known jurist from the Baltic, Dr. J. Robinson, is the most learned and lucid analysis. An indispensable reference source is J. Robinson and P. Friedman's *Guide to Jewish History under Nazi Impact* (New York: Yivo Institute for Jewish Research, 1960). The most recent additions to this literature, based primarily on secondary sources, are N. Levin's *The Holocaust* (New York: T. Y. Crowell Co., 1968), and A. H. Friedlander's *Out of the Whirlwind* (Garden City, N.Y.: Doubleday & Co., 1968).

55. M. I. Dimont, *op. cit.*, pp. 373, 388. Dimont adds a footnote on the so-called "quantification of the murder" problem: "The figure usually quoted for the number of Jews murdered by the Nazis is 6,000,000 but facts tend to support a figure of 5,000,000. Justice Jackson at the Nuremberg trials cited 4,500,000 Jews killed by the Germans. Today, the highest estimate is 5,600,000, the lowest 4,200,000. This difference is accounted for by guessing Jewish losses in territories held by the Soviet Union." G. Reitlinger, giving a figure of 5,000,000 says: "I believe it does not make the guilt of the living Germans any less if the figure of six million turns out to be an overestimate" (*The Final Solution*: New York, Beechhurst Press, 1953, p. 469). Howard M. Sachar quotes the total as 4,200,000 to 4,600,000, stating that "the figure of 6,000,000, released at the end of the war, has since been discounted" (*The Course of Modern Jewish History*: New York, The World Publishing Co., 1958, p. 457). For another source,

see N. Levin, *op. cit.,* pp. 715–718. E. Davidson, in *The Death and Life of Germany* (New York: Alfred A. Knopf, 1959), p. 306, cited a figure of four million, while in a later work (*The Trial of the Germans, op. cit.,* p. 23), he cited the figure of 5.7 million.

56. N. Robinson, "Spoliation and Remedial Action," *Institute Anniversary Volume* (New York: Yivo Institute for Jewish Research, 1962), p. 163.

57. B. Wyler, "Reparations Are Not Handouts," *The Jerusalem Post,* September 23, 1966.

58. Israel, Ministry of Foreign Affairs, *Documents Relating to the Agreement Between the Government of Israel and the Government of the Federal Republic of Germany* (Jerusalem: Government Printer, 1953), pp. 9–12.

59. K. Adenauer, *Erinnerungen, 1953–1955* (Stuttgart: Deutsche Verlags-Anstalt, 1966), p. 135.

60. E. Davidson, *The Trial of the Germans,* p. 8.

61. For a recent survey of Stalin's terror in the 1930s, see R. Conquest, *The Great Terror: Stalin's Purge in the Thirties* (New York: The Macmillan Co., 1968).

62. F. Simiand, "Causal Interpretation and Historical Research," in F. C. Lane and J. C. Riemersma, eds., *Enterprise and Secular Change* (Homewood, Ill.: Richard D. Irwin, 1953), p. 475.

63. N. Levin, *op. cit.,* p. 719.

64. Q. Wright, *A Study of War* (Chicago: The University of Chicago Press, 1942), p. 8.

65. W. W. Rostow, *The Stages of Economic Growth* (Cambridge: The University Press, 1960), p. 106.

66. Q. Wright, *op. cit.,* p. 479.

67. K. Lorenz, *On Aggression* (New York: Harcourt, Brace & World, 1963).

68. *Ibid.,* pp. 20–21, 35 and *passim.* See also, in this connection, Anthony Storr, *Human Aggression* (New York: Atheneum, 1968); for an opposite viewpoint, M. F. Ashley Montagu, ed., *Man and Aggression* (New York: Oxford University Press, 1968).

69. K. E. Boulding, *The Meaning of the Twentieth Century* (New York: Harper Colophon Books, 1965), p. 90.

70. H. E. Barnes, *Social Institutions* (New York: Prentice-Hall, 1946), p. 321.

71. From Q. Wright, *op. cit.,* p. 653.

72. W. K. Hancock, *Four Studies of War and Peace in this Century* (Cambridge: The University Press, 1961), p. 1.

73. R. Aron, *War and Industrial Society* (London: Oxford University Press, 1958), p. 3.

74. K. E. Boulding, *op. cit.*, p. 88.

75. A. D. Sakharov, *Progress, Coexistence and Intellectual Freedom* (New York: W. W. Norton, 1968), p. 37.

Chapter 2

1. Quoted by I. Vasarhelyi, *Restitution in International Law* (Budapest: Akademiai Kiado, 1964), p. 21.

2. *Ibid.*, p. 23.

3. A. Held, "Kriegsentschädigungen und die Reparationen der grossen Friedensverträge des Weltkrieges," in *Wörterbuch des Völkerrechts und der Diplomatie* (Berlin: 1927), p. 722.

4. F. Heichelheim, "Tribute," *Encyclopedia of the Social Sciences*, 15 (1935), 102.

5. *Ibid.*, 103.

6. E. Lipson, *The Growth of English Society* (New York: Henry Holt and Co., 1950), p. 158. For a broader definition, see G. Schmoller, *The Mercantile System and Its Historical Significance* (New York: Macmillan and Co., 1896), p. 51.

7. C. Wilson, "Treasure and Trade Balances: The Mercantilist Problem," *Economic History Review*, 2 (1949), 152–161.

8. H. F. Fraser, "Indemnity, Military," *Encyclopedia of the Social Sciences*, 7 (1935), 642.

9. A. Held, "Wirtschaftskrieg," in *Wörterbuch des Völkerrechts und der Diplomatie* (Berlin: 1927), p. 726.

10. L. H. Gipson, *The Coming of the Revolution, 1763–1775* (New York: Harper and Bros., 1954), New American Nation series, Vol. IX.

11. W. Treue, *Deutsche Geschichte* (Stuttgart: A. Kröner Verlag, 1965), pp. 598–599.

12. M. Howard, *The Franco-Prussian War* (London: Rupert Hart-Davis, 1961), p. 441.

13. B. Graefrath, *Zur Geschichte der Reparationen* (Berlin: Deutscher Zentralverlag, 1954), pp. 13, 17.

14. J. M. Keynes, "The German Transfer Problem," in *Readings in the Theory of International Trade* (Philadelphia: The Blakiston Co., 1949), p. 165.

15. F. Machlup, *International Payments, Debts and Gold* (New York: Charles Scribner's Sons, 1964), pp. 378–379.

16. For the composition of French payments, see H. G. Moulton and C. E. McGuire, *Germany's Capacity to Pay* (New York: McGraw-Hill,

1923), p. 220. See also C. P. Kindleberger, *International Economics,* 3rd edition (Homewood, Ill.: Richard D. Irwin, 1963), pp. 373–375.

17. H. Neisser, *The Problem of Reparations* (New York: The American Labor Conference on International Affairs, 1944), pp. 13–14 (mimeo).

18. G. Bielschowsky, "War Indemnities and Business Conditions I," *Political Science Quarterly,* 44 (1929), 334.

19. B. C. Jensen, *The Impact of Reparations on the Post-War Finnish Economy: An Input-Output Study* (Homewood, Ill.: Richard D. Irwin, 1966), p. 23.

20. H. G. Moulton and C. E. McGuire, *op. cit.,* p. 229.

21. G. Bielschowsky, *op. cit.,* 337.

22. G. Bielschowsky, "War Indemnities and Business Conditions II," *Political Science Quarterly,* 44 (1929), 529–530.

23. W. Treue, *op. cit.,* p. 599.

24. J. W. Angell, "Reparations," *Encyclopedia of the Social Sciences,* 13 (1935), 300–308.

25. G. Stolper, *German Economy, 1870–1940* (London: Allen & Unwin, 1940), p. 176.

26. P. Mantoux, *Paris Peace Conference 1919. Proceedings of the Council of Four, March 24–April 18* (Geneva: Librairie Droz, 1964), p. 28.

27. J. W. Angell, *The Recovery of Germany* (New Haven, Conn.: Yale University Press, 1929), p. 8.

28. P. Mantoux, *op. cit.,* p. 79.

29. *Loc. cit.*

30. J. M. Keynes, *A Revision of the Treaty* (New York: Harcourt, Brace and Co., 1922), p. 107.

31. J. W. Wheeler-Bennett and H. Latimer, *Information on the Reparation Settlement* (London: Allen & Unwin, 1930), p. 24.

32. J. W. Angell, *The Recovery of Germany,* p. 12.

33. L. Loucher, "The Essentials of a Reparations Settlement," *Foreign Affairs,* 2 (1923–24), 1.

34. J. M. Keynes, *A Revision of the Treaty,* p. 64.

35. C. Bergmann, *The History of Reparations* (Boston: Houghton Mifflin Co., 1927), pp. 21, 48.

36. C. Bergmann, *op. cit.,* p. 7.

37. F. W. Taussig, "Germany's Reparation Payments," *American Economic Review,* 10 (1920), Supplement, 33.

38. *Ibid.,* 36.

39. P. Mantoux, *op. cit.,* p. 14.

40. *Ibid.,* p. 15.

41. J. M. Keynes, *A Revision of the Treaty,* p. 180.

42. *Ibid.,* pp. 185, 201.

43. H. Schacht, *The Stabilization of the Mark* (New York: The Adelphi Co., 1927), p. 43.

44. For a brief summary of the various stages of the reparations, see B. Röper, "Reparationen," in *Handwörterbuch der Sozialwissenschaften,* 8 (1964), 812–821.

45. J. W. Wheeler-Bennett, *The Wreck of Reparations* (London: Allen & Unwin, 1933), pp. 210–253.

46. J. F. Dulles, "The Reparation Problem," *Economic Journal,* 31 (1921), 179.

47. F. Machlup, *op. cit.,* p. 383.

48. H. L. Lutz, "Inter-Allied Debts, Reparations, and National Policy," *The Journal of Political Economy,* 38 (1930), 45.

49. F. W. Taussig, *op. cit.,* 41.

50. J. F. Dulles, *op. cit.,* 180–181.

51. H. D. Gideonse, "Comment on Reparation Payments," *American Economic Review,* 20 (1930), 692.

52. J. F. Dulles, *op. cit.,* 184.

53. *Ibid.,* 185.

54. C. Bresciani-Turroni, *The Economics of Inflation* (London: Allen & Unwin, 1937), pp. 95–96.

55. H. Schacht, *op. cit.,* p. 49.

56. James W. Angell, "Reparations," *op. cit.,* 301.

57. C. Bresciani-Turroni, *op. cit.,* p. 97.

58. Moulton and McGuire, *op. cit.,* p. 86.

59. J. M. Keynes, *A Revision of the Treaty,* p. 103.

60. *Ibid.,* p. 86.

61. H. L. Lutz, *op. cit.,* 39.

62. C. Bergmann, *op. cit.,* pp. 85–91.

63. P. Cagan, "The Monetary Dynamics of Hyperinflation," in M. Friedman, ed., *Studies in the Quantity Theory of Money* (Chicago: The University of Chicago Press, 1956), p. 26.

64. R. Stucken, *Deutsche Geld- und Kreditpolitik, 1914 bis 1953* (Tübingen: J. C. B. Mohr, 1953), p. 33.

65. C. Bresciani-Turroni, *op. cit.,* p. 61.

66. L. A. Hahn, *Fünfzig Jahre zwischen Inflation und Deflation* (Tübingen: J. C. B. Mohr [Paul Siebeck], 1963), p. 16; and R. Stucken, *op. cit.,* p. 37.

67. C. Bresciani-Turroni, *op. cit.,* pp. 203–216. See also G. Stolper, K. Häuser, K. Borchardt, *The German Economy, 1870 to the Present* (New York: Harcourt, Brace & World, 1967), pp. 87–88.

68. *Ibid.,* p. 83.

69. R. Gaetten, *Inflationen* (Munich: R. Pfaum Verlag, 1955), p. 255.

70. France, Ministry of Foreign Affairs, *Diplomatic Correspondence. Reply of the French Government to the Note of the British Government of August 11, 1923, Relating to Reparations* (Paris: Imprimerie Nationale, 1923), p. 11.

71. W. Treue, *op. cit.,* pp. 712–713.

72. F. Lütge, *Deutsche Sozial- und Wirtschaftsgeschichte: Ein Überblick,* 3rd edition (Berlin: Springer-Verlag, 1966), p. 542.

73. A. Murad, *Private Credit and Public Debt* (Washington, D.C.: Public Affairs Press, 1954), p. 122.

74. U.S. Senate Committee on War Mobilization, *A Program for German Economic and Industrial Disarmament,* 1946, pp. 578–579.

75. J. Robinson, "The Economics of Hyper-Inflation," in *Collected Economic Papers* (New York: A. M. Kelley, 1951), p. 74.

76. *Ibid.*

77. M. J. Bonn, *Wandering Scholar* (New York: The John Day Co., 1948), pp. 286–287.

78. Redistributive effects of inflation have been analyzed in M. Bronfenbrenner and F. D. Holzman, "A Survey of Inflation Theory," in *Surveys of Economic Theory* (New York: St. Martin's Press, 1965), Vol. I, pp. 94–99.

79. R. F. Harrod, *The Life of John Maynard Keynes* (New York: Harcourt, Brace and Co., 1951), pp. 272–273.

80. W. Treue, *Wirtschaftsgeschichte der Neuzeit* (Stuttgart: A. Kröner Verlag, 1962), p. 678.

81. W. S. Churchill, *The Gathering Storm* (Boston: Houghton Mifflin Co., 1948), p. 7.

82. Alpha (anonymous), "Reparations and the Policy of Repudiation: An American View," *Foreign Affairs,* 2 (1923–24), 58.

83. S. P. Gilbert, "The Meaning of the 'Dawes Plan,'" *Foreign Affairs,* 4:3 (1925–26), iv, viii.

84. H. D. Gideonse, *op. cit.,* 693. See also J. W. Angell, "The Payment of Reparations and Inter-Ally Debts," *Foreign Affairs,* 4 (1925–26), 94.

85. A. Comstock, "Reparation Payments in Perspective," *The American Economic Review,* 20 (1930), 203.

86. W. Holzer, *Transfer und Transferpolitik im Rahmen des Dawesplanes* (Weiler in Allgäu: G. Holzer, 1929).

87. For some of the literature on the German transfer problem see Friedrich List-Gesellschaft, *Zu der Aussprache in Pyrmont am 5. und 6. Juni 1928. Thema 1–7; Gutachten über den Transfer und die Kommerzialisierung der Reparationszahlungen;* A. Lösch, "Eine Auseinandersetzung über das Transferproblem," *Schmollers Jahrbuch,* 54 (1930), 1093–1106; A. Lösch, "Die Lehre vom Transfer neu gefasst," *Jahrbücher*

für Nationalökonomie und Statistik, 154 (1941), 385–402; G. Haberler, "Transfer und Preisbewegung," *Zeitschrift für Nationalökonomie,* 1 (1930), 547–554; S. Helander, "Zur Theorie der Transferierung," *Weltwirtschaftliches Archiv,* 20 (1924), 589–616; J. C. Stamp, A. Pirelli, A. DeChalendar, *Reparation Payments and Future International Trade* (Paris: International Chamber of Commerce, 1925), pp. 10–12.

88. C. Bergmann, "Germany and the Young Plan," *Foreign Affairs,* 8 (1929–30), 583.

89. B. Röper, *op. cit.,* 815.

90. F. Machlup, *op. cit.,* p. 382.

91. B. Röper, *op. cit.,* 815.

92. F. Lütge, *op. cit.,* p. 545; L. A. Hahn, *op. cit.,* pp. 62–67.

93. Bruno Suviranta, "War Reparations and Trade Policy," *Kyklos,* 5 (1951–52), 334.

94. T. Balogh, *Unequal Partners* (Oxford: Basil Blackwell, 1963), Vol. 2, p. 134.

95. B. Graefrath, *op. cit.,* p. 90.

96. U.S. Department of State, *Germany, 1947–1949: The Story in Documents* (Washington, D.C.: Government Printing Office, 1950), p. 44.

97. *Ibid.,* pp. 50–51.

98. B. Suviranta, "Reparation Payments in Kind," *Economica,* 18 (1950), 424.

99. Anonymous, "Das finnische Reparationsproblem," in *Österreichisches Bank-Archiv,* 3 (1955), 165.

100. B. Suviranta, "Reparation Payments in Kind," *op. cit.,* 425.

101. J. Auer, "Finland's War Reparation Deliveries to the Soviet Union," in *Finnish Foreign Policy Publications,* 1963, p. 76. See also B. C. Jensen, *op. cit.,* p. 4.

102. B. Suviranta, "Reparation Payments in Kind," *op. cit.,* 426.

103. B. C. Jensen, *op. cit.,* p. 18.

104. B. Suviranta, "Reparation Payments in Kind," *op. cit.,* 429.

105. N. Spulber, *The Economics of Communist Eastern Europe* (New York: John Wiley and Sons, 1957), p. 39.

106. H. Köhler, *Economic Integration in the Soviet Bloc* (New York: Frederick A. Praeger, 1965), pp. 5–30.

107. "Reparatsii," in *Diplomaticheskii Slovar,* 3 (Moscow: Politizdat, 1964), pp. 51–53.

108. B. Graefrath, *op. cit.,* p. 114.

109. N. Spulber, *op. cit.,* p. 205.

110. House Select Committee on Foreign Aid, *Final Report of Foreign Aid, 1948,* pp. 143–144.

111. W. Treue, *Die Demontagepolitik der Westmächte nach dem zweiten Weltkrieg* (Göttingen: Musterschmidt-Verlag, 1967).

Chapter 3

1. H. C. Wallich, *Mainsprings of the German Revival* (New Haven, Conn.: Yale University Press, 1955), p. 82.

2. K. Adenauer, *Erinnerungen, 1953–1955* (Stuttgart: Deutsche Verlags-Anstalt, 1966), p. 141.

3. R. Murphy, *Diplomat Among Warriors* (Garden City, N.Y.: Doubleday and Co., 1964), pp. 240–242. For another important volume on the last few months of the Third Reich, see C. Ryan, *The Last Battle* (London: Collins, 1966).

4. C. A. Zebot, *The Economics of Competitive Coexistence* (New York: Frederick A. Praeger, 1964), p. 3.

5. R. Murphy, *op. cit.,* p. 208.

6. J. M. Mackintosh, *Strategy and Tactics of Soviet Foreign Policy* (New York: Oxford University Press, 1963), pp. 1–17.

7. A. Z. Rubinstein, ed., *The Foreign Policy of the Soviet Union* (New York: Random House, 1960), pp. 202–216.

8. According to Professor Joseph A. Schumpeter, the Soviet Union was the real victor of World War II; see his *Capitalism, Socialism and Democracy,* 3rd edition (New York: Harper and Bros., 1950), p. 398.

9. Writers such as Ronald Steel, Marcus G. Raskin, Richard J. Barnett, Gar Alperovitz, and D. F. Fleming have accused the United States of provoking the Cold War. Steel is the author of *Pax Americana* (New York: Viking Press, 1967).

10. A. Schlesinger, Jr., "Origins of the Cold War," *Foreign Affairs,* 46:1 (1967), 26.

11. Of the numerous volumes on the subject that could be cited or recommended to the specialist, only the following shall be mentioned here: M. F. Herz, *Beginnings of the Cold War* (Bloomington: Indiana University Press, 1966); H. Feis, *Between War and Peace: The Potsdam Conference* (Princeton: Princeton University Press, 1960); and W. L. Neumann, *After Victory: Churchill, Roosevelt, Stalin and the Making of the Peace* (New York: Harper & Row, 1967).

12. Schlesinger, *op. cit.,* 41.

13. For the official text of the Potsdam Agreement, see U.S. Department of State, *Germany 1947–1949: The Story in Documents* (Washington, D.C.: Government Printing Office, 1950), pp. 45–57.

14. *Ibid.,* p. 44.

15. H. Köhler, *Economic Integration in the Soviet Bloc* (New York: Frederick A. Praeger, 1965), p. 7.

16. U.S. Department of State, *op. cit.,* pp. 50–51.

17. H. Köhler, *op. cit.,* p. 8.

18. For the intense pressure generated by the American and British press for the elimination of the Dönitz government, see M. G. Steinert, *Die 23 Tage der Regierung Dönitz* (Düsseldorf-Vienna: Econ-Verlag, 1967), p. 334. See also K. Dönitz, *Zehn Jahre und zwanzig Tage* (Bonn: Anthenäum Verlag, 1958), p. 473.

19. E. E. Nobleman, "Quadripartite Military Government Organization and Operations in Germany," *The American Journal of International Law*, 41 (1947), 650–655.

20. N. J. G. Pounds, *The Economic Pattern of Modern Germany* (Chicago: Rand McNally, 1963), pp. 4–6.

21. F. Lütge, *Deutsche Sozial- und Wirtschaftsgeschichte. Ein Überblick*, 3rd edition (Berlin: Springer-Verlag, 1966), p. 565.

22. G. Stolper, K. Häuser, K. Borchardt, *The German Economy, 1870 to the Present* (New York: Harcourt, Brace and World, 1967), p. 180.

23. G. Stolper, *German Realities* (New York: Reynal & Hitchcock, 1948), p. 102, and H. Mendershausen, *Two Postwar Recoveries of the German Economy* (Amsterdam: North-Holland Publishing Company, 1955), p. 27.

24. W. Treue, *Deutsche Geschichte* (Stuttgart: A. Kröner Verlag, 1965), p. 769.

25. A. J. Heidenheimer, *Adenauer and the CDU* (The Hague: M. Nijhoff, 1960), p. 30.

26. W. Leonhard, *Child of the Revolution* (Chicago: Henry Regnery Co., 1958), pp. 297–358, and W. Leonhard, "Es muss demokratisch aussehen," *Die Zeit*, May 14, 1965, p. 8.

27. L. D. Clay, *Decision in Germany* (New York: Doubleday and Co., 1950), p. 50.

28. H. Zink, *The United States in Germany, 1944–1955* (Princeton, N.J.: D. Van Nostrand Co., 1957), pp. 93–97.

29. W. H. Chamberlin, *The German Phoenix* (New York: Duell, Sloan & Pearce, 1963), p. 40; see also H. Grabert, *Sieger und Besiegte* (Tübingen: Verlag der Deutschen Hochschullehrer-Zeitung, 1966), pp. 82–83.

30. D. C. Watt, *Britain Looks to Germany* (London: Oswald Wolff, 1965), pp. 54–55.

31. F. R. Willis, *France, Germany, and the New Europe* (Stanford, Calif.: Stanford University Press, 1965), pp. 15–25. For a basic work on the various attitudes of the four Allies in Germany, see M. Balfour and J. Mair, *Four Power Control in Germany and Austria* (London: Oxford University Press, 1956), pp. 14–48.

32. A. D., "War Damage in Germany: Economic Consequences and Allied Policy," *World Today*, 2 (1946), 201.

33. T. Pünder, *Das Bizonale Interregnum, Die Geschichte des Vereinigten Wirtschaftsgebietes, 1946–1949* (Waiblingen: Grote, 1966), p. 70. This is an indispensable work on West Germany from 1945 to 1949.

34. R. Murphy, *op. cit.*, p. 304. See also K. Adenauer, *Erinnerungen, 1945–1953* (Stuttgart: Deutsche Verlags-Anstalt, 1965), pp. 104–105.

35. U.S. Department of State, *op. cit.*, pp. 91–92. See also K. Adenauer, *op. cit.*, pp. 162–164.

36. *Ibid.*, p. 234.

37. A. Tedder, *Without Prejudice: World War II Memoirs* (Boston: Little, Brown, 1967).

38. F. M. Davis, *Come as a Conqueror* (New York: The Macmillan Co., 1967), p. 108.

39. P. Schöller, *Die Deutschen Städte* (Wiesbaden: Franz Steiner Verlag, 1967), pp. 76–77.

40. W. Westecker, *Die Wiedergeburt der deutschen Städte* (Düsseldorf-Vienna: Econ-Verlag, 1962), p. 382.

41. G. Stolper, K. Häuser, K. Borchardt, *op. cit.*, p. 203.

42. Statistisches Bundesamt, *Statistisches Jahrbuch für die Bundesrepublik Deutschland 1952* (Stuttgart-Cologne: Verlag W. Kohlhammer, 1953), p. 30. See also H. C. Wallich, *op. cit.*, p. 267.

43. G. C. Paikert, *The German Exodus* (The Hague: M. Nijhoff, 1962), p. 29.

44. West Germany, Bundesministerium für Vertriebene, Flüchtlinge und Kriegsgeschädigte, *Zeittafel, Band 2. Vertriebenenproblem: Recht auf die Heimat und Selbstbestimmung im Deutschen Parlament (von 1949 bis Mitte 1960)* (Bonn: 1960), pp. 5–29.

45. The German literature on this subject is enormous. Of the numerous volumes on this tragic subject, only the following shall be recommended here: M. Dönhoff, *Namen die keiner mehr kennt* (Cologne: Eugen Diederichs Verlag, 1962) and H. Mönnich, *Der vierte Platz, Chronik einer westpreussischen Familie* (Munich: Kindler Verlag, 1964).

46. H. C. Wallich, *op. cit.*, pp. 272–273.

47. R. Luza, *The Transfer of the Sudeten Germans* (New York: New York University Press, 1964), p. 287.

48. For a comprehensive survey of the expellee and refugee problems, see E. Lemberg and F. Edding, eds., *Die Vertriebenen in Westdeutschland* (Kiel: F. Hirt, 1959), 3 volumes.

49. *Statistisches Jahrbuch 1952*, p. 30.

50. F. Lütge, *op. cit.*, p. 567.

51. For some yearly figures, see G. Stolper, K. Häuser, K. Borchardt, *op. cit.*, p. 305.

52. EMNID, *Jeder Dritte hat kein Bett,* Untersuchung 12, July 1949 (mimeo).

53. West Germany, Federal Ministry for the Marshall Plan, *Twelfth, Final Report of the German Federal Government on the Progress of the Marshall Plan for the Period until June 30, 1952, and First and Second Report on the Continuation of U.S. Economic Aid (MSA) for the Period from July 1, 1952, until December 31, 1952* (Bonn: 1953), p. 72 (hereafter referred to as *Final Report*).

54. H. Hoover, *The President's Economic Mission to Germany and Austria, Report No. 1* (Washington, D.C.: 1947), p. 3.

55. H. Zink, *op. cit.,* p. 293.

56. *Ibid.,* p. 295.

57. F. S. V. Donnison, *Civil Affairs and Military Government North-West Europe, 1944–1946* (London: Her Majesty's Stationery Office, 1961), pp. 338–339.

58. H. Schlange-Schöningen, *Im Schatten des Hungers* (Hamburg: P. Parey, 1955), p. 310.

59. Senate Committee on Appropriations, *European Interim Aid and Government and Relief in Occupied Areas,* Hearings, November 1947, p. 551. See also House Committee on Foreign Affairs, *United States Foreign Policy for a Post-War Recovery Program,* Hearings, December 1947–March 1948, p. 362.

60. H. Schlange-Schöningen, *op. cit.,* p. 192. See also W. Niklas, *Ernährungswirtschaft und Agrarpolitik* (Bonn: *Ernährungswirtschaft und Agrarpolitik,* 1949), p. 13.

61. U.S. House Select Committee on Foreign Aid, *Final Report on Foreign Aid* (Washington, D.C.: Government Printing Office, 1948), p. 121.

62. N. Balabkins, *Germany Under Direct Controls: Economic Aspects of Industrial Disarmament, 1945–1948* (New Brunswick, N.J.: Rutgers University Press, 1964).

63. M. Pyke, *Industrial Nutrition* (London: Macdonald and Evans, 1950), p. 4, and International Labor Office, *Nutrition and Industry* (Montreal: 1946), p. 10.

64. M. Pyke, *op. cit.,* p. 161.

65. Testimony of D. A. Fitzgerald, Secretary General of the International Emergency Food Council. See House Committee on Appropriations, *First Deficiency Appropriation Bill for 1947,* Hearings, p. 793.

66. For effects of starvation and semistarvation on man, see J. Brozek, "Experimental Neurosis Resulting from Semistarvation in Man," *Psychosomatic Medicine,* 10:1 (1948), 31–50, and J. Brozek, "Psychology of Human Starvation and Nutritional Rehabilitation," *The Scientific Monthly,* 70:4 (1950), 270–274.

67. P. A. Sorokin, *Man and Society in Calamity* (New York: E. P. Dutton and Co., 1942), p. 51.

68. President's Committee on Foreign Aid, *European Recovery and American Aid* (Washington: GPO, 1947), p. 121.

69. The problem of hunger and its effects on man and society was reflected in the early postwar German literature, as, for instance, in W. Borchert's play, *Draussen vor der Tür* (Hamburg: Rowohlt Verlag, posthumous, 1956) and H. Böll, *Das Brot der frühen Jahre* (Frankfurt: Ullstein-Bücher, 1960).

70. H. A. Kraut and E. A. Muller, "Calorie Intake and Industrial Output," *Science,* 104:2709 (1946), 497; and W. D. Keller and H. A. Kraut, "Work and Nutrition," in *World Review of Nutrition and Dietetics* (London: Pitman Medical Publishing Co., 1947), pp. 69–81.

71. M. J. Bonn, "The Potsdam Reparation Plan," *World Affairs,* 3 (1949), 10.

72. M. J. Bonn, "The Reparation Fiasco," *Banker's Magazine* (London), 167 (1949), 406.

73. A. D., *op. cit.,* 204.

74. M. J. Bonn, "The Potsdam Reparation Plan," *op. cit.,* 11.

75. Absolutely indispensable is U.S. Senate, Committee on the Judiciary, Subcommittee to Investigate the Administration of the Internal Security Act and Other Internal Security Laws, *Morgenthau Diary (Germany),* Volumes I and II (Washington, D.C.: Government Printing Office, 1967). In another volume of his diaries, Mr. Morgenthau said that "the thing up at Quebec, all together, was unbelievably good. And as far as I went personally, it was the high spot of my whole career in the Government. I got more personal satisfaction out of those forty-eight hours than with anything I have ever been connected with": see U.S. Senate, Committee on the Judiciary, Subcommittee to Investigate the Administration of the Internal Security Act and Other Internal Security Laws, *Morgenthau Diary (China)* (Washington, D.C.: Government Printing Office, 1965), Volume II, p. 1234.

76. For the step-by-step development of the Morgenthau Plan, see J. M. Blum, *From the Morgenthau Diaries, Years of War, 1941–1945* (Boston: Houghton Mifflin Co., 1967), pp. 343–359. For some secondary accounts, see A. Armstrong, *Unconditional Surrender* (New Brunswick, N.J.: Rutgers University Press, 1961), pp. 69–77, and H. G. Gelber, "Der Morgenthau-Plan," in *Vierteljahrshefte für Zeitgeschichte,* 13:4 (1965), 372–402.

77. D. C. Watt, *op. cit.,* pp. 94, 114.

78. H. Zink, *op. cit.,* p. 252.

79. U.S. Department of State, *op. cit.,* pp. 22–33.

80. J. M. Blum, *op. cit.*, p. 356. For a German reaction to the chapters dealing with the making of the Morgenthau Plan, see K. Keppler's review, "Morgenthau und die Ruhr," *Industriekurier*, 5 (January 30, 1968), p. 2.

81. W. Treue, *Die Demontagepolitik der Westmächte nach dem zweiten Weltkrieg* (Göttingen: Musterschmidt-Verlag, 1967), p. 24.

82. G. Moltmann, "Zur Formulierung der Amerikanischen Besatzungs-politik in Deutschland am Ende des Zweiten Weltkrieges," in *Vierteljahrs-hefte für Zeitgeschichte,* 15:3 (1967), 299–322. See also Paul Y. Ham-mond, "Directives for the Occupation of Germany: The Washington Controversy," in H. Stein, ed., *American Civil-Military Decisions* (Bir-mingham: University of Alabama Press, 1963), pp. 314–343.

83. E. Plischke, "Denazification Law and Procedure," *The American Journal of International Law,* 41 (1947), 812.

84. R. Murphy, *op. cit.*, p. 294. The idea that industrial managers should also be treated as war criminals was first advocated by Emil Ludwig, in his 1943 volume, *How to Treat the Germans.* He demanded that the German industrial captains should not escape unpunished. He reminded his readers that it was the leading industrialists who sabotaged the implementation of the Versailles Treaty, and he feared that they would try again. Louis Nizer, in his book *What to Do with Germans,* charged that all of German big industry conspired against world peace, and thus should be treated as "war criminals." Joseph Pulitzer, owner of the St. Louis *Post-Dispatch,* Elbert D. Thomas, Chairman of the Armed Services Committee of the Senate, and Senator Harley M. Kilgore also demanded that the leading German businessmen and industrialists be treated as war criminals.

85. E. Plischke, *op. cit.*, 814–815.

86. K. Keppler, "Die deutschen Industrielle als 'Kriegsverbrecher,'" *Industriekurier,* 70 (May 6, 1965), 6.

87. R. Murphy, *op. cit.*, p. 251.

88. C. B. Hoover, *Memoirs of Capitalism, Communism, and Nazism* (Durham, N.C.: Duke University Press, 1965), pp. 240–241.

89. D. C. Watt, *op. cit.*, p. 53.

90. C. B. Hoover, *op. cit.*, p. 246. For the same point see L. D. Clay, *op. cit.*, p. 50.

91. R. Murphy, *op. cit.*, p. 227. See also E. Davidson, *The Death and Life of Germany: An Account of the American Occupation* (New York: Alfred A. Knopf, 1959), pp. 23–46.

92. C. B. Hoover, *op. cit.*, p. 224.

93. M. Balfour and J. Mair, *op. cit.*, p. 14–18.

94. F. M. Davis, *op. cit.*, p. 79.

95. U.S. Department of State, *op. cit.*, p. 51.

96. B. Ruhm von Oppen, ed., *Documents on Germany Under Occupation, 1945–1954* (London: Oxford University Press, 1955), pp. 113–118.

97. Anonymous, "Germany Under Allied Control II," *The Round Table,* 36 (1945–46), 22–23.

98. R. P. Schwarz, "Reparations and Politics," *The Fortnightly,* 159 (1946), 368.

99. E. S. Mason, "Has Our Policy in Germany Failed?" *Foreign Affairs,* 24 (1945–46), 586.

100. M. J. Bonn, "The End of Reparations?" *The Banker,* 93 (1950), 194.

101. "Spectator," "Dismantling in Western Germany," *The Fortnightly,* 166 (1949), 146.

102. B. U. Ratchford and W. D. Ross, *Berlin Reparations Assignment* (Chapel Hill: The University of North Carolina Press, 1947), p. 69.

103. C. B. Hoover, *op. cit.,* p. 223.

104. U.S. Department of State, *op. cit.,* paragraphs 15 and 16, pp. 33–41.

105. *Ibid.,* pp. 356–359.

106. House Committee on Foreign Affairs, *Plants and Parts of Plants Listed for Reparations from United States and United Kingdom Zones* (of Germany), 1947.

107. W. Hasenack, "Bilanz der Demontage," *Jahrbuch für Sozialwissenschaften,* 2 (1951), 23–24.

108. See American statements on the reparations debate in U.S. Department of State, *op. cit.,* pp. 411–426.

109. W. Hasenack, *op. cit.,* 34.

110. M. J. Bonn, "Reparations and Partition," *The Banker,* 84 (1947), 173.

111. M. Riedel, *Vorgeschichte, Entstehung und Demontage der Reichswerke im Salzgittergebiet* (Hanover: 1966), pp. 158–159. See also D. Bolster, "The End of Reparations," *Contemporary Review,* 178 (1950), 339.

112. B. Ruhm von Oppen, *op. cit.,* p. 442 (paragraph VIII of the Petersburg Agreement).

113. Inter-Allied Reparation Agency, *Report of the Assembly of the Inter-Allied Reparation Agency to its Member Governments,* Brussels, p. 15. By the end of 1949, the Inter-Allied Reparation Agency had distributed German merchant shipping and industrial equipment in the amount of 600 million marks; see D. Bolster, *loc. cit.*

114. M. J. Bonn, "The End of Reparations?" *op. cit.,* 196.

115. F. G. Reuss, *Fiscal Policy for Growth Without Inflation: The German Experiment* (Baltimore, Md.: The Johns Hopkins Press, 1963), p. 10,

and G. Stolper, K. Häuser, K. Borchardt, *op. cit.*, p. 191. See also W. Hasenack, *op. cit.*, 50.

116. Inter-Allied Reparation Agency, *loc. cit.*, and F. G. Reuss, *loc. cit.*

117. R. Krengel, "Some Reasons for the Rapid Economic Growth of the German Federal Republic," *Banca Nazionale del Lavoro Quarterly Review*, 64 (1963), 5.

118. W. Kirner, *Zeitreihen für das Anlagevermögen der Wirtschaftsbereiche in der Bundesrepublik Deutschland* (Berlin: Duncker & Humblot, 1968), pp. 87, 88.

119. R. Krengel, *op. cit.*, 4. See also K. W. Roskamp, *Capital Formation in West Germany* (Detroit: Wayne State University Press, 1965), p. 36.

120. M. M. Postan, *An Economic History of Western Europe, 1945–1964* (London: Methuen and Co., 1967), p. 24.

121. W. Hasenack, *op. cit.*, 47.

122. J. S. Mill, *Principles of Political Economy* (New York: The Colonial Press, 1899), Vol. I, p. 75.

123. R. Krengel, *op. cit.*, 5.

124. B. Ruhm von Oppen, *op. cit.*, pp. 117, 118.

125. Professor Albert Schweitzer of Indiana University has used this term repeatedly: see his reviews in *The Journal of Economic History*, 28:3 (1968), 495, and *The Southern Economic Journal*, 31 (1965), 262.

126. A. Dallin, *German Rule in Russia 1941–1945* (New York: St. Martin's Press, 1957), pp. 39–40, and V. Petrov, *Money and Conquest: Allied Occupation Currencies in World War II* (Baltimore, Md.: The Johns Hopkins Press, 1967), pp. 29–34.

127. T. Balogh, *Unequal Partners* (Oxford: Basil Blackwell, 1963), Vol. 2, pp. 130, 136.

128. See N. Balabkins, *op. cit.*, pp. 135–138.

129. Potsdam Agreement, Section B, paragraph 14c: see U.S. Department of State, *op. cit.*, p. 50.

130. J. Gimbel, *A German Community under American Occupation* (Stanford, Calif.: Stanford University Press, 1961), pp. 117–132. See also E. Liefmann-Keil, *Die wirtschaftliche Verarmung Deutschlands: Verarmungsprozess oder Aufbau?* (Stuttgart: 1947), pp. 18–19 (mimeo).

131. L. Erhard, *Prosperity Through Competition* (London: Thames & Hudson, 1958), p. 10.

132. H. Sauermann, "The Consequences of the Currency Reform in West Germany," *The Review of Politics*, 12 (1950), 178–179.

133. For examples, see U.S. Office of Military Government, *Monthly Report*, No. 8 (March 1946), p. 44, and No. 31 (January 1948), p. 16.

134. Köln Industrie- und Handelskammer, *Bericht für das Jahr 1947*, p. 5; Ludwigsburg Industrie- und Handelskammer, *Denkschrift: Grund-*

sätzliche und aktuelle Probleme unserer wirtschaftpolitischen Aufgabe (1947), p. 20.

135. IFO-Institut für Wirtschaftsforschung, *Fünf Jahre Deutsche Mark* (Berlin and Munich: Duncker & Humblot, 1954), p. 32.

136. F. A. Burchardt and K. Martin, "Western Germany and Reconstruction," *Bulletin of the Oxford University Institute of Statistics,* 9:12 (1947), 405.

137. T. Balogh, *Germany: An Experiment in "Planning by the 'Free' Price Mechanism"* (Oxford: Basil Blackwell, 1950), p. 12.

138. U.S. Office of Military Government, Manpower Division, *Unemployment and Underemployment in the Bizonal Area of Germany* (1949), p. 18 (mimeo).

139. W. Eucken and F. W. Mayer, "The Economic Situation in Germany," *The Annals of the American Academy of Political and Social Science,* 260 (1948), 59.

140. W. Röpke, "Das Deutsche Wirtschaftsexperiment: Beispiel und Lehre," in A. Hunold, ed., *Vollbeschäftigung, Inflation und Planwirtschaft* (Zürich: E. Rentsch Verlag, 1953), p. 271.

141. "The German Lesson," *The London Economist,* 221:6425 (1966), viii.

142. F. B. Jensen and I. Walter, *The Common Market: Economic Integration in Europe* (Philadelphia: J. B. Lippincott Co., 1964), p. 4.

143. H. Hoover, *The President's Economic Mission to Germany and Austria, Report No. 3* (Washington, D.C.: 1947), p. 15.

144. J. F. Dulles, *War or Peace* (New York: The Macmillan Co., 1950), pp. 102–106. For another source, see G. Wettig, *Entmilitarisierung und Wiederbewaffnung in Deutschland, 1943–1955* (Munich: R. Oldenbourg Verlag, 1967), pp. 196–198.

145. R. F. Harrod, *The Life of John Maynard Keynes* (New York: Harcourt, Brace and Co., 1951), p. 489. This memo of Keynes is still subject to the Foreign Office Rule, which denies access to documents.

146. M. Saeter, *Eine Analyse der Deutschen Frage, Okkupation, Integration, Gleichberechtigung* (Oslo: Norsk Utenrikspolitisk Institut, 1967), p. 14.

147. J. Hennessy, "The German Miracle," in *Economic 'Miracles'* (London: Andre Deutsch, 1964), p. 32.

148. K. W. Roskamp, *op. cit.,* p. 45. For other relevant literature see H. Möller, *Zur Vorgeschichte der DM* (Tübingen: J. C. B. Mohr, 1961), pp. 16–18.

149. For some literature on the currency reform, see E. Davidson, *op. cit.,* pp. 222–232; H. Behr, *Vom Chaos zum Staat* (Frankfurt a/M.: Verlag Frankfurter Bücher, 1961), pp. 232–235; F. A. Lutz, "The German Cur-

rency Reform and the Revival of the German Economy," *Economica,* 16 (1949), 122–142; and Bank Deutscher Länder, *Report of the Bank Deutscher Länder for the Years 1948 and 1949* (1950), pp. 1–8.

150. L. Erhard, *op. cit.,* pp. 3–5; H. C. Wallich, *op. cit.,* pp. 73–78; L. Erhard, *Deutsche Wirtschaftspolitik* (Frankfurt a/M.: Knapp, 1962), pp. 62–68; A. Müller-Armack, *Wirtschaftsordnung und Wirtschaftspolitik* (Freiburg i. Breisgau: Verlag Rombach, 1966), pp. 171–199.

151. G. Stolper, K. Häuser, K. Borchardt, *op. cit.,* p. 228. See also F. Lütge, *op. cit.,* pp. 574–575.

152. J. Rueff, *The Age of Inflation* (Chicago: Henry Regnery Co., 1964), pp. 86–105.

153. L. Erhard, *The Economics of Success* (London: Thames & Hudson, 1963), p. 36.

154. K. G. Pfleiderer, *Politik für Deutschland* (Stuttgart: Deutsche Verlags-Anstalt, 1961), p. 86.

155. Appendix of "British Military Government Ordinance No. 88: Agreement for Reorganization of Bizonal Economic Agencies," reproduced in B. Ruhm von Oppen, *op. cit.,* pp. 227–231.

156. U.S. Office of Military Government, *German Government Organization and Civil Administration,* No. 23 (April–May 1947), p. 5.

157. According to one observer of the scene, McCloy was "a guide and counselor of the new half-free state": see E. Davidson, *op. cit.,* p. 248.

158. P. Noack, *Die Deutsche Nachkriegszeit* (Munich and Vienna: G. Olzog Verlag, 1966), pp. 194–197.

159. M. Saeter, *op. cit.,* p. 22.

160. K. G. Pfleiderer, *op. cit.,* p. 36.

161. West Germany, *Statistisches Jahrbuch für die Bundesrepublik Deutschland 1952* (Stuttgart: Verlag W. Kohlhammer, 1953), p. 209.

162. U.S. Office of Military Government for Germany, *The European Recovery Program: US/UK Occupied Area of Germany* (September 1948), pp. 15–16.

163. J. Semler, *Kommentare zu meiner Erlanger Rede* (n.p.: 1948), pp. 34–36 (mimeo).

164. West Germany, Federal Ministry for the Marshall Plan, *Recovery Under the Marshall Plan, 1948–1952* (Bonn: 1953), p. 79.

165. H. C. Wallich, *op. cit.,* p. 230.

166. *Ibid.,* p. 231.

167. F. Friedrich, *Westdeutsche Zahlungsbilanzpolitik von 1948 bis 1951* (Zürich: Polygraphischer Verlag, 1955), p. 24.

168. Bank Deutscher Länder, *op. cit.,* p. 34.

169. West Germany, Federal Ministry for the Marshall Plan, *op. cit.,* p. 23.

170. A. Yoder, "The Ruhr Authority and the German Problem," *The Review of Politics,* 17 (1955), 352.

171. U.S. Department of State, *op. cit.,* p. 343.

172. West Germany, Federal Ministry for the Marshall Plan, *op. cit.,* p. 23.

173. H. C. Wallich, *op. cit.,* p. 107. See also P. M. Boarman, *Germany's Economic Dilemma: Inflation and the Balance of Payments* (New Haven, Conn.: Yale University Press, 1964), p. 105.

174. West Germany, Federal Ministry for the Marshall Plan, *Report of the German Federal Government on the Progress of the Marshall Plan: General Survey, October 1, 1949–March 31, 1951* (Bonn: 1951), p. 27.

175. *Ibid.,* p. 92.

176. West Germany, Federal Ministry for the Marshall Plan, *What Happened in Germany? A Preliminary Balance* (Bonn: 1951), p. 19. See also Office of the U.S. High Commissioner for Germany, Historical Division, *The Liberalization of West German Foreign Trade, 1949–1951* (Bonn: 1952), pp. 102–107.

177. West Germany, Federal Ministry for the Marshall Plan, *Ninth Report of the German Federal Government on the Progress of the Marshall Plan: October 1, 1951–December 31, 1951 and Annual Survey of 1951* (Bonn: 1952), p. 29.

178. R. Salomon, *Begriff und Problematik der wirtschaftlichen Engpässe: Dargestellt am Beispiel der Bundesrepublik Deutschland in den Jahren 1948 bis 1952* (Kiel: Institut für Weltwirtschaft, 1954), pp. 60–70.

179. West Germany, Federal Ministry for the Marshall Plan, *Tenth Report of the German Federal Government on the Progress of the Marshall Plan: January 1, 1952–March 31, 1952* (Bonn: 1952), p. 33.

180. *Ibid.*

181. F. A. Lutz, *op. cit.,* 142.

182. K. Friedrich, *op. cit.,* p. 51.

183. West Germany, Federal Ministry for the Marshall Plan, *Recovery Under the Marshall Plan, 1948–1952* (Bonn: 1953), p. 89.

184. See P. M. Boarman, *op. cit.,* p. 239, and H. Mendershausen, *op. cit.,* p. 51.

185. West Germany, Federal Ministry for the Marshall Plan, *op. cit.,* p. 107.

186. *Ibid.*

187. L. Erhard, *op. cit.,* p. 33.

188. West Germany, Federal Ministry for the Marshall Plan, *Recovery Under the Marshall Plan, 1948–1952, op. cit.,* p. 23.

189. P. M. Boarman, *op. cit.,* p. 66.

190. F. Schäffer, *Ein Rechenschaftsbericht über die deutsche Finanzpolitik 1949 bis 1953* (Bonn: 1953), p. 17.

191. Interview with Robert Murphy (author of *Diplomat Among Warriors*) on June 6, 1966, in New York City.

Chapter 4

1. The American Jewish Committee, Research Institute on Peace and Post-War Problems, *Preliminary Announcement* (New York: 1941).

2. *Ibid.*, p. 9.

3. Institute of Jewish Affairs, *The Institute Anniversary Volume (1941–1961)* (New York: World Jewish Congress, 1962), p. ix.

4. Dr. Goldmann, a Lithuanian-born Jew, who lived for many years in Germany and went to the United States in the 1930s, was president of the World Jewish Congress from 1951 to 1968.

5. U.S. Department of State, *Bulletin*, 8:185 (January 9, 1943), 21–22.

6. G. Landauer, *Der Zionismus im Wandel Dreier Jahrzehnte* (Tel Aviv: Bitaon Verlag, 1957), p. 42.

7. *Ibid.*, p. 278.

8. S. Moses, *Die jüdischen Nachkriegsforderungen* (Tel Aviv: Bitaon Verlag, 1944).

9. *Ibid.*, pp. 16–21.

10. N. Bentwich, "Siegfried Moses and the United Restitution Organization," in *In Zwei Welten: Siegfried Moses zum Fünfundsiebzigsten Geburtstag*, H. Tamer, ed. (Tel Aviv: Bitaon Verlag, 1962), p. 193.

11. F. Gillis and H. Knopf, *The Reparation Claim of the Jewish People* (Tel Aviv: M. Feuchtwanger, 1944).

12. H. Muller, "Aus der Gründungszeit des Council of Jews from Germany," in *In Zwei Welten, op. cit.*, pp. 184–192. For additional details on the early part of the collective claim against Germany see S. Adler-Rudel, "Aus der Vorzeit der kollektiven Wiedergutmachung," *ibid.*, pp. 200–217.

13. F. E. Shinnar, "Konzeption und Grundlage der Wiedergutmachung," *ibid.*, pp. 233–235.

14. E. Munz, "Restitution in Postwar Europe," *Contemporary Jewish Record*, 6:4 (1943), 371–380.

15. G. Weis, *Restitution Through the Ages* (London: The World Jewish Congress, British Section, 1962).

16. Schweizerischer Israelischer Gemeindebund, *Jüdische Nachkriegsprobleme* (Zürich: Verlag, 'Die Gestaltung,' 1945), pp. 37–38.

17. *Ibid.*, p. 44.

18. World Jewish Congress, War Emergency Conference, *Summary of Proceedings*, Atlantic City, N.J., November 26–30, 1944, pp. 4, 15.

19. *Ibid.*, p. 32.

20. *Ibid.*, p. 33.

21. N. Goldmann, *The Autobiography of Nahum Goldmann: Sixty Years of Jewish Life* (New York: Holt, Rinehart and Winston, 1969), p. 251 (hereafter *Autobiography*).

22. World Jewish Congress, *Resolutions; War Emergency Conference of the World Jewish Congress,* Atlantic City, N.J., November 26–30, 1944, pp. 30–31.

23. N. Robinson, *Indemnification and Reparations* (New York: Institute for Jewish Affairs of the American Jewish Congress and World Jewish Congress, 1944).

24. N. Goldmann, "Nehemiah Robinson: Dedicated and Faithful Servant of the Jewish People," in N. Robinson, *Ten Years of German Indemnification,* Memorial Edition (New York: Conference on Jewish Material Claims Against Germany, 1964), p. 8.

25. N. Robinson, *Spoliation and Remedial Action: The Material Damage Suffered by Jews Under Persecution. Reparations, Restitution, and Compensation* (New York: Institute of Jewish Affairs, 1962), p. 163. For another study, published during the war, see H. Marx, *The Case of the German Jews vs. Germany* (New York: The Egmont Press, 1944).

26. For the contents of this letter, see Israel, Ministry of Foreign Affairs, *Documents Relating to the Agreement Between the Government of Israel and the Government of the Federal Republic of Germany* (Jerusalem: Government Printer, 1953), pp. 9–12 (hereafter cited as *Documents*).

27. The initial estimate made by Dr. Robinson in 1944, this figure was used by Dr. Bernard Joseph in preparing a memorandum on the Jewish losses for the use of the Jewish Agency: see Adler-Rudel, *op. cit.,* p. 211.

28. American Jewish Committee, Committee on Peace Problems, *Abrogation of Nazi Legislation; Restitution and Indemnification; A Review of Developments in 1945,* New York, Second Session, January 31–February 1, 1946, p. 14 (mimeo).

29. D. Peretz, *The Middle East Today* (New York: Holt, Rinehart and Winston, 1964), and N. H. Bentwich, *Mandate Memories, 1918–1948* (New York: Schocken Books, 1965).

30. The best source on this matter is Chancellor Adenauer's account in *Erinnerungen, 1953–1955* (Stuttgart: Deutsche Verlags-Anstalt, 1966), pp. 132–162. Another good source is a volume edited by R. Vogel, *Deutschlands Weg nach Israel* (Stuttgart: Seewald Verlag, 1967): see p. 77.

31. R. Giordano, ed., *Narben, Spuren, Zeugen* (Düsseldorf: Verlag Allgemeine Wochenzeitung der Juden in Deutschland, 1961), p. 207.

32. K. R. Grossmann, *Die Ehrenschuld* (Frankfurt a/M.: Ullstein, 1967), p. 17.

33. World Jewish Congress, *Unity in Dispersion: A History of the World Jewish Congress* (New York: World Jewish Congress, 1948), pp. 270–271.

34. N. Barou, *The Story Behind Reparations* (4 pages, typewritten manuscript). This sketch, written by Dr. Barou after the Wassenaar negotiations were completed, is at the Institute of Jewish Affairs, London.

35. K. R. Grossmann, *op. cit.,* p. 19.

36. K. Adenauer, *op. cit.,* p. 133.

37. N. Goldmann, *Autobiography,* p. 253.

38. A. L. Easterman, "Monument Without An Epitaph," *World Jewry,* 5:3 (1962), 5.

39. N. Barou, *op. cit.,* p. 1.

40. *Ibid.*

41. For the details of these contacts, see R. Vogel, ed., *op. cit.,* pp. 19–21 and 28.

42. H. van Dam, *The Problem of Reparations and Indemnification for Israel* (Hamburg: July 1, 1950), p. 1 (mimeo).

43. Interview, July 20, 1966, in Düsseldorf, West Germany.

44. For the full text, see Appendix A.

45. Appendix A, p. 280.

46. A. L. Easterman, Germany, Note of conversation with Lord Henderson, Under-Secretary of State for Foreign Affairs (accompanied by Mr. Wilson), at the Foreign Office, London, on Thursday, January 11, 1951, from 11 A.M. to 12:45 P.M. (mimeo). This note is printed in full in Appendix B.

47. Appendix B, p. 291. At the then prevailing rate of exchange of $2.80 for £1, the above sum came to a total of $1.4 billion.

48. For the significance of this note in the history of the Jewish claim for collective compensation, see The World Jewish Congress, *Survey of Policy and Action, 1948–1953* (Presented to the Third Plenary Assembly of the World Jewish Congress at Geneva in August 1953), p. 43.

49. K. R. Grossmann, *Germany's Moral Debt* (Washington, D.C.: Public Affairs Press, 1954), p. 9.

50. *Documents,* pp. 9–91. See also F. E. Shinnar, *Bericht eines Beauftragten* (Tübingen: R. Wunderlich Verlag, 1967), pp. 23–24.

51. This is the wording of the U.S. Note of July 5, 1951: see *Documents,* pp. 34–36. The British Government also replied in the negative, saying that it could not see its way clear to "impose upon the German Federal Government the task of making reparation to the Government of Israel. . . .": *ibid.,* p. 37.

52. N. Goldmann, *Autobiography,* p. 255.

53. G. Landauer, *op. cit.,* p. 312.

54. N. Goldmann, *Autobiography*, p. 257.

55. Anglo-Jewish Association, *The Future of European Jewry and Other Papers* (London: 1946), pp. 44–45.

56. F. E. Shinnar, *op. cit.*, p. 18.

57. *New York Times*, December 29, 1950, quoted in H. Volle, "Das Wiedergutmachungsabkommen zwischen der Bundesrepublik Deutschland und dem Staate Israel," *Europa-Archiv*, 8 (1953), 5619.

58. The World Jewish Congress, *Survey of Policy and Action, 1948–1953, op. cit.*, p. 44.

59. W. Hausenstein, *Pariser Erinnerungen* (Munich: Günter Olzog Verlag, 1961), p. 76.

60. N. Barou, *op. cit.*, p. 2.

61. N. Goldmann, *Autobiography*, p. 255. Also N. Barou, *op. cit.*, p. 3.

62. N. Barou, "Origin of the German Agreement," *Congress Weekly*, October 13, 1952, pp. 6–7.

63. J. Fraenkel, "Noah Barou: The Man from Poltava," in H. F. Infield, ed., *Essays in Jewish Sociology, Labour, and Co-operation in Memory of Dr. Noah Barou, 1889–1955* (London: T. Yoseloff, 1962), p. 7.

64. N. Barou, *The Story Behind Reparations, op. cit.*, p. 2.

65. Interview with Governor Horowitz in Jerusalem, January 18, 1966.

66. Dr. Herbert Blankenhorn, a witness at this first official contact, has thus far not published his account of it.

67. Bundesrepublik Deutschland, *Verhandlungen des Deutschen Bundestages: Stenographische Berichte*, 9 (1951), 6697–6700.

68. According to E. Davidson, *The Trial of the Germans* (New York: The Macmillan Co., 1966), p. 8, 80,000 people served in the extermination apparatus, and not all were Germans.

69. For a full collection of the press reviews on this matter, see Bundesrepublik Deutschland, Presse- und Informationsamt der Bundesregierung, *Deutschland und das Judentum* (Bonn: Deutscher Bundes Verlag, 1951), pp. 11–18.

70. R. Giordano, ed., *op. cit.*, pp. 212–213.

71. M. Bar-Zohar, *Ben-Gurion: The Armed Prophet* (Englewood Cliffs, N.J.: Prentice-Hall, 1968), p. 174.

72. Anonymous, "German Reparations to Israel: The 1952 Treaty and Its Effects," *The World Today*, 10 (1954), 260.

73. M. Bisgyer, *Challenge and Encounter* (New York: Crown Publishers, 1967), pp. 118–119.

74. F. E. Shinnar, *op. cit.*, pp. 26–28.

75. N. Goldmann, "A Noble Son of Jewry," in H. F. Infield, ed., *op. cit.*, p. 11.

76. N. Goldmann, *Autobiography*, p. 256.

77. J. B. Schechtman, "Case Against Negotiations with Germany," *The Jewish Herald,* 15:19 (1951), 7.

78. J. B. Schechtman, "Direct Israel-German Negotiations? No," *The Zionist Quarterly,* 1:3 (1952), 15.

79. *Ibid.*

80. M. Nurock, "To Negotiate Is to Condone," *The Jewish Horizon,* January 1952, p. 5.

81. J. B. Schechtman, "The Case Against Negotiations with Germany," *The Alliance Review,* 6:24 (1951), 8.

82. Anonymous, "Around Negotiations with Germany," *Bulletin of the United Zionist-Revisionists of America,* 5:3 (1952), 2.

83. Anonymous, "Germany's First Offer of Amends," *The Reconstructionist,* 17:2 (1951), 3.

84. Anonymous, "Around Negotiations with Germany," *op. cit.,* 2.

85. J. B. Schechtman, "Direct Israel-German Negotiations? No," *op. cit.,* p. 13.

86. J. B. Schechtman, "The Case Against Negotiations with Germany," *loc. cit.*

87. I. H. Levin, "Reparations from Germany," *Jewish Life,* 19:4 (1952), 32–33.

88. M. Nurock, *op. cit.,* p. 4.

89. J. B. Schechtman, "Direct Israel-German Negotiations? No," *op. cit.,* p. 20.

90. Amalek was the first foe to attack the people of Israel after they had come out of Egypt as a free nation. The name is a byword for the arch-enemy of Israelites: "Remember what Amalek did unto thee" (Deut. 25:17–19) is read in the synagogue on the Sabbath preceding Purim. Amalek is also a popular term for a Jew-hater: see *The Jewish Encyclopedia* (New York: Funk & Wagnalls Co., 1901), Vol. I, 482–483.

91. N. Goldmann, "Direct Israel-German Negotiations? Yes," *The Zionist Quarterly,* 1:3 (1952), 10.

92. N. Goldmann, "Why I Favor Direct Israel-German Negotiations," *Jewish Observer and Middle East Review,* 1:3 (1952), 9.

93. S. Daniel, "Shall We Demand Reparations from Germany?" *The Jewish Horizon,* January 1952, p. 3.

94. N. Goldmann, "Direct Israel-German Negotiations? Yes," *op. cit.,* 12.

95. R. L. Halprin, "Shall Jews Negotiate with Germany for Restitution?" *Hadassah Newsletter,* 32:3 (1952), 2.

96. J. H. Justman, "Conference Will Weigh Bonn 'Restitution' Offer," *Israel Speaks,* 5:18 (1951), 4.

97. Anonymous, "A Bill That Must Be Paid," *Congress Weekly*, 18:12 (1951), 3.

98. I. Ivry, "Reparation But Not Reconciliation," *Congress Weekly*, 19:7 (1952), 6.

99. N. Goldmann, "Bonn-Israel Claims Settlement Opens Way to Economic Expansion," *Israel Economic Horizons*, 5:4 (1953), 3.

100. N. Goldmann, "Why I Favor Direct Israel-German Negotiations," *op. cit.*, 11.

101. D. Courtney, "The German Reparations Agreement," *Jewish Frontier*, 19:10 (1952), 9.

102. M. Shtrigler, "Less Enthusiasm, Please!" *Jewish Frontier*, 19:10 (1952), 12.

103. Bank of Israel, *Hashilumim Vehashpaatam al Hameshek Haisrael* (Jerusalem: 1965), p. 30. See also N. Halevi and R. Klinov-Malul, *The Economic Development of Israel* (New York: Frederick A. Praeger, 1968), pp. 6, 141.

Chapter 5

1. M. Sicron, *Immigration to Israel, 1948–1953* (Jerusalem: Central Bureau of Statistics, 1957), p. 35. For more data, see N. Halevi and R. Klinov-Malul, *The Economic Development of Israel* (New York: Frederick A. Praeger, 1968), pp. 52–54.

2. J. T. Shuval, *Immigrants on the Threshold* (New York: Atherton Press, 1963), p. 6.

3. A. Hovne, *The Labor Force in Israel* (Jerusalem: 1961), pp. 13–29.

4. R. L. Frey, *Strukturwandlungen der Israelischen Volkswirtschaft global und regional, 1948–1975* (Basel: Kyklos-Verlag, 1965), p. 41.

5. D. Horowitz, "Israel," in H. V. Prochnow, ed., *World Economic Problems and Policies* (New York: Harper & Row, 1965), pp. 224–225.

6. *Statistical Abstract of Israel*, 16 (1965), p. 95, Table D/3.

7. For this point, see D. Patinkin, *The Israel Economy: The First Decade* (Jerusalem: Jerusalem Post Press, 1960), p. 21.

8. H. Lehrman, "The Economic Test Facing Israel," *Commentary*, 7 (1949), 513.

9. J. Nasmyth, "Israel's Distorted Economy," *The Middle East Journal*, 8 (1954), 393–394.

10. C. Bresciani-Turroni, *The Economics of Inflation* (London: Allen & Unwin, 1937), pp. 107–207.

11. United Nations, "Inflation and the Mobilization of Domestic Capital in Underdeveloped Countries in Asia," in G. M. Meier, ed., *Leading*

Issues in Development Economics (New York: Oxford University Press, 1964), p. 173.

12. R. D. Ottensooser, *The Palestine Pound and the Israel Pound* (Geneva: Librairie E. Droz, 1955), p. 107.

13. S. Riemer, "Inflation in Israel," *Public Finance,* 12 (1957), 264.

14. Israel, *Government Yearbook 5711 (1950)* (Jerusalem: Government Printer, 1950), p. 198.

15. J. T. Shuval, *op. cit.,* p. 19.

16. D. Patinkin, "Monetary and Price Developments in Israel, 1949–53," *Scripta Hierosolymitana,* 3 (1956), 23.

17. D. Horowitz, "Israel," *op. cit.,* p. 227.

18. D. Horowitz, "Economic Problems of the State of Israel," *Israel Economic Bulletin,* 2:16–17 (1950), i.

19. Israel, *Government Yearbook 5711, loc. cit.*

20. M. Michaely, "Domestic Effects of Devaluation under Repressed Inflation," *The Journal of Political Economy,* 63 (1955), 512.

21. On the theory of repressed inflation, see B. Hansen, *A Study in the Theory of Inflation* (New York: Rinehart & Co., 1951), pp. 1–21, 83–114. See also H. Brems, *Output, Employment, Capital, and Growth* (New York: Harper & Row, 1959), pp. 77–82; R. Turvey, "The Inflationary Gap," *Ekonomisk Tidskrift,* 50 (1948), 10–17; and R. Turvey, "A Further Note on the Inflationary Gap," *ibid.,* 51 (1949), 92–97.

22. H. K. Charlesworth, *The Economics of Repressed Inflation* (London: Allen & Unwin, 1956), pp. 35, 39.

23. Bank of Israel, *Annual Report 1955* (Jerusalem: 1956), p. 156; see also *Statistical Abstract of Israel,* 16 (1965), pp. 506–507.

24. D. Patinkin, *The Israel Economy, op. cit.,* p. 108, where this is calculated at 36 per cent for a slightly different period.

25. S. Riemer, *loc. cit.;* and S. Riemer (S. E. Ahuvah), "Israel's New Economic Policy (NEP): The Background," *Public Finance,* 9 (1954), 286.

26. S. Riemer (S. E. Ahuvah), *op. cit.,* 289–290, 294–295.

27. Israel, *Government Yearbook 5711, op. cit.,* p. 204. See also A. Rubner, *The Economy of Israel: A Critical Account of the First Ten Years* (New York: Frederick A. Praeger, 1960), p. 58, and W. Schick, *Das Bankwesen in Israel* (Basel: Kyklos-Verlag, 1964), pp. 108–109.

28. Israel, *Government Yearbook 5711, op. cit.,* p. 205.

29. Israel, *Government Yearbook 5712 (1951/52)* (Jerusalem: Government Printer, 1951), pp. 410, 421; and A. Rubner, *op. cit.,* p. 55.

30. R. D. Ottensooser, *op. cit.,* p. 124.

31. E. Goldberger, *Preisbewegungen in Israel, 1949–1953* (Zürich: Polygraphischer Verlag, 1956), pp. 127, 131.

32. S. Riemer (S. E. Ahuvah), *op. cit.,* 286.

33. For other discussion of this period, see A. L. Gaathon, "Israels Wirtschaft," in *Israel: Kultur der Nationen* (Nuremberg: Glock und Lutz, 1963), Vol. 13, pp. 174–176, and by the same author, "Das Wirtschaftliche Wachstum Israels von 1950 bis 1964," *Konjunkturpolitik,* 11:4 (1965), 223–224, 244.

34. D. Patinkin, "Monetary and Price Developments in Israel, 1949–1953," *op. cit.,* 49. For data on official and free-market prices of margarine, edible oil, and butter, see F. Ginor, *Uses of Agricultural Surpluses* (Jerusalem: Bank of Israel, 1963), p. 451.

35. R. D. Ottensooser, *op. cit.,* p. 125.

36. M. E. Kreinin, *Israel and Africa, A Study in Technical Cooperation* (New York: Frederick A. Praeger, 1964), p. 113.

37. Israel, *Government Yearbook 5711, op. cit.,* p. 202.

38. *Ibid.,* p. 203.

39. From 1940 to 1960, the U.S. civilian consumption per capita per day of proteins was 90 grams, of fat 140 grams.

40. F. Ginor, *op. cit.,* pp. 400–401.

41. A. Rubner, *op. cit.,* p. 163.

42. *Ibid.,* pp. 59, 267.

43. *Ibid.,* pp. 262–267.

44. W. L. Crum, J. F. Fennelly, L. H. Seltzer, *Fiscal Planning For Total War* (New York: National Bureau of Economic Research, 1942), pp. 107–111.

45. For a recent work on this matter, see A. G. Mazour, *Soviet Economic Development. Operation Outstrip: 1921–1965* (Princeton, N.J.: D. Van Nostrand, 1967).

46. D. Horowitz, *The Economics of Israel* (Oxford: Pergamon Press, 1967), p. 120.

47. *Ibid.,* p. 33.

48. M. Kreinin, *op. cit.,* p. 113, and N. Halevi and R. Klinov-Malul, *op. cit.,* p. 96.

49. S. Riemer, "Inflation in Israel," *op. cit.,* p. 275; *Israel Economic Bulletin,* 2:5–6 (1950), 9, estimated that the total of investment in 1949 was I£ 86 million or $240.9 million.

50. The values for "realistic" exchange rates were taken from *Israel Economic Bulletin, loc. cit.*

51. For other data, see A. Rubner, *op. cit.,* p. 39, whose total for gross investment comes to $713 million for the 1949–1951 period. Still another source is D. Patinkin, *The Israel Economy, op. cit.,* p. 96.

52. A. Rubner, *op. cit.,* p. 34.

53. N. Halevi and Klinov-Malul, *op. cit.,* p. 155.

54. S. Riemer, *op. cit.*, p. 275.

55. D. Cohen, "Israel's Inflow of Capital and Its Institutional Impact," *The Israel Yearbook 1961* (Tel Aviv: 1961), p. 67. From 1949 to 1951, the total of capital imports was $895 million.

56. S. Riemer (S. E. Ahuvah), *op. cit.*, p. 279.

57. N. Halevi and R. Klinov-Malul, *op. cit.*, p. 96.

58. D. Patinkin, *The Israel Economy, op. cit.*, p. 84.

59. *Ibid.*, p. 87.

60. *Israel Economic Bulletin*, 2:3–4 (1949), 5.

61. H. Margulies, preface to "Some Industrial Problems of New Immigrants in Israel," *Economic News*, 3:7–8 (1950), 129.

62. Israel, *Government Yearbook 5711, op. cit.*, p. 198.

63. A. L. Gruenbaum, *Four Year Development Plan for Israel 1950–1953. Summary and Conclusions* (Jerusalem: Prime Minister's Office, 1951), p. 16.

64. The data on Israel's industry in 1949 are difficult to come by. It is known that in 1950 the Ministry of Trade and Industry was compiling information on equipment, number of workers, types of products, raw materials required, etc., for more than 4,000 industrial enterprises. Since mandatory registration for every industrial firm was introduced only in 1950, the data for the first few years of statehood are incomplete. In addition, there existed close to 20,000 artisan shops, each employing a few people; see Israel, *Government Yearbook 5711, op. cit.*, p. 97. The industrial census of 1952 covered 20,301 establishments employing 100,275 persons, an average of 5 persons per establishment; see United Nations, Department of Economic and Social Affairs, *Economic Developments in the Middle East, 1945–1954* (New York: United Nations, 1955), p. 131.

65. *Israel Economic Bulletin*, 2:16–17 (June 1950), 3.

66. Israel, *Government Yearbook 5712, op. cit.*, p. 52.

67. *Ibid.*, p. 49.

68. *Ibid.*, p. 50.

69. J. L. Mosak, *Inflationary Pressure and Price Control in Israel* (New York: United Nations, 1953), pp. 4–5, 20.

70. Israel, *Government Yearbook 5711, op. cit.*, p. 203.

71. D. Patinkin, *The Israel Economy, op. cit.*, p. 109.

72. E. Goldberger, *op. cit.*, p. 124.

73. A. Rubner, *op. cit.*, p. 65.

74. E. Levy, *Israel Economic Survey, 1953–54* (Jerusalem: The Economic Department of the Jewish Agency, 1955), p. 16.

75. W. Röpke, "Das Deutsche Wirtschaftsexperiment: Beispiel und Lehre," in A. Hunold, ed., *Vollbeschäftigung, Inflation und Planwirtschaft* (Zürich: E. Rentsch Verlag, 1953), p. 271.

76. E. Levy, *op. cit.*, p. 15.

77. J. L. Mosak, *op. cit.*, p. 12.

78. G. De Gaury, *The New State of Israel* (New York: Frederick A. Praeger, 1952), p. 162.

79. E. Kaplan, "The Budget for 1950–1951," in *Government Yearbook 5711, op. cit.*, p. 228. Eliezer Kaplan was the first Minister of Finance.

80. *Ibid.*

81. J. L. Mosak, *op. cit.*, p. 5. According to N. Halevi and R. Klinov-Malul, *op. cit.*, p. 100, aggregate private consumption in 1951 was 22.6 per cent higher than in 1950.

82. D. Patinkin, *The Israel Economy, op. cit.*, pp. 46, 109, 122.

83. For a listing of these practices, see A. Rubner, *op. cit.*, pp. 62–66, 262–266.

84. S. N. Eisenstadt, "The Process of Absorption of Immigrants in Israel," in C. Frankenstein, ed., *Between Past and Future* (Jerusalem: The Henrietta Szold Foundation for Child and Youth Welfare, 1953), pp. 53–81; see also S. Z. Klausner, "Immigrant Absorption and Social Tension in Israel," in *The Middle East Journal*, 9 (1955), 281–294.

85. E. Kaplan, *op. cit.*, p. 227.

86. D. Horowitz, *The Economics of Israel* (Oxford: Pergamon Press, 1967), pp. 171–172.

87. L. B. Yeager, *International Monetary Relations* (New York: Harper & Row, 1966), p. 117.

88. I. Walter, *International Economics: Theory and Policy* (New York: The Ronald Press Co., 1968), p. 377.

89. E. Levy, *op. cit.*, p. 14.

90. N. Halevi and R. Klinov-Malul, *op. cit.*, p. 155.

91. *Ibid.*

92. Israel, *Government Yearbook 5715 (1954)* (Jerusalem: Government Printer, 1954), p. 229.

93. Israel, Ministry of Finance, *The Development Budget 1953–54* (Jerusalem: 1953), p. 8.

94. E. Levy, *op. cit.*, p. 33.

95. Israel, Ministry of Finance, *The Economic Report of the Minister of Finance* (Jerusalem: 1955), p. 11.

96. *Ibid.*, p. 12. According to Bank of Israel, *Hashilumim Vehashpa-atam al Hameshek Haisrael* (Jerusalem: 1965), p. 212, the short-term indebtedness in 1953 was $70.8 million.

97. Israel, Central Bureau of Statistics, *Statistical Abstract of Israel*, 16, p. 239. For some early data, covering the years from 1948 to 1950, see Israel, *Government Yearbook 5712, op. cit.*, p. 326. The ratio of exports to imports in 1948 was 5.8 per cent; in 1949, 12.0 per cent; in

1950, 12.8 per cent. In 1951, this ratio was supposedly 18 per cent; see Israel, *Government Yearbook 5714 (1953/54)* (Jerusalem: Government Printer, 1954), p. 271.

98. N. Halevi and R. Klinov-Malul, *op. cit.*, p. 142.

99. Israel, Ministry of Finance, *The Development Budget 1953–54, op. cit.*, p. 20.

100. A. Rubner, *op. cit.*, pp. 48–51, and N. Halevi and R. Klinov-Malul, *op. cit.*, pp. 229–230.

101. D. Patinkin, *The Israel Economy, op. cit.*, p. 121.

102. E. Goldberger, *op. cit.*, p. 133.

103. R. D. Ottensooser, *op. cit.*, p. 131.

104. Bank of Israel, *Hashilumim, op. cit.*, p. 39.

105. N. Halevi, "Housing in Israel," in *The Economic Problems of Housing* (London: Macmillan, 1967), p. 216.

106. R. Cale, "Rents: Ceilings Fixed in 1940 Due for Rise Under Pending Legislation," *Israel Speaks,* 7 (1953), 8.

107. H. Lowenberg, "Rent and Housing," *Zionist Newsletter,* 4:12 (1952), 11.

108. *Ibid.*, p. 12.

109. *Ibid.*

110. "The Failure of Rent Control," *The Israel Economist,* 8:12 (1952), 270.

111. Israel, Ministry of Justice, "Tenant's Protection Law, 5714 (1954)," in *Laws of the State of Israel,* vol. 8 (1953–54), pp. 75–89.

112. R. D. Ottensooser, *op. cit.*, p. 131.

113. C. Abrams, "Israel Grapples with Its Housing Crisis," *Commentary,* 11 (1951), 349.

114. A. Rubner, *op. cit.*, p. 72.

115. N. Halevi, *op. cit.*, p. 220.

116. H. Drabkin-Darin, *Housing in Israel: Economic and Sociological Aspects* (Tel Aviv: Gadish Books, 1957), p. 9.

117. Israel, *Government Yearbook 5719 (1958)* (Jerusalem: Government Printer, 1958), p. 356.

118. J. T. Shuval, *op. cit.*, p. 7.

119. N. Halevi, *op. cit.*, p. 217.

120. Israel, Ministry of Finance, *The Development Budget 1953–1954, op. cit.*, p. 19.

121. J. T. Shuval, *op. cit.*, pp. 64, 71. For the basic work on the experiences of immigrants in the early years of the state, see R. Bachi, *Immigration to Israel, 1948–1953* (Jerusalem: 1957). The literature on this subject is enormous, but for a highly revealing account of that difficult period, see B. Halpern and S. Wurm, eds., *The Responsible Attitude:*

The Life and Opinions of Giora Josephthal (New York: Schocken Books, 1966), pp. 105–146.

122. N. Halevi and R. Klinov-Malul, *op. cit.*, p. 66.

123. G. A. Lincoln, *Economics of National Security* (Englewood Cliffs, N.J.: Prentice-Hall, 1954), pp. 506–511. See also B. Hansen, *op. cit.*, pp. 16–17.

124. N. Halevi and R. Klinov-Malul, *op. cit.*, p. 272.

125. M. Derber, "Israel's Wage Differential: A Persisting Problem," *Midstream,* 9 (1963), 8.

126. R. D. Ottensooser, *op. cit.*, p. 120, and D. Patinkin, *The Israel Economy*, pp. 38–39.

127. D. Patinkin, *The Israel Economy*, *op. cit.*, p. 109.

128. *The Gates of Zion,* 8 (October 1952–September 1953), 2.

129. O. Remba, "Can Israel Support Herself?" *Commentary,* 22 (1956), 434.

Chapter 6

1. R. Vogel, ed., *Deutschlands Weg nach Israel* (Stuttgart: Seewald Verlag, 1967), p. 39.

2. N. Goldmann, *The Autobiography of Nahum Goldmann: Sixty Years of Jewish Life* (New York: Holt, Rinehart and Winston, 1969), p. 257.

3. *Ibid.*

4. *Ibid.*, p. 260.

5. *Ibid.*

6. K. Adenauer, *Erinnerungen, 1953–1955* (Stuttgart: Deutsche Verlags-Anstalt, 1966), pp. 137–138.

7. I. H. Levin, "Reparations from Germany," *Jewish Life,* 19:4 (1952), 29.

8. Anonymous, "Thunder from the Left," *Jewish Frontier,* 19:2 (1952), 5.

9. H. Abiam, "Should Israel Seek Reparations from Germany?" *Jewish Vanguard* (London), 85 (1952), 4.

10. For an interesting survey of the Israeli press on these attitudes, see *The Jerusalem Post,* January 4, 1952.

11. H. Dan, *B'Derekh Lo Selula* (On an Unpaved Way) (Tel Aviv: Schocken Publishing Co., 1963), p. 329. This work is available only in Hebrew.

12. For a comprehensive summary of the government's position, see M. Sharett, *Staatsprobleme* (Jerusalem: Informationsdienst des Staates Israel, 1952).

13. M. Bar-Zohar, *Ben-Gurion: The Armed Prophet* (Englewood Cliffs, N.J.: Prentice-Hall, 1968), pp. 174–175.

14. B. Litvinoff, *David Ben Gurion* (New York: Oceana Publications, 1960), p. 135.

15. *The Jerusalem Post*, January 8, 1952.

16. *The Jewish Herald* (South Africa), 15 (January 11, 1952); and R. St. John, *Ben-Gurion* (Garden City, N.Y.: Doubleday and Co., 1959), p. 242.

17. *Ibid.*, p. 242.

18. *Ibid.*

19. *The Jerusalem Post*, January 9, 1952.

20. B. Litvinoff, *loc. cit.*; M. Bar-Zohar, *op. cit.*, p. 175.

21. *The Jerusalem Post*, January 10, 1952.

22. N. Goldmann, *op. cit.*, p. 262.

23. *Ibid.*

24. R. Vogel, ed., *op. cit.*, pp. 40–41.

25. Collection of newspaper clippings at the Institut für Weltwirtschaft, Kiel, West Germany, under the title "Finanzen und Reparationen," files 1 and 2, 1952–1966.

26. Society for Christian and Jewish Cooperation, *September 10, 1952– September 10, 1962, Agreement Between the Federal Republic of Germany and the State of Israel* (Düsseldorf: 1962), pp. 3–17.

27. B. Halpern and S. Wurm, eds., *The Responsible Attitude: The Life and Opinions of Giora Josephthal* (New York: Schocken Books, 1966), p. 147.

28. F. Böhm, "Die Luxemburger Wiedergutmachungsverträge und der arabische Einspruch gegen den Israelvertrag," in *Franz Böhm: Reden und Schriften* (Karlsruhe: Verlag C. F. Müller, 1960), pp. 221–222.

29. Bundesrepublik Deutschland, Presse- und Informationsamt der Bundesregierung, *Bulletin,* 40, April 5, 1952.

30. F. E. Shinnar, *Bericht eines Beauftragten* (Tübingen: R. Wunderlich Verlag, 1967), p. 24.

31. Interview with Dr. Jacob Robinson of the Yivo Institute, June 22, 1967, in New York City.

32. B. Halpern and S. Wurm, eds., *op. cit.*, p. 146; F. E. Shinnar, *op. cit.*, p. 37.

33. B. Halpern and S. Wurm, eds., *op. cit.*, p. 147.

34. R. Vogel, *op. cit.*, p. 46.

35. Interviews with Dr. Shinnar in Tel Aviv, January 6 and 15, 1966.

36. *The Jerusalem Post*, March 26, 1952.

37. Bank Deutscher Länder, *Report for the Year 1951*, pp. 1, 7.

38. Bank Deutscher Länder, *Report for the Year 1952*, p. 71.

39. Abs' mission was successful. His delegation gained a reduction of the German obligations from a total of DM 13.5 billion to 7.3 billion. In other words, West Germany had to pay only slightly more than 50 per cent of the total external debt. However, as Dr. Abs pointed out, this large reduction *was brought about only by the cancellation of accrued interest;* there was no reduction in the nominal prewar indebtedness. See Hermann J. Abs, "Das Londoner Schuldenabkommen," in *Zeitfragen der Geld- und Wirtschaftspolitik* (Frankfurt a/M.: F. Knapp Verlag, 1959), pp. 11–42, and in an interview in Frankfurt a/M., July 21, 1966.

40. Interview with Professor Franz Böhm in Frankfurt a/M., December 7, 1965.

41. Information from Dr. H. J. Abs.

42. R. Vogel, *op. cit.,* pp. 42–44.

43. Interview with Dr. Abs in Frankfurt a/M., August 4, 1966.

44. Bundesrepublik Deutschland, Presse- und Informationsamt der Bundesregierung, *Bulletin,* 46, April 24, 1952.

45. K. R. Grossmann, *Die Ehrenschuld* (Frankfurt a/M.: Ullstein, 1967), p. 33.

46. *The Jewish Herald* (South Africa), 15, March 28, 1952.

47. *The Jewish Chronicle,* November 30, 1951.

48. *Ibid.*

49. *Der Spiegel,* 6 (May 28, 1952), 15.

50. *The Jerusalem Post,* April 2, 1952.

51. F. E. Shinnar, *op. cit.,* p. 37.

52. N. Goldmann, *op. cit.,* p. 263.

53. K. Adenauer, *op. cit.,* p. 141.

54. R. Hilberg, *The Destruction of the European Jews* (Chicago: Quadrangle Books, 1961), p. 757.

55. B. Halpern and S. Wurm, eds., *op. cit.,* p. 150.

56. K. R. Grossmann, *op. cit.,* p. 37.

57. *The Jerusalem Post,* April 6, 1952.

58. B. Halpern and S. Wurm, eds., *op. cit.,* p. 149.

59. N. Goldmann, *op. cit.,* p. 264.

60. F. E. Shinnar, *op. cit.,* p. 39.

61. *The Jerusalem Post,* April 11, 1952.

62. Israel, Ministry of Foreign Affairs, *Documents Relating to the Agreement Between the Government of Israel and the Government of the Federal Republic of Germany* (Jerusalem: Government Printer, 1953), pp. 88, 90.

63. N. Barou, "Origin of the German Agreement," *Congress Weekly,* October 13, 1952, p. 7.

64. Interview with Dr. F. Schäffer in Ostermünchen, West Germany, August 5, 1966.

65. F. E. Shinnar, *op. cit.,* p. 39.

66. N. Goldmann, *op. cit.,* p. 264.

67. D. G. Acheson, *Sketches from Life of Men I Have Known* (New York: Harper & Brothers, 1960), p. 180.

68. K. R. Grossmann, *op. cit.,* p. 36.

69. N. Goldmann, *op. cit.,* p. 264.

70. *Ibid.*

71. F. E. Shinnar, *op. cit.,* p. 38.

72. R. Vogel, *op. cit.,* pp. 49–52.

73. K. Adenauer, *op. cit.,* p. 142.

74. B. Halpern and S. Wurm, eds., *op. cit.,* pp. 154–155 and *passim.*

75. What Josephthal actually said was, "The Germans got iberge-schrekt" (scared).

76. Interview with Dr. h.c. Jacob Blaustein in Baltimore, September 4, 1968. Blaustein talked to the President in early April. His letter to the President was sent on April 11, and Truman's reply was received on April 15. See K. R. Grossmann, *op. cit.,* p. 40; and J. Blaustein, *A Dramatic Era in History* (New York: American Jewish Committee, 1966), p. 12.

77. B. Halpern and S. Wurm, eds., *op. cit.,* p. 154.

78. J. Blaustein, *op. cit.,* p. 7.

79. N. Goldmann, *op. cit.,* p. 265.

80. F. E. Shinnar, *op. cit.,* p. 40. According to Grossmann, Abs had supposedly offered DM 100 million a year for the next twelve years: K. R. Grossmann, *op. cit.,* p. 37. For an explanation of what Dr. Abs really said and why, see R. Vogel, *op. cit.,* p. 44.

81. B. Halpern and S. Wurm, eds., *op. cit.,* p. 158.

82. Interview with Dr. F. E. Shinnar in Tel Aviv, January 13, 1966.

83. B. Halpern and S. Wurm, eds., *op. cit.,* p. 158. See also F. E. Shinnar, *op. cit.,* p. 40, and K. Adenauer, *op. cit.,* p. 145.

84. K. Adenauer, *op. cit.,* p. 146. The full text of the letter has been reproduced in R. Vogel, *op. cit.,* pp. 52–54. See also N. Goldmann, *op. cit.,* p. 265.

85. Interview with Dr. F. E. Shinnar, Tel Aviv, January 13, 1966, and his book, *op. cit.,* p. 41.

86. *Ibid.,* p. 42.

87. N. Goldmann, *op. cit.,* p. 266, and K. Adenauer, *op. cit.,* p. 147.

88. N. Goldmann, *op. cit.,* p. 266.

89. Dr. F. Schäffer's information, Ostermünchen interview, August 5, 1966.

90. Interview with Professor F. W. Meyer, Bonn, July 27, 1966. The two documents are still not available to the public.

91. H. J. Abs, *op. cit.*, p. 38.

92. K. Adenauer, *op. cit.*, pp. 147–150 and *passim*.

93. For the contents of Böhm's report, see R. Vogel, *op. cit.*, pp. 54–58.

94. K. Adenauer, *op. cit.*, p. 150.

95. F. E. Shinnar, *op. cit.*, p. 43.

96. R. Vogel, *op. cit.*, p. 59, and N. Goldmann, *op. cit.*, p. 268.

97. I. Kirkpatrick, *The Inner Circle* (London: Macmillan, 1959), p. 244.

98. N. Goldmann, *op. cit.*, p. 268.

99. K. Adenauer, *op. cit.*, p. 151.

100. N. Goldmann, *op. cit.*, p. 268.

101. F. E. Shinnar, *op. cit.*, p. 43.

102. N. Goldmann, *op. cit.*, p. 268.

103. F. E. Shinnar, *op. cit.*, p. 45.

104. K. Adenauer, *op. cit.*, p. 152.

105. R. Vogel, *op. cit.*, p. 59.

106. F. E. Shinnar, *op. cit.*, p. 48.

107. R. Vogel, *op. cit.*, p. 56.

108. F. E. Shinnar, *op. cit.*, p. 57.

109. Interviews with Dr. Shinnar in Tel Aviv, January 6 and 13, 1966.

110. Dr. Goldmann speaks of DM 500 million: *op. cit.*, pp. 262, 269. The original request was for $500 million: see, for example, K. R. Grossmann, *op. cit.*, p. 41.

111. N. Goldmann, *op. cit.*, p. 269.

112. *Ibid.*, pp. 269–270.

113. *Ibid.*, p. 271.

114. B. Halpern and S. Wurm, eds., *op. cit.*, p. 161.

115. N. Goldmann, *op. cit.*, p. 271.

116. K. Adenauer, *op. cit.*, p. 153.

117. N. Goldmann, *op. cit.*, p. 272.

118. Information from J. Blaustein.

119. Interview with Dr. Robinson, New York City, June 22, 1966.

120. B. Halpern and S. Wurm, eds., *op. cit.*, p. 162.

Chapter 7

1. *The New York Times*, September 11, 1952.

2. *The Jerusalem Post*, April 2, 1952.

3. F. E. Shinnar, *op. cit.*, p. 54.

4. N. Goldmann, *The Autobiography of Nahum Goldmann: Sixty Years of Jewish Life* (New York: Holt, Rinehart and Winston, 1969), p. 274.

5. For speeches made by Finance Minister Moshe Sharett and Dr. F. E. Shinnar after the signing ceremony, hear the recording, in German, *Brücke in die Zukunft: Das deutsch-israelische Abkommen vom 10. September 1952*, edited by Rolf Vogel, September 1965.

6. *The Jerusalem Post*, January 10, 1952.

7. N. Goldmann, *op. cit.*, p. 274.

8. Conference on Jewish Material Claims Against Germany, *Five Years Later, 1954–1958* (New York: 1959), p. 18 (this author's italics).

9. *The New York Times*, September 11, 1952.

10. P. Giniewski, "Germany and Israel: The Reparations Treaty of September 10, 1952," *World Affairs Quarterly*, 30 (1959–60), 180.

11. *The New York Times*, September 22, 1952, Letter to the Editor by Joseph B. Schechtman, Member of the General Council, World Zionist Organization.

12. N. Goldmann, *op. cit.*, pp. 274–275.

13. E. Lüth, *Welt ohne Hass* (Hamburg: Gesellschaft für christlich-jüdische Zusammenarbeit, 1958).

14. N. Robinson, "Germany's Balance Sheet," *Congress Weekly*, 18:24 (1951), 14.

15. E. Lüth, *Viele Steine lagen am Weg* (Hamburg: Marion von Schröder Verlag, 1966), pp. 270–274. See also R. Giordano, ed., *Narben, Spuren, Zeugen* (Düsseldorf: Verlag Allgemeine Wochenzeitung der Juden in Deutschland, 1961), pp. 125–127.

16. M. Shtrigler, "Less Enthusiasm, Please!" *Jewish Frontier*, 19:10 (1952), 11.

17. K. R. Grossmann, "Is Germany Repenting," *Congress Weekly*, 20:16 (1953), 11. See also *ibid.*, pp. 23, 35.

18. F. Rodens, *Konrad Adenauer* (Munich: Droemersche Verlagsanstalt, 1963), pp. 34, 38, 114.

19. See C. C. Aronsfeld, "Not All Germans Are Guilty," *The Gates of Zion*, 8 (1954), 17–20; H. D. Leuner, *When Compassion Was A Crime: Germany's Silent Heroes, 1933–1945* (London: O. Wolff, 1966); and K. R. Grossmann, *Die unbesungenen Helden* (Berlin: Arani Verlags GmbH, 1957).

20. P. Weymar, *Konrad Adenauer* (London: Andre Deutsch, 1957), p. 432.

21. Bundesrepublik Deutschland, Bundestag, *Verhandlungen des Deutschen Bundestages: Stenographische Berichte*, 15 (March 4, 1953), 12093 (hereafter *Verhandlungen*).

22. W. Hausenstein, *Pariser Erinnerungen* (Munich: Günter Olzog Verlag, 1961), p. 73.

23. T. Prittie, *Germany Divided: The Legacy of the Nazi Era* (Boston: Little, Brown and Co., 1960), p. 220.

24. *Ibid.*, p. 205. For political advice he went to Hans Globke and Heinrich Krone, see R. Hiscocks, *The Adenauer Era* (Philadelphia: J. B. Lippincott Co., 1966), p. 118.

25. D. G. Acheson, *Sketches from Life of Men I Have Known* (New York: Harper & Brothers, 1960), p. 179.

26. *Ibid.*

27. F. Rodens, *op. cit.*, p. 100.

28. N. Robinson, "How We Negotiated with the Germans and What We Achieved," *Information on Germany*, 3:2–3 (Fall 1952), 1.

29. R. Hiscocks, *op. cit.*, p. 33.

30. This is available in the Wiener Library, London, file 2BF.

31. Communist views on the Luxemburg Treaty may be found in the Wiener Library, London, file 2(0) /B/.

32. H. Wallich, *Mainsprings of the German Revival* (New Haven, Conn.: Yale University Press, 1955), p. 342.

33. R. Hagelstange, "Dort, wo wir leben, ist Vaterland," *Frankfurter Hefte,* 7 (1952), 160.

34. R. Hiscocks, *op. cit.*, p. 29.

35. H. Wewer, "Die Deutsch-Israelischen Beziehungen: Ende oder Neubeginn," *Frankfurter Hefte,* 18 (1963), 457.

36. The full title of the Luxemburg accord was "Agreement Between the State of Israel and the Federal Republic of Germany. Signed on 10 September 1952, at Luxemburg." It appears in, Israel, Ministry of Foreign Affairs, *Documents Relating to the Agreement Between the Government of Israel and the Government of the Federal Republic of Germany* (Jerusalem: Government Printer, 1953), pp. 125–151 (hereafter cited as *Documents*). The entire text of the Luxemburg Treaty was reprinted in *Die Haager Vertragswerke* (Düsseldorf-Benrath: Verlag "Allgemeine Wochenzeitung der Juden in Deutschland," 1952), pp. 23–36 (hereafter referred to as *Vertragswerke*).

37. B. Halpern and S. Wurm, eds., *The Responsible Attitude: The Life and Opinions of Giora Josephthal* (New York: Schocken Books, 1966), p. 165. See also K. Adenauer, *op. cit.*, p. 157, and M. Selzer, "The Diplomacy of Atonement: Germany, Israel and the Jews," *Issues* (vol. 21, #2, 1967), 33.

38. *Vertragswerke*, p. 37.

39. These deliveries were popularly called reparations. However, the term is a misnomer, and for that reason the term Shilumim deliveries or

payments will be used instead. See Bank Deutscher Länder, *Report for the Year 1952* (Frankfurt a/M.: 1953), p. 90, for the estimated period of deliveries.

40. F. Honig, "The Reparations Agreement Between Israel and the Federal Republic of Germany," *The American Journal of International Law*, 48 (1954), 564–578.

41. *Documents*, p. 125.

42. *Vertragswerke*, Letter 4a, p. 34. See also F. E. Shinnar, *Bericht eines Beauftragten* (Tübingen: R. Wunderlich Verlag, 1967), p. 56.

43. For full details and explanations of the above provisions, see F. Honig, *op. cit.*, 570.

44. Article 10 (c).

45. Article 5 (e).

46. Article 8 (c).

47. Annex to Article 7; see also *Documents*, p. 141.

48. Article 13.

49. Articles 14 and 15.

50. For a revealing analysis of the ratification, see K. R. Grossmann, *Die Ehrenschuld* (Frankfurt: Ullstein, 1967), pp. 44–47, and N. Goldmann, *op. cit.*, p. 275.

51. R. Vogel, ed., *Deutschlands Weg nach Israel* (Stuttgart: Seewald Verlag, 1967), p. 60.

52. Nah- und Mittelost-Verein, Hamburg, *Rundschreiben, September 10, 1952*, p. 1 (mimeo).

53. Press report in *Die Welt*, Hamburg, November 1, 1952.

54. *Deutsche Zeitung und Wirtschaftszeitung*, 88, November 1, 1952.

55. K. R. Grossmann, *Die Ehrenschuld, op. cit.*, p. 46.

56. K. Adenauer, *op. cit.*, p. 155.

57. F. E. Shinnar, *op. cit.*, p. 61.

58. *Die Neue Zeitung*, January 16, 1953.

59. F. Böhm, "Die Luxemburger Wiedergutmachungsverträge und der arabische Einspruch gegen den Israelvertrag," in *Franz Böhm: Reden und Schriften* (Karlsruhe: Verlag C. F. Müller, 1960), p. 228.

60. M. Shtrigler, *Jewish Frontier*, 20 (1953), 8–11.

61. F. E. Shinnar, *op. cit.*, p. 65.

62. N. Goldmann, *op. cit.*, p. 275.

63. *Die Zeit*, November 20, 1952.

64. Bundesrepublik Deutschland, Presse- und Informationsamt der Bundesregierung, *Bulletin*, 76, 1952.

65. *Verhandlungen*, 15, 12093–94.

66. *Verhandlungen*, 15, 12280–81.

67. E. Ollenhauer, "German Social Democracy and Reparations," in

H. F. Infield, ed., *Essays in Jewish Sociology, Labour, and Co-operation in Memory of Dr. Noah Barou, 1889–1955* (London: T. Yoseloff, 1962), pp. 94–95.

68. *Verhandlungen,* 15, 12293.

69. *Daily Telegraph* (London), July 26, 1963.

70. Bundesrepublik Deutschland, Bundesrat, *Sitzungsbericht,* 103 (March 20, 1953), 134.

71. Bundesrepublik Deutschland, Bundesminister der Justiz, *Bundesgesetzblatt II* (1953), 128.

72. N. Goldmann, *op. cit.,* p. 258.

73. F. Böhm, *op. cit.,* p. 225.

74. N. Goldmann, *op. cit.,* p. 252.

75. M. Selzer, *op. cit.,* 23. See also E. Berger, . . . *Who Knows Better Must Say So!* (New York: American Council for Judaism, 1955).

76. F. Böhm, "Die Deutsch-Israelischen Beziehungen," *Frankfurter Hefte,* 20 (1965), 602.

77. "Ein völkerrechtliches Novum in Den Haag," *Bulletin* des Presse- und Informationsamtes, 39, 1952.

78. F. Böhm, "Die Luxemburger Wiedergutmachungsverträge," *op. cit.,* pp. 224–225.

79. *Encyclopaedia Britannica,* 19 (1962), 1571.

80. P. Giniewski, *op. cit.,* 169.

81. Bundesrepublik Deutschland, Presse- und Informationsamt der Bundesregierung, *Bulletin,* 153, 1952.

82. Anonymous, "Should We Negotiate with Germany?" *The American Hebrew* (August 25, 1950), pp. 9, 14.

83. A. Bahod, "The Ethics of German Reparations," *The Jewish Chronicle,* January 18, 1952.

84. A. L. Easterman, "Nahum Goldmann—The Man and Statesman," *The Gates of Zion,* 8 (1954), 23.

85. N. Goldmann, *op. cit.,* p. 280.

86. *Ibid.*

87. N. Robinson, "Spoliation and Remedial Action," in *The Institute Anniversary Volume, 1941–1961* (New York: Institute of Jewish Affairs, 1962), pp. 199–204. See also R. Hilberg, *The Destruction of the European Jews* (Chicago: Quadrangle Books, 1961), pp. 747–750.

88. "Wiedergutmachung ohne Ende?" *Industriekurier,* May 26, 1964. See also L. Köllner, "Grenzen der Wiedergutmachung," *Deutsche Korrespondenz,* May 11, 1963.

89. *Daily Telegraph* (London), July 26, 1963.

90. N. Goldmann, *op. cit.,* p. 261.

Chapter 8

1. R. Lekachman, *The Age of Keynes* (New York: Random House, 1966), p. 36.

2. Anonymous, "Germany at Work," *Roundtable,* 44 (1953–54), 154.

3. G. Stolper, K. Häuser, K. Borchardt, *The German Economy, 1870 to the Present* (New York: Harcourt, Brace and World, 1967), p. 222.

4. Calculated as $147(r)^{14} = 333$, $r = 6$ per cent, where the 147 and 333 are G.N.P.s at constant 1954 prices in 1953 and 1966, respectively. From 1950 to 1966, also in 1954 prices, r was 7 per cent: see W. Vogt, *Die Wachstumszyklen der westdeutschen Wirtschaft* (Tübingen: J. C. B. Mohr, 1968), pp. 3 and 16.

5. Bank Deutscher Länder, *Report of the Bank Deutscher Länder for the Year 1952,* p. 10.

6. *Ibid.,* p. 1.

7. *Ibid.,* p. 4.

8. *Ibid.,* 1954, p. 3.

9. *Ibid.,* 1955, p. 1.

10. *Ibid.,* 1956, p. 3.

11. Deutsche Bundesbank, *Report of the Deutsche Bundesbank for the Year 1957,* p. 13. In 1957, Deutsche Bundesbank became the central bank of West Germany, replacing the former Bank Deutscher Länder.

12. *Report of the Deutsche Bundesbank for the Year 1958,* p. 1.

13. *Ibid.,* p. 5.

14. For comparison, see K. W. Roskamp, *Capital Formation in West Germany* (Detroit: Wayne State University Press, 1965), p. 63, where the author calculates a 3.3 per cent growth rate for that year.

15. *Report of the Deutsche Bundesbank for the Year 1959,* p. 2.

16. *Ibid.,* p. 16.

17. *Report of the Deutsche Bundesbank for the Year 1961,* p. 1.

18. *Ibid.,* p. 46.

19. *Ibid.,* 1960, p. 6.

20. *Ibid.,* 1962, pp. 3, 10–11.

21. *Ibid.,* 1963, pp. 1, 7.

22. *Ibid.,* 1964, pp. 2, 70.

23. *Ibid.,* 1966, p. 2.

24. For a discussion of the particularly rapid growth of per capita income during the first half of the 1950s, see L. Erhard, *The Economics of Success* (London: Thames and Hudson, 1963), p. 70. The rate of growth of per capita G.N.P. during 1950–1960 was 6.5 per cent, according to A. Maddison, *op. cit.* (in Table 8-1, note *c,* above), p. 30. For the 1949–

1959 period, see C. P. Kindleberger, *Europe's Postwar Growth* (Cambridge, Mass.: Harvard University Press, 1967), pp. 25, 27.

25. *The London Economist,* 22:6425 (October 15, 1966), xiv. See also M. M. Postan, *An Economic History of Western Europe, 1945–1964* (London: Methuen & Co., 1967), p. 12, which gives the compounded annual growth rate of the Gross Domestic Product from 1948 to 1963 as 7.6 per cent. For other computations for different periods, see *ibid.,* pp. 19–20, 86.

26. E. Sohmen, "Competition and Growth: The Lesson of West Germany," *American Economic Review,* 49:5 (1959), 986–1003.

27. P. M. Boarman, *Germany's Economic Dilemma: Inflation and the Balance of Payments* (New Haven, Conn.: Yale University Press, 1964), p. 33.

28. F. G. Reuss, *Fiscal Policy for Growth Without Inflation: The German Experiment* (Baltimore, Md.: The Johns Hopkins Press, 1963), pp. 35, 49.

29. West Germany, Presse- und Informationsamt der Bundesregierung, *Ein Rechenschaftsbericht über die deutsche Finanzpolitik 1949 bis 1953* (Bonn: 1953), pp. 23, 27.

30. K. W. Roskamp, *op. cit.,* pp. 162–207.

31. J. Hennessy, "The German Miracle," in *Economic "Miracles"* (London: Andre Deutsch, 1964), pp. 30–31.

32. R. G. Opie, "Western Germany's Economic Miracle," *Three Banks Review,* 53 (1962), 6, 12.

33. H. C. Wallich, *Mainsprings of the German Revival* (New Haven, Conn.: Yale University Press, 1955), pp. 288–297. See also F. M. Davis, *Come as a Conqueror* (New York: The Macmillan Co., 1967), pp. 141–142, where the author speaks of manifestations of German discipline in the form of "hewing to routine" and "go to work—start small and build big."

34. "The German Lesson," *The London Economist,* 22 (October 15, 1966), xv–xix. See also R. G. Opie, *op. cit.,* p. 13.

35. L. B. Yeager, *International Monetary Relations* (New York: Harper & Row, 1966), pp. 404–405.

36. C. P. Kindleberger, *op. cit.,* p. 30.

37. L. G. Reynolds, *Economics,* revised edition (Homewood, Ill.: Richard D. Irwin, 1964), p. 621.

38. J. S. Mill, *Principles of Political Economy* (New York: The Colonial Press, 1899), Vol. I, p. 75.

39. West Germany, Statistisches Bundesamt, *Statistisches Jahrbuch für die Bundesrepublik Deutschland,* 1967 (Stuttgart: W. Kohlhammer Verlag, 1967), p. 234. 1958 = 100.

40. $67.0(r)^{14} = 161.0$, $r = 7$ per cent, where 67.0 and 161.0 are the total production indices (1958 = 100) in 1953 and 1966, respectively.

41. A. Maddison, *op. cit.* (in Table 8-1, note *c,* above), p. 28. P. M. Boarman, *op. cit.,* p. 215, gives the very high rate of 13 per cent per annum for the growth of total production.

42. G. Stolper, K. Häuser, K. Borchardt, *op. cit.,* pp. 240–244.

43. N. Macrae, "Twentieth Century Trade Unions," *The London Economist,* 22 (October 15, 1966), xv.

44. H. Spiro, *The Politics of German Codetermination* (Cambridge, Mass.: Harvard University Press, 1958), pp. 38–43, 62–67. See also H. Deist, "Wirtschaftsdemokratie," in *Grundfragen moderner Wirtschaftspolitik* (Frankfurt a/M.: Europäische Verlagsanstalt, n.d.), pp. 220–226.

45. *Report of the Bank Deutscher Länder for the Year 1952,* p. 2.

46. *Report of the Bank Deutscher Länder for the Year 1955,* pp. 8–9.

47. For some useful material on the prevailing labor shortage, see C. P. Kindleberger, *op. cit.,* pp. 34–36, and W. Fellner *et al., The Problem of Rising Prices* (Paris: OEEC, 1961), pp. 321–333.

48. *Report of the Deutsche Bundesbank for the Year 1960,* p. 11.

49. *Report of the Deutsche Bundesbank for the Year 1961,* p. 10.

50. *Ibid.,* p. 15.

51. *Ibid.,* p. 59.

52. *Report of the Deutsche Bundesbank for the Year 1962,* pp. 2–3.

53. *Report of the Deutsche Bundesbank for the Year 1966,* pp. 79–80. See also Bundesanstalt für Arbeitsvermittlung und Arbeitslosenversicherung Nürnberg, *Ausländische Arbeitsnehmer: Beschäftigung, Anwerbung, Vermittlung. Erfahrungsbericht 1968,* 1969, p. 3.

54. *Statistisches Jahrbuch 1964,* p. 489, and *Statistisches Jahrbuch 1966,* p. 495.

55. Verein Deutscher Maschinenbau-Anstalten, *Statistisches Handbuch für den Maschinenbau 1964* (Frankfurt a/M.: Maschinenbau-Verlag, 1964), pp. 118–119.

56. C. P. Kindleberger, "Germany's Persistent Balance-of-Payments Disequilibrium," in R. E. Baldwin, ed., *Trade, Growth, and the Balance of Payments* (Chicago: Rand McNally, 1965), p. 236.

57. *Report of the Deutsche Bundesbank for the Year 1962,* p. 3.

58. For some policy implications, especially with regard to the so-called Phillips curve, which shows the tradeoff between inflation and unemployment, see M. Bronfenbrenner and F. D. Holzman, "A Survey of Inflation Theory," in *Surveys of Economic Theory* (New York: St. Martin's Press, 1965), Vol. I, pp. 83–84, and J. Kromphardt and R. Müller, "Uberstrapazierte Theorie," *Der Volkswirt,* 33 (August 15, 1969), 31–32.

59. H. C. Wallich, *op. cit.,* p. 224.

60. P. M. Boarman, *op. cit.,* p. 158.

61. If $18.5(r)^{14} = 80.6$, $r = .13$, where the 18.5 and 80.6 are exports in billions of marks in 1953 and 1966, respectively.

62. If $16.0(r)^{14} = 72.7$, $r = .11$, where the 16.0 and 72.7 are imports in billions of marks in 1953 and 1966, respectively.

63. K. Roskamp, *op. cit.,* p. 71.

64. J. B. Yeager, *op. cit.,* p. 405.

65. C. P. Kindleberger, "Germany's Persistent Balance-of-Payments Disequilibrium," *op. cit.,* pp. 232–233.

66. K. Holbik and H. A. Myers, *West German Foreign Aid, 1956–1966* (Boston: Boston University Press, 1968), p. 24.

67. W. Krause, *International Economics* (Boston: Houghton Mifflin Co., 1965), p. 61, and P. T. Ellsworth, *The International Economy,* third edition (New York: The Macmillan Co., 1964), pp. 272–278.

68. This term is used by P. T. Ellsworth, *ibid.,* p. 279, as a contrast to "induced transactions," such as capital movements and unilateral transactions (donations).

69. *Statistisches Jahrbuch 1968,* p. 510. See also P. Boarman, *op. cit.,* pp. 38–39.

70. K. Holbik and H. A. Myers, *op. cit.,* p. 42.

71. K. Häuser, "Das Inflationselement in den deutschen Exportüber-schüssen," *Weltwirtschaftliches Archiv,* 83 (1959), 169–173.

72. P. Boarman, *op. cit.,* p. 61.

73. *Report of the Bank Deutscher Länder for the Year 1952,* p. 62.

74. Deutsches Institut für Wirtschaftsforschung, *Wochenbericht,* 20 (1953), 65–66.

75. *Report of the Deutsche Bundesbank for the Year 1957,* p. 21.

76. For a lucid presentation of the technical aspects of foreign trade multiplier, including the literature on the subject, see I. Walter, *International Economics: Theory and Policy* (New York: The Ronald Press Co., 1968), pp. 312–324. See also K. K. Kurihara, *Introduction to Keynesian Dynamics* (London: Allen & Unwin, 1956), pp. 147–153.

77. *Report of the Deutsche Bundesbank for the Year 1960,* p. 4, stated that foreigners were buying German securities because of high yield and the expectation of re-evaluation of the Deutsche Mark. The influx of foreign capital was repeated in 1968.

78. *Report of the Deutsche Bundesbank for the Year 1961,* p. 2.

79. *Report of the Deutsche Bundesbank for the Year 1963,* p. 2, and p. 18.

80. M. Michaely, *Balance-of-Payments Adjustment Policies: Japan, Germany, and the Netherlands* (New York: National Bureau of Economic Research, 1968), p. 83.

81. K. Richenbächer, "Germany's Unsought Surplus," *The Banker*, 114:458 (1964), 224.

82. F. E. Shinnar, *Bericht eines Beauftragten* (Tübingen: R. Wunderlich Verlag, 1967), p. 65.

83. In one year, 94.3 pfennigs will grow into DM 1.00, at 6% a year, according to the following formula:

$$p_1 = \frac{A}{1 + r} = \frac{DM\ 1.00}{1 + 0.06} = DM\ .943$$

where r is the annual rate of interest, and A is the pfennig value (p_1) one year later. One mark due in 14 years is worth only .442 pfennigs today, according to the same formula:

$$p_{14} = \frac{A}{(1 + r)^{14}} = \frac{DM\ 1.00}{(.06)^{14}} = \frac{DM\ 1.00}{2.26} = .442$$

84. The prevailing formula would read:

$$A_n = Pr^n$$
$$(3.45)(1.06)^{14} = 3.45 \times 2.26$$

85. Bundesminister der Justiz, *Bundesanzeiger*, 5, June 19, 1953.

86. A total of 18 protocols, numbered in sequence, were signed on the following dates: June 16, 1953; March 4, 1954; August 5, 1954; February 17, 1955; February 22, 1955; March 14, 1956; February 25, 1957; March 10, 1958; March 12, 1959; March 3, 1960; July 22, 1960; August 8, 1960; March 2, 1961; April 5, 1962; April 5, 1962; March 20, 1963; March 17, 1964; March 16, 1965. See J. Ebeling, *Bericht über die Durchführung des Abkommens zwischen der Bundesrepublik Deutschland und dem Staate Israel vom 10. September 1952* (Bonn: Bundesminister für Wirtschaft, 1966), pp. 7–8 (hereafter referred to as *Ebeling's Report*).

87. Bundesminister der Justiz, *Bundesanzeiger*, 8 (1956), 2. This refers to *Runderlass Aussenwirtschaft*, 18/56.

88. Letter from Dr. Hans A. Goers of the Economics Ministry, May 13, 1966. The minutes and debates of the Mixed Commission have, unfortunately, not yet been made public.

89. For details, see Bundesminister der Justiz, *Bundesanzeiger*, 5, June 19, 1953. See also *Ebeling's Report*, pp. 13–16, and Appendix 2 to this book.

90. *Ebeling's Report*, p. 25.

91. The Chatham House of the Royal Institute of International Affairs and the Wiener Library, both in London, have excellent files of press clippings on the Shilumim Agreement from 1952 on.

92. *Ebeling's Report*, pp. 7, 23, 38.

93. F. E. Shinnar, *op. cit.*, pp. 73–74.

94. Bundesminister der Justiz, *Bundesanzeiger*, 7:49 (March 11, 1955).

95. *Ibid.*, 8:68 (April 7, 1956), 2.

96. *Ibid.*

97. Bundesminister der Justiz, *Bundesanzeiger*, 9 (March 19, 1957); 10 (March 19, 1958); 11 (March 18, 1959); 12 (March 23, 1960); 13 (March 30, 1961); 14 (April 21, 1962).

98. *Frankfurter Allgemeine Zeitung*, November 5, 1962.

99. Dr. F. E. Shinnar in an interview in the Israeli newspaper *Haaretz*, February 21, 1965.

100. *Report of the Bank Deutscher Länder for the Year 1953*, p. 99, stated that "For the 1954–55 financial year the amount to be delivered by the German Federal Republic was fixed at DM 250 million, of which DM 175 million was to be for the purchase of goods, while DM 75 million was to be provided in sterling to pay for the procurement of oil."

101. *Bundeshaushaltsplan für das Rechnungsjahr*, Title 681, p. 1912.

102. *Report of the Bank Deutscher Länder for the Year 1953*, p. 8.

103. *Ibid.*, 1954, p. 77. By 1957, the budget surpluses and unspent appropriations came to DM 7 billion. F. G. Reuss, *op. cit.*, p. 159, lists yearly budget surpluses.

104. F. E. Shinnar, *op. cit.*, p. 67. This transaction took place after the ratification of the Shilumim Agreement by the West German parliament on March 20, 1953, and not before, as was asserted by the official East German organ *Neues Deutschland*, July 9, 1957, which reported that Chancellor Adenauer permitted a payment of DM 94 million for American-delivered oil to Israel prior to the parliamentary ratification of the Agreement. The story was probably due to the writer's ignorance of the difference between a calendar and fiscal year.

105. West Germany, Bundesminister für Wirtschaft, *Bericht über die Durchführung des Abkommens zwischen der Bundesrepublik und dem Staate Israel vom 10. September 1952* (Bonn: 1966), pp. 34–35 (mimeo).

106. *Ibid.*

107. Title 67 in the Federal Budgets of West Germany from 1955–1956 on reported the interest earnings of the Treasury from the Israel Mission. See, for example, *Bundeshaushaltsplan 1956*, p. 2215; *1957*, p. 2506; *1958*, p. 1960; *1959*, p. 2110; *1960*, p. 2182; *1961*, p. 2309; *1962*, p. 2461 (there were no prepayments in 1962); *1963*, p. 2429; *1964*, p. 2504; *1965*, p. 2522.

108. F. E. Shinnar, *op. cit.*, p. 73.

109. Interview with the late Hillel Dan, first Director of the Shilumim Corporation of Tel Aviv, in January 1966. The same point was also made by Dr. Zvi Sussman, Director of Research, Bank of Israel, Jerusalem, in December 1965.

110. F. Biderman, "Reparations and Our Economy," *Israel Youth*

Horizon, 3 (November–December 1952), 8. See also "Reparations in Perspective," *The Israel Economist,* 8:10 (1952), 223.

111. *Ibid.*

112. R. Cale, "Reparation Funds," *Israel Speaks,* 6:15 (September 12, 1952), 3.

113. "Reparations Agreement and Development Plan," *Review of Economic Conditions in Israel,* 1 (November 1952).

114. "Reparations Deliveries Proceeding on Schedule," *Israel Speaks,* 7:22 (1953), 2.

115. S. Shapiro, "Reparations Program To Cut Trade Deficit 60%," *Israel Speaks,* 7:11 (1953), 2.

116. "Reparations," *The Israel Economist,* 9 (1953), 186.

117. *Ibid.*

118. A. Rubner, *The Economy of Israel: A Critical Account of the First Ten Years* (New York: Frederick A. Praeger, 1960), p. 46.

119. Dr. Hans A. Goers of the West German Economics Ministry in an interview in Bonn, July 27, 1966.

120. West Germany, Bundesminister für Wirtschaft, *op. cit.,* p. 24.

121. *Ibid.,* p. 54.

122. F. E. Shinnar, *op. cit.,* p. 74.

123. Interview with Mr. Friedrich Bernard of the Finance Ministry, Bonn, July 29, 1966.

124. Interview with Dr. Shinnar, January 13, 1966, in Tel Aviv. See also his memoirs, *op. cit.,* pp. 48, 79–82.

125. Interview, January 13, 1966, Tel Aviv.

126. For a fictional account of such a possibility, see R. Z. Chesnoff, E. Klein, and R. Littell, *If Israel Lost the War* (New York: Coward-McCann, 1968).

127. Interview with Dr. H. J. Abs, August 4, 1966, Frankfurt am Main.

128. *Ibid.*

129. West Germany, Bundesminister für Wirtschaft, *op. cit.,* p. 20.

130. *Ebeling's Report,* p. 25.

131. *Nachrichten für den Aussenhandel,* Frankfurt a/M., December 19, 1957.

132. *Ebeling's Report,* p. 27.

133. *Ebeling's Report,* pp. 28–30. See also Society for Christian and Jewish Cooperation of Düsseldorf, *September 10, 1952—September 10, 1962: Agreement Between the Federal Republic of Germany and the State of Israel* (Düsseldorf: 1962).

134. *Ebeling's Report,* p. 27.

135. Society for Christian and Jewish Cooperation of Düsseldorf, *op. cit.,* pp. 13–14.

136. The agreement was signed on June 1, 1962. See Bundesrepublik Deutschland, Bundesminister der Justiz, *Bundesgesetzblatt II,* 14:107 (1962), 3.

137. *Ibid.,* 38 (1965), 1305–1333.

138. *Ebeling's Report,* p. 35.

139. *Die Haager Vertragswerke* (Düsseldorf-Benrath: Verlag "Allgemeine Wochenzeitung der Juden in Deutschland," 1952), pp. 34–35.

Chapter 9

1. For an analysis of these considerations, see B. Goldmann, *Die Bedeutung des Abkommens zwischen der Bundesrepublik Deutschland und dem Staate Israel vom 10. September 1952 für die wirtschaftliche Entwicklung der Bundesrepublik und Israels, dargestellt am Beispiel der Erfüllungsperiode 1952–53 bis 1955–56* (Mainz: 1956), pp. 36–37 (dissertation).

2. N. Goldmann, *The Autobiography of Nahum Goldmann: Sixty Years of Jewish Life* (New York: Holt, Rinehart and Winston, 1969), p. 254.

3. Paraphrase of J. A. Schumpeter, *History of Economic Analysis* (New York: Oxford University Press, 1954), pp. 12–13.

4. These are the usual questions economic historians ask. See J. Clapham, "Economic History as a Discipline," *Encyclopedia of the Social Sciences,* 5 (1930), 327–330.

5. *Deutschland-Bericht,* 5:1 (1969), 12–13.

6. Deutsche Bundesbank information in 1969.

7. R. Vogel, ed., *Deutschlands Weg nach Israel* (Stuttgart: Seewald Verlag, 1967), p. 112.

8. This method has been developed by F. Machlup. See his *International Payments, Debts and Gold* (New York: Charles Scribner's Sons, 1964), p. 384.

9. B. J. Cohen, "Reparations in the Postwar Period: A Survey," *Banca Nazionale del Lavoro Quarterly Review,* 82 (September 1967), 274–275.

10. R. Hilberg, *The Destruction of the European Jews* (Chicago: Quadrangle Books, 1961), p. 758, observed that by 1958 the reparations (Shilumim) amounted to "about" one-fifth of one per cent.

11. See earlier, page 41.

12. Deutsche Bundesbank. For comparable data, see R. Vogel, ed., *op. cit.,* p. 112.

13. West Germany, Presse- und Informationsamt der Bundesregierung, *Regierung Adenauer, 1949–1963* (Wiesbaden: Franz Steiner Verlag, 1963), pp. 212, 519.

14. F. G. Reuss, *Fiscal Policy for Growth Without Inflation: The German Experiment* (Baltimore, Md.: The Johns Hopkins Press, 1963), p. 120.

15. *Ibid.*, p. 121.

16. *Ibid.*

17. West Germany, Presse- und Informationsamt, *op. cit.*, pp. 66–67.

18. *Statistisches Jahrbuch 1967*, p. 414.

19. *Bundeshaushaltsplan 1954*, p. 136.

20. *Bundeshaushaltsplan 1955*, p. 198.

21. *Finanzbericht 1963*, p. 145.

22. *Finanzbericht 1966*, p. 286.

23. West Germany, Presse- und Informationsamt, *op. cit.*, p. 521.

24. *Ibid.*

25. For a simple presentation of the input-output table, see R. T. Bye, *Principles of Economics* (New York: Appleton-Century-Crofts, 1956), pp. 427–428, and R. W. Campbell, *Soviet Economic Power*, 2nd edition (Boston: Houghton Mifflin Co., 1966), pp. 36–52.

26. For example, if we assume a change in autonomous investment of $20 billion, in conjunction with a given marginal propensity to consume of $2/3$, the investment multiplier being 3, the new level of national income will be 3 times $20 billion, or $60 billion. The ratio of the change in national income to the change in autonomous investment is known as the multiplier or, more precisely, the "instantaneous" multiplier in the Keynesian analysis of comparative statics. The Keynesian investment multiplier establishes a precise relationship between aggregate income and the change in investment. It also shows how much change in expenditure is likely to result in employment changes: see K. K. Kurihara, *Introduction to Keynesian Dynamics* (London: Allen & Unwin, 1956), pp. 23, 87, 93–102.

27. *Bundesanzeiger*, 6:68 (April 7, 1954).

28. R. Krengel *et al.*, *Ausgenutztes Brutto-Anlagevermögen: Brutto-Anlagevermögen* (Indexziffern d. Anlagenausnutzung) (Berlin: Deutsches Institut für Wirtschaftsforschung). The figures for 1950–1961 were prepared in 1964 and those for 1958–1966 in the fall of 1967. See also W. Vogt, *Die Wachstumszyklen der westdeutschen Wirtschaft* (Tübingen: J. C. B. Mohr, 1968), p. 16.

29. K. Häuser, "West Germany," in *Foreign Tax Policies and Economic Growth* (New York: National Bureau of Economic Research, 1966), p. 106.

30. *Ibid.*, p. 109.

31. W. Vogt, *op. cit.*, p. 16.

32. Bundesamt für gewerbliche Wirtschaft, *Die Durchführung des Ab-*

kommens vom 10. September 1952 zwischen der Bundesrepublik Deutschland und dem Staate Israel in den Jahren 1952–1962 (Frankfurt a/M.: 1962), p. 60.

33. B. Goldmann, *op. cit.*, p. 45.

34. Anonymous, "Probleme der westdeutschen Werftindustrie," *Wirtschaftsdienst,* 31 (1951), 47–48.

35. *Ibid.*

36. H. Glembin, "Die Situation der Hamburger Werften," *Wirtschaftsdienst,* 40:1 (1960), 42.

37. United Nations, *Statistical Yearbook 1960* (New York: 1961), p. 253; *ibid. 1962,* p. 267; *ibid. 1966,* p. 312. For the number of ships produced in this period, see Organization for Economic Co-operation and Development, *The Situation in the Shipbuilding Industry* (Paris: OECD, 1965), p. 82. The figure was 10.6 million GRT over the fourteen-year period.

38. J. Ebeling, *Bericht über die Durchführung des Abkommens zwischen der Bundesrepublik Deutschland und dem Staate Israel vom 10. September 1952* (Bonn: Bundesminister für Wirtschaft, 1966), pp. 29–30 (hereafter *Ebeling's Report*).

39. Bank of Israel, *Hashilumim Vehashpaatam al Hameshek Haisrael* (The Shilumim: Impact on the Economy of Israel) (Jerusalem: 1965), pp. 89–90 (hereafter *Shilumim Report*).

40. Verband Deutscher Schiffswerften, *Bericht über das Geschäftsjahr 1953,* p. 7.

41. *Ibid. 1954,* p. 6.

42. *Shilumim Report,* p. 90.

43. H. Heeckt, "Die Schiffbauindustrie der Bundesrepublik Deutschland im internationalen Wettbewerb," *Weltwirtschaftliches Archiv,* 95–96 (1965–66), 323.

44. Kreditanstalt für Wiederaufbau, *Eleventh Annual Report for 1959* (Frankfurt a/M.: 1960), p. 36.

45. *Ibid. 1960,* p. 40, and F. G. Reuss, *op. cit.*, pp. 202–203.

46. Kreditanstalt für Wiederaufbau, *Thirteenth Annual Report for 1961,* pp. 39–40.

47. H. Glembin, *op. cit.,* 43.

48. *Ibid.*

49. H. Heeckt, *op. cit.,* 353.

50. Calculated from the yearly reports of the Verband Deutscher Schiffswerften, 1953–1962.

51. *Ebeling's Report,* p. 30.

52. *Ebeling's Report,* p. 26.

53. F. E. Shinnar, *Entwicklung und Stand der Wirtschaft Israels,* Deutscher Industrie- und Handelstag, Schriftenreihe 52 (1958), p. 16.

54. Interview with Herr Friedrich Bernard of the Finance Ministry, November 1965, in Bonn.

55. Interview with Dr. H. A. Goers, November 1965, in the Economics Ministry, Bonn.

56. T. M. Loch, " 'Shilumim': die deutsche Wiedergutmachung als Stimulanz der israelischen und der deutschen Wirtschaft," *Europa-Archiv* (April 10, 1963), 247.

57. *Ebeling's Report,* p. 39.

58. An interested reader may consult the ample folders of press clippings at the Royal Institute of International Affairs, London.

59. *The Scotsman,* September 17, 1954.

60. *Financial Times,* September 12, 1957.

61. *Observer Foreign News Service,* November 15, 1962.

62. *The New York Times,* September 11, 1962.

63. *Financial Times,* April 13, 1965.

64. March 17, 1965.

65. N. Goldmann, *op. cit.,* p. 249.

66. *Die Haager Vertragswerke* (Düsseldorf-Benrath: Verlag "Allgemeine Wochenzeitung der Juden in Deutschland," 1952), p. 54.

67. *Deutschland-Bericht,* 2:9 (August 1966), the entire issue.

68. N. Goldmann, "Introductory Remarks," *World Jewish Congress Fifth Plenary Assembly* (Brussels: 1966), 2 (mimeo).

69. *Ibid.,* 5.

70. *Ibid.,* 4 (author's emphasis).

71. *Ibid.,* 6.

72. R. Vogel, *op. cit.,* p. 225.

73. *Ibid.,* pp. 223–224.

74. *Ibid.,* p. 225.

75. *Ibid.,* pp. 224–225.

76. *Deutschland-Bericht,* 2:9, 10–21. See also R. Vogel, *op. cit.,* pp. 229–241.

77. *Deutschland-Bericht,* 2:9, 21.

78. *Ibid.,* 22. See also R. Vogel, *op. cit.,* pp. 241–250.

79. *Ibid.*

80. K. Jaspers, "Germans and Jews," *World Jewish Congress Fifth Plenary Assembly* (Brussels: 1966), 1 (mimeo). See also R. Vogel, *op. cit.,* pp. 266–272.

81. K. Jaspers, *op. cit.,* 2.

82. *Ibid.,* 5.

83. E. Gerstenmeier, "Deutsche und Juden," *World Jewish Congress Fifth Plenary Assembly* (Brussels: 1966), 1 (mimeo). See also R. Vogel, *op. cit.,* pp. 262–266.

84. K. Adenauer, *Erinnerungen, 1953–1955* (Stuttgart: Deutsche Verlags-Anstalt, 1966), p. 160.

85. *Ibid.,* p. 161. See also K. Adenauer, "Bilanz einer Reise," *Die politische Meinung,* 11:115 (1966), 15–19.

86. T. Prittie, *Eshkol: The Man and the Nation* (New York: Pitman Publishing Corp., 1969), p. 228.

87. R. Vogel, *op. cit.,* p. 199.

88. *Ibid.* (. . . no good can come from your denying us at least recognition for our efforts.)

89. T. Prittie, *loc. cit.*

90. *The Jerusalem Post* (weekly), September 2, 1966.

91. R. Vogel, *op. cit.,* p. 280.

92. E. Jünger, *Tagebücher III: Strahlungen, Zweiter Teil* (Stuttgart: Ernst Klett Verlag, 1962), pp. 603–604.

93. H. C. Meyer, *Five Images of Germany* (New York: The Macmillan Co., 1960), p. 52. See also F. T. Epstein, "Germany and the United States: Basic Patterns of Conflict and Understanding," in G. L. Anderson, ed., *Issues and Conflicts* (Lawrence: University of Kansas Press, 1959), pp. 284–314.

94. K. Mehnert, *Der deutsche Standort* (Stuttgart: Fischer Bücherei, 1969), pp. 185, 188.

95. K. Epstein, "Das Deutschlandbild der Amerikaner," in H. Ziock, ed., *Sind die Deutschen wirklich so?* (Stuttgart: Horst Erdmann Verlag, 1965), pp. 186–187.

96. H. Eich, *Die unheimlichen Deutschen* (Düsseldorf: Econ-Verlag, 1963), p. 48.

97. R. Breitenstein, *Der hässliche Deutsche?* (Munich: Verlag Kurt Desch, 1968), pp. 10–12.

98. K. Epstein, "Shirer's History of Nazi Germany," *Review of Politics,* 23 (1963), 230–245.

99. M. F. Connors, "Current Germanophobia: The Transmission Belt of Communist Propaganda?" *Social Justice Review,* 55 (December 1962), 260–261.

100. K. Jaspers, *The Future of Germany* (Chicago: The University of Chicago Press, 1967), pp. 62, 163, 165, 172.

101. Quoted in H. Stenzel, "Deutsche im Urteil des Auslandes: Abgewertet," *Der Volkswirt,* 23:17 (April 25, 1969), 21.

102. "Eine heilige Pflicht," *Frankfurter Allgemeine Zeitung,* October 1, 1965.

103. H. Eich, *op. cit.,* p. 83.

104. D. C. Watt, *Britain Looks to Germany* (London: Oswald Wolff, 1965), pp. 114–118.

105. *Ibid.* See also T. Prittie, "Sind die 'unbelehrbaren' belehrbar?" in H. Ziock, ed., *op. cit.,* pp. 273–293.

106. K. Mehnert, *op. cit.,* p. 199.

107. R. Breitenstein, *op. cit.,* p. 158.

108. For revealing observations on this issue, see A. Roy and Alice L. Eckardt, "Again, Silence in the Churches," parts I and II, *The Christian Century,* 84:30–31 (1967), 970–973, 992–995.

109. For a listing of the most important actions taken in the various West German cities in support of Israel, see R. Vogel, *op. cit.,* pp. 330–337.

110. *Ibid.,* p. 338.

111. R. Breitenstein, *op. cit.,* p. 105.

112. A. Hodes, "Implications of Israel's Nuclear Capability," *The Wiener Library Bulletin,* 22:4 (1968), 6.

113. J. Gross, *Die Deutschen* (Frankfurt a/M.: Verlag Heinrich Scheffler, 1969), p. 285.

Chapter 10

1. Interview with Hillel Dan at his home in Tel Aviv, January 19, 1966.

2. S. Trone, *German Payments: Basic Development Programme* (Jerusalem: June 30, 1952), 11 (mimeo). See also "Master Plan Set to Develop Israel," *The New York Times,* August 12, 1952.

3. S. Trone, *loc. cit.*

4. H. Dan, *B'Derekh Lo Selula* (Tel Aviv: Schocken Publishing Co., 1963), pp. 323–324.

5. K. Loewy, "Israel: Nach dem ersten Jahr der Deutschen Reparationen," *Aussenpolitik,* 6:3 (1955), 183.

6. S. Trone, *op. cit.,* p. 7.

7. *Ibid.,* p. 13.

8. *Ibid.*

9. In 1949 another observer reported that Israel's administrators suffered from the lack of responsible economic experience and that they were still less concerned with learning their duties than jockeying for position and making themselves "indispensable": see H. Lehrman, "The Economic Test Facing Israel," *Commentary,* 7 (1949), 517, 523.

10. S. Trone, *op. cit.,* p. 13.

11. *Ibid.,* p. 16.

12. Israel, State Comptroller's Office, *Annual Report No. 4. Report of the State Comptroller for the Fiscal Year 1952–53: Selected Chapters* (Jerusalem: 1953), p. 174 (mimeo) (hereafter cited as *Comptroller's Report No. 4*).

13. C. P. Kindleberger, *Economic Development,* 2nd edition (New York: McGraw-Hill, 1965), p. 85.

14. R. Jochimsen, *Theorie der Infrastruktur* (Tübingen: J. C. B. Mohr, 1966), p. 100.

15. Kindleberger, *loc. cit.*

16. A. O. Hirschman, *The Strategy of Economic Development* (New Haven, Conn.: Yale University Press, 1967), pp. 82–84.

17. R. Jochimsen, *op. cit.,* pp. 133–135.

18. For a discussion of many facets of innovational and authoritarian personalities, constituting "human capital," see E. E. Hagen, *On the Theory of Social Change* (Homewood, Ill.: Dorsey Press, 1962), pp. 86–98.

19. T. W. Schultz, "Investment in Human Capital," *The American Economic Review,* 51 (1961), 1–17. See also G. Myrdal, *Asian Drama: An Inquiry into the Poverty of Nations* (New York: The Twentieth Century Fund, 1968), pp. 1533–1650.

20. "Investment in Human Capital," in G. M. Meier, ed., *Leading Issues in Development Economics* (New York: Oxford University Press, 1964), p. 267.

21. F. H. Harbison, "Human Resource Development," in G. M. Meier, ed., *op. cit.,* p. 273.

22. R. Jochimsen, *op. cit.,* pp. 117–118.

23. For the significance of institutional infrastructure, see G. Myrdal, *op. cit.,* pp. 71–125.

24. H. Myint, "Investment in the Social Infrastructure," in G. M. Meier, ed., *op. cit.,* p. 282.

25. W. W. Rostow, *The Stages of Economic Growth* (Cambridge: The University Press, 1960), p. 25.

26. A. J. Youngson, *Overhead Capital: Study in Development Economics* (Edinburgh: Edinburgh University Press, 1967), pp. 34, 80 and *passim.*

27. J. Stohler, "Zur rationalen Planung der Infrastruktur," *Konjunkturpolitik,* 11:5 (1965), 294.

28. L. J. Fein, "The Israeli Road from Underdevelopment to Affluence," in Harry G. Shaffer and Jan S. Prybyla, eds., *From Underdevelopment to Affluence* (New York: Appleton-Century-Crofts, 1968), pp. 353–354.

29. W. R. Espy, *Bold New Program* (New York: Harper and Bros., 1950), p. 144.

30. N. Halevi and R. Klinov-Malul, *The Economic Development of Israel* (New York: Frederick A. Praeger, 1968), p. 35.

31. For a presentation of Palestine's economic problems, see R. R. Nathan, O. Gass, D. Creamer, *Palestine: Problems and Promise* (Wash-

ington, D.C.: Public Affairs Press, 1946). See also A. Bonne, *The Economic Development of the Middle East: An Outline of Planned Reconstruction After the War* (New York: Oxford University Press, 1945), pp. 115–121, and T. Prittie, *Israel: Miracle in the Desert* (New York: Frederick A. Praeger, 1967), pp. 3–26.

32. N. Bentwich, ed., *A New Way of Life: The Collective Settlements of Israel* (London: Shindler & Golomb, 1949).

33. M. Turnowsky-Pinner, *Die zweite Generation mitteleuropäischer Siedler in Israel* (Tübingen: J. C. B. Mohr, 1962), p. 136.

34. H. Gerling, "Das Ethos der Wiedergutmachung," *Mitteilungsblatt* (Israel), 27:6 (1959), 3. The actual figure was 8.1 million pounds sterling: see L. Pinner, "Vermögenstransfer nach Palästina, 1933–1939," in *In Zwei Welten: Siegfried Moses zum Fünfundsiebzigsten Geburtstag,* H. Tramer, ed. (Tel Aviv: Bitaon Verlag, 1962), p. 157. For other literature on this matter, see W. Feilchenfeld, *Fünf Jahre Deutsche Palästinawanderung und Havarah-Transfer, 1933–1938* (Tel Aviv: 1939), p. 39, and G. Krojanker, *The Transfer: A Vital Question of the Zionist Movement* (Tel Aviv: 1936), p. 20.

35. R. A. Easterlin, "Israel's Development: Past Accomplishments and Future Problems," *Quarterly Journal of Economics,* 75 (1961), 70.

36. *Ibid.,* p. 71. For other sources on education, see J. S. Bentwich, *Education in Israel* (Philadelphia: The Jewish Publication Society of America, 1965), and J. Baruch, "Investment in Education and Human Capital in Israel," *Bank of Israel Bulletin,* 23 (1965), 3–27.

37. H. Dan, *op. cit.,* p. 325.

38. Interview with the late Hillel Dan in Tel Aviv, January 19, 1966. See also his memoirs, *op. cit.,* p. 326.

39. *Ibid.,* pp. 326–327.

40. See F. E. Shinnar, *Bericht eines Beauftragten* (Tübingen: R. Wunderlich Verlag, 1967), p. 73, for his attitudes in early 1953.

41. For other details see H. Dan's memoirs, *op. cit.*

42. For a description of the initial organization of the Shilumim Corporation, see A. Lazarson, "Execution of Shilumim," *Rivon Lekalkala,* 5–6 (1954), 75–79. For the subsequent reorganization, see Bank of Israel, *Hashilumim Vehashpaatam al Hameshek Haisrael* (Jerusalem: 1965), p. 61 (hereafter *Hashilumim*).

43. *The Jerusalem Post,* November 17, 1953.

44. *Hashilumim,* p. 61.

45. "Reparations and Development," *The Israel Economist,* 9:6 (1953), 118.

46. "Reparations," *The Israel Economist,* 9:9 (1953), 186.

47. *Comptroller's Report No. 4,* p. 173.

48. J. Ebeling, *Bericht über die Durchführung des Abkommens zwischen der Bundesrepublik Deutschland und dem Staate Israel vom 10. September 1952* (Bonn: Bundesminister für Wirtschaft, 1966), p. 38.

49. For a detailed account of these administrative frictions, see *Comptroller's Report No. 4*, pp. 168–169. See also A. Lazarson, *op. cit.*, 76.

50. *The Jerusalem Post*, December 8, 1953.

51. *Ibid.*

52. *The Jerusalem Post*, July 9, 1954.

53. *Comptroller's Report No. 4*, p. 168.

54. *Ibid.*

55. For a brief discussion of the meaning of economic dependence, see D. Horowitz, "The Attainment of Economic Independence," in *Israel Today, A New Society in the Making* (Tel Aviv: Hamenora, 1967), pp. 67–75.

56. *The Jerusalem Post*, November 1, 1954.

57. F. E. Shinnar, *op. cit.*, p. 47.

58. N. Halevi, "Economic Policy Discussions and Research in Israel," *The American Economic Review*, 59:4, part 2 (1969), 78.

59. "Short-sighted Revisions," *The Israel Economist*, 8 (1953), 240.

60. E. Laserson, "Reparations: Their Role in Long-Range Planning," *Israel Speaks*, 8:3 (1954), 5.

61. *The Jerusalem Post*, November 4, 1954.

62. H. Dan, *op. cit.*, pp. 332–333. See also *Hashilumim*, p. 220.

63. *Ibid.*

64. H. Dan, *op. cit.*, pp. 332–333.

65. S. Trone, *op. cit.*, p. 35.

66. Interview with H. Dan, Tel Aviv, January 19, 1966.

67. H. Dan, *op. cit.*, p. 333.

68. *Comptroller's Report No. 4*, p. 171.

69. *Hashilumim*, p. 207.

70. H. Dan, *op. cit.*, pp. 324–325.

71. "Reparations and the Histadrut," *The Israel Economist*, 11:8 (1955), 144.

72. H. Dan, *op. cit.*, p. 326.

73. A. Rubner, *The Economy of Israel: A Critical Account of the First Ten Years* (New York: Frederick A. Praeger, 1960), p. 46.

74. *Hashilumim*, p. 62.

75. *Ibid.*, p 79.

76. *Ibid.*, p. 65.

77. *Ibid.*, p. 64.

78. "The Sale of Reparations Goods," *The Israel Economist*, 9:6 (1953), 125.

79. "Reparations and Planning," *The Israel Economist,* 8:11 (1952), 247.

80. "The Sale of Reparations Goods," *op. cit.,* p. 125.

81. Israel, Ministry of Finance, *The Development Budget 1953–54* (Jerusalem: 1953), p. 47. The calculation is my own.

82. Computed from Ministry of Finance, *Progress and Prospects* (Jerusalem: 1960), p. 30, and Ministry of Finance, *Achievements and Objectives* (Jerusalem: 1960), p. 31.

83. *The Jerusalem Post,* April 15, 1966.

84. For details, see *Hashilumim,* pp. 66–69.

85. F. E. Shinnar, *op. cit.,* p. 70.

86. *Hashilumim,* p. 70.

87. *Frankfurter Allgemeine Zeitung,* March 17, 1955.

88. *Hashilumim,* p. 71.

89. *Ibid.,* p. 75. ZIM lines discontinued this practice in 1960.

90. B. Boxer, *Israeli Shipping and Foreign Trade* (Chicago: University of Chicago, 1957), pp. 122–123. For a discussion of Haifa's inadequacies, see "Haifa Port Enquiry," *The Israel Economist,* 8:8 (1952), 176–179.

91. *Hashilumim,* p. 76.

92. F. E. Shinnar, *op. cit.,* pp. 74–75.

93. *Hashilumim,* p. 87.

Chapter 11

1. D. Rahman, "Development of the Israel Shipping Industry," *Israel Economic Bulletin,* 8:2 (1956), 7–9, and *passim.*

2. J. Ebeling, *Bericht über die Durchführung des Abkommens zwischen der Bundesrepublik Deutschland und dem Staate Israel vom 10. September 1952* (Bonn: Bundesminister für Wirtschaft, 1966), p. 28 (hereafter *Ebeling's Report*). The official Israeli figure was given as DM 569 million: see Bank of Israel, *Hashilumim Vehashpaatam al Hameshek Haisrael* (Jerusalem: 1965), p. 89 (hereafter *Hashilumim*).

3. *Ebeling's Report,* pp. 29–30, and *Hashilumim,* pp. 226–227.

4. "Israel Acquires New Ships," *The Israel Economist,* 11:1 (1955), 13.

5. "Shipbuilding for Israel," *The Israel Economist,* 11:4 (1955), 75.

6. "New Shipbuilding Program," *The Israel Economist,* 11:12 (1955), 220.

7. "Big Programme for Israel Fleet," *The Israel Economist,* 12:6 (1956), 122.

8. Interview with H. Dan at his home in Tel Aviv, January 19, 1966.

9. The Israel Export and Trade Journal, *Ten Years Restitution Agreement Israel-Federal Republic of Germany* (Tel Aviv: 1962), p. 47.

10. *Hashilumim,* pp. 71–72.

11. "Delivery of First Restitution Ship," *The Israel Economist,* 10:11 (1954), 215. See also "Shipping Orders from Germany," *The Israel Economist,* 10:12 (1954), 235.

12. Israel, State Comptroller, *Report on the ZIM Navigation Company* (Jerusalem: August 1965), p. 41 (translation from Hebrew). For delivery dates, see *Hashilumim,* pp. 226–227.

13. Bank of Israel, *Annual Report 1956* (Jerusalem: 1957), p. 235.

14. "Big Programme for Israel Fleet," *loc. cit.*

15. Bank of Israel, *op. cit.,* p. 236.

16. Bank of Israel, *Annual Report 1957* (Jerusalem: 1958), p. 161.

17. Bank of Israel, *The Israel Merchant Marine: An Economic Appraisal* (Jerusalem: 1962), p. 23.

18. *Ibid.*

19. Bank of Israel, *Annual Report 1964* (Jerusalem: 1965), p. 308.

20. Israel, State Comptroller, *op. cit.,* p. 44.

21. *Hashilumim,* p. 90.

22. Bank of Israel, *Annual Report 1958* (Jerusalem: 1959), p. 158.

23. Israel, State Comptroller, *op. cit.,* p. 44.

24. *Hashilumim,* p. 96.

25. *Ibid.,* p. 100.

26. "More Ships from Germany?" *The Israel Economist,* 11:3 (1955), 54.

27. Bank of Israel, *The Israel Merchant Marine, op. cit.,* p. 17.

28. *Ibid.*

29. Y. Friedler, "ZIM Steers 4-Way Course in Drive to Cut Losses," *The Jerusalem Post,* November 28, 1966, p. 4.

30. Bank of Israel, *Annual Report 1959* (Jerusalem: 1960), pp. 194–195.

31. "The Problems of Passenger Shipping," *The Israel Economist,* 13:6 (1957), 85.

32. Y. Friedler, "Shalom Means Goodbye," *The Jerusalem Post,* April 3, 1967, p. 12. See also L. Ben Dor, "Post Mortem on S.S. Shalom," *The Jerusalem Post,* May 8, 1967, p. 9.

33. Y. Friedler, "ZIM Steers 4-Way Course . . . ," *op. cit.,* p. 4.

34. L. Ben Dor, *op. cit.,* p. 9.

35. *Ibid.*

36. *Hashilumim,* p. 33.

37. "Israel Shipping News," *The Israel Economist,* 13:10 (1957), 156.

38. Bank of Israel, *Annual Report 1963* (Jerusalem: 1964), p. 274.

39. "Was haben wir mit den Reparationsgeldern gemacht?" (1962, mimeographed, translated from a series of articles in the Israeli newspaper *Maariv*), p. 1.

40. Bank of Israel, *The Israel Merchant Marine, op. cit.,* p. 18.

41. *Ebeling's Report,* p. 26.

42. *Hashilumim,* p. 89.

43. *Ebeling's Report,* p. 26.

44. G. DeGaury, *The New State of Israel* (New York: Frederick A. Praeger, 1952), p. 199.

45. *Ibid.,* p. 200.

46. M. J. Deutsch, *Report on a Preliminary Survey of Industrial Conditions in Israel with Regard to Potential Projects in the Chemical, Petroleum and Utility Fields,* prepared for the Industrial Institute of Israel, Washington, August 31, 1949, pp. 68–70 (mimeo).

47. *Israel Economic Bulletin,* 13 (May 1949), 7.

48. G. Fischler, *Energiewirtschaft in Israel* (Basel: Kyklos-Verlag, 1965), p. 11.

49. Israel, Ministry of Finance, *The Development Budget 1953–54* (Jerusalem: 1953), p. 7 (hereafter *Development Budget 1953–54*).

50. S. Trone, *German Payments: Basic Development Programme* (Jerusalem: June 30, 1952), p. 50.

51. *Ibid.,* p. 47.

52. *Ibid.,* p. 49.

53. The Israel Export and Trade Journal, "The Development of Israel's Power Supply Under the Aspect of the Israel-German Reparations Agreement," *op. cit.,* pp. 54–55.

54. Bank of Israel, *Annual Report 1956,* pp. 206–207.

55. *Ibid.,* p. 205.

56. Israel, Ministry of Finance, *Progress and Prospects* (Jerusalem: 1959), p. 9.

57. Bank of Israel, *Annual Report 1956,* p. 205.

58. Bank of Israel, *Annual Report 1957,* pp. 142–143.

59. *Ibid.,* p. 143.

60. Bank Leumi Le-Israel, "Reparations," *Review of Economic Conditions in Israel,* 53 (May 1966), 5. See also *Ebeling's Report,* p. 31.

61. G. Fischler, *op. cit.,* p. 54.

62. *Ibid.,* p. 61.

63. *Ibid.,* p. 10.

64. *The Jerusalem Post Economic Annual 1962–63* (Jerusalem: 1963), p. 204.

65. G. Fischler, *op. cit.,* p. 15.

66. T. T. Kermani, *Economic Development in Action: Theories, Problems and Procedures as Applied to the Middle East* (Cleveland: The World Publishing Co., 1967), p. 20.

67. *The Jerusalem Post Economic Annual 1962–63, op. cit.,* p. 205.

68. G. Fischler, *op. cit.*, p. 51.

69. Bank Leumi Le-Israel, *loc. cit.*

70. G. Fischler, *op. cit.*, p. 52.

71. F. E. Shinnar, *Bericht eines Beauftragten* (Tübingen: R. Wunderlich Verlag, 1967), p. 73.

72. *Hashilumim,* p. 93.

73. Bank Leumi Le-Israel, *op. cit.*, 6.

74. *Ibid.,* and "Was haben wir mit den Reparationsgeldern gemacht?" *op. cit.*, p. 3.

75. *Hashilumim,* pp. 65, 198–199.

76. Dr. Hans A. Goers, information at the West German Wirtschaftsministerium.

77. G. Fischler, *op. cit.*, p. 12.

78. S. Trone, *op. cit.*, pp. 21–33.

79. For similar arguments, see D. Regling and R. Voss, *Die Bahn der Drei Meere* (Basel: Kyklos-Verlag, 1963), pp. 9–15, 27, 46–47.

80. S. Trone, *op. cit.*, p. 29.

81. *Hashilumim,* p. 147.

82. The Israel Export and Trade Journal, "Reparations Equipment Revolutionized Israel Railways," *op. cit.* (Tel Aviv: 1962), pp. 42–43.

83. *Hashilumim,* p. 147.

84. Bank of Israel, *Annual Report 1958,* p. 168.

85. "Was haben wir mit den Reparationsgeldern gemacht?" *op. cit.*, p. 4.

86. Bank of Israel, *Annual Report 1959,* p. 209.

87. *Ibid.,* p. 206.

88. Bank of Israel, *Annual Report 1963,* p. 283.

89. Bank of Israel, *Annual Report 1961,* p. 257.

90. Bank of Israel, *Annual Report 1956,* p. 247.

91. The Israel Export and Trade Journal, "Reparations Equipment Revolutionized Israel Railways," *op. cit.*, p. 42.

92. *Hashilumim,* p. 155.

93. "Was haben wir mit den Reparationsgeldern gemacht?" *op. cit.*, p. 4.

94. S. Trone, *op. cit.*, p. 45.

95. The Israel Export and Trade Journal, "Reparations for Communications Equipment," *op. cit.*, pp. 40–41.

96. *Ibid.,* p. 40.

97. *Hashilumim,* p. 155.

98. S. Trone, *op. cit.*, pp. 41–42.

99. B. Menzinger, *Der Hafen Haifa* (Basel: Kyklos-Verlag, 1966), pp. 3–4.

100. "Repairs and Construction," *The Israel Economist,* 10:1 (1954), 13.

101. H. Dan, *B'Derekh Lo Selula* (Tel Aviv: Schocken Publishing Co., 1963), p. 341. He also stressed this point in an interview in Tel Aviv on January 19, 1966.

102. "Ship Overhaul in Haifa," *The Israel Economist,* 10:5 (1954), 93.

103. *Hashilumim,* p. 154.

104. The Israel Export and Trade Journal, "Haifa Port: Faster and More Efficient," *op. cit.,* pp. 44–45.

105. "Floating Dock Looks for Work," *The Israel Economist,* 11:2 (1955), 38.

106. "Kishon and Ship Repair," *The Israel Economist,* 11:5 (1955), 92.

107. *Hashilumim,* pp. 152, 154.

108. B. Menzinger, *op. cit.,* pp. 14–17, 52.

109. "Ports Regraded," *The Israel Economist,* 13:4 (1957), 61. See also "Reparations from West Germany," *Israel Investor's Report,* 47 (January 15, 1963), 5.

110. H. Worst, "Der Negev," *Geographische Rundschau,* 16 (1964), 448–449.

111. "The Dead Sea Industry," *The Israel Economist,* 10:6 (1954), 107.

112. *Hashilumim,* p. 135.

113. "Composition of the Value of Purchases of Equipment as in the Industrial and Development Group," tables provided by Dr. F. E. Shinnar from the Shilumim Corporation, p. 13 (mimeo).

114. "The Dead Sea Industry," *The Israel Economist, op. cit.,* p. 106.

115. *Development Budget 1953–54,* p. 19.

116. "Some Unsolved Transport Problems," *The Israel Economist,* 8 (1952), 202.

117. *Ibid.*

118. J. K. Allen, W. Bredo, H. J. Robinson, C. A. Trexel, Jr., *Industrial Economy of Israel: Final Report* (Menlo Park, Calif.: Stanford Research Institute, 1955), p. 227 (mimeo). Prepared for the United States Operations Mission in Israel and Ministry of Commerce and Industry, Government of Israel.

119. "Prospects of Mineral Exports to Japan," *The Israel Economist,* 12:8 (1956), 156.

120. *Hashilumim,* p. 135.

121. *Development Budget 1953–54,* p. 35.

122. *Ibid.*

123. Bank of Israel, *Annual Report 1956,* p. 211.

124. *Hashilumim,* p. 135.

125. The Israel Export and Trade Journal, "Copper Mining," *op. cit.,* p. 51.

126. *Hashilumim,* p. 141.

127. *Ibid.*

128. M. Bentov, "Development of Natural Resources," *Israel Economic Bulletin,* 9:3–4 (1957), 13.

129. I. Hoffman and B. C. Mariacher, "Beneficiation of Israeli Phosphate Ore," *Mining Engineering,* 13 (1961), 472.

130. *Ibid.*

131. "The Negev," *The Israel Economist,* 11:1 (1955), 8.

132. I. Hoffman and B. C. Mariacher, *op. cit.,* p. 473.

133. G. Schultze, "Bergbau und Bodenschätze Israels," *Glückauf: Bergmannische Zeitschrift,* 99 (1963), 460.

134. The Israel Export and Trade Journal, "Phosphates," *op. cit.,* p. 52.

135. *Hashilumim,* p. 135.

136. *Development Budget 1953–54,* p. 32.

137. H. Worst, *op. cit.,* 451.

138. *Ebeling's Report,* p. 26.

139. A. Kahane, "Zwölf Jahre Planung in Israel," *Schweizer Zeitschrift für Landes-, Regional- und Ortsplanung,* 17 (1960), 84.

140. *Hashilumim,* pp. 139, 244.

141. *Ebeling's Report,* p. 26.

142. E. Levy, *Israel Economic Survey 1953–54* (Jerusalem: The Economic Department of the Jewish Agency, 1955), p. 29.

143. *Ibid.,* p. 33.

144. *Israel Economic Bulletin,* 5:7–8 (May–June 1953), 3.

145. Israel, Prime Minister, Economic Advisory Staff (Bernard R. Bell), *The Israel Economy in 1954* (Jerusalem: July 1955), p. 5 (mimeo).

146. *Ibid.,* p. 26.

147. Israel, Ministry of Finance, *The Economic Report of the Minister of Finance Mr. Levi Eshkol Before the Knesset, February 8th, 1955* (Jerusalem: 1955), p. 12.

148. *Ibid.,* p. 11.

149. *Hashilumim,* p. 39.

150. *Ibid.,* p. 212. See also *The Israel Economist,* 10:7 (1954), 132. According to this source, Israel's short-term debts in mid-1953 were 18.2 per cent of the total indebtedness. A year later they came to 10.5 per cent.

151. *Ebeling's Report,* p. 26.

152. I. M. Kirzner, *Market Theory and the Price System* (Princeton, N.J.: D. Van Nostrand Co., 1963), pp. 150–153.

153. *Israel Economic Bulletin,* 8:2 (1956), 3.

154. *Ebeling's Report,* pp. 27–28.

155. *Hashilumim,* p. 113.

156. *Ibid.*

157. "The 'Koor' Steel Project," *The Israel Economist*, 13:7 and 8 (1957), 105, 123.

158. Israel, Ministry of Finance, Industrial Advisory Group, *First Interim Report on the "Steel Town" Pig Iron and Steel Project in Israel: An Economic Appraisal* (Jerusalem: July 1957), p. 8 (mimeo).

159. *Ibid.*, pp. 1, 29.

160. *Ibid.*, p. 65.

161. *Ibid.*, p. 68.

162. A. Rubner, *The Economy of Israel: A Critical Account of the First Ten Years* (New York: Frederick A. Praeger, 1960), p. 233.

163. "Was haben wir mit den Reparationsgeldern gemacht?" *op. cit.*, p. 5.

164. Bank of Israel, *Annual Report 1956*, p. 197.

165. Bank of Israel, *Annual Report 1959*, p. 172.

166. "Was haben wir mit den Reparationsgeldern gemacht?" *op. cit.*, pp. 5, 8.

167. "The Negev," *The Israel Economist*, *op. cit.*, 8.

168. J. K. Allen *et al.*, *op. cit.*, p. 42.

169. For an overview of the changes in the country's industry, see "Industrial Development Program," *The Israel Economist*, 13:9 (1957), 151.

170. J. Kleiner, *Die Textilindustrie in Israel* (Basel: Kyklos-Verlag, 1966), pp. 10–12.

171. The Israel Export and Trade Journal, "Equipment for Israel's Modern Textile Industry," *op. cit.*, pp. 67–73.

172. *Ibid.*, p. 67.

173. N. Intertar, "Shilumim in the Development of Industry," *Rivon Lekalkala*, 8 (1955), 494.

174. *Hashilumim*, p. 113, gives the exact details.

Chapter 12

1. This was the author's impression while in Israel in December 1965 and January 1966.

2. N. Goldmann, *The Autobiography of Nahum Goldmann: Sixty Years of Jewish Life* (New York: Holt, Rinehart and Winston, 1969), p. 249.

3. F. E. Shinnar, *Bericht eines Beauftragten* (Tübingen: R. Wunderlich Verlag, 1967), p. 87.

4. B. Wyler, "Reparations Are Not Handouts," *The Jerusalem Post*, September 23, 1966.

5. Bank of Israel, *Hashilumim Vehashpaatam al Hameshek Haisrael* (Jerusalem: 1965), pp. 28, 208–209 (hereafter *Hashilumim*).

6. *Ibid.*, p. 30.

7. *Ibid.*, p. 10.

8. Calculated from Israel, Ministry of Finance, *Annual Reports of the Accountant General.*

9. "Reparations: We Might Have Done Without," *The Jerusalem Post,* April 15, 1966.

10. "The Reparations Agreement," *The Israel Economist,* 19 (April 1953), 80.

11. "Reparations: We Might Have Done Without," *op. cit.*

12. *Ibid.*

13. "German Projects," *The Jerusalem Post,* April 15, 1966.

14. F. E. Shinnar, "What Reparations Did for Israel," *The Jerusalem Post,* April 22, 1966.

15. "Reparations and Growth," *The Jerusalem Post,* April 29, 1966.

16. J. Bension, "The More 'Honourable' Way," *The Jerusalem Post,* April 29, 1966.

17. M. Raami, "The More 'Honourable' Way," *The Jerusalem Post,* April 29, 1966.

18. Bank Leumi Le-Israel, "Reparations," *Review of Economic Conditions in Israel,* 53 (1966), 6.

19. F. E. Shinnar, *Bericht eines Beauftragten,* p. 87.

20. For a discussion of this problem, see Bank of Israel, *Annual Report 1955* (Jerusalem: 1956), p. 57.

21. F. Ginor, *Uses of Agricultural Surpluses* (Jerusalem: Bank of Israel, 1963), pp. 17–18.

22. N. Halevi, "Economic Policy Discussion and Research in Israel," *The American Economic Review,* 59:4, part 2 (1969), 84.

23. *Hashilumim,* pp. 32–43.

24. *Ibid.*, p. 46.

25. *Ibid.*, p. 48.

26. *Ibid.*, pp. 44–45.

27. *Ibid.*, p. 49.

28. *Commerce (Palnews),* 20:8–9 (August–September 1952), 3.

29. Israel, Prime Minister's Office, Economic Planning Authority, *Israel Economic Development: Past Progress and Plans for the Future* (Jerusalem: 1968), p. 9.

30. *Ibid.*, p. 10. Another work computed the average annual rate of growth of Israel's Gross Domestic Product at 9.6 per cent from 1952 to 1960. See D. Horowitz, *The Economics of Israel* (Oxford: Pergamon Press, 1967), p. 26. According to still another source, "between 1952 and 1965

the average annual rates of growth were 8.7 per cent for domestic resources and 10.4 per cent for G.N.P., while the per capita rates were 4.9 and 6.5 per cent, respectively." See N. Halevi and R. Klinov-Malul, *The Economic Development of Israel* (New York: Frederick A. Praeger, 1968), p. 92. The dean of Israeli statisticians, Dr. A. L. Gaathon, calculated that from 1950 to 1964 the G.N.P. rose on the average 10.8 per cent annually. See A. L. Gaathon, "Das wirtschaftliche Wachstum Israels von 1950 bis 1964," *Konjunkturpolitik,* 11:4 (1965), 231. And, lastly, according to Dr. Ginor, the annual rate of growth of G.N.P. at constant prices from 1950 to 1960 was 10.6 per cent. See F. Ginor, *op. cit.,* p. 17.

31. D. Patinkin, *The Israel Economy: The First Decade* (Jerusalem: Jerusalem Post Press, 1960), p. 92.

32. N. Halevi and R. Klinov-Malul, *op. cit.,* p. 97.

33. *Ibid.,* p. 155.

34. Israel, Prime Minister's Office, Economic Planning Authority, *op. cit.,* p. 168.

35. *Ibid.,* p. 174.

36. *Ibid.,* p. 169.

37. *Hashilumim,* p. 29.

38. G. Landauer, *Der Zionismus im Wandel Dreier Jahrzehnte* (Tel Aviv: Bitaon Verlag, 1957), p. 430.

39. D. Cohen, "Israel's Inflow of Capital and Its Institutional Impact," *The Israel Yearbook 1961* (Tel Aviv: 1961), p. 67.

40. *Ibid.,* p. 68.

41. *Ibid.*

42. H. Lubell, "The Public and Private Sectors and Investment in Israel," *Middle Eastern Affairs,* 12:4 (1961), 105. For comparable data, although for different years, see D. Patinkin, *op. cit.,* pp. 86–87.

43. Israel, Prime Minister's Office, Economic Planning Authority, *op. cit.,* p. 104.

44. H. Lubell, *op. cit.,* p. 98.

45. *Ibid.,* p. 99.

46. "The Reparations Agreement," *The Israel Economist, op. cit.,* p. 80.

47. J. Nasmyth, "Israel's Distorted Economy," *The Middle East Journal,* 8 (1954), 391–402.

48. D. Patinkin, *op. cit.,* p. 132, quoted by N. Halevi and R. Klinov-Malul, *op. cit.,* p. 168.

49. N. Halevi and R. Klinov-Malul, *op. cit.,* pp. 168–175, evaluate the most important findings of the debate. See also D. Horowitz, "The Attainment of Economic Independence," in *Israel Today* (Tel Aviv: Hamenora, 1967), p. 67, and A. L. Gaathon, *op. cit.,* 229. According to the latter, in the long run foreign financing of investments cannot be

objected to if (1) the new facilities raise the G.N.P. more than the costs of extra foreign indebtedness and (2) the new investments must raise the export potential of the country at least by as much as the increase in foreign indebtedness.

50. M. Tzur, "Industrial Development in Israel," in A. Winsemius and J. A. Pincus, eds., *Methods of Industrial Development* (Paris: OECD, 1962), p. 131.

51. *Ibid.*, p. 128.

52. Israel, Central Bureau of Statistics, *Statistical Abstract of Israel,* 18 (Jerusalem: 1967), p. 97.

53. "Israel Suffers From Immigration Pains," *The World Journal Tribune,* February 5, 1967.

54. For some interesting discussions of this matter, see D. Patinkin, "A 'Nationalist' Model," in W. Adams, ed., *The Brian Drain* (New York: The Macmillan Co., 1968), pp. 92–108, and A. Hovne, "On the Brain Drain from Israel," *Jewish Journal of Sociology,* 9:1 (1967), 58–65.

55. S. Amir, "The National Income of Israel, 1950–1956," *Middle Eastern Affairs,* 9 (1958), 208–212.

56. "Tod aus der Textilfabrik," *Der Spiegel,* 23:19 (May 5, 1969), 147.

57. *The Jerusalem Post,* May 12, 1969.

58. A. Hodes, "Implications of Israel's Nuclear Capability," *The Wiener Library Bulletin,* 22:4 (1968), 5.

59. *Ibid.*

60. *Ibid.*, p. 6.

61. L. Laufer, *Israel and the Developing Countries: New Approach to Cooperation* (New York: The Twentieth Century Fund, 1967), and M. E. Kreinin, *Israel and Africa, A Study in Technical Cooperation* (New York: Frederick A. Praeger, 1964).

62. For some quantitative aspects of this program, see L. Laufer, *op. cit.*, p. 20.

63. International Bank for Reconstruction and Development, International Development Association, *Current Economic Position and Prospects of Israel* (Washington, D.C.: March 17, 1965) (mimeo).

64. P. M. Boarman, *Germany's Economic Dilemma: Inflation and the Balance of Payments* (New Haven, Conn.: Yale University Press, 1964), p. 221.

65. *Ibid.*, p. 157.

66. E. M. Bernstein, "Economic Policy for a Working Economy: The Case of Israel," *Bank of Israel Bulletin,* 5 (1957), 13–14, 35–36. See also A. P. Lerner, "Planning for Israel's Solvency," *Midstream,* 4:3 (1958), 56, and N. Halevi and R. Klinov-Malul, *op. cit.*, p. 252.

67. P. M. Boarman, *op. cit.*, p. 116.

68. International Bank for Reconstruction and Development, International Development Association, *Current Economic Position and Prospects of Israel* (Washington, D.C.: March 17, 1965), Recommendation VII (mimeo).

69. Israel, Prime Minister's Office, Economic Planning Authority, *op. cit.*, p. 21. See also A. Sherman, "Israel's Economic Problems," *The World Today*, 15:10 (1959), 398.

70. N. Halevi and R. Klinov-Malul, *op. cit.*, p. 149.

71. E. A. Tenenbaum, *Israel's Industrial Finances: A Second Look* (Washington, D.C.: Report to the Government of Israel and U.S. International Cooperation Administration, 1960), p. 132.

72. N. Halevi and R. Klinov-Malul, *op. cit.*, p. 158.

73. N. Goldmann, *op. cit.*, pp. 274–275.

74. C. Landauer, *Contemporary Economic Systems* (Philadelphia: J. B. Lippincott, 1964), p. 252.

75. The interested reader may consult, for example, A. L. Gaathon, *Capital Stock, Employment, and Output in Israel, 1950–1959* (Jerusalem: Bank of Israel, 1961), pp. 80–82, and D. Horowitz, *op. cit.*, pp. 181–188.

76. A. Sherman, *op. cit.*, 405–406.

77. U.S. Bureau of the Census, *Statistical Abstract of the United States: 1967* (Washington, D.C.: Government Printing Office, 1967), pp. 862–864.

78. S. Dell, *Trade Blocs and Common Market* (New York: Alfred A. Knopf, 1963), p. 218.

79. *The Philadelphia Inquirer,* August 10, 1969.

80. On this question, see D. S. Pearson, "Income Distribution and the Size of Nations," *Economic Development and Cultural Change,* 13 (1964–65), 472–478; S. Kuznets, "Economic Growth of Small Nations," *The Challenge of Development* (Jerusalem: 1958), pp. 9–25; M. Michaely, *Concentration in International Trade* (Amsterdam: North-Holland Publishing Company, 1962), p. 16; D. Vital, *The Inequality of States* (Oxford: Clarendon Press, 1967), p. 8; W. G. Demas, *The Economics of Development in Small Countries with Special Reference to the Caribbean* (Montreal: McGill University Press, 1965), p. 22; E. A. G. Robinson, "Introduction," in *Economic Consequences of the Size of Nations* (New York: St. Martin's Press, 1960), p. xvii; D. R. Raynolds, *Rapid Development in Small Countries* (New York: Frederick A. Praeger, 1967), pp. x, 100–108, 111; P. J. Lloyd, *International Trade Problems of Small Nations* (Durham, N.C.: Duke University Press, 1968), pp. 9, 31–32.

81. D. Vital, *op. cit.*, p. 8.

82. I. Svennilson, "The Concept of the Nation and Its Relevance to Economic Analysis," in E. A. G. Robinson, ed., *op. cit.*, p. 1.

83. G. Marcy, "How Far Can Foreign Trade and Custom Agreements Confer upon Small Nations the Advantages of Large Nations?" in E. A. G. Robinson, ed., *op. cit.,* p. 266.

84. S. Kuznets, *op. cit.,* p. 10, and D. Vital, *op. cit.,* p. 40.

85. W. G. Demas, *op. cit.,* p. 22.

86. E. A. G. Robinson, "Introduction," *op. cit.,* p. xviii. See also P. J. Lloyd, *op. cit.,* p. 37.

87. W. G. Demas, *op. cit.,* p. 51.

88. S. Kuznets, *op. cit.,* p. 12.

89. M. Michaely, *op. cit.,* pp. 16–17.

90. Committee for Economic Development, *Economic Development of Central America* (New York: CED, 1964), p. 24.

91. N. Halevi and R. Klinov-Malul, *op. cit.,* p. 149.

92. G. A. Duncan, "The Small State and International Economic Equilibrium," *Economia Internazionale,* November 1950, p. 937.

93. J. Robinson, *The New Mercantilism* (Cambridge: The University Press, 1966), p. 11.

94. D. Vital, *op. cit.,* pp. 43–44.

95. C. Weststrate, *Portrait of Modern Mixed Economy, New Zealand* (Wellington: New Zealand University Press, 1959), pp. 255–256.

96. S. Kuznets, *Economic Growth and Structure* (London: Heinemann Educational Books, 1965), p. 205.

97. T. Scitovsky, "International Trade and Economic Integration as a Means of Overcoming the Disadvantages of a Small Nation," in E. A. G. Robinson, ed., *op. cit.,* p. 282.

98. H. B. Chenery, "Patterns of Industrial Growth," *American Economic Review,* 50:4 (1960), 646. For some recent evidence on the difficulty of producing heavy capital equipment, even in large countries, see A. Cilingiroglu, *Manufacture of Heavy Electrical Equipment in Developing Countries* (Baltimore: The Johns Hopkins Press, 1969), pp. 7, 29, 82.

99. E. M. Bernstein, *op. cit.,* 47.

100. W. G. Demas, *op. cit.,* p. 51.

101. Israel, Ministry of Finance, *The Development Budget, 1953–54* (Jerusalem: 1953), p. 3.

102. N. Halevi and R. Klinov-Malul, *op. cit.,* p. 168.

103. D. Avramovic and R. Gulhati, *Debt Servicing Problems of Low-Income Countries, 1956–1958* (Baltimore: The Johns Hopkins Press, 1960), p. 11.

104. H. S. Ellis, ed., *Economic Development for Latin America* (New York: St. Martin's Press, 1961), p. 164.

105. D. Avramovic and R. Gulhati, *op. cit.,* p. 47.

106. "Poorer Nations Face a Debt Crisis," *Business Week*, December 7, 1963, p. 110.

107. A. Basch, *Financing Economic Development* (New York: The Macmillan Co., 1964), p. 265.

108. International Bank for Reconstruction and Development and International Development Association, *Current Economic Position and Prospect of Israel* (Washington, D.C.: March 17, 1965) (mimeo).

109. W. G. Demas, *op. cit.*, pp. 49–51.

Index

Abs, Hermann J., 44, 45, 93, 156; Israel Mission loan and, 181–82; Wassenaar and, 125, 126–27, 128, 129, 130, 131–32, 133, 134

Acco, Israel, 252, 254

Achdut Haavoda-Poale-Zion, 207

Acheson, Dean, 133

Adenauer, Konrad, 44, 53, 212; Abs and, 45, 93, 125, 126–27, 128, 129, 130, 131–32, 133, 134; election of 1949 and, 75; election of 1953 and, 156; on Jewish property losses, 14, 85, 86, 90–91, 92, 119–20, 123, 125, 128, 153, 194, 289, 290; Luxemburg Treaty and, 3, 137, 138, 140–43, 147, 148, 149, 151, 169, 206, 208–209, 210; Petersburg Agreement and, 76

Africa, 96

Afula, Israel, 246, 255

agriculture: German, 10, 49, 55–56, 59, 66; Israeli, 106, 109, 111, 219, 262, 263, 265, 268; West German product deliveries to Israel, 144, 170, 172, 183, 184(*tab*), 185, 204, 222, 252, 253

airplanes, 51, 62, 236; Israeli, 264, 268

Akko (vessel), 232(*tab*)

Alan (vessel), 232(*tab*)

alcohol tax, 37

Algeria, 96

Al Hamishmar (periodical), 120

Allied Bipartite Board, 75

Allied Control Council, 46, 52; deindustrialization and, 49, 61–62

Allied High Commissioners, 53, 64, 75–76, 286; Wassenaar and, 131, 133

Allied Joint Export and Import Agency, 49, 77

Allied Military Security Board, 64

Allied Occupation Statute, 273, 275, 276, 277, 278, 279

Allied Powers (World War I), 24–39, 41, 58, 66, 221. *See also specific countries*

Allied Powers (World War II): Cold War and, 46–50, 52, 66, 73, 85; food and, 55–58, 69, 74; Jewish restitution issue and, 82, 84–85, 86, 87–89, 93, 94, 124, 131, 141, 148, 273–91; occupation of Germany by, 40–43, 45–46, 49, 50–52, 53, 62, 68–71, 72, 85, 273, 275, 276, 277, 278, 281, 283–84, 285. *See also specific countries*

Allied Powers-Federal Republic Contractual Agreement (1952), 133, 285, 287, 291

Allied Reparations Commission (1921), 128

Alsace, 22, 50

Amal (vessel), 232(*tab*)

American Jewish Committee, 122, 131; Committee on Peace Studies, 81

American Jewish Congress, 122

About the Author

Nicholas Balabkins is a native of Latvia. He came to the United States in 1951 and began graduate study at Rutgers University, where he earned the M.A. and Ph.D. degrees. He became a United States citizen in 1956.

Dr. Balabkins has taught at Washington and Jefferson College and since 1962 has been a member of the economics faculty at Lehigh University. On a sabbatical leave and during several summer trips he did research at Hamburg, Kiel, Cologne, Bonn, London, Stockholm, and in Israel, in preparation for his first book, *Germany Under Direct Controls* (1964), and the present volume.

Dr. Balabkins has contributed articles to a number of journals both in the United States and foreign countries.

The text of this book was set in Baskerville linotype and printed by offset on P & S Special XL manufactured by P. H. Glatfelter Co., Spring Grove, Pa. Composed, printed and bound by Quinn & Boden Company, Inc., Rahway, New Jersey.